# CHARIOTS
# RETURN

## MARK RYAN

First published by Keep It Real Publishing in 2024

© Mark Ryan 2024

Mark Ryan has asserted his right under the Copyright, Designs
and Patents Act 1988 to be identified as the author of this work.

ISBN: 978-1-7396052-1-6

Design and layout by Tim Underwood

Printed and bound in Great Britain by Clays Ltd, Elcograf S.p.A.

MIX
Paper | Supporting
responsible forestry
FSC
www.fsc.org    FSC® C018072

Dedicated to Luca Ryan –
and all who play their sport with passion


With special thanks to Kate Rossi

# Contents

# Chariots of Fire:
# The Ending They Filmed and Discarded

It's the final scene in *Chariots of Fire*. But this one never made it to the silver screen. Aubrey and Lord Lindsay have just left the memorial service for Harold Abrahams. They stop outside a TV rental shop and watch a few moments from the Moscow Olympics.

'A bit different from our day, old chap,' Lindsay mutters, and they wander on.

The scene was cut because, Lord David Puttnam explained, 'It somehow felt too anti-climactic.'

But the thinking behind this little postscript to the *Chariots* action was fascinating. Puttnam added this:

*The intention however was to make a point that the Olympics had, to a great extent, become professionalised and politicised, and had rather lost its soul and an important aspect of its purpose. Exactly the thing the Paris organisers and the IOC [International Olympic Committee] seem to be trying to regain.*

With Paris 2024 in mind, it's a good thing that scene was dropped. The film's feel-good factor has eternal appeal. Happily, Puttnam and his team resisted the temptation to dilute the euphoria when it came to the final cut. The movie stayed true to itself. The way it was left, *Chariots* remained a pure and effective antidote to any less admirable aspects of modern Games. If Paris 2024 wanted to call on the glory of *Chariots of Fire*, it was because Paris 1924 remained the film's only Olympic focus.

Hats off to Eric Liddell, Harold Abrahams and David Puttnam – the Paris Centenary Trio. These three men personified, protected and promoted the true spirit of the Olympic movement between 1924 and 2024. It sounds dramatic: but they might just have saved the soul of the Games. Ironic in Puttnam's case, because he was always terrible at running. Yet the way this trio combined to inspire a century had the feel of a relay. With his own purity of spirit, Eric Liddell set the perfect tone a hundred years ago. His old rival, Harold Abrahams then shaped the modern Olympics and ensured their survival through troubled times. And just as Harold's strength was leaving him, Lord Puttnam took the baton and conjured a magic that lasts to this day.

Eric Liddell and Harold Abrahams are the British athletes immortalised by David Puttnam in a movie that never seems to age. A hundred years after the events so gloriously depicted in *Chariots of Fire*, the Olympics prepared to return to Paris. The Centenary Celebrations promised to be special – and *Chariots* would not be forgotten.

Perhaps fittingly, given the origins of the Olympic movement, the race to capture the essence of the Games featured a Greek protagonist at the centre of the action. And that particular race went down to the wire. For a few silent seconds, no one was quite sure who had won.

Lord Puttnam kindly edited the following true-life scene from 1980, so that we could start our journey back in time as he remembered it.

PROLOGUE:

# A Greek's Race Against Time

David Puttnam and his wife Patsy are enjoying a quiet dinner in a Chinese restaurant in North Audley Street, London.

After a pretty stressful year, it's a moment to relax. The production of *Chariots of Fire* is at last complete. Done and dusted.

Except it isn't.

Walking into the restaurant in a state of excitement comes the Greek composer Vangelis. He has left his Rolls Royce outside the restaurant, where he's managed to track down Puttnam.

'David! David! Is it too late?'

They've known each other since he started composing commercials for the director Hugh Hudson in the early 70s. They'd tried to work together on the score of an earlier film Puttnam produced, *Midnight Express*, but conflicting recording contracts got in the way.

However for the past few months Vangelis has worked his synth magic in composing an atmospheric score for *Chariots*.

It's just as well David and Patsy are relaxing between courses, or their food would have been left half-eaten. Before they know it, Vangelis is directing them out to his Rolls Royce.

Resistance is futile, but then so is the untimely intrusion. Puttnam has already answered the question a dozen times.

Yes it's too late. Of course it's too late.

Vangelis knows it's too late. The movie is practically ready for release. Yet Vangelis isn't taking no for an answer. Not until Puttnam has heard what he has just created.

The composer's father, who has recently passed away, was something of an athlete and had known the exhilaration that came with the poetry of human movement.

Vangelis had badly wanted to conjure something magical to both honour his father and capture the soaring spirit of the film.

This highly-strung perfectionist felt he had failed, deep down.

Until now.

David and Patsy sit in the back of the car. Puttnam knows this could be embarrassing. He will almost certainly like the latest offering – and say so to ease the tension.

But then he'll have to remind his friend that the ship has sailed.

He knows that's going to hurt. And so a relaxing evening is likely to end in awkwardness and frustration.

Vangelis pushes a cassette into the slot and presses the button. The music begins with that low throb.

Puttnam can feel the hairs on the back of his neck leap to tingling attention. Vangelis looks at them both through the rear view mirror and waits.

Silence in the car. Only the music, which goes straight to the soul. This is what exhilaration should sound like. It's exactly the theme *Chariots of Fire* needs.

There's joy at the magic the music can add. There's pity, too – because this defining moment really has come too late.

The only work remaining on the film involves the front and end titles.

The central body of the score can't be changed now. But Vangelis has created something so remarkable that it deserves to be heard, if only acompanything the titles.

It's unusual, but it's clearly worth trying.

Puttnam tells Vangelis they'll give it a go. There are tears in the Greek's eyes. They all sense how memorable his theme could become.

The composer lets out a huge sigh of relief. His last-ditch gate-crashing seems to have worked.

He smiles apologetically at Patsy. She gets it.

# Part I: Chariots 24

*The most important thing is to be students of your sport. Understand the history of your sport and the adversity others had to overcome.*

Olympic gold medallist Seb Coe's message to young athletes who want to become champions.

## CHAPTER ONE

# Left for Dead before Eric Liddell

Eric Liddell is watching. He knows these are huge moments. Soon enough it will be his turn to shine. But for now, he is reduced to the role of spectator. Eric knows it could have been him down there. Unfortunately, the heats for the 100m were scheduled for the previous day. The day of rest.

It's three o'clock on Monday afternoon, July 7, 1924. This is the Colombes Stadium, Paris, and Harold Abrahams is out on the track at the Games of the Eighth Olympiad. His face looks gaunt, as if the enormity of the moment has just hit him. He has always been highly strung, and a few weeks ago he almost broke down completely before a big race. This race is much bigger. He comes across as arrogant, but he is also insecure and perhaps too intelligent for his own good. His high forehead and deep-set eyes make him look older than his twenty-four years. His lips, plump when relaxed, are thin with tension. Sport has a habit of distorting him, just as it has always made him feel special.

'Crack-a-Jack and twinkle-footed,' his coach Sam Mussabini calls him. His enemies prefer 'conceited and big-mouthed' but they don't know how kind and generous he can be. Harold is full of contradictions; gloomy one moment, so happy the next that his smile can light up a room and his blue eyes sparkle like the sea on a summer's day.

There will be no smiles today, not this side of the tape anyway. And even if he safely negotiates the Olympic semi-final, there will be no reward – except the certainty of an even tougher ordeal that evening.

Harold feels a little sick. He describes it as a sinking feeling, just as if his stomach were taking a walk up to his mouth and leaving a vacuum behind it. He always feels sick before a race, and he is trying not to let the occasion get to him. 'Avoid fussing like the plague,' coach Mussabini always tells him. 'If you are becoming increasingly worried, it is a good idea to sit down quietly, close your eyes, and relax all your muscles for about ten minutes.'

There isn't time for that now. But he must master his fear of failure; the fear that he will make a fool of himself in front of thousands of spectators. Most seem to be packed into the covered stand hugging the straight. Harold can hear them, a buzzing mass, the tone rising as the noise grows more persistent. They can't contain their excitement and soon the starter will need to calm them down again. But Harold's excitement is tenfold, the sensation hard to control. Abrahams intends to use this extra nervous energy to his advantage. He is determined not to let the sinking feeling get the better of him. Otherwise it will give rise to panic. Surprisingly, considering that he is about to take part in an Olympic semi-final, he manages to settle. This could be a good day.

Harold is still wearing his blazer over his white vest, which sports the image of a neat Union Flag waving in the wind. The vest, which looks like a twenty-first-century T-shirt, is just the way he likes it; not too high in the neck, a snug fit but not too tight. Harold's broad shoulders and powerful torso can live comfortably inside this one. The number 419 has been pinned across his belly and he has memorised it. If the starter or stadium announcer mentions 'quatre cents dix-neuf', Abrahams knows they are talking about him. He wears his own pair of shorts, roomy and loose. His legs are toned and unusually long, as if specifically built for extreme speed. He looks down at his running shoes. He has rejected a recently purchased pair in favour of some springy old shoes. The decision has been taken after advice from Mussabini. Both pairs were made to measure, much like the shorts he is wearing. But by now the older track shoes fit like a second skin. Each shoe hides six strategically placed, half-inch spikes below. They are designed to give maximum grip on a cinder track.

He surveys his lane, a private kingdom defined by straight lines of string tied to shin-high pegs. He is still waiting to begin his pre-race ritual, hoping it will compose him for the second semi-final of the 100 metres. His captain and roommate in the British team's hotel, Philip Noel-Baker, has come to watch the race. Sitting alongside Eric Liddell, Philip also feels the tension of the moment, because he knows semi-finals carry a greater risk of oblivion than finals:

*To a sprinter, an Olympic final is the supreme moment of his athletic life. In all probability, it comes to him just once. To a sprinter's friends, a semi-final is even more exciting, in the strain it imposes on their emotions and their nerves. If their man goes through, he joins the immortal ranks of the first six finalists in the Olympic Games. If he fails, his name may be forgotten, and he himself feel the sharp, though temporary, bitterness of defeat . . . I was sharing Harold's bedroom in our Paris hotel, and I knew at first hand the intensive training, with its minute attention to every detail, which he had done. I had seen, and I had tried to help with his psychological preparation. As he himself says, no wise man will venture a firm prediction on Olympic victories.*

Down on the starting line, Harold is ready to dig his footholds with a trowel. He can almost hear his coach, Mussabini whispering in his ear, 'Be careful about the measurements of those holes to the fraction of an inch.' Each hole must be big enough to contain the ball of the foot, and yet not too wide. If the foot has room to move around then stability is lost. The athlete will be unsteady at the first stride. The fit has to be snug, and then there are the angles to consider. The front wall must slant forward to remove the sharp edge. Otherwise the toe is apt to catch as the foot comes through for the completion of that all-important first stride. The back wall presents the opposite challenge. It has to be sloped at such an angle that Harold's foot can fit firmly against the wall in the "set" position. 'The back wall of the rear hole should be slanting at 75 degrees,' Harold always tells himself.

Trowel work done ...
Harold Abrahams is ready to go.

Abrahams works diligently. He seems pleased with his efforts. Now he takes a piece of cord out of his blazer. It is just less than three feet long. He places one end of the cord on the starting line in the centre of his lane, and marks the spot where the cord finishes. Then he takes that point and draws a line parallel with the starting line. That is where his first stride will land. The first stride will either reinforce the poise of the runner or throw him slightly off balance. Get it wrong and it is almost impossible to recover. Harold's first stride is always just under three feet when he gets it right. The cord should help him achieve his customary precision.

Such intricacies are lost on the French crowd, who rioted in the same Colombes stadium just a couple of months earlier, when their rugby heroes somehow managed to lose the gold medal game to a rag-tag bunch from the USA. The Parisians have packed the Stade Colombes to support the Frenchman, Maurice Degrelle. An eyewitness account tells how 'the loud-speaker had to appeal for silence among the clamorous, gesticulating crowd'. In this environment, composure doesn't come easily. There had been three false starts prior to the first semi-final, eventually won by the "New York Thunderbolt", Jackson Scholz. Degrelle was the offender in each case – and now he has been eliminated.

As Harold removes his jacket for the second semi-final, Philip Noel-Baker can suddenly sense the massive potential for something to go wrong. 'I felt a growing, urgent tension as he and his five opponents stripped and went to their marks. My instinct was not mistaken. What really happened, only Harold – and perhaps the starter – can say.'

The competitors are jumpy after a further false start. They are called again.

'A vos marques,' says the starter, Dr Moir from Manchester, in the best French accent he can muster. Harold knows how important it is that Dr Moir, in his long white coat and summer hat, shows composure too. 'I have always felt that what counts more than anything else with starting is the personality of the starter, who above all must inspire confidence in the competitor. It must, of course, be conceded that there are some people who deliberately attempt to "beat the pistol" but they are few and far between and a starter who knows his job will have them "stone cold" every time.'

Abrahams and the other athletes, who are waiting a few yards behind the starting line, walk forward again purposefully. A hush finally falls across the stadium. Harold recalled the scene, 'I had to face the two Americans, Charley Paddock and Chester Bowman, "Slip" Carr of Australia and Cyril Coaffee, the Canadian champion. I was in fact sandwiched in between Carr and Coaffee, with the two Americans on my extreme right.' Giovanni Frangipane of Italy is on the inside.

Harold reaches for his footholds in the cinder track and places his right foot in its temporary home first. Then he puts his left in the front hole. His running shoes nestle snugly like rockets on launch pads. Now his hands are on the starting line, the width of his body apart. His thumbs point inward, his index fingers touching the line itself. The other fingers spread out just short of the line. Harold looks down his lane again. Each lane is separated from the next by those stretches of string connected to low posts. That should help to focus the mind. It's what you do that matters, not the next man. It's all down to you. This is it.

'Run a sprint race as if you were the only competitor.' That is what Harold always tells others, because that is what Mussabini has told him. But it is easier said than done. Harold's rivals are real enough, and they want to destroy his dreams, just as he must try to destroy theirs. Harold is aware of a longing; 'the enormous amount of hope one concentrates in ten brief seconds', as he puts it. He feels the adrenalin coursing through his veins. Yet he must achieve calm, so that his muscles are relaxed, his position comfortable. He must not hurry unduly and he must not let the starter or anyone else fluster him. Nothing must distract his attention one iota. If he feels irritated by a speck of grit on his right knee he must brush it away while he has time. If he feels something is wrong, he is entitled to stand up and call the starter's attention to it. On this occasion there is no need. All is well.

'Prêt!' calls the starter with urgency, preparing to pull the trigger right behind the racers. Harold and the others raise their bodies, predators ready to hunt. He remains in the set position for what seems an eternity, yet his control over his body is total. Senses are magnified. For the rest of his life Harold will 'remember every millimetre of the semi-final'.

His whole world should now be focused on the starter's gun and his first stride. His head is down yet his eyes are glued to the spot where that first stride must land. He sees the mark he has made. No margin for error. The sound of the gun is coming, he knows it. Harold is used to holding this position for ten or twenty seconds at a time. Poised, sharp, patient; Harold later boasted, 'I spent many hours perfecting starting, and am proud to record that during the whole of my athletic career, I never once caused a false start.'

Since reaching Paris, Abrahams has been taught an old French proverb, *C'est peu de courir; il faut partir a point*. He translates it like this: There is nothing in running; the real trouble is to start at the right moment. Many sprint races are won and lost in the first second after that pistol has been fired.

Grainy shot of Harold (centre) on the start line in Paris

Something suddenly invades Harold's peripheral vision. Later he explained:

*Slip Carr was immediately on my right, and he had the reputation of being faster off the mark than any man alive. Before the pistol was fired, I saw him out of the corner of my eye. I definitely saw Carr on the move. 'Bang!' went the pistol, and for a fraction of a second I did not react, believing there would assuredly be a recall.*

His sense of precision, his quest for perfection, demands similar standards of others.

He knows the starter will call the others back; he will soon stand up and walk around again, maintaining his focus. He thinks he knows. Harold recalled, 'Dr Moir was a very good starter indeed; but in Paris I think he was a little overawed with the occasion – and who would not be?'

Dr Moir does not call the others back. In those same dreadful fractions of a second there is a grim realisation. Moir has ruled the start legitimate. The others have gone. The race to reach the Olympic final has started without him.

An astonished Eric Liddell winces at what he sees. He understands the pressure Abrahams has been feeling. The sheer weight of expectation.

Now what?

The horror of these moments stayed with Harold forever. 'I waited for the second gun, but none came. There was no recall. In front of me I could see three backs. To my horror, I was at least one-and-a-half yards behind the others. For a fraction of a second I began to panic.'

Similarly horrified, Harold's captain, Philip Noel-Baker looked on helplessly. 'Certain it is that he was "left" – left by a yard and a half – a yard and a half that might have been two yards. Who could give so great a start to sprinters good enough to reach the semi-final?'

The next few seconds would be definitive, not just for the race but for the rest of his life. They would also provide the most dramatic moments the 1924 Olympics saw on the cinders track of Stade Colombes...until Eric Liddell put a near-suicidal plan into action in the 400 metres final a few days later.

CHAPTER TWO:

# Born to Run

For a man who never made a false start in his entire sprinting career, Harold Abrahams showed a remarkable lack of discipline at birth. In fact he was so impatient that he almost didn't survive his opening minutes at 30 Rutland Road in Bedford, England. Harold insisted on joining his three brothers and two sisters so prematurely on a mid-December Friday in 1899 that it was almost the end of him. To be born a few weeks early is sometimes acceptable. To be born in the wrong century is asking for trouble.

'I ought to have been born in February 1900 because I was a seven-month baby and weighed three-and-a-half pounds. I oughtn't to have stayed very long, I'm told.'

Somehow, he escaped the ultimate punishment for jumping the

gun, and sounded quite proud of the way he had broken the rules. 'I wasn't disqualified for a false start,' he explained. But it was touch and go for quite a while. 'He was not expected to live,' said Harold's adopted daughter Sue Pottle more than a century later. 'His mum Esther and his sister Dorothy fed him milk on a "drip" by soaking it through cotton wool. He survived – so he showed plenty of fighting spirit from the start.'

Harold probably inherited that grit from one of the most brutish men in Bedford at the time – his father Isaac.

The sprinter's nephew, Tony Abrahams explained that Isaac, normally flint-hearted, became uncharacteristically emotional about the little baby's struggle for survival, and always retained a soft spot for his youngest son. 'He was extremely sentimental about Harold, because he was not much more than three pounds when he was born.'

Isaac holding Harold as a baby is the first picture of the future Olympic hero. The infant has clearly won his fight for life by then and put on a few more pounds.

Baby Harold with father Isaac

The pride with which Isaac shows off his youngest child for the camera does suggest that he possessed a warmer side of sorts. But those who knew Isaac might have been surprised to hear him described as 'sentimental' or 'warm' about anything. A tough refugee who couldn't speak English, he didn't place being nice high on his list of priorities. Finding a way to make money came first.

Isaac Klonimus was born in Vladyslovovo in Suwalki, Lithuania, or Russo-Poland as it was then. Klonimus proclaimed himself a Lithuanian Jew and escaped to Britain to avoid persecution. He arrived virtually penniless as a 15-year-old and changed his name to Abrahams, in recognition of his father – Abraham Klonimus.

It didn't take Isaac long to meet Harold's mother, Esther Isaacs, a distant cousin who was born in Merthyr Tydfil in Wales. Her father Samuel had been born in Poland but had emigrated to Britain, living briefly in Wales before setting up in Birmingham as a bedding manufacturer.

The eldest of eight siblings, Esther was introduced to Isaac as her family helped the newcomer to find his feet in the Midlands. Isaac began to make a living in Birmingham too; but he didn't like the place enough to want to stay. He took a shine to Esther, though, and the young couple married there in 1880.

It took Isaac a while to put down fresh roots. They moved to Brighton, by which time they had two children, Adolphe and Solomon or "Solly." The family finally settled in Bedford, where the remaining four children – Lionel, Dorothy, Ida and Harold – were added to the line-up. The three eldest boys – Adolphe, Sidney and Lionel – were educated at Bedford Modern, while Harold went to Bedford School, which was regarded as the better of the two.

Harold's father could barely speak English and he certainly couldn't write it – not even his name. So his rise was remarkable, as his grandson Tony Abrahams explained. 'He showed a good deal of native wit. He was very shrewd. He made a lot of money.' Isaac had a stall in Bedford market, where he sold tobacco and certain precious stones. He gradually began to lend money to selected people, including minor Bedfordshire aristocracy. At this stage, business was done at home or in the market; there was no pawnbroker's shop. As he succeeded, he took as collateral the houses or businesses of his debtors. He opened an office. Then he opened several – in Bedford, Luton, Ipswich, Watford and London. They made him richer still, and by the time the twentieth century was into its stride he had founded the Bedfordshire Loan Company.

Harold was sixteen years younger than Adolphe, and fourteen years younger than Solly. By the time Harold went into education, his father felt rich enough to call himself a 'financier and jeweller'. Yet behind the scenes Isaac was still renewing his pedlar's licence, almost as if he feared waking up one day to find that his astonishing success had been a dream. The fact that he was still classified as a foreigner – a Russian – couldn't have made him feel much more secure. Even when he became a British national later, Isaac was still something of an outsider – a feeling Harold inherited.

As a small boy, Harold discovered that he had little else in common with his father, though they did share one passion. Harold's nephew, Tony, revealed, 'The Gilbert and Sullivan interest came first from Harold's father, who sang with a very thick Jewish accent any "G and S" he could get hold of. The rest of the family were thus brought up on the "G and S" operas.'

Three quarters of a century later, *Chariots of Fire* writer Colin Welland – another Gilbert and Sullivan fan – would pick up on this very English musical passion in the Abrahams family. In the movie, it becomes one of Harold's most likeable traits. In reality, it may well have been his father's only likeable trait. Tony explained, 'Otherwise Harold's father was a bit of a swine. There is no evidence of any athleticism – I don't know if the "Old Man" was fast – he was very portly and not very tall. One of my colleagues once told me, 'I remember your grandfather at his stall – a funny little chap, very fat.'

But there was nothing funny about Isaac when he drank, because he became abusive and violent. Fortunately, as Tony pointed out, 'There were enough older siblings to protect Harold. I think his mother Esther and his sister Dorothy would protect Harold against the Old Man. He was a brute and they definitely feared him. I don't think Harold was beaten by his father, in terms of really being clouted, though.'

The great Eric Liddell used to say, 'Seldom did a proper athlete come from a drunken family.' He obviously didn't know the full story behind his rival Harold Abrahams' tricky background.

Eric liked to tell people he stood there before them as a representative of either the third or fourth generation of non-drinkers and tee-total folk. He would never be able to quantify the contribution his forefathers had made to the success he had enjoyed, but he knew this much:

'They had given their contribution.'

Harold couldn't say Isaac had passed any great physical fitness down the line. But he still appreciated the opportunities Isaac's financial success afforded his sons. 'My father couldn't write a letter until the day he died, but he could sign a cheque. It was through his efforts that we were given such a fine chance in life.' The problem, as Harold's brother Solly put it when reflecting on their childhood, was this: 'We had comfort but no happiness.'

There were six Jewish families in Bedford at the time. They were not persecuted but they would, according to Tony Abrahams, have felt 'set apart', simply because they were different from the majority. Since they weren't subjected to antisemitism in Bedford, Harold's family didn't seem to mind this feeling of being different. And when Isaac wasn't around, the athlete wasn't a complete stranger to fun. For example, a photo survives from this period which can be said to show Harold's first race – even though his legs weren't doing the running.

Harold's First Race: Abrahams (circled centre)
on brother Lionel's back against siblings.

The older children are hurdling over garden obstacles with the younger ones on their backs. Everyone concerned seems ready to collapse with laughter, yet there is also a competitive edge. Harold has long, curly locks, is clinging to Lionel's back in the "middle" lane and clearly loving every moment.

'I was almost born sprinting!' Harold was able to reflect later. And he was delightfully unpretentious when asked much later why he had taken up running as a boy. 'Well certainly in the early days. . . it's just exciting moving fast, you know? In my earliest days I wanted to run. I was plunged into athletics almost from the start.'

In that regard, Abrahams had a head start over a young man who would become such an unsettling rival.

CHAPTER THREE:

## Made for China

Eric Liddell wasn't born until January 16, 1902, a second son to his Scottish missionary parents, James and Mary.

He was supposed to be Christened Henry Eric Liddell. Then someone realised "H.E.L." weren't ideal initials for the latest arrival in a devout Christian family. Eric came into the world in Tientsin, China, where his father James was highly respected for his fearless commitment to his missionary work.

*Courtesy of Eric Liddell Community*

James and Mary's wedding.

As with Abrahams and his siblings, Eric would develop a degree of athletic rivalry with his elder brother, Robert in time. Only one would become an Olympian, though. And

Courtesy of Eric Liddell Community

Eric and father James.

given what a momentous event Liddell's birth ultimately was for the Olympic movement, it's strange to think it took place in a country that was still in a state of sporting obscurity. China didn't take part in the Olympics for some time.

The Liddell family didn't mind feeling remote from mainstream life. Indeed, the London Missionary Society sent them on a journey of some 700 miles out to Siaochang on the Great Plain not long after Eric was born. They lived in a gated compound, but Eric was immersed in Chinese culture for his first five years. He had a Chinese "amah" or nanny. And despite the love he developed for Scotland, he would always regard the Chinese as his people.

'God made me for China,' Eric would often say. He'd prove it by returning to that land at the height of his fame.

Liddell the infant learned Mandarin – and saw no reason why appearances should make him any less Chinese than any other child growing up around him. He ate like a Chinese boy, he felt at home. China was where his little sister Jenny had been born, too. It was where the family took on its identity. And from his earliest years, Eric was acutely aware of the love and esteem the local community had for his father.

Most sons want to be like their dad somehow, especially if what they see in their father is overwhelmingly admirable. The father-son bond strengthened the intensity of the ties between Eric and China, creating a love that would last a lifetime. In Liddell's family, missionary work was more than just a family trade, it was a calling. In truth, it had to be. There was danger involved in spreading the Christian word in a country reeling from the Boxer Rebellion. Violent crime was rife. Intense bravery and integrity were required to thrive in this challenging environment. James Liddell had both – and he won people over. All these things combined to leave an indelible impression on Eric Liddell. They created loyalties and dreams in Eric that could never be shaken. Even his first burgeoning romance, and the prospect of a long-term athletic career at the highest level would not distract him. The firm belief that he was made for China would also, tragically, bring Eric Liddell's life to a premature end. And yet China was soon left behind, for almost two decades.

At the age of six, Eric was enrolled at the School for the Sons of Missionaries in Blackheath, south-east London. Now he only had the presence of his elder brother Robert for security. It isn't hard to imagine the emotional pain that being left in England caused the brothers – and Eric in particular. The family had arrived in Britain together as one, to enjoy the year's furlough James had been given.

Eric had enjoyed the rugged open spaces and spectacular scenery of Scotland. But at some point, it must have sunk in that Eric and Robert weren't going back to China with their parents when the time came. They weren't even going to stay in their father's beloved Scotland. Poor Eric Liddell was only a small child when he was left behind, knowing his parents were returning to the only place he had ever called home without him. The family would sometimes spend time in Edinburgh going forward,

Early Liddell family.

precious reunions taking place when his parents were back again on furlough. Sadly, for a young boy who adored his mother and father, those treasured family moments were few and far between. Indeed, over the next seven years, poor Eric spent less than a third of a year in the company of both parents. His new kid brother Ernest got more attention when he arrived towards the end of that period.

The first year of being away from his father and mother was the hardest for Eric. Most boys cry the first time they are left by their parents. And Eric missed them terribly. In fact, he struggled to adapt to his English school in those tough early months, going into a shell and looking to his brother for comfort. It didn't help that he was 'weedy' as one member of staff rather unkindly put it. And with disease rife in that cramped school environment, it was a wonder Liddell found his feet at all.

A school photo of the two brothers from 1908 has survived. Most of Robert's hair has been cut off and his pose borders on the casually rebellious. He seems to be doing his best to create "don't-mess-with-me" vibes for the camera. Eric is right next to him; but he could hardly look more different. The younger brother stands up straight with his hands behind his back, the same pose he will adopt when Harold Abrahams takes a photo of him at the Paris Olympics sixteen years later. Eric, the smaller boy in the school photo, looks round-faced and healthy enough.

Courtesy of Eric Liddell Community

Robert and Eric at school 1908.

The moving thing is that he forces a little smile, though the pain is just detectable in his deep-set eyes.

It took about two years to mend Eric – and rugby helped. You had to toughen up and find a way to survive out on those muddy English fields; and little Eric discovered that he could run faster than the others when he had the ball. Given enough space, he could leave potential tacklers for dead as he raced for the try-line. When not given space, he would more likely be flattened; but he was ready for that. Neither was little Liddell too scared to try and take down boys twice his size in the tackle. He had seen other minnows show a bravery that would stay with him for the rest of his life.

He later told an audience that he 'could remember at school watching a little back limping across the field to tackle a person three times his size – and then limping back to the other side to tackle another person.' That little back could just as easily have been Eric Liddell himself. He knew from an early age what he had to do in sport – and why. Others set the early example; and soon enough it was Eric Liddell setting that same example for others.

'It's the spirit of the whole thing that matters,' Eric would explain later. 'And the first element in sportsmanship is courage. The sights I best remember on a rugby field are situations where sheer courage has been the best element.'

The result of applying his own personal courage was that a more robust Eric Liddell emerged after about two years. And it wasn't just teamwork on the rugby field that gradually gave him a sense of belonging.

There were only about sixty children in the entire school. They were all in the same boat and one big family; all left by their parents, who had returned to the missionary life indefinitely.

Eric Liddell already felt a sense of destiny, though; the inner certainty that he would return home to China one day too. This feeling also seems to have helped him through. The fact that James and Mary had left him behind and returned to the Far East didn't leave any lingering resentment. Absence only made the heart grow fonder. Meanwhile Eric's faith in God was never in doubt. A personal calling seems to have taken shape at a younger age than most. He was said to have told a close friend at the age of eight or nine that he was going to become a Missionary in China. A lot of the boys in the school would have harboured similar ambitions to follow in their fathers' footsteps across the globe. But Eric was already putting Christianity into practice. At the same age, he saved a new boy from a nasty, familiar welcome to the school. The ritual would see the newcomer run a gauntlet of older boys, as they aimed blows at him with knotted handkerchiefs. Eric already knew right from wrong, and this was clearly wrong. He didn't care how long it had been a school tradition. For as long as he was going to be around the school, that tradition was over.

The funny thing was, when he had to take a stand for good against bad, the shyness temporarily fell away. Excruciatingly, it always returned when those sudden and spontaneous tests of character were over. Much of the time, the rest of the boys would hardly have known little Eric was there.

Then he was given the role of the dormouse in the school drama, "Alice in Wonderland." Liddell stole the show in his own unassuming way. It didn't mean he had faced and cured his stage fright for life. But he had given a good account of himself – and provided the other boys with the opportunity to give him a nickname that would stick – "The Mouse." It wasn't the most masculine or muscular tag a boy could be given; and playing any role in front of an audience must have terrified Eric. Little by little, he would grow into the person he wanted to be, though. What a mighty mouse Liddell would become as the years went by and his physical prowess came to the fore.

Actions and words always counted for Eric Liddell. Sporting excellence and even captaincy couldn't shake off his discomfort when it came to speaking publicly, though. In that regard, he would remain more mouse than man for his childhood and early adulthood.

At his school, the boys voted every year for the pupil they considered to be the best influence within the school community. It was called the Bayard Prize. Interestingly Eric Liddell, the man who would grow to influence Olympic and Christian communities indefinitely, never won that prize. And he would avoid further opportunities to face down his stage fright at school if he could.

Eric simply dreaded the thought of public speaking. And for a youngster who only ever wanted to be like his father, that presented a major problem. How could he become a preacher when he hated standing up in front of an audience? His professional dreams for adult life collided with a shyness bordering on phobia for the first twenty years of his life. One can only imagine what that conflict did to him deep inside.

CHAPTER FOUR:

# A First Brush with Mussabini

For his first twenty years, the inner race Harold Abrahams ran was against his brothers. He wanted to be like them. And once he realised he had at least as much talent, he wanted to be better than them.

Harold explained, 'One of my brothers [Sidney] was a Cambridge Blue in the long jump and British Champion, and another [Adolphe] was a good all-round athlete, inter-hospitals champion and a doctor. Their interest in athletics meant that almost literally from my cradle I was guided and encouraged to perform. I was surrounded by this atmosphere of running. Sidney and Adolphe used to train me when I was tiny – even six years old. Whether they knew I'd got a lot of ability I don't know.'

Harold was used as a pacemaker during Sidney's training. 'He used to give me half a minute's start in the quarter-mile and woe betide me if I glanced behind in the straight,' the youngest brother recalled. Whatever recriminations he suffered, Harold had already decided the pressure was a price worth paying for the thrill of a race and the distant hope of a fancy jacket. He revealed later:

*My brother Sidney got his 'Blue' in 1904. I liked the Blue blazer very much and I determined – I should think at the age of six – that I was going to wear one as soon as I could get it. I saw this pale-blue blazer and I thought how terribly good I'd look in it. Already at six, seven, eight, I lived athletics – I used to ask my brothers to let me run. I suppose I also resented their athletic fame and was determined to do better.* 

Harold with Cambridge Blue Sidney (right).

*As a very tiny boy I would, I suppose, have been described as a phenomenon.*

Adolphe and 'S.S.' (Sidney Solomon) weren't about to let that talent go to waste. Tony Abrahams knew how hard his uncle had been pushed. 'The moment Harold started showing great athletic ability, the brothers would make him run everywhere. Their favourite game was to make him run around the houses in Bedford, and they would give him a time to beat and if he didn't make it they would hit him over the head with rolled newspapers.'

Though Harold respected all his brothers, it seems that 'S.S.' was his favourite. And by the age of six, he must have sensed the excitement as Solly prepared for the biggest athletic event of the century so far. 'S.S.' competed in the 100 metres and the long jump in the Olympic celebration at Athens in 1906. Frustratingly for Harold, it was another brother, Lionel, who accompanied Solly to Athens, where he came fourth in the semi-final of the 100 metres in a time of 11.8sec.

Harold was determined to do better; and he was barely seven when he first experienced the thrill of victory in an organised event.

*The first prize I ever received, for winning a fifty yards race on the sands at Hunstanton, was a copy of The Pilgrim's Progress. I was given a long start, because I looked such a miserable little fellow. They never saw me for sand. I came home with The Pilgrim's Progress, and I never looked back from that moment until I was lucky enough to run in the Olympic Games some thirteen years later.*

Harold's next challenge was to negotiate his early school days in Bedford, where his father's growing wealth gave Harold a better start than his brothers. He explained, 'I went to the Bedford Junior School – known as the "Incubator" – of what was then the Bedford Grammar School for £5 a term. The Grammar subsequently became Bedford School.'

Harold enjoyed life in 'the 'Incubator', not least because it offered him stability at a time when his father's behaviour became erratic. Tony Abrahams explained, 'Isaac was a heavy drinker and a womaniser. He slept with anyone he could get hold of – and he was a bully.'

With so much tension at home, athletics also offered a welcome escape. Harold won a handsome mug, his prize for winning an Under-10, 440-yard race at school. Bedford's sporting community already knew it was nurturing a special talent. Elsewhere in England, that talent sometimes came as a nasty surprise. Brighton made the same mistake as Hunstanton. Harold's daughter Sue explained, 'Again they gave him a head start because he was smaller than the others. He ran off and that was it. No one caught him. I still have the mug he won – it says "1910 Quarter-Mile. Over-Ten. First – Abrahams."'

Soon Harold was ready for his first big race in a recognised athletics arena, one which is now more famous for football. He recalled, 'I won my first gold medal at ten at Stamford Bridge. It was 1910 and it was an event called the Lotinga Cup, which was for the sons and brothers of members of the London Athletic Club. They gave you so many yards per year that you were under fifteen.'

A photograph survives of that summer event, which was run over 150 yards. A skinny Harold, legs bent, almost appears to be jumping at the tape in his huge shorts. In second place trails a much smaller boy who looks no more than six.

Aged eleven, Harold won his school 100 yards in a time of 14sec. But a more important race was the traditional dash from the playing fields back to the main school building. It was measured at 300 yards, and Harold won the 1911 race in 47.4sec.

Victories soon became less spectacular, much to the disappointment of his demanding brother Adolphe, who wrote later, 'As a little

Lotinga Cup glory at Stamford Bridge.

boy, up to the age of ten, H.M. Abrahams was really remarkable. The little boy ran like a man. But later in boyhood and early adolescence he was of hardly more than average ability.'

Academically he was also unexceptional, though his classics teacher described his work as 'quite promising'. English was 'very fair',

All the time he longed to emulate Solly, the family Olympian. Instead he was excluded from his brother's sporting adventures, and never forgot the feeling of frustration. He explained, 'I was at Bedford up to the age of twelve . . . I can remember my mother, my sister and my two brothers going to Stockholm for the 1912 Olympic Games, and I desperately wanted to accompany them.'

This time Solly only competed in the long jump; and although he was still unable to win a medal, at least he had been part of it. And Harold hadn't even been able to watch. Three Olympic Games had passed Harold by; he intended to put that right one day. For the moment there was only upheaval, though. He recalled, 'I came away [from Bedford] for four terms in order to go to a Jewish Prep School at Brighton to be confirmed. Then I went back to Bedford and did one term in the Upper School.'

Tony Abrahams explained later, 'Harold was Bar Mitzvahed at the appropriate age, but joined no congregation.'

Sent back and forth between schools of contrasting cultures, these were the first in a series of unsettling moves. Later he claimed they created within him a tendency to leave things unfinished in his life. And an even more destabilising event was just around the corner.

Tony added, 'Something happened between his parents and they separated. I don't know if it was a civilised separation or not, but Esther established the new family home in Fulham Palace Road, West London.' Isaac left Bedford for London too, and moved into a flat in Rodney Court, Maida Vale. Before long, his daughter Dorothy was getting an allowance to look after him.

Life in Fulham Palace Road brought a new family dynamic. Harold's elder brothers were often out working or living the lives of adults in their prime. So Harold was sometimes left to play the 'man' of the house as his mother adapted to the separation. That must have brought a fresh set of pressures – and as a new boy at St Paul's school in Kensington, he was the outsider again.

Sidney 'Solly' Abrahams won the long jump title at the Amateur Athletic Association Championships in 1913. Harold felt proud and jealous of his brother in the same moment. They began to frequent a track at Herne Hill in South London. There, Harold saw his future coach at work. 'I met Sam Mussabini, who was going to play a very great part later in my running. He was training Applegarth.'

Willie Applegarth had taken the 200 metres bronze medal at the Olympic Games of 1912. 'I was a great admirer of Applegarth,' Abrahams said later. He would become an even greater admirer of Willie's coach in time.

Mussabini was a wily forty-six-year-old with a generous grey moustache and intense, sparkling eyes. He had been working his magic down at Herne Hill for so long that he was almost part of the furniture. When Harold met him, he was being employed two evenings per week as the

Polytechnic Harriers' senior coach. He lived in a house almost over-looking the track – at 84 Burbage Road.

'I think Harold's brothers introduced them' said Rosemary Warne, a companion to Harold much later in his life. In the fullness of time, Harold Abrahams and Sam Mussabini would be linked forever in athletics history. Although Sam must have known all about the Abrahams' family pedigree, Harold didn't shine sufficiently at that tricky stage in his physical development to command much immediate attention. He found his new, adolescent body strange and awkward. Nevertheless, Mussabini saw enough to know that Harold and his long legs might hold some promise for the future. Old Sam began to keep an eye on Harold too.

No one can say for sure that Mussabini's influence helped Harold to return to winning ways in 1914 at St Paul's. But it happened – and Abrahams confirmed, 'I was the long-jump champion there with 15ft 3in.' He also won the 100 yards in 11.8sec, a decent time for a 14-year-old who hadn't done any serious running for two years. And all the while, Harold's sprinting role model continued to inspire him.

'As a schoolboy, on July 4, 1914, I visited my first AAA Championship meeting. I well remember the thrill of seeing Willie Applegarth in the inside string tearing round the bend on a banked track at Stamford Bridge. He equalled the world's 220 yards record in 21.2sec, his strides following one another with incredible rapidity. Applegarth beat Vic D'Arcy, another great sprinter, by four yards.'

What kind of superman would Mussabini have made of Harold too, had the outbreak of World War One not ended their loose association? We will never know, and Abrahams would have to wait nine long years for his turn to work intensively under the studious gaze of the magician with the Midas touch.

CHAPTER FIVE:
## Liddell's Imperfections

The seemingly incurable shyness of Eric Liddell was facing fresh challenges. More children arrived to test him. His school grew when it moved to a new home and changed its name. The School for the Sons of Missionaries became Eltham College when it upped sticks to Mottingham in 1912. Eric Liddell is said to have walked the entire way across the park and fields from Blackheath to the school's new location. The trauma of leaving the familiar comfort of the old, intimate place to face life within a larger school population did at least carry the compensation of a far more spacious and healthier environment.

The loss of the word "Missionary" in the new school's name didn't dim Eric's sense of self, either. He was still very much the son of a missionary and a future one too, if only he could overcome his dread of public speaking. His return to China would only have purpose if he could leave his inhibitions behind, as all preachers must. It was like wanting to be a great footballer, and not being able to kick a ball straight. How was it going to work, when push came to shove?

Apart from that one significant problem, Eric Liddell was not a complicated character. He had already seen the light. He was a good guy, pure and simple. This is why David Puttnam once said: 'Chariots of Fire would have been a thin brew without Harold.' Sure, the moral stand that Eric Liddell took at the Paris Olympics of 1924 was going to be defiant and dramatic. The personal sacrifice he would choose to make was destined to stand out as extraordinary. But deep down, Abrahams was the more complex individual.

He was insecure. And that insecurity comes almost as a relief to observers of his life, given that he was so physically gifted. We can relate to imperfection more easily than perfection. We can relate to not always having that comforting feeling of belonging. Abrahams spent his entire life searching for true acceptance. And because he never quite found it, he spent years compensating in ways that weren't always likeable.

Liddell's search ended when he knew he was accepted and loved by God. The key to understanding Eric Liddell lies in the intensity of his love for God and for China. And the origins for both lie in his love and admiration for his father. What captures our imagination and delights us so much in *Chariots of Fire* is the way Liddell's personal conviction collides with the 1924 Olympic Games and the sheer pomposity of his critics in Paris.

Producer David Puttnam and writer Colin Welland are quite masterful in that regard. In his early notes for the screenplay, Welland points out: 'There are of course other influences, other textures, active within the movie – the British Ruling Class in the person of Lord Birkenhead [played so brilliantly by Nigel Davenport] and his fellow Olympic Committee men…'

And they help create the conflict that is of course the essence of all drama. But the unwavering nature of Liddell's longer journey in real life is still hard to grasp. The idea that someone's path through life can be so completely predestined from such an early age, with barely a hint of exploratory deviation or adolescent rebelliousness, is almost beyond comprehension.

And so it almost comes as a relief to discover an example of a mischievous streak on display at Eltham when Eric "pranked" his head-master one day at school. There was a strict rule not to cycle in the Eltham College quadrangle, the focal point of the school. Eric saw the headmaster breaking his own rule and shouted down from what he thought was the safe anonymity of a window above:

'Hey! No cycling there!'

By jumping away from the window before the angry headmaster could spot the culprit, Liddell thought he had got away with it. Unfortunately for him, the headmaster recognized his voice and obtained a confession. Sent to bed with no supper for that piece of cheek, young Liddell wasn't about to make the same mistake again.

If that was Eric's biggest moment of naughtiness, then he wasn't very naughty. Disrespect aside, you could even argue he had been in the right for exposing the head's hypocrisy. No one is perfect. But from start to finish, Eric simply made it his mission to be the very best person he could be, whatever the situation. He visited a nearby hospital to offer what comfort and company he could to the sick and lonely there. What he lacked in obvious leadership skills, he found ways to make up for. He led by example, by his actions; and if others followed then all the better. Liddell was already a thoroughly "good egg," as they might have put it in his day. For the moment, he had to make no great sacrifices to be the person he wanted to be. But there was one inescapable aspect to school life that he didn't particularly love – lessons. Yes, like many of us, poor Eric had to endure class after class when he wasn't particularly academic.

'I don't think much of lessons, but I can run,' Liddell confided to his sister Jenny once.

Children usually don't think much of lessons when they are not particularly good at them. In this regard, we can assume Eric was also less than perfect at this young age. Thankfully, the extensive sports programme the school provided gave Liddell a happy daily outlet to do things he was becoming extremely good at. And all in all, the British

Rob, Jenny, Ernest and Eric Liddell.

Courtesy of Eric Liddell Community

educational environment was far less challenging than any that would await him on his return to China.

For now, he remained in England, steadily growing stronger. As the younger man, he was still behind his future rival, Harold Abrahams in physical and athletic development. But that disparity would gradually disappear. Time was on Eric Liddell's side. And one day, the moment would come to face Abrahams on the track. Years of school races and rugby would help Eric build and prepare for that showdown.

He was building towards greatness in a happy environment, free from prejudice. Harold Abrahams was not so lucky. And there were times in his own childhood when he could have done with a friend who possessed the unwavering compassion of Eric Liddell.

## CHAPTER SIX:

# A Jew at Repton

It's strange to think that Englishman Abrahams spent most of his adolescence further north than Scotsman Liddell. Repton in Derbyshire was grim, though not as appalling as the prospect of fighting in the fields of northern France. Many unfortunate boys moved swiftly from one to the other, their young lives obliterated in an instant. At least the antisemitism Harold had to face at Repton wasn't life-threatening.

In every sense, Repton was a long way from the life Harold Abrahams knew. The school still dominates a little village in Derbyshire, where the Midlands meets the North of England. Harold was given a place there because his brother Adolphe had the right contacts. Through his doctor's practice, the eldest sibling had come to know a top Liberal politician called Sir John Simon. Adolphe was physician to Lady Simon, who campaigned against persecution of any kind. She knew the staff at Repton and used her connections on Harold's behalf.

Abrahams later claimed he was rejected by one Repton boarding house because he was the son of a moneylender. Instead, he joined Old Mitre House, which had played host to the Sherlock Holmes actor, Basil Rathbone, a few years earlier. They didn't much care for the new Jew there either. Luckily Abrahams had a way to fight back. 'As a schoolboy, at my public school, I think that I used athletics for covering up that sense of inferiority. I was determined to demonstrate my superiority over others. And what better way than in athletic distinction?' The irony was that Abrahams had no great desire to defend the Jewish faith and didn't wish to be defined by it. He once joked, 'I lost my Jewishness the first time I smelt bacon and eggs at Repton.' In truth, he never entirely lost his Jewishness – partly because others would not let him. There is no doubt that Harold was hurt by antisemitism as a teenager, because he referred to it so consistently in later interviews. On another occasion he reflected:

*I was good at athletics even at Repton, and found an opportunity, really for self-expression. I wanted something to justify myself. There was quite a deal of anti-Semitism at schools in those days and I had to find something where I could score off people. And by running of course you can do it, you can get first and you can win and I was determined to do so.*

Before he had the chance to show his athletic prowess, Harold had to play football. Unfortunately he had more speed than skill. Harold admitted later, 'I was moderate at other games – I played soccer for the house and I got into Second XI at outside right. But I can't really say I was any good at soccer.'

He had to wait before he could show the bigots what he was really made of. By then he felt a burning anger at the prejudice he was suffering on a regular basis. 'There was much more antisemitic feeling in those days and it provided one with the driving force to succeed in athletics. I never sought grievances, it was more a question of "this animal is dangerous when attacked". And I was attacked a few times.'

Some of the 'attacks' may have been more than verbal. Harold had to find a way to survive in a world where the absence of girls reduced the options for boys seeking sexual expression.

Harold at Repton.

Unable to escape the homosexual advances of a stronger, older boy, Harold succumbed. Much later he told his nephew about the incident. Tony explained delicately, 'The question as to whether we had any homosexual experience came up. And he said there had been an occasion at Repton when a more senior boy had sexual experience with him one night. But Harold certainly wasn't homosexual.'

That incident probably took place in the Old Mitre House itself, a three-storey building and former pub which can still be seen when you look out through the ancient, arched school entrance, in the direction of the village shops. Harold's temporary 'alliance' with the older boy may have earned him protection – or simply invited further abuse. To an extent the law of the jungle applied, and if you were weak you had to become strong quickly. Only then could you determine your own path as you progressed through the school.

When the chance to show his strength finally came, Harold took it. He was a better long-jumper than a runner in his mid-teens; and on Sports Day in March 1915, he produced a leap to be proud of. It also started a numbers game in Harold's head, one that would continue for his entire athletics career. Harold explained, 'When I was just fifteen years old, I managed to long-jump 18ft 1½in. My age (within a few days) runs conveniently with the years, and I resolved that I would set my ambition as a long-jumper to keep for as long as possible ahead in feet of the date.'

He had until 1919 to jump in excess of 19ft, a good four years to build up more strength. But the prospect of future physical maturity wasn't necessarily comforting, because it meant war.

Many a young man felt obliged to join up and fight even before he was fully grown. Others waited in trepidation for their turn to face the German guns. Harold braced himself for the ghastly conveyor belt of war, just like everyone else in his school. He was part of the Repton School Officer Training Corps, and in October 1916 he learned the art of 'Signalling', proud to join those who had 'qualified for their flags'.

He might have been a warrior-in-waiting, but there was still time for tenderness. After receiving a parcel he wrote, 'My darling mother, not many people have such good and kind mothers as I have, I am sure.'

Esther was the one constant in a life that looked destined to be cut short. Nothing was geared to a normal future – least of all the school's academic programme. Abrahams reflected later:

*I started off with Classics. And here is another thing which would recur again and again, you see. One of the things where I found I had a disadvantage early on was that I went to so many schools – Bedford, Brighton, Bedford, St Paul's. I then went to Repton in war time, with no future ahead of us because the war was on, and we were all – I certainly was – extremely frightened of the future. So that I never really felt I had to finish anything. And you get that time and time again, that one doesn't go thoroughly into things. I think that has something to do with the fact that I never had to exert myself to the utmost. We had no exams at all at Repton during the war.*

The wholesale slaughter left a strain on the educational system. Besides, there was little point in putting teenagers through exams when they probably wouldn't live to benefit from their academic success. A former Classics classmate called Donald McLeod Innes, whose sister Harold would soon know so well at Cambridge, lost his brother Patrick to that war in April 1917. So many Repton boys had to suffer similar news of lost loved ones.

Donald came to terms with his grief by writing a haunting poem called The Young Dead, which began like this and summed up the mood of the time.

> Those whom we loved are gone; and at their going
> We, who so ill could spare them needs must stay.
> They were our best and brightest: it was they
> On whom our hopes were builded, all unknowing
> The destiny that was theirs; we watched them growing,
> Learning where joy is found, and day by day
> Happier, worthier.
> Now – they are fled away,
> They are blotted out, beyond all human showing.

Tragically, Donald was to join 'the young dead' in the final year of that same war, before he could reach the sanity and serenity of Cambridge. Like his brother, he had earned a place at Trinity College, and would never have the chance to go.

This was the sort of sadness that threatened to engulf Repton in Harold's final years there, as he heard what he described as 'seemingly endless rollcalls' of the fallen. Harold would soon feel the loss of Patrick and Donald McLeod Innes acutely, through the sister they left behind.

For the moment, Abrahams clung to any sense of normality that sport could offer. Athletics provided the escape from all things ugly. It always had, it always would. And after a couple of mediocre years, Harold's speed had returned with a vengeance, because he won the 100 and 220 yards at Repton in 1917. His time for the 100 yards was a searing 10.8sec, while he took a respectable 25sec for the 220 yards.

Looking back on this period of Harold's life, his brother Adolphe wrote with a scarcely suppressed excitement, 'At about the age of seventeen a change became evident.'

If only Abrahams' school head had been impressed. The outer arrogance Harold displayed was almost certainly a result of his inner insecurity, a protective mechanism designed to cope with the undercurrents of antisemitism and that pervasive feeling of not quite belonging. By his final year, Harold had overcome most of his difficulties, and there were no older boys left to intimidate him. He moved from House Prefect to Head of House and School Prefect. He was also a Sergeant in the Corps. And his growing authority was built in no small measure on his athletic prowess, a highly respected commodity in such a competitive environment.

But Abrahams still felt his religious roots unfairly restricted his role within the school. His nephew Tony explained:

*Harold disliked the headmaster, Geoffrey Fisher, who was an anti-Semite. Harold was irritated when the headmaster picked him out early to become a prefect but then said he wasn't allowed to read the prayers. The headmaster made him Head of House; but as for reading in assembly, he wasn't allowed to read the lesson. He was only allowed to read various items of administration.*

The sticking point was the fact that the Jewish faith does not consider Jesus to be the Son of God. The headmaster decided that Harold was therefore unfit to utter the words 'through Jesus Christ our Lord, Amen'. Feeling that he was going to be discriminated against whatever solution he found, Harold approached the problem with a humour that only thinly masked his exasperation. Tony added, 'Harold told the headmaster that he was quite prepared to read prayers in the normal way but end them by saying "through Jesus Christ YOUR Lord".'

The headmaster declined his offer.

Abrahams focused on the Repton Sports Days of 1918 instead. They were to provide a fitting symbol for the way Harold had risen above the abuse he had suffered, without entirely leaving it behind.

Harold remembered, 'I had an interesting experience in the long jump because [for a pit] they used to take just the turf off the top to jump into. And the distance from the take-off board to the end of the pit was 22ft and I landed on the grass! And I sat back and my measured jump from my bottom was 20ft 5½in.'

Abrahams ended the school sports on a high with victories in the 100 and 220 yards. He could go to the 1918 Public Schools Championship at Stamford Bridge feeling confident. Sure enough, he claimed two big prizes there too. *The Sportsman* newspaper's correspondent, well aware of all four Abrahams brothers, wrote:

*The last of the athletics quartet, Harold, who by winning the 100 yards public schools title at Stamford Bridge on a heavy track in 11sec, and the long jump with 20ft 3¾in, proved himself to be a worthy holder of dual honours. He has excellent nerve, judgement and steadiness for one so young and if some day he secures the titles that his brother S.S. once held, and with an even better performance to his credit, I for one shouldn't be surprised.*

But Evelyn A. Montague, portrayed in the film *Chariots of Fire* as Aubrey, the good-natured narrator and steeplechaser, remembered souring his rival's moment of glory. Harold's future friend explained:

*It was a weak year, and each of us won two events without much trouble. In the dressing room afterwards Harold and I eyed each other with interest and, in Harold's case, with a touch of bitterness, for I had done his school, Repton, out of the championship cup. In those days only first places counted towards the cup, or second in the case of a tie. His two victories and mine made Repton and Rugby equal, but Rugby had also gained second place in the mile, and Harold had only managed third in the quarter.*

Abrahams had an important consolation. He explained, 'At the Public Schools Sports in 1918 Sir John Simon came with my brother to watch me.' Harold was in awe of the politician, who had already been

Home Secretary and went on to become Chancellor of the Exchequer, Foreign Secretary and finally Lord Chancellor. Simon asked Harold what he intended to do for a living. Still undecided over the path he should follow, the schoolboy suddenly made up his mind. 'He [Sir John] had been Attorney General and I suppose partly one tries to imitate people. My father was a money-lender and I didn't want to go into that. I wanted to go to Cambridge and I had to select something to read so I chose law.'

Down at Eltham, Eric Liddell wasn't ready for university yet. But he was certainly making his mark.

## Chapter Seven:
# Liddell in the Limelight

Young Eric Liddell was excelling in all kinds of sports on the playing fields of Eltham. He had already played in the First XV rugby team at the tender age of fourteen.

A photo shows Eric in the back row, noticeably shorter and seemingly less equipped to deal with the sort of violent rugby played by young men, yet standing proudly on the right anyway. One can only imagine that his raw speed had already helped him to escape many a blow to that underdeveloped body of his.

The same early breakthrough happened with cricket that year. There's a picture of Eric sitting on the ground to the front and right of the group. It's almost as though the photographer has decided that, by placing Eric there, his lesser physical frame won't be so noticeable against the stature of the other boys.

No wonder Eric was already school captain by the time he reached 16. True, the drain on fine young men created by the Great War would have played its part in Eric's early rise to the top. Within the school,

Courtesy of Eltham College

1916 rugby team (Eric back row far right).

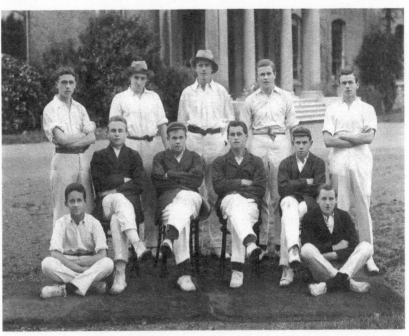

Courtesy of Eltham College

1916 cricket team (Eric front right on grass).

however, there can be little doubt that the younger Liddell became revered as some kind of sporting phenomenon. All first teamers are worshipped at private schools, particularly among the younger children. Since Liddell was one of their own in that regard, the feeling could only have intensified. And it would have been all too easy for Eric to succumb to this adulation and become too fond of himself for his own good.

Yet Liddell's headmaster by then, George Robertson, said he was 'entirely without vanity', despite being more physically talented than any of the others. Eric took their approval in his stride; and he would probably have swapped all their cheers for one warm smile of approval from the man he idolised – his father.

It must have hurt Eric that James Liddell was never there to witness his sporting exploits, as the entire school began to sit up and take notice. All Eric and Robert could do was to impress him from afar. And the Liddell brothers made sure they had plenty to write home about

In fact their last school championships as a pair were always remembered as the "Liddell Games".

Eric won the 100 yards in 10.8 seconds – and he was pushed all the way by Rob. Eric also took the 440 yards, showing that he was no stranger to what proved to be his best Olympic distance. As with many fast athletes, Eric was able to rule the long jump too. Meanwhile Rob took the sprint hurdles and cross country races, adding the high jump to even up the family honours

As Robert Liddell said farewell to the school, looking every inch the dashing young adult, Eric knew he would face a more

Courtesy of Eltham College

Dashing young men: sprinters Eric and Rob.

intense sporting spotlight than he had known before. He was the community's last remaining Liddell phenomenon, after all.

Everything was relative, though. He could hone his skills away from pressures of the outside world. And Eric had his faith to compensate for the loss of daily contact with his brother. His path through life was already clearly defined. And Eric had been confirmed in the Scottish Congregational Church at the age of fifteen. His religious zeal and his athletic prowess would go hand in hand, until an Olympic schedule a few years later forced a jarring decision. For now, he thrived on a smaller stage, still an unknown.

Meanwhile Harold Abrahams soon had access to the kind of sporting stage from which Olympic honours could be won. And there was a chance to make a real name for himself. His athletic ability, his father's money and his brothers' contacts assured him a place at Cambridge to read law. But would the war finish in time to allow him to take up that place?

Harold knew it was touch and go. He explained, 'I went from Repton to a Cadet Battalion in the First War – and I won some events and represented the Army for the long jump against the Americans.' Mercifully, he didn't have to fight because the war ended. He knew just how lucky he had been; and he reckoned the army was lucky too. 'I'd have been an incredibly bad soldier,' he once said. 'Hated it.'

Abrahams was demobilised at the end of 1918; but just when he thought he had cheated death, it almost claimed him. He contracted Spanish flu, which went on to kill more young Brits than the war itself. His natural physical prowess helped to save him.

Regaining his strength once more, Harold began to train with other sprinters on a track in Paddington, West London. That summer he took part in the first post-war AAA Championships. 'I ran a very long way behind W.A. Hill in the furlong [220 yards],' he recalled. However, in late August 1919, shortly before going up to Cambridge, Harold had the chance to race against his boyhood hero, Willie Applegarth, the sprinter Mussabini had trained to an individual 200 metres bronze medal and relay gold in the 4 × 100 metres at the Stockholm Olympics in 1912. Applegarth had lost none of his pre-war confidence and no wonder, with times to his name of 10.6sec for the 100 metres and 9.8sec for the 100 yards. Willie's reputation alone was enough to worry most opponents.

It was the 29-year-old veteran against the 19-year-old wonderkid. Since the race was to be decided over 100 yards, Applegarth gave his Herne Hill apprentice a two-yard head start. As soon as he heard the pistol, Applegarth set about trying to eat away Harold's slender advantage. Surprisingly, however, the master failed to make much impression on the pupil he was stalking. The gap stayed at two yards. Then, to everyone's astonishment, Abrahams started to pull away. Three yards, four; then five as a shocked Applegarth tightened. When Harold hit the tape, he was six yards ahead. Abrahams had come of age.

He still had plenty to learn, though – and not just about sprinting. Harold prepared for university – and life beyond – by taking up an offer from Sir John Simon to watch him at work in the law courts of London.

He recalled, 'I listened to cases even before I went up to Cambridge; a very famous court case called Isaacs against Hobhouse in which [Sir John Simon] was taking part. I was thrilled to look at the papers and to be there and to feel terribly important, sitting behind one of the leading advocates of the day.'

Sir John asked for something in return – Harold's support in the general election. Abrahams obliged, though his heart wasn't entirely in his work. He confessed, 'I think there again I wasn't genuinely drawn towards politics, but I was asked to help him in the elections. I took part in the 1918 election – Walthamstow. There was also a by-election in 1919 in Spen Valley, in which I took part, canvassing, beginning to speak – though my speeches were not very profound.'

Having lost his Spen Valley seat in 1918, Sir John was trying to get himself elected back into Parliament a year later in the same constituency. Harold played his role in the campaign as enthusiastically as he could. And though he didn't fall in love with politics, he did embrace the attention and the opportunity to show his quick wit.

He recalled, 'My capacity or incapacity for "punning" was evident very early. I remember in the 1919 election, somebody saying, "Mr Lloyd George is a great artist," and I remember saying, "Ah yes, but we want the country governed, not the House of Commons decorating," and I was very pleased with myself because people laughed. I got a lot of election experience.'

How Eric Liddell would have loved to possess such natural verbal agility. And how Sir John Simon must have wished that Abrahams wit had made more difference to the by-election result. He still lost to Labour.

As for Harold Abrahams, the political ladder wasn't to prove sufficiently inviting. What he wanted above all was a light-blue blazer, the one he had seen his brother Solly wearing during his Cambridge days. A symbol of sporting excellence and a very fine colour, something the six year-old Harold had decided would suit him very nicely. In thirteen long years, Harold's opinion hadn't changed. He was determined to get his hands on one.

CHAPTER EIGHT:

# The Cambridge Freshman

If Harold Abrahams was trying to follow in the footsteps of his brothers at Cambridge, the plan seems to have encountered a hitch even before he reached the university.

His nephew Tony said, 'Something funny happened because two of his elder brothers had been up at Emmanuel but he didn't go to that college. And there was a rumour that Emmanuel had not accepted him. At any rate, Harold went to Gonville and Caius.'

Caius wasn't as spectacularly beautiful as nearby King's or Trinity; but it was cosy and atmospheric all the same. Harold's task, in time, was to progress through the symbolic Caius gates – the Gate of Humility, the Gate of Wisdom, the Gate of Virtue; and finally the Gate of Honour, the little wooden door through which students still pass to receive their degree at the Senate House. The journey would not be without its trials and tribulations, especially for a Jew like Abrahams.

Lord Puttnam insisted there was an unsavoury undercurrent at Caius. He maintained:

*One of the reasons I had problems filming at Caius was that antisemitism had been rife during Harold's time. It was probably evident in all of Cambridge and Oxford for all I know, but certainly in Caius College. It is a fact. And Caius got very, very neurotic about us filming there, because they thought we would go further in our portrayal of the antisemitism. Caius were hypersensitive. I remember a phrase was, 'We don't want all that being dragged up again.'*

An article for the college magazine of Harold's era, *The Caian*, reflects the pervading antisemitic feeling of the age. Entitled 'Shylock the Jew', it salutes Shakespeare's creation of the central character in *The Merchant of Venice*. But the reason Shakespeare has been so brilliant, the college magazine seems to argue, is that he has suspended a natural loathing for the worst characteristics of Jews.

The writer, who signs himself only 'MJO', says of Shylock:

*He is not there, so that the British public may indulge themselves in a few minutes' quiet hate and contempt, so that they may become flattered into a comfortable belief in their own virtue and in the degradation of others . . . In the character of Shylock, Shakespeare has accomplished the feat of putting himself in complete sympathy with a personality some aspects of which he must have loathed with an wholesome loathing.*

If such views formed the backdrop to Harold's time at Caius, he could at least be grateful that Cambridge students considered themselves too well bred to exercise that prejudice blatantly. He would not be physically attacked or verbally abused for being a Jew, or even prevented from climbing most social ladders at the university. Neither, on the other hand, would he often find an enthusiastic audience when he described his Jewish father's rise to financial power from nothing. Harold remained grateful nevertheless.

As his great friend Norris McWhirter recalled, 'He would sometimes tell the astonishing story of a father who arrived all but penniless from Eastern Europe without a word of English – but whose burning conviction about higher education propelled his sons through Cambridge.'

So Abrahams didn't want to betray his father; nor did he want to be restricted or disadvantaged by his Jewish roots, for which he felt no great passion. No wonder he suffered such insecurity and angst about his identity and the way others perceived him. He must have sensed that an open-minded approach to Christianity would help him at Cambridge. And when he signalled that open-mindedness to others, it sparked a fierce battle for his soul.

Like other freshmen, Harold became an instant target for recruitment by various religious groups and societies within the university. And he was ready to take part in a post-war Cambridge search for a way to avoid the carnage of recent years. The loss of a bright young generation cried out for a formula to prevent future wars. Religion was "in". Abrahams, for all his bluster, was still discovering himself. He was impressionable, even vulnerable, and many things were worth exploring before he settled on one. Harold was spiritually rudderless but trying to do the right thing, hoping to find ways to be accepted among his peers.

The Cambridge Inter-Collegiate Christian Union – or CICCU – was the group most determined to capture the souls of freshmen. Rivals to the evangelical CICCU were the more moderate Student Christian Movement, which endeavoured to combine in one association those who are seeking and those who find.

Overtures from the likes of CICCU and the SCM sparked something inside Harold. Perhaps it was here in his first year that he took his initial steps towards Christianity. Realising that actions speak louder than words, he did what he could to live a "Christian" life at Cambridge.

Writer A.J. Wallis later said of Harold, 'He devoted much of his time while at Cambridge to a group of young working men who had not had an undergraduate's advantages in life. He ran in their sports, wrote for their magazine, and helped them to produce a play. This eagerness to help those less fortunate than himself has remained throughout his life.'

He was referring to the Caius Mission in Battersea, South London, where boxing, football and athletic clubs thrived, and Cambridge students visited whenever time allowed. Harold maintained his links with the Mission until long after he left the University. He served on the Caius Mission London Committee at the height of his fame in 1924. And he was still serving on that same committee, for the benefit of those less fortunate than himself, nearly ten years later. The place clearly impressed him from the first time he saw it as a student. And if they ever had time to discuss such matters, Eric Liddell would have been impressed by the way Harold Abrahams let his actions do the talking for him in that regard.

Not that Harold's love of talking was ever in doubt. He polished up his public speaking skills with one eye on the future. He revealed, 'I took lessons in elocution for the Bar at Cambridge. It's very important to avoid saying "er" every few seconds.' It would help his athletics commentary later in life, too. In fact, this was a key decision, and not just for the fluency of his speech. Elocution lessons effectively guaranteed the removal of any Jewish intonation in Harold's delivery, giving him the opportunity to mix with the Cambridge social elite with less fear of prejudice. Outwardly at least, those lessons would give him the vocal authority of an upper-class student from an established British family.

Norris McWhirter later recalled a conversation he had with Abrahams about his smooth exterior. 'I remember saying on a journey with him, "The trouble with you, Harold, is you are so effortlessly superior." He replied, with that ever-youthful twinkle reserved for confidences, "Effortlessness has nothing to do with it." That was the remark of a man of consummate modesty and gentleness.' It may also have been the remark of a man who was remembering his elocution lessons as a Cambridge student.

It was only a matter of time in that first year before Harold exploded onto the university track and field scene. After all, as he pointed out, 'I lived athletics in the sense that if I were going along the street and there was an entry to a yard about fifteen feet wide, I would always jump across.'

The recognised venue for such demonstrations of athletic prowess was Fenners. The track is long gone, but during the summer it tries to return like a ghost from the past. When the ground is dry, the old cinder outlines rise to the surface, almost as though athletes long forgotten wish to push their achievements into the present. 'The cinder track comes back, even though we filled it in with soil,' confirmed the head groundsman, John Moden in 2010. 'It's fascinating.'

Harold's first challenge at Fenners was to make a big impact at the Freshman's Sports, held in his first term. To do that, he would have to blaze down the 100-yard stretch of track which hugged tightest to a row of horse-chestnut trees. With spectators pressing in on the other side of the track, competitors ran the gauntlet in an atmosphere of passionate intensity. Undaunted, Abrahams fed off that pressure to win his first big race in 10.2sec. He also jumped an impressive 21ft 3in and ran 52.8sec for the quarter-mile.

A prestigious clash between Cambridge University and the Amateur Athletic Association was next on the calendar. Harold was one of the stars of the show. Evelyn Montague explained, 'When at the end of his first term he beat W.A. Hill, the reigning AAA Champion, in 10.2sec over 100 yards, there could no longer be any doubt that a future champion had arrived.'

The News of the World clearly thought that Cambridge University's coach, Alec Nelson, was responsible, calling him 'the greatest athletic coach we have in England.'

In fact Harold wasn't very impressed with Nelson's sprint coaching. 'Thanks to my brothers, I knew far more about it than he did. He was a good chap for jollying you along.'

Harold jumps at Fenners.

Whatever Nelson's abilities, the conceited Abrahams didn't think he could be taught much about sprinting by anyone. He felt he already knew it all; and later he freely admitted that as a young man he could hardly have been cockier. 'I would say that an enlarged head is much more common in youth than an enlarged heart,' he said of his early Cambridge days. Harold certainly wasn't as modest about his stunning triumphs and rave reviews as convention demanded at the time. But then what was the point in pretending that he wasn't good when he clearly was? The problem lay in the fact that his honesty gave jealous rivals and the anti-semitic element ammunition with which to snipe at him.

Even if he had been the modest type, Harold's talent alone would probably have antagonised those around him. As Harold's future friend Norris McWhirter put it in the *Dictionary of National Biography* (DNB): 'If the road to popularity at university lies in never inculcating a sense of inferiority into one's contemporaries, Abrahams stood little chance of being popular.'

It wasn't just his enviable talent or big mouth that antagonised others, but the way he took his sport so very seriously. Bevil Rudd, a brilliant South African all-rounder who was at Oxford before and after the First World War, described the acceptable training ethic of the day: 'I belonged primarily to the pre-war era, when training was essentially casual, and competition very occasional. We conformed to a traditional training schedule which, while it kept us fit, in no way tested our individual abilities or polished our style. A faulty style was regarded as a fascinating idiosyncrasy, and misplaced energy as a sign of guts.'

It would be a while before Harold Abrahams ironed out his own style with the help of the brilliant Sam Mussabini. But even during his first year at Cambridge, he must have seemed rather too intense in his sporting ambitions to fit in with the prevailing ethos of the day. In November, for example, Abrahams had written, 'A man or boy should never be out of training. "The sports are over for now" seems to be a most repulsive attitude . . . Take a cold bath every morning (winter and summer) . . . Do some exercises before retiring to bed at night for about ten minutes – press-ups, etc. Lead a clean life; always be in training.'

But to some this 24/7 commitment to sporting excellence was cheating, pure and simple.

Sport was still amateur, sport was for fun. Harold and his new athletic intensity were on collision course with Rudd and his old-style courage.

CHAPTER NINE:

# Showdown at Queen's

The Queen's Club in West Kensington, London, beckoned for the big Varsity showdown against Oxford. The athletics rivalry between the universities dated back to 1864. The race venue – now famous for tennis – wasn't for the faint-hearted. It drew so many fans from Oxford and Cambridge that they could have filled the little stand closest to the newly constructed cinder track twice over. A report explained, 'The revival, after the suspension during the war, of the inter-Varsity sports drew a large and enthusiastic assembly of spectators. Indeed, at 1 o'clock, over an hour before the first contest, the ground was well filled.'

Harold's race was the very first, scheduled for 2.15 p.m. The crowd pressed so close to the athletes that the runners must have heard almost every whisper, and smelt the cigarette smoke as they prepared for their big moment. Weather conditions were far from ideal. One report mentioned an 'adverse wind' for the '100 yarders'. Harold could deal with the wind. But the atmosphere, both intimidating and exhilarating, was new. The clamour of an all-Cambridge crowd was one thing. The claustrophobic effect of this Varsity mix at the start of the biggest race of Harold's career was quite another. And to make matters worse, Abrahams had drawn the lane closest to the stand.

Later he claimed, 'I know of no other greater ordeal than the sensation – fear and joyful anticipation mixed – as one goes to the start of a race at Queen's Club. Somehow, the fact that one is representing a great University with centuries of traditions is both terrible and wonderful.'

Harold would carry the hopes of the Cambridge fans, just as he drew the hostility of Oxford's. In a way this was the future racing the past; but Abrahams was still effectively a boy, racing against a man.

Bevil Rudd, the veteran who favoured the amateur ethos of the pre-war era, was waiting for him. Born in Cornwall but educated mainly in South Africa, Rudd had been a war hero. He returned to Oxford with a Military Cross, and knew better than most why sport should never be regarded as a matter of life and death. That didn't mean he wasn't keen to beat Abrahams, the young upstart from the rival university.

The start, of course, had to be right. For Abrahams, it wasn't – and this would become a common theme. The little Queen's Club stand was packed to the rafters as the pistol cracked and Rudd, Oxford's President, tore through the air like a bullet. The shorter man's compact arms were already pumping furiously as Harold's arms flailed loosely. In this instant the crowd went wild and students of Oxford were strident.

Harold recalled, 'I received a rude shock. I got a good start, but Bevil had a better one. Bevil gave me the fright of my sweet young life ... After thirty yards he was perhaps half a yard ahead. Time seemed to stand still.' Harold explained, 'Ten seconds is not after all very long, but it can seem an eternity on occasions, and this was one of such. Thirty yards from the tape I was still perhaps six inches to the bad.'

*The Times* seemed to know why and said of Harold, 'He is certainly not a graceful runner, with so very marked and curious a roll. But he runs low, with a fine stride, and his body well forward, and any amount of dash and resolution.'

As they neared the tape, it seems that Rudd thought he had the edge in all departments. He raised his arms, perhaps in triumph; but in that moment the joy turned to anguish as he realised that Abrahams, pushing out his torso, may have broken the tape first. Now it was the turn of the Cambridge fans to go wild.

Harold said, 'He led me for 80 yards of the 100, and but somehow I just managed to thrust myself ahead in the last stride or two to win by a very, very short six inches.' Given the conditions, the time was as extraordinary as the sheer drama of it all. One report claimed, '[Abrahams] won a clear, though very narrow, victory. [His] hundred in 10sec dead, with the wind certainly not helping him, was a fine achievement.'

When Abrahams looked back on his life, he saw those ten seconds at Queen's as make-or-break moments in his climb towards the top. The two protagonists knew straight away that their tussle had been something special. Whatever their preconceptions, they had won each other's lasting respect. Harold explained, 'My exciting race with Bevil was the beginning of a friendship which lasted until he died. Had I lost that race, my whole athletic career might have been different. And it is no exaggeration to say that a victory in an inter-Varsity contest means more to its proud possessor than a world's championship.'

Adrenalin and gritty determination had seen Harold through. But what would the effort cost him when it came to the long jump? His leap of 22ft 7in carried the day.

Evelyn Montague, running for the "enemy" in his first Varsity, later conceded, 'Harold jumped straight into the limelight.'

He had more than earned his Blue in both the 100 yards and long jump. Even though Oxford won the contest overall, Abrahams was still the toast of Cambridge. And ordinarily, his heroics would have earned him an invitation to join one of the university's most prestigious organisations – the Hawks Club. After his Varsity triumph, Hawks members would doubtless have debated his suitability, if not for immediate nomination then for the following academic year, as was the norm. You could only join if you were a sportsman who had won a "Blue" by representing Cambridge against Oxford. On the face of it, therefore, Abrahams fitted the bill. But a Blue alone didn't win you membership to the Hawks; you had to be nominated and accepted by the committee, you had to be socially acceptable, clubbable – even popular. And even by his own admission, Harold wasn't popular.

Later he seemed to want to sweep what happened under the carpet. He said, 'I didn't belong to the Hawks Club, I belonged to another club called the Pitt Club, where the food was better.' Yet in the *Dictionary of National Biography*, Norris McWhirter was quite adamant about what had really happened. 'His election to the Hawks Club was opposed due to a contribution to *The Times*, which the committee regarded as immodest.'

Harold still didn't see any merit in false modesty. In fact he was positively full of himself. 'That's one of the problems of being prominent when one is too young in a limited sphere like athletics,' he admitted later. 'You get very easily a swelled head. Some people probably think I never recovered from it.' But he was in an awkward position, because he was one of the few athletes – perhaps the only one – who sometimes wrote about races in which he himself had taken part. Harold explained, 'I'd started journalism in 1920. I wrote for a journal called *All Sports* and for the *Evening News* in those days.'

So when did he write the offending article for *The Times*? He couldn't have penned that newspaper's description of his victory at the Queen's Club, because the article criticised his style. So the source of the controversy must have been something as innocuous as a brief description of his University Sports win a few weeks earlier, which had appeared without a by-line. The contests weren't important enough to warrant the presence of a staff reporter from *The Times*. So Abrahams appears to have volunteered to further his fledgling journalistic career by covering the occasion himself.

Under the headline: 'SPORTS AT CAMBRIDGE – SOME PROMISING PERFORMANCES' it read: 'H.M. Abrahams did well to win the Hundred Yards race in 10.2sec against this wind, and his winning leap in the Long Jump was a good effort . . . G.M. Butler did not extend himself fully in the heat of the Quarter-Mile Race and Abrahams, having won two events, ran only a little more than half way before retiring.'

The degree of "immodesty" shown here was negligible. But Abrahams had committed a cardinal sin: he had dared to compliment himself in writing. It didn't seem to matter that he had gone on to praise R.S. Woods, who was 'in fine form in Putting the Weight', E.S. Burns, who 'did well' in the High Jump' and H.B. Stallard, who 'won the Mile easily'. Three mentions of Abrahams in as many paragraphs amounted to a shameful piece of self-publicity. Why bother to refer to himself in the Quarter-Mile, for example, when he hadn't even finished the race? It simply wasn't on; and something had to be done.

Even if there was no antisemitic aspect to Harold's rejection, he might still have perceived there to have been one. He once acknowledged that perceived prejudice soon became magnified in his head:

*I think that being Jewish has played a very big part . . . There wasn't a lot of antisemitism when I was young and of course one imagines that a lot of things you don't get are not because you don't deserve to get them but because you are Jewish. You can distort it quite easily. And I was determined I was going to show myself superior in something where there could be no argument about it. And I WAS good at athletics. And this was a method of self-expression.*

Later Harold confessed to journalist Neil Allen, 'There was some antisemitism at university, in my early days as a Cambridge athlete, but I think I had a bit of a chip on my shoulder about it.' Colin Welland, who wrote the screenplay for *Chariots of Fire*, claimed that 'Harold had a chip on his shoulder the size of a synagogue'. Less fortunate people might wonder what all the fuss was about. Even Harold's son Alan pointed out, 'it was a little strange that my father complained of discrimination because he went to Cambridge University and was not entirely down-trodden. He didn't exactly lead a tough life.' But once you are in any environment, even at a lofty and privileged level of English society, you want to be accepted by your peers and welcomed into every corner of that environment. So rejection by the Hawks must have hurt Abrahams all the same. His critics probably wounded him too. At various events he was accused by newspaper critics of being 'quite unable to keep his stride', of 'dawdling over the first paces' in both 100 and 220 yards races, of being a 'slovenly starter', and of 'fiddling about to strike the take-off board' in the long jump. When the AAA Championships at Stamford Bridge came around, he flopped.

Later he admitted, 'I am convinced that a phenomenal success may hang like a millstone round a young man's neck. Modern publicity is responsible for a tremendous amount of failure on the athletic track. Could it be that this results in the athlete in question being over-anxious and failing to do himself justice?'

Harold had been full of himself at Cambridge; now he had been cut down to size in the wider world.

With the Olympics approaching the England selectors were wise enough to know that Abrahams was a work in progress. Understandably, they decided to make him no more than a reserve in the 100 yards for an international against Ireland and Scotland on July 10. But they gave Harold a chance to shine in other disciplines. He did just that, winning the 220 yards race. And he had one last chance to perform – for Polytechnic Harriers against The Rest at Stamford Bridge on Saturday, July 17. He was second to Harry Edward in the 100 yards; but he won the long jump with a solid leap of 22ft 1½in. And Abrahams impressed in the relays, teaming up with Harry Edward and two others to beat The Rest there too.

Three days later, on July 20, 1920, a letter from the Amateur Athletic Association arrived for Harold Abrahams. He began to open it with some trepidation.

## Chapter Ten:

# Christina's Olympian

Harold Abrahams sliced open the letter, knowing the first two lines would give him his answer:

Dear Sir,
RE OLYMPIC GAMES AT ANTWERP

I have the pleasure to advise you that at a meeting of the Special Olympic Committee of this Association you have been selected to represent Great Britain in the 100 and 200 metres and 400 metres [4 × 100m] relay at Antwerp at the VIIth Olympiad from the 15th to the 23rd of August next. I need hardly point out to you the desirability of continuing to train, so as to be thoroughly fit in order that Great Britain may be represented with credit...

For Harold, this letter was more than enough. He had done it; he had achieved every athlete's dream, to represent his country at the Olympic Games. He recalled, 'It was a Wednesday morning in July, 1920, when I received a letter from the Amateur Athletic Association telling me that I had been selected to represent my country at the Olympic Games at Antwerp the following month. I can still remember the thrill.'

For Eric Liddell, the date with Olympic desitiny was still four years away. He was only seventeen years old, and he hadn't reached anything like his full potential yet. Then again neither had Harold. Still, to follow in the footsteps of his brother Solly was a big enough personal prize in itself – and not lost on Harold

*For my interest in Olympic matters went back to my early childhood. My brother, S.S. Abrahams, had travelled to an Olympic celebration in Athens in 1906, and competed for Great Britain at the Stockholm Games in 1912. I knew, or thought I knew, all there was to know about Olympic performances, and here I was going not only to see the world's best athletes in action, but to compete against some of them. I was a sufficient realist to appreciate that I had no earthly chance of any success. I was a very, very long way behind the world standard in these events.*

Antwerp 1920: Harold's limbs lack the strength to be a world-beater.

He wasn't wrong. The appearance, for the first time in history, of the Olympic flag, with its five coloured circles entwined, didn't inspire him at the time. When the competitions began, Harold won the tenth heat of the 100 metres from Alexandre Penton, Canada, and Giorgio Croci, of Italy, in 11sec. 'That's about 10.2sec for 100 yards,' pointed out Abrahams somewhat guiltily. He failed by inches to reach the semi-final, so he was a spectator for that race and the final itself.

For the most part, Harold masked the pain of mediocrity with customary humour. 'My own performances were not at all good. I had a very good back view of Charley Paddock in the second round of the 100 metres – in fact I needed a very powerful pair of field glasses to see him at all.'

Perhaps it was a sense of inferiority in such formidable company that also led Harold to take a verbal swipe at the way Paddock finished with such an extravagant flourish. He said, 'Paddock did a ridiculous jump at the finish, you've probably seen a picture of it at the 1920 Olympics. But you can't jump faster than you can run. He slowed up to make the jump. He had a terrible style.'

Paddock – the "California Flash" – was aware of this sort of criticism and was quite happy to hear his jump described as 'the freak finish of a freak performer'. But he added: 'The "jump finish" has won so many more races than it has lost for me. You have to run high, "bounding" along, before the exaggerated final stride of 10-14 feet. It requires patience to learn it and courage to use it.' Only 5ft 8in tall, Paddock's knee action was so high that he sometimes struck his own chin. His efforts were fuelled by a raw egg and a glass of sherry.

Abrahams may not have liked him, but Paddock ran 10.8 in the final for his gold. A 5ft 7in, cigar-smoking American called Jackson Scholz also shone, but was ultimately relegated to fourth. At twenty-three, Scholz would have time to come again at the next Olympics, if only he could go easy on those cigars. Harry Edward, Abrahams' fellow Brit, had a bronze medal to show for his efforts at the end of that final.

Harold saw his Varsity rival Bevil Rudd win the 400m. But he was even more impressed by another GB performer. He explained, 'Albert Hill gained a wonderful "double event" in the 800 and 1500 metres... Hill, like Edward, was trained by Sam Mussabini. What a great little man

"Sam" was.' Hill's achievement was all the more remarkable because of a crazy schedule. Abrahams remembered:

*The semifinal and finals of the 800 metres were held on the same afternoon and within half an hour of one another. This was an incredibly ignorant piece of organisation, but the whole organisation at Antwerp was rather primitive; races were actually run at half past nine in the morning, which meant that competitors either had to get up about six in order to have breakfast a sufficiently long time before the race to permit it to digest or go without breakfast altogether. In 1920, athletics were still suffering a little from the 1914-18 war.*

One day he would put such things right as an athletics administrator – and introduce the sort of schedules that would be seen in Paris in 2024. But at Antwerp 1920 he had played no more than a bit-part in the drama. It must have been tough to watch lesser-rated stars do better. In the 4 × 400 metres relay, Harold's Cambridge friend and rival, Guy Butler, anchored the British victory, and therefore returned to university with a gold medal to his name. Abrahams returned with little more than envy and respect for those who had taken their big chance better. He dismissed his first Olympics as a casual learning curve, perhaps to numb the pain.

*As far as I was concerned in 1920, I attached far more importance to getting my "Blue" at Cambridge, than being chosen to represent Great Britain at the Olympics. It was just a trip to Belgium and an athletic meeting – that was all.*

He wouldn't have said that if he had won a medal; but he had at least experienced the pressures of Olympic participation. And though he regarded himself as something of a failure at the time, he acknowledged later, 'I had an experience which served me well later on. I benefited enormously from that experience.'

Yet he had always known there was more to life than athletics, whatever his brothers had told him. And where Harold still had very little experience was with the opposite sex. His world turned upside down when he met Christina McLeod Innes early in his first term back at Cambridge. Christina was eighteen years old, petite and pretty, with blue-grey eyes and red-brown hair.

'Her brothers always called it "rusty", so that she shouldn't get conceited,' said Christina's daughter, Sue Smithson, many decades later. 'Typical older brothers.'

By the time Harold met Christina at Cambridge, her brothers were dead. From her expression in photographs of the period, you can almost feel her sadness. As Sue put it later, 'There was an abiding sorrow to her.' There was a quiet determination and strength about her too; the kind sometimes born of intense personal suffering. Life had hurt her horribly; and yet she wasn't ready to give up on life so young. Harold saw all this in Christina, and learned of her connection to Donald, his tragic Repton school chum. He became captivated.

From Christina, Harold heard what had happened to the young man who had written so movingly of his elder brother's death not long before he met his own. Donald had joined the Black Watch in the summer of 1918, was wounded in September and died in a French hospital in October, barely a month before hostilities ceased. To have lost one brother would already have been devastating for Christina. To lose a second, the one to whom she was closest, must have been as much as she could bear.

Sue Smithson explained:

*Donald, the brother my mother was particularly fond of, was wounded in the leg, and got gangrene. The leg had to come off. This was in hospital at Amiens. And my grandmother, Margaret Innes, went over to nurse him until he died in that hospital aged just nineteen. It is just so awful that I can't bear to think about it even now.*

Though Christina was desolate, she was determined to receive the education she thought she deserved – the one her brothers had been denied. There were only two women's colleges at Cambridge at that time – Girton and Newnham. Christina was at Girton, where she was studying modern languages. The women's colleges were not considered part of the university fabric in quite the same way as the male colleges. Women were not awarded degrees as such. Yet the Girton and Newnham students were still connected to the university; and they were allowed to join some of the university clubs.

Christina did so, and her younger daughter, Peregrine Morley, said later, 'I believe she met Harold through the Student Christian Movement at the University. I remember my mother explaining that Harold was a member of the SCM and was therefore not a practising Jew.'

His adopted daughter, Sue Pottle, believed that Harold's decision to embrace Christianity was influenced by his need for acceptance beyond the Jewish community. She said, 'He always wanted to fit in. I don't think he was incompatible with being Jewish, more incompatible with the restrictions it put on him. He used to tell his brothers, "What's the point in not eating bacon or pork?" He ate them. I never remember him going to a synagogue, and we never celebrated Jewish festivals. He was up on Jewish things but not really immersed in them.'

But it was also the depth of Harold's feelings for Christina McLeod Innes which led him towards the Christian causes of post-war Cambridge. There was something about her brave spirit which brought out the best in him. And his philanthropic efforts during their first months as friends could have done nothing but impress the deep-thinking teenager. It wasn't long before Christina became Harold's first girlfriend. His nephew Tony was convinced that she contributed to Harold's religious fervour.

A Cambridge student after the Second World War, Tony heard all the stories about his uncle from staff who were still there and recounted:

*As an undergraduate at Cambridge in his second year, Harold formed a romantic attachment. The attraction became quite serious and this led for a short time to an interest in Christianity. There was some anecdotal evidence up at Cambridge of Harold "getting religion". Harold had a phase when he preached in public. That was Christianity. He was preaching – my recollection of the description given me is that he was out in the open; on the streets. I think Harold's enthusiasm for this girl conditioned the fact that he actively started giving public utterances in favour of Christianity.*

It may surprise many *Chariots of Fire* fans to know that Harold Abrahams was a preacher years before Eric Liddell ever became one. How completely Harold felt driven by any new-found faith remains open to question. But he genuinely tried to be that person he thought he should be. Eric's religious fervour would always come from a higher and purer place, uncomplicated by the need to impress and belong. But in eloquence as a speaker, he probably never hit Harold's heights. And it would be unfair simply to dismiss this phase in Harold's life with a cynical wave of a hand, or condemn him as any kind of fraud. Sure, passion for God and passion for Christina may have become conflated. But Abrahams really tried to be the man Christina wanted him to be.

Sue Pottle also heard that her father became quite evangelical in his younger days. 'A long time ago a vicar wrote to me, saying that he had managed to get a lot of these Cambridge athletes converted. He said that he, my father and the others had gone round the East End of London "proselytising". That's the way he put it.'

That meeting in the Student Christian Movement had sparked something powerful between Harold Abrahams, star university athlete, and Christina, broken-hearted intellectual. As for Eric, he didn't need a woman to draw him towards Christianity. It was in his blood from the start.

CHAPTER ELEVEN:

# The Proposal

The bond between Harold and Christina was strong. Deep down, however, Harold must have suspected that it wasn't entirely of their own making. He was a living link to Donald, who had been the same age as Abrahams. Christina's daughter Sue explained, 'I'm sure this is how

Harold came into the bosom of the family. I think it was this emotional bond, through having known her brothers.'

Christina's father Hugh may not have been so instantly welcoming. He was probably taken aback by how quickly she fell for Abrahams. Hugh McLeod Innes was Bursar of Trinity College, a dour Scot whose father, General James John Mcleod Innes, had won a Victoria Cross during the Indian Mutiny. Hugh was not a man to be messed with either, despite his genteel surroundings. His office was in the King's Hostel, just below the Big Clock in Trinity's famous Great Court. A few years later, Harold's friend Lord Burghley succeeded in running round the Great Court in less time than it took the college bells to strike twelve.

What Hugh McLeod Innes couldn't see from his office, he could deploy spies to help him see.

Harold's daughter, Sue Pottle said, 'I met Christina and she told me she always used to visit my father in the halls of residence at Cambridge with a chaperone. I don't think Christina and my father were having sex.' Christina's youngest daughter Perry suggested, 'It's unlikely that they got beyond hand-holding and the occasional kiss.'

Instead of seeking physical pleasure, the lovers put their combined energies into campaigning for various causes. Looking back on his university days with the benefit of a lifetime's hindsight, however, Harold gave the impression that he was being swept along at a pace with which he was not entirely comfortable. Christina, who had a great personal interest in the plight of Russia, is thought to have played a leading role in the way Cambridge Christians reacted to the Russian Famine of 1921-22.

Harold also played a prominent role in the Russian Famine Relief Campaign. As images of the starving Russian millions reached Britain, it was impossible not to be moved by the suffering. Harold was no exception, yet part of him remained strangely detached from the unfolding tragedy. He knew he was doing the right thing by getting involved. But he didn't feel quite so passionately about the situation as many others did; and all the time there was the sneaking suspicion that he was being manipulated.

In a moment of typically brutal self-analysis, Harold said much later, '...I was very susceptible. You see, I was all the time trying to find a means of self-expression. I did an awful lot of work helping to collect money for Russian relief. But I can't, if I'm honest with myself, say that I felt emotionally terribly sincere about it. I did the work, I helped to get the money, and I was appalled by the pictures of starving.'

But he wasn't so deeply moved that he would have given all his spare time to the cause had he not loved Christina. And he was conscious that he sometimes spread himself too thinly, as he devoted his energies to the latest causes in a troubled world.

Harold added, 'I once made a speech on "Parker's Piece" [a big open green in Cambridge] for Dr Barnardos. You see, one was roped into a tremendous number of things, all of which one skated over the surface of.'

Picture Harold Abrahams, preaching good things even before Eric Liddell began to speak publicly of God's love. Harold ultimately lacked the moral strength of Liddell, but then so did pretty much everyone. The Scotsman's innate and colossal goodness was unbeatable. But what would Liddell have given for some of those Abrahams speaking skills? And we can be sure of one thing. Having seen talented and physically blessed young men leave Repton for the battlefields of Flanders, only to become a lifeless name on a school notice board within months, Harold Abrahams did not want another war. He would support anything he hoped would prevent that.

Indeed, Abrahams spent his lifetime truly believing the Olympic Games were a vehicle for peace. And if in fact they are, who is to say that Harold Abrahams did not make a greater contribution to the pursuit of world peace than Eric Liddell, for all the Scotsman's heroic and selfless acts? For now, however, Christina had become his great passion, above and beyond the Olympic movement. On the face of it, they seemed made for each other.

Christina even helped Harold to train. She used to ride a bicycle beside Harold while he was running. You can imagine Christina cycling as fast as she could ahead of him, so that the greyhound had a rabbit to chase. Her eagerness to break the monotony of Harold's training might have given him new athletic impetus. Instead Harold's passion for athletics began to dwindle, at roughly the same rate as his passion for Christina grew.

Harold soon became unwell, the precise nature of his illness undisclosed. Whether this low point was physical, mental or a combination of both is unknown. One report stated at the start of 1921, 'Harold Abrahams, the Cambridge Blue, is at present indisposed and will not be able to go into residence at Cambridge at the end of the month. Caius, favourites for the Inter-Collegiate Cup, will suffer seriously from his absence.'

On February 3, 1921, his low-key return to action was described like this: 'Abrahams, the Blue, who has been ill and only took up residence on Monday, turned out for Caius against St Johns and won the hundred and long jump without fully extending himself.'

Later that month there was a big showdown between Trinity and Caius. Harold's great Cambridge University rival and Athletics Club President, Guy Butler of Trinity, beat him in the 100 yards in a time of 10.2sec. Abrahams came second in the high jump and 120 yards hurdles, which was no good because both events were also won by Trinity. It was something of a shock that Caius were defeated so soundly. Abrahams and his great reputation had been well and truly dented. Perhaps there had been too big a weight of expectation after his first Cambridge year. At a misty Fenners in the University Sports of March 3 and 5, Harold was beaten yet again. Guy Butler defeated Abrahams, by now his Cambridge University Athletic Club Secretary, with such ease in the 100 yards that Harold's style looked a mess. He was even beaten in the long jump. What was going on?

'I went back and back,' he acknowledged later, reflecting on this confusing period.

'Paying too much attention to my mother, yes. I can see it all!' joked Christina's daughter Sue later.

Harold's pushy brother Adolphe referred to this sporting crisis in his book, *Fitness for the Average Man*. Speaking of Harold, he wrote: 'As a freshman at the age of nineteen he was accepted as the fastest runner who had ever represented the Varsity. At the age of twenty-one he slumped badly enough to invite the "burnt out" explanation, which would (as is usual) have been accepted had he not been encouraged to continue.'

Harold later put it this way: 'Some people may argue that every human being possesses a certain amount of innate energy, and if he uses up an excessive amount of it in his early years, he will have to pay the bill later on. I doubt very much if the problem is as simple as that. I do think competition of a strenuous kind has a very subtle effect on the nervous system.'

There was nothing wrong with his nervous system for the Varsity showdown. At the Queen's Club in London, Harold found himself locked in battle yet again with his greatest Varsity rival over the 100 yards. One report claimed that Bevil Rudd 'led to within yards of the tape', until he was hunted down once more. This time both Harold and his president, Guy Butler swept past at the death. Another report explained that 'last year's winner made a great effort in the last twenty yards and beat his president by two feet'. Abrahams had triumphed over Butler in a Cambridge one-two. Harold's time of 10.2sec didn't set the world alight. But it wasn't the time that mattered when you were racing Oxford. Winning was everything. Harold raised his arms high in the air while the ever-popular Rudd shook his head in fresh disappointment.

For a second successive year, Harold returned to Cambridge as a hero. But that Varsity victory was put in sharp perspective when news arrived from America to crush any Englishman with the slightest Olympic sprint ambitions for 1924. In April 1921, on a cold and rainy day in Redlands, California, Charley Paddock did something almost incredible. Finishing tapes awaited him at both the 100-yard and 100-metre stages of the race in question. Outstanding American reporter Maxwell Stiles wrote an eye-witness account of Paddock's progress, starting with his 9.6sec for 100 yards. 'Fifteen feet from the tape Paddock gave a mighty bound, and fairly flew over the finish line, coming down heavily. Recovering, he took two quick strides and leaped for the tape at 100m.' The time, 10.4sec, was a new world record. Stiles declared, 'Two such leaps as these made it appear that the boy must have wings or a kangaroo hoof.'

Later that day Paddock ran 21.2sec for the 200 metres, on his way to a world record 33.4sec for 300 metres. He had already clocked 20.8sec for the 220 yards a few weeks earlier.

Harold Abrahams could say what he liked about Charley Paddock; but in 1921 the Englishman wasn't in the same league. Harold recharged his batteries and wondered whether there was any point in persevering with athletics. As the weather became warmer, he decided to race for the hell of it – and his times picked up a little. They still didn't represent the sort of breakthrough he needed to make an impact on the world stage, though.

The university year was reaching the home straight. Soon the summer sun began to rise a few short hours after it had set, and the Caius May Ball came around. It was an occasion which seemed made for lovers, though it could test a relationship too. A party which began at 9.30pm and lasted till after 6am, the May Ball tended to leave many of its revellers drunk or exhausted. And the sensitivity some students showed towards their partners could become impaired. This seemed to happen in Harold's

Harold and Christina (circled) at the May Ball.

case, a story captured by the photographer when it was time to take the official survivors' picture.

Frozen in time is Christina's faint annoyance as she realises that Harold is posing for the camera without paying her any attention what-soever. Christina has no time to rectify this slight, because the picture is taken as she is left in limbo.

Perhaps the feisty Miss Innes let her feelings be known soon after-wards. We will never know, but Harold and Christina seemed insepa-rable. Then Harold let slip that he hoped to run in the USA during the summer holidays – and Christina wouldn't be able to join him. For a vulnerable young woman deeply scarred by the loss of two brothers, the prospect of this separation may have created a disproportionate sense of anxiety. A reassuring gesture from Harold was required; but he came up with more than a mere gesture.

Harold asked Christina to marry him . . . and Christina said yes.

CHAPTER TWELVE:

# A Pivotal Decision

Eric Liddell's academic adventures had switched from Eltham College to Edinburgh University, where his elder brother was already stud-ying medicine. The long-term goal was to teach science at the Anglo-Chinese College in Tientsin – and use that base as a springboard for his preaching activities in surrounding areas. Eric had chosen a four-year Bsc degree in Pure Science at Edinburgh – and knew it was a demanding academic programme.

At first, he wasn't convinced there would be much room in his life for athletics. He let slip to someone that he had played a lot of rugby at school; and he was persuaded to train with the university "rugger" squad, without possessing any firm ambition to progress.

It's strange to think that a photo of Eric and his siblings at Christmas 1920 marked the close of an Olympic year, during which Liddell hadn't even shown a passing interest in trying to get near the Olympic team.

But by the spring of 1921, he had changed his mind and was back in training. The University Sports of May 1921 were his focus, though he never considered them so important that he couldn't set off for a cycling holiday to Ben Nevis with friends shortly before the big week. Later in life, Eric would have to

Eric and siblings, Christmas 1920.

brave machine gun fire while cycling out on mercy missions in China. But his first trainer in Scotland considered a mere pleasure ride so dangerous to his muscular health that machine guns might as well have been waiting.

Cycling to Ben Nevis: Eric Liddell (second left) and friends.

He warned Liddell that cycling was the worst possible thing he could do so close to the University Sports. Maybe Eric didn't quite have enough faith in his trainer at first.

'I was a novice then, and a novice was my trainer,' he wrote.

Liddell learnt his lesson the hard way, much as he enjoyed that trip to the mountains. He recalled, 'Arriving back, I went to see if I would be able to run, but, alas! What I had been told was only too true. I was stiff, and there was no spring in my muscles, and only three or four more weeks before I was to make my first appearance in public as a runner.'

Eric was young and his body adaptable, though. When he raced the 100 yards at the University Sports, he exploded into life and beat the favourite, G. Innes-Stewart by inches. When his rival returned the compliment in the 220 yards, it was the only time Liddell ever lost a race in Scotland. No matter. He had announced himself on the public stage. He was going places.

University Sports rapidly became inter-university sports – and Liddell showed enough promise to make him take his athletic talent seriously. Training switched to a cinders track – the surface for proper sprinters – at the memorably named Edinburgh stadium of Powderhall. And that's where Eric began his partnership with the coach who would take him to the very top – Tom McKerchar.

He may not have had quite the reputation of the legendary Sam Mussabini down in London, but craggy-faced McKerchar knew his stuff alright. He told Liddell that his muscles were too tough and tight. They needed to be softened to achieve enough elasticity to avoid serious injuries such as snapped hamstrings. Extensive massage and exercise programmes gave Liddell's hardy, stocky body enough flexibility for him to take a serious shot at sprinting.

Like Musssabini, Tom McKerchar was a stickler for repetitive training. It was the only way to perfect a speedy start. The problem for Liddell was not so much his inability to react quickly to the gun. He was more irked by the cynical tendency in others to set off prematurely.

Liddell found false starts indescribably tedious and unnecessary. They dulled the edge he needed when the real start finally came. Subconsciously he paused for a split second, probably anticipating yet another attempt to cheat from among his fellow competitors.

McKerchar struggled to give his charge the psychological tools to cope with this problem.

Like Harold Abrahams, Eric Liddell also suffered from pre-race nerves early in his career. He was supposed to be running to honour God with a purely joyful display of the talents he had been given. And that would cure his nerves later in his career. But as his first Scottish championships drew near in that summer of 1921, the 19-year-old Liddell was stricken in a way that Harold would have recognised all too easily.

Later Eric wrote: 'At last, the day dawned. Needless to say I was excited. Excited is a very mild word to use in order to try to explain the various emotional tremors that vibrated through my system. My dinner [lunch] that day was not a success, in fact it was a nasty failure. The food would not slide down the alimentary canal with any degree of ease, and any that did manage to get down hadn't a dog's chance of being digested. This is an experience most athletes go through some time in their career, and it makes you ask yourself if it was all worth it.'

Harold Abrahams had asked himself that question many times already. Now Eric had also reached a level of competition where nerves became a factor. But could he use them to his advantage?

Liddell was the star of those Scottish Championships with commanding performances in the 100 yards and 220 yards. The extra adrenalin worked its magic. And as time went on, a quiet confidence in his athletic ability, coupled with his firm Christian faith would help control those nerves as the big races kept coming.

Meanwhile Harold's anxiety would not be helped when he heard the name "Eric Liddell" with increasing frequency in sprinting circles. And if Harold Abrahams didn't increase his own focus and keep his eyes on the prize, the young pretender was going to be coming for him. Someone at the *Glasgow Herald* saw how it might unfold:

*E.H. Liddell, Edinburgh University A.C., is going to be a British champion ere long, and he might even blossom into an Olympic hero.*

Harold couldn't see it yet, but then he had romantic distractions. Aware that there might be strong opposition from their families, it appears that Harold and Christina decided to keep the news of their engagement to themselves for the time being. But there is little doubt they became engaged, albeit unofficially.

Sue Smithson explained, 'Harold wished to marry my mother. I think the word engagement probably was used. But I don't think they were ever formally engaged. Still, it is an important strand to his story.'

If Abrahams didn't feel any great urge to rush round to her family home at 6, St Eligius Street and ask Hugh McLeod Innes for his daughter's hand in marriage, there was another reason. As if the Bursar of Trinity College wasn't formidable enough, Harold was even more intimidated by the Bursar's wife, Margaret. In fact, he let it be known that he was rather frightened of her.

Did he feel guilty? He hadn't fought in the war, while Donald, just six months older, had fought and died. Margaret McLeod Innes must have felt like a war veteran herself, having dashed to France to nurse her youngest son through his final weeks. She had seen the horror of war first-hand and yet Harold, a fine physical specimen, hadn't suffered at all. Now he was enjoying Cambridge, the reward that should have been waiting for Margaret's two sons. This gulf in human experience couldn't have created much common ground between them.

Then there were Harold's chauvinist tendencies; not uncommon for the day, but dangerous if they surfaced in any shape or form in front of Margaret, who was very keen on feminism. While he contemplated a lifetime with a mother-in-law he feared, Harold's focus on his racing wasn't all it might have been. Would a trip to America bring back the passion? In the summer of 1921 Harold recalled:

*I was selected to compete for Oxford and Cambridge against the American Universities of Harvard and Yale and Princeton and Cornell, and I made my one and only visit to the United States.*

The sense of anticipation among the men of Oxford and Cambridge must have been immense as they prepared for the six-day voyage across the Atlantic Ocean. The English team sailed on what Harold described as 'that luxurious liner, the Olympic'. The razzamatazz of the most energetic city on earth was felt even before they reached dry land. 'About half an hour before we actually landed in New York a host of press photographers and "movie" men came alongside in a tender, and, having wormed their way on board, bombarded us with questions and shutters for quite a time,' Abrahams recalled. With prohibition in force, he added, 'This was our first experience of American methods; our first experience of America had taken place some few hours earlier when we entered American territorial waters, and the bar closed.'

His account of events in Boston didn't suggest much more fun was had there either. He explained for the local media, 'Against Harvard and Yale the English Universities won only two events out of ten. I had heard a great deal about American hospitality and how considerate you were; but I don't think you were very kind to me. I had to jump against Ed Gourdin and he was ungracious enough to jump 25ft 3in – a new world's record – at his first effort.'

A good performance in the forthcoming contest against Princeton and Cornell would salvage some pride. Harold was determined to play his part, even though there were those on his own side who thought him so conceited that they preferred to see him beaten by their American hosts. Abrahams explained:

*At Travers Island [not far from New York] I competed in the first duel between Oxford and Cambridge and Princeton and Cornell. Anglo – American rivalry in athletics has produced Anglo-American friendship; that these friendships matter so much more than the result of the contest is, perhaps, best exemplified by an incident which occurred in the first Oxford and Cambridge against Princeton and Cornell meet in 1921. An Oxford man said to a Princeton man, 'I don't even care a damn who wins this sprint, so long as that blighter from Cambridge doesn't'.*

But 'that blighter from Cambridge' did. And even *The New York Times* hailed Abrahams. It wrote:

*The bright particular star in the visitors' demonstration was Harold M. Abrahams, wearer of the Cambridge Light Blue. He contributed two victories to the cause of his countrymen and paved the way for the unexpected recovery shown by the lads from across the sea. Abrahams started England off auspiciously by capturing the 100-yard dash, which opened the program. It was the work of this same athlete [Abrahams] in the broad jump which pulled the visitors within a single point of an even break in the honors of the day . . . The hero of the day was Abrahams, who was the only man to win two events.*

Neither his sprint time, nor the distance he jumped were anything to write home about; but this was a team event and allowed the drama of the day to reach a rousing climax. A spectacular run by Rudd in the half-mile gave the English universities a share of the spoils. *The New York Times* highlighted the 'remarkable recovery and surprising strength' of the English universities after their 'overwhelming setback of last Saturday'. Each side scored five wins and British honour had been restored. And yet, as he sailed home, Harold already had other matters on his mind.

Imagine Adolphe's mounting horror as his little brother dropped the bombshell; that he intended to announce his engagement to Christina. Her younger daughter Perry Morley was later told how that piece of news went down. 'My mother told us that Harold's brother was very strict with him – and he wouldn't hear of them becoming engaged while Harold was a student and had not established himself in some profession. I don't know whether the fact that my mother was not Jewish had anything to do with it.'

Sue Pottle, Harold's daughter, knew what the longer-term consequences would be. 'Christina told me she thought the brothers had put an end to her relationship with my father because it was harming his athletics. She used the word "brothers" in the plural. That suggested

"S.S." had backed Adolphe on this particular issue, though he was generally more kind-hearted.'

It was time for Harold to show his fiancée what he was made of. If he loved her enough, then surely he would tell his brothers to respect his wishes or stay out of his business? Instead, he wavered and even relented. Few women would be impressed if they saw their man's resolve buckle under pressure from his family. Sue Pottle recalled, 'The sense I got was that Christina might have thought Harold was being a bit meek by accepting the decision of his brothers.'

Adolphe, the lesser athlete, still wanted to live out his Olympic fantasies through his youngest brother. He wasn't about to watch Harold, who was blessed with so much more talent, throw away "their" Olympic dream.

'I think later in life he was competing, he lived through me many of the dreams which he himself had not the prowess to achieve,' Harold reflected.

Adolphe claimed he was playing an active part in making this dream a reality. 'The will to win telepathically influences others, even superior.'

It's hard to escape the conclusion that Adolphe used his own ambition to destroy Harold's romantic happiness.

CHAPTER THIRTEEN:

## Eileen and Christina

Eric Liddell faced no pressure from his family to abandon his personal life – because he didn't have one yet. Eric's shyness had ensured there was no girlfriend for siblings to assess. Maybe he already had the beginnings of a feeling for a member of the opposite sex, though. There was a talented young artist down in England by the name of Eileen Soper. The previous year, at the age of fifteen, she had become the youngest artist to exhibit at the Royal Academy. That exhibition had brought her acclaim on both sides of the Atlantic.

Eric wasn't one to be attracted by fame. Besides, he had known her since his school days. There must have been some kind of family connection for that acquaintance to have been made. And Eileen, it appears, had already developed a crush on the older boy. Since she was three years Eric's junior, the attraction

Courtesy of the Chris Beetles Gallery on behalf of the Artists General Benevolent Institution (AGBI)

A young Eileen Soper.

hadn't been mutual back then. But now Eileen was blossoming in every way. Her high cheekbones, plump lips and sensitive eyes could create quite an effect, even in someone who had barely noticed her before. Eileen didn't have a string of suitors, though; she was by no means a socialite. She lived with her family in a house called Wildings in Harmer Green, Hertfordshire. But at some point, Eric had noticed the change in her. And if he hadn't already come up with some fresh excuse to visit her, it wouldn't be too long before he did.

As Eric's first romance was showing tentative signs of life, Harold's was suddenly in its death throes. It had always been complicated. But Abrahams was never going to be left to work out the underlying issues in his private life by himself. And since he showed no obvious signs of being able make sense of it, perhaps that was just as well. Even so, the way his brothers went to work and effectively brushed Christina aside wasn't pleasant.

Adolphe may have used Isaac's will as leverage to scupper the engagement before it was formalised. There were financial implications to consider – consequences which seemed better suited to a Jane Austen novel. Adolphe may have felt compelled to warn his little brother that, by getting engaged, he might throw away his inheritance as well as his athletics career. Harold's father, Isaac would have to be told; and that carried considerable risk. Sidney Abrahams, whose wife had converted to Christianity, had already been cut out of the family estate when a codicil was added to Isaac's will. Adolphe would have been alert to such danger, because he and Lionel were executors of their father's will.

Tony Abrahams, Sidney's son, suggested, 'It may have been significant that Adolphe didn't marry until after his father's death and then he soon married a Catholic. It is possible to speculate that, when Harold told Adolphe (or indeed Lionel) that he wanted to marry Christina, Adolphe advised against it, knowing what was in the will and codicil. Lionel might have expressed the same view.'

The legalities sounded complicated, but the threat was very simple. It would only require Harold's father to dislike Christina or her religion, and the runner could lose his inheritance. Added to his brothers' disapproval, this was a serious setback for Harold and Christina's hopes of marriage. There could be no wedding if Harold had no means to support his prospective wife, because women of a certain social standing didn't usually work. Besides, they were both still students.

So Adolphe Abrahams seems to have undermined Harold's engagement on two fronts, using the inheritance issue and his younger brother's athletics career as twin sticks with which to beat him. Adolphe was a controlling character and often interfered in Harold's life. He admitted in one letter to Harold that he possessed 'a natural disposition to suspect everybody and everything', and advised his little brother to 'cut out ruthlessly the things that are too trivial and which won't advance you personally'. Though he probably didn't go so far as to call Christina trivial, Adolphe didn't see how the engagement could advance Harold personally – quite the reverse.

'To an extent Adolphe inherited some of his father's nastiness,' Tony Abrahams said. 'Isaac adored Harold but all the sons were fairly scared of him and, in the same way Adolphe didn't marry a Catholic until after his father died, I would not expect Harold to have broached the subject of marriage with Isaac. It seems Isaac continued to have a strong influence over the situation indirectly, even without being consulted.'

There is evidence that Harold's brother Solly adopted a gentler approach to his youngest brother's romance when he visited the McLeod Innes home. In a letter Christina later wrote to Harold about Solly, she described her 'personal recollection of his kindness and friendliness to me [when] you brought him and his wife, whom I also liked extremely, to 6 St Eligius Street'.

It shows that the families had recognised and accepted the relationship to a point. Solly might even have discussed Harold's situation with Christina's parents in their pretty walled garden at the back of their modest property. But his diplomacy could have changed little; Adolphe was never going to allow that engagement.

Part of Harold may even have felt relieved when the matter was taken out of his hands. He once said, 'I've got that sort of psychological temperament about things, I don't like getting too involved in something, I don't like caring too much about something.'

His love for Christina probably made him feel insecure. Even for one of the fastest men in England, things were moving too quickly. What if their love suddenly died just as quickly? For a young man like Harold, it was all a little frightening. Tony Abrahams concluded, 'He was serious about her; but it was not a definitive relationship.'

Harold's inner confusion may have led to his poor performance at the Freshmen's Sports in early November. But soon there were signs that he was back in the groove and leaping enthusiastically towards a future free of responsibility. He dominated an inter-collegiate contest, winning no fewer than four events. Trotting off triumphant after achieving a personal best 23ft in the long jump, Harold was saddened by some unexpected news. Old Isaac had died that very day.

No matter how much trauma Isaac had caused during Harold's childhood, he had given his son the perfect platform to showcase his talents. Harold would always be grateful. In time, the numbness he felt at the loss of his father gave way to an even greater sense of freedom. In theory, it could have put Harold's engagement to Christina back on the agenda. It didn't. Yet, for the moment, she remained close to him – and took a keen interest in his sporting activities.

On Friday February 24, 1922, when Caius beat St Catharine's in what Christina described as the 'Finals' of the 'Inter-collegiate Sports Div 1', she was definitely present. We know this because Christina took advantage of the clear blue skies to photograph her man in action. 'H.M.A. High-jumping at Fenners. Caius v Cats' Christina wrote on the back of a photo good enough to have been taken by a professional.

Perfect shot by Christina – Harold leaps sky-high.

Harold appears to be jumping higher than the head of a man watching. There was no "Fosbury Flop" in those days and Abrahams achieved his clearance using a simple 'scissors' style – making his jump all the more remarkable.

His former fiancée kept those photographs for the rest of her life, a visual record of an exceptional young man in his prime. Even as she captured her boyfriend's magnificent athleticism in the cold sunshine, she may have known deep down that their days together were numbered. And yet, whatever the extent of their underlying problems, Harold seemed untroubled in those pictures, as he casually put his opponents to the sword.

Abrahams was a complex character, someone who could be buzzing one moment and desolate the next. It was at around this time that a Cambridge student called Walter Ashley was ushered into Harold's rooms in Caius to meet the great sporting hero. Ashley wrote, 'I shall never forget our first meeting. He was like a racehorse – highly trained, impulsive, eager to be off. Exultant one minute; depressed the next (but usually the former). An artist in life, no less than in sport. An artist too, with real genius in both spheres.'

~

A truer and more talented artist, Eileen Soper had been keeping her eye on Eric Liddell's progress. And in many ways, what Eric was achieving was even more impressive – because it earned him international acclaim in another sport beyond track and field. Eileen must have been thrilled when news reached her of her close friend's latest sporting honour. Eric Liddell had worked his way up through the Edinburgh University rugby ranks by playing at centre three-quarter. First-team rugby allowed him to shine. An inter-city showdown followed in November – and brought him to the attention of the Scotland selectors. Eric was moved out to the wing, to make the most of his obvious speed. And he was lucky enough to form a good partnership with Leslie Gracie, another old boy from Eltham college, during trials. Gracie was already a star for the London club Harlequins – and didn't have much to prove.

When Scotland played The Rest in a trial match at Netherdale in December, Liddell ran in no fewer than five tries from left wing, some of them gifted by the trickery of Gracie. One final trial match at Inverleith saw the Liddell-Gracie partnership continue to blossom. They say if you're good enough, you're old enough. Eric Liddell was good enough alright, so his tender years didn't count against him in the selectors' eyes.

On January 2, 1922 Eric played his first international against France in Paris. Eric looks a little nervous in the team photo – and he is still a teenager when the snap is taken. Yet he is destined to hold his own at the Stade Colombes, the scene of his greatest triumph little more than two years later.

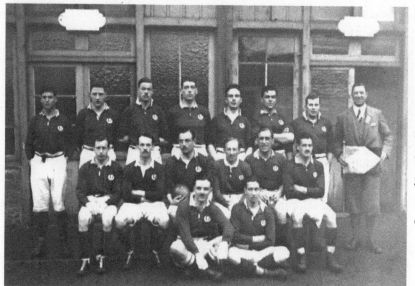

Proud moment: Eric Liddell (seated far left) represents Scotland at rugby.

Liddell did well enough in a low-scoring Parisian draw to stay in the squad. He even scored a try in an international against Ireland not long afterwards. By then he had turned twenty, and everyone could see he had a long and bright future in big-time rugby, if only he chose to stick at it. For the moment, at least, he did. Indeed, Eric was set to distinguish himself even more markedly the following season. Edinburgh University already seemed to know by the summer of 1922 that an international star had been born in its midst. In June, *The Student* magazine wrote of Liddell:

> *He has that rare combination, pace and the gift of rugby brains and hands; makes openings, snaps opportunities, gives the dummy to perfection, does the work of three (if necessary) in defence, and carries unselfishness almost to a fault.*

The second half of that appraisal could have summed him up just as well in his final years, when he was interned in a Japanese camp in China.

Whether he played team sports or took part in individual events, Liddell shone just the same. Later in 1922, Eric was also photographed representing Scotland at athletics.

Eric Liddell was strikingly consistent. Brilliant at sport, selfless in life. But who would share that life? Eileen Soper was seventeen by now – and turning into a desirable young woman. Distance would prevent the friendship from developing into anything more serious for the moment. Sooner or later, however, Eric Liddell might have a decision to make. Just as well there would soon be an excuse to visit her more frequently, so that he could make up his mind about what he was feeling.

Courtesy of Eric Liddell Community

Proud double:
Eric Liddell runs for Scotland too!

CHAPTER FOURTEEN:

# The Hero They Hated

Though Harold Abrahams had the temperament of an artist, he showed no talent for the arts. That didn't stop him from taking centre stage on March 9 to pay homage to one of his great loves – Gilbert and Sullivan. Christina, who was also a devoted fan, must have known what a fool Harold risked making of himself on Caius' College Hall stage. A musical genius he wasn't.

As Harold told radio presenter Roy Plomley on *Desert Island Discs* later in life, 'I love music Roy. I love Gilbert and Sullivan. I'm not musical in the sense that I can't play a single instrument, and I sing out of tune. I change key, I do everything that's wrong.'

At least there was no danger of him forgetting his words on that Caius stage. As his friend in athletics administration, Sir Arthur Gold said much later, 'He would produce apposite quotes from G & S as readily as any biblical scholar quoting from the Testaments.' Yet this was to be a duet; and his inability to hold his half of the tune threatened to sound almost tragically awful – especially when set against the skill of a good singer.

Despite the clear risk of offence to the ears of Cambridge music-lovers, Harold went ahead with his performance. Mercifully there is no recording of the result. The college magazine, *The Caian*, reviewed it:

*The Gilbert and Sullivan Concert was given on Thursday, March 9, in the College Hall, by kind permission of the Master and Fellows. The chief interest in the programme was due to the fact that many of the items were chosen from the less known operas, and many thus seemed quite new. It was a long programme, but it was, on the whole, quite successful. Much might be said, but there is no room for it here, and a detailed criticism would be as tedious as it would be out of place now that the concert is already buried in the past. H.K.P. Smith, in his solos and the duet with H.M. Abrahams, was enthusiastically received.*

The review didn't suggest that Harold was similarly appreciated. But perhaps his energy just about carried him through. And Harold's love for Gilbert and Sullivan was still appreciated nearly sixty years later in *Chariots of Fire*. It was written by Colin Welland, who loved Gilbert and Sullivan just as passionately.

But what of Harold's passion for athletics? It began to return, just as his love for Christina began to fade. And his next competitive experience was to go down as one of the most famous in Cambridge history.

The Varsity Sports, held as usual at the Queen's Club in London, were so one-sided that it was almost embarrassing. Abrahams set the tone, with typical victories in the 100 yards and long jump. It was Harold's sprinting that caught the imagination of The Times, whose perceptive correspondent also noticed just how highly strung Abrahams was. On March 27, 1922 the newspaper wrote: 'Abrahams is undoubtedly a fine sprinter. He runs low with a big raking stride, and he has that touch of splendid frenzy which has been well described in the saying that "to be a sprinter a man must run like a madman".'

Mad or not, Abrahams was too much for Oxford. And by the time the mismatch was over, Cambridge had crushed their rivals completely. In his book *Cambridge Doctor*, Rex Salisbury Woods wrote: 'In 1922 Cambridge beat Oxford in the Sports by nine events to one, a record victory of which Harold Abrahams, already a sporting journalist, never failed to remind the "House of Lost Causes" for years afterwards, and, on the standard displayed, members of the Cambridge team and myself were invited to give demonstrations in Aldershot's newly-built stadium.'

It was probably no coincidence that Harold had just been freed from the worst of the pressure surrounding his hasty engagement to Christina. And soon he would leave this romance behind. He felt bad about it. In fact, he felt terrible. In their first university year together, Harold and Christina had been so in love. Their second university year had been full of problems and complications. The fun had gone; and the love began to die. Harold later referred to 'that hopeless feeling that you can't prevent love just vanishing'. It was a feeling that he never forgot.

For more than a decade he was tormented by the dreadfulness of that feeling. He knew what Christina had been through, losing her brothers in the war, and felt awful about the collapse of their romance. He also developed a morbid fear that he might one day suffer a repeat of love's 'vanishing act' with someone else. It meant he avoided serious involvement with women for many years to come.

Sue Smithson believes her mother accepted the break-up without lasting bitterness. 'I don't think my mother ever held it against him. In a way she was probably quite relieved herself. I don't know, that's speculation on my part. But I know she always spoke very warmly of Harold. I think they were serious about each other, but I think it was a first love thing which doesn't always last very long.'

Harold rediscovered his independence and built on his athletic excellence over the course of the following year. Fast forward to late March 1923, as Harold prepared for his last shot at Oxford in the Varsity athletics. This time it felt different. Now President of the Cambridge University Athletic Club, everything depended on Abrahams and the pressure was terrific. He even picked the team, and there was no room for sentiment. Harold left S.E. Nelson of Fitzwilliam House out, even though his father Alec Nelson was coach of CUAC.

Arthur Marshall, one of Harold's teammates at the time, didn't like the decision. As first choice for the 440 yards, Marshall expected to be consulted before his "support act" for the Varsity race was selected. After all, the "second string," as the second pick for any contest was known, traditionally danced to the tune of the better man. On the record, Marshall only admitted to 'surprise'. But privately he told friends how dissatisfied he was with Harold's unilateral approach.

No wonder Marshall gravitated towards Eric Liddell as the 1924 Olympic Games drew near, rather than Harold Abrahams.

It was particularly audacious of Abrahams to pick himself for the 440, because Cambridge were facing a vastly superior opponent – on paper at least – in Oxford's talented American, Bill Stevenson. Two years earlier, Stevenson had won the amateur championship of the United

States, and he seemed a class apart. Stevenson had defeated Bevil Rudd on the East Coast earlier that year. He had broken 49 seconds in the USA and he had never been beaten in England, where he was a Rhodes scholar. It was as though Harold, a comparative novice in quality races at this distance, had just challenged Superman. Stevenson was the AAA Champion, and Evelyn Montague – Aubrey the narrator in *Chariots of Fire* – admitted, 'We of Oxford roared with laughter at the idea of Harold's taking on Bill Stevenson.'

Later Abrahams tried to claim that he didn't have much more faith in the decision than Oxford.

*I was not only burdened with the responsibility of being Captain of the Cambridge Team, but much against my will I had been persuaded to compete in the quarter-mile as well as the 100 yards and long jump.*

Who would have done the persuading? After all, ultimately it was Harold's decision. One can only guess that his brother Adolphe, an ex-Cambridge man, had come up with the idea, and then exerted the usual pressure as 'father figure'. Whoever was behind the decision, it nearly backfired even before race-day. Twenty-four hours before Cambridge faced Oxford, Harold came close to suffering a mental breakdown. The weight of responsibility on his shoulders became almost unbearable; so many people were waiting to shoot him down if his plan failed. Abrahams revealed:

*The morning before my farewell performance at Cambridge, I woke up with a ghastly sore throat, felt feverish and ached in every part of my body. I was so bad that I called round on my brother Adolphe at his Brook Street practice for a complete check-up. He spent a good half-an-hour examining me and then he said, 'You bloody fool – it's nerves.' He informed me that I had never been fitter in my life. I had the 'wind up vertical'. The intense 'wind up' had caused me to create all sorts of imaginary ailments. Of what was I afraid?*

The answer, of course, was failure and humiliation. Harold explained, 'I had jumped 23ft in the Varsity trials and injured my heel, and I was down to represent Cambridge in three events: 100 yards, quarter mile and long jump. I was expected by many experts to win both the 100 and long jump.' But in that moment Harold didn't feel equipped to do so, either mentally or physically. He knew that in some ways his years at Cambridge would be defined by how he performed against Oxford on this final occasion. And he didn't feel fit to meet the challenge.

Big brother Adolphe helped Harold to pull himself together and recover his composure. Slowly a semblance of confidence returned to the younger man. Gradually, that confidence turned into a familiar, strutting arrogance.

Arthur Marshall revealed, 'In Kensington on the morning of the Varsity match, Harold suggested a walk to the Peter Pan statue. On the way he said, "Do you think you have any chance of beating Stevenson in the quarter mile?" I said I didn't think I had a dog's chance. Harold said, "Will you give up any chance of winning and let me have a go then?"'

Having already walked into Harold's trap by playing down his own chances, Marshall could hardly refuse. Abrahams revealed what Marshall later described as 'cunning tactics, pre-agreed'. They may have sounded clever, but Arthur was the one being asked to sacrifice himself.

All the training the superior quarter-miler had done to prepare for the big race was going to count for nothing if Harold had his way. There was no argument between them, merely an unspoken tension as they headed to the Queen's Club. Soon they would put Harold's plan into action against the old enemy; and it would either be hailed as a masterstroke or ridiculed as selfish lunacy.

First Harold had to set the tone for the day in the most glamorous event of them all, the 100 yards. Abrahams revealed later, 'A study of past University records showed that no athlete had ever won the 100 yards outright four times...I wanted four clear wins, which was something which could never be beaten...No athlete can represent his University at athletics more than four times.'

The weather was described as 'exceptionally fine', as Abrahams carved out his starting holes. No one wanted to win more than he

Harold wins at London's Queen's Club.

did. When he heard the gun, Harold exploded into action and raced into a decisive three-yard lead. No one came close to catching him. Abrahams had won the most glamorous sprint for the fourth successive year – and equaled the Varsity record of 10sec in doing so. 'Another youthful ambition achieved,' he said of his Fantastic Varsity Quadruple. The *Daily Mail* even claimed he was 'easing up' at the end. His nearest opponent was Rex Alston, who later became famous as a BBC sports commentator. According to the *Daily News*, 'Had Abrahams been pushed he could have got inside even time, a feat not yet recorded in Varsity Sports.'

But his day was only starting. Twenty minutes later, 'keyed up by his sprint victory', as *The Observer* put it:

*[Abrahams] went all out for his second record of the day ... Conscious of a damaged heel, he banked on his first long-jump effort as probably his last. A magnificent leap, a yell from the crowd, and a wave of the hand from the judge. The Cantab had cleared 24 feet but with his foot three inches over the board. Yet, after this heartbreaking misfortune, and with his heel 'gone', he tried again: 23ft 7¼in in a jump plumb off the board, and the Light Blue President confidently trotted back to the pavilion.*

Abrahams had just beaten H.S.O. Ashington's 1914 record for the long jump of 23ft 6¼in. Even in 1959, Harold was able to say wryly, 'I am still lucky enough to hold the Oxford and Cambridge record, a miserable twenty-three feet seven-and-a-quarter.'

Now it was time for Harold to face his biggest challenge of all – the 440 race against Stevenson. Abrahams was drawn on the outside, usually a disadvantage for any runner. On this occasion, it rather fitted his plan. Lanes were quickly forgotten under the rules of the day, as competitors vied for the inside track. When Harold heard the crack of the pistol, he 'at once dashed for the lead'. Abrahams had told Marshall, 'I'll go off like a dingbat for the first hundred yards.' Though it looked like a foolish rush of blood to the head from Harold, his opponents still had to quicken their pace initially. But they seemed to be caught in two minds over whether or not to cover his move.

The Oxford men knew that Marshall was the chief Cambridge threat, so to an extent they judged their reaction by his. Marshall said of Harold, 'he started the race at a very fast speed for the first 50 yards, and I didn't follow, so Stevenson was watching me as first string and hanging back with me.' One report described how, 'When Abrahams had drawn the two Oxford men after him, he dropped back . . . but lengthened his stride.' Harold had already explained this phase to Marshall, 'I'll try to slow the race down until the open straight.' He did just that, acting like a whirlwind that had blown itself out too early. That was Marshall's cue to take over. An eyewitness account described how Harold 'went wide to allow Marshall to go through, and the public thought he was finished. Stevenson, the Princeton crack, no doubt thought he was too.'

Forgetting Abrahams, Stevenson stayed with Marshall, who seemed reluctant to take the race on with any great vigour. Arthur admitted, 'Abrahams slowed the race right down until we came round the final bend when he ran wide, with a view to letting me, his first string, through; but I didn't make any effort, and Stevenson didn't make any particular effort.' At this point the American must have known that he had the measure of his chief rival. Stevenson didn't need to kick hard for home to beat Marshall; so he went into cruise control, thinking the race was won. There was no reason to consider Abrahams, who was ten yards behind at that point. The American's overconfidence was, of course, exactly what Harold had hoped for. Marshall explained his president's strategy. 'His idea was to run wide as if to let me through, then come up on the inside, staying behind Stevenson until the last few yards. "Then," said Harold, "I'll go for it." Which he did.'

Evelyn Montague described what happened next. 'I shall never forget my feeling of incredulous horror as I stood beside the straight and watched Harold, all arms and legs, rushing past Stevenson like an animated windmill.' He caught the American about fifteen yards from the post. Reports said that '[Stevenson] couldn't hold Abrahams down the all-important final straight', where Harold 'quickly overhauled the first strings'. With a mixture of admiration and envy, Marshall explained, 'Abrahams came up with a very fast finish in the last 30 yards and won the race. Harold came first, Stevenson second, and I was third.'

The time was astonishing, and one onlooker described how Abrahams 'wore [Stevenson] the Balliol man down in the straight and finished full of running in 50.8sec, probably a second faster than he has achieved in his life.' It wasn't just the impudence Harold had shown to run away with the quarter, as second string. The time was as good as any done in the next three or four years by 'proper' 440 Varsity runners. Harold's raking stride brought him home, though in reality brains had played as big a part as pace. Having won by about three yards, the Cambridge President received a tremendous ovation, which doubled when it was known he had broken yet another record. These were, as the *Sporting Life* put it, 'superhuman efforts'. As far as the Varsity was concerned, he had gone out in a blaze of glory.

Abrahams had established a new individual record of eight inter-Varsity firsts in total. No one seemed to care that Oxford had defeated Cambridge by seven events to four. Harold had stolen the show, just as he had planned. He was the hero of the hour, and even his enemies had to admit it.

Would he have been capable of such exploits at the height of his romance with Christina? Probably not, and now she could only watch with the rest as the Queen's Club went wild. Abrahams saw through the wild celebrations:

*We all like to jump on the bandwagon. I can remember when I was carried off in my last year at Oxford and Cambridge sports noticing the sort of people who were joining in that probably hated my guts really. I wasn't a popular person in the team. I knew that and that hurt a lot.*

He wasn't a popular person in Oxford's team, either. Montague wrote to his mother after the race and said, 'They chaired Harold Abrahams from the track, and I was just waiting for them to drop him on his arse.'

Ironic, therefore, that Montague's letters home from the 1924 Olympics would effectively immortalise Harold in *Chariots of Fire* after the screenplay writer, Collin Welland used them to create "Aubrey," his narrator.

And Welland had it right when he wrote in his provisional notes for *Chariots of Fire* that Montague was conflicted when it came to Harold: 'Abrahams, like many others, he finds difficult to warm to, even, at times, craving his fall. And yet in later years the same man is to godfather his sons.'

An intelligent man, Montague had no doubt worked out by then that Harold's arrogance was just a front.

CHAPTER FIFTEEN:

# Breakthrough

Eric Liddell was about to face a make-or-break moment in an area of his life that had been unresolved for some time. Ever since he had been a boy, Eric had wanted to follow in his father's footsteps and become a preacher in China. But he had always feared he was too shy to achieve his ambitions.

To have the missionary life in your blood, and to be educated in a school with "missionary" in its name allowed little respite for a young man who worried that he didn't have the speaking skills to succeed as a missionary. Even now, while at university, he was staying at the Edinburgh Medical Missionary Society hostel in George Square. But would he ever have what it took to be a missionary? Eric was brave enough, he was pretty sure of that. And there was no question that his faith was strong enough. To be a missionary, however, you had to be able to preach. And Eric Liddell was so painfully shy in big crowds that he found it a struggle to speak at all, let alone preach. Life changed for Liddell at the end of March 1923, when he was visited by an evangelical Christian called David Patrick "D.P." Thomson. D.P. had a request. Would Eric speak publicly about his faith in the industrial town of Armadale in central Scotland, and try to appeal to the ordinary folk there to follow the ways of Christ? Factory men might listen to a rugby international and athletics star more readily than a more established man of the cloth, he reasoned. It was a clever and timely approach.

Only the previous month, Eric Liddell had scored a try in Scotland's 11-8 win at Cardiff Arms Park, their first at that ground since 1890. A team photo survives, taken just before the match.

Eric is standing on the far left of the back row in that team photo. You can see how much shorter than the rest of his team he appears to be. Compared to the year before, however, he looks more confident and self-assured. That's what international experience had done for him. And perhaps Eric had an inkling of just how well that match was going to go.

A crowd of 40,000 had entered the Arms Park before the gates were locked. It was a tremendous occasion for those taking part, and for the packed spectators too. Eric had not been unnerved by the highly charged atmosphere for a second. He had thrived in the cauldron of rugby that Wales was fast becoming. But then again, he hadn't been required to

Courtesy of Scottish Rugby with special thanks to Laura Tinch

What he lacks in size he makes up for in heart.
Liddell (standing far left) prepares for Wales v Scotland.

speak to the crowd at Cardiff Arms Park. Playing, when you knew you had the skills to please, and speaking, when you knew deep down you didn't have the required skills, were two different things entirely.

Liddell must have felt mildly terrified by Thomson's Armadale invitation, and yet also compelled to accept. How could he really say no? He had always known this day would come; and now at last he had to face his fears. There would be a week to prepare; to think about what he would say. You can just picture him praying to God to find the right words for a challenge far scarier than anything he had attempted before.

He described this period later:

*My whole life had been one of keeping out of public duties; but the leading of Christ seemed now to be in the opposite direction and I shrank from going forward. At this time, I finally decided to put it all on Christ. After all, if He called me to do it, then He would have to supply the necessary power.*

At that point a letter dropped onto his doormat. It was from Tientsin, where his sister Jenny had returned to live while her brothers were educated in Britain. And although the letter must have been written some time before Eric received his invitation to speak, the timing of its arrival felt like a sign. Particularly when Liddell opened the letter and saw the passage Jenny had selected from the Bible. It was from Isaiah and read: 'Fear not, I am with thee; do not dismay, for I will guide thee.' It was so appropriate for these moments of doubt that it felt almost uncanny. Eric couldn't have asked for greater comfort.

In *Chariots of Fire*, Jenny comes across almost as the nagging voice of religious obligation and formality. Whenever Liddell starts to let his hair down and express his individuality, she is there to keep him in check. In the film, Jenny isn't in favour of Eric's running or the hero-worship it seems to create. She feels athletic stardom will clash with his plan for a humble life devoted solely to serving God back in China. But gradually she comes to understand that athletics need not compromise Eric's commitment to Christianity. And her ultimate approval of Liddell's Olympic adventure is part of the movie's joyous finale.

The reality was different. Jenny was never against Eric's running – and there was never any underlying tension between them. Liddell wanted to choose the life of a missionary over everything else, he simply didn't know if he had what it took. Far from raining on his parade, Jenny inspired Eric to follow his dream and face his fears.

Just as Harold Abrahams was afraid of letting down a huge athletics crowd, so Eric Liddell was worried about losing any member of his audience due to his lack of talent for speaking. Many years later, Eric's future wife Florence approached David Puttnam at the *Chariots of Fire* premiere and told him that his actor, Ian Charleson possessed an eloquence that Liddell, the man he played in the movie, could only have yearned for.

'Eric wasn't a good speaker,' she explained. 'He had a real problem with crowds and getting his deep conviction across to large groups of people. He knew it and regretted it.'

If we accept that Liddell never became a great orator, despite two decades of doing his best, how excruciating must his discomfort have been at the prospect of trying for the first time? And imagine his nerves in the first week of April when he entered Armadale Town Hall for his first ever public engagement.

Eric admitted later in life:

*When I was at the University, I wanted to help Christ. I wanted to use any talents I had, and I did not feel I could. Mr Thomson came to me one day and asked if I would go out to an area and speak. I think the bravest thing I did in my life was to accept that invitation. It was something positive.*

Eric was probably relieved to see fewer than a hundred people there. And he was under no illusions: this would be a tough crowd to convert to his way of thinking. Half had probably turned up just to see a sporting hero in the flesh; and they may not have been remotely interested in what he had to say about religion. They had read about his heroics in Wales and the glory he had brought Scotland. That probably meant more to most than the glory of God. If Liddell misjudged his tone, he might lose the non-believers inside the first two minutes.

But Eric did a very clever thing and chose a path all novices should walk, in any field. He kept it simple and spoke only about what he knew. That was the guidance he must have felt he had received, when he had asked God to show him the way during the nervous days leading up to the event. Eric just talked about his everyday life; how he introduced elements of his Christian beliefs into little situations he encountered, where simple choices had to be made.

He applied his beliefs to the sporting arena, as well. Life and sport were all about being the best you can be – and forgiving yourself if you fell short sometimes. Courage and sportsmanship mattered.

As he explained later,

*That was the spirit to keep on the field and in everyday life. It was when courage was applied to everyday life that it reached its very highest form. It was for young men to get hold of that spirit and carry it, not only into the sporting field, but into everyday life.*

His audience listened because he didn't talk down to them. He didn't demand anything they might consider impossible for them to give.

This wasn't the sort of preaching ordinary men were used to hearing. Eric wasn't poetic or bombastic. But his bright blue eyes carried a kind intensity that mesmerised his audience – and most future crowds – in their own passionate way. Those eyes were windows to a bright soul; and the informality of the message held the audience well enough until the very end of his talk.

By the time Eric Liddell left Armadale that night, he knew something very important. After years of doubting his ability to do it at all, Eric realised he could preach. He was under no illusions about his talent for public speaking. He knew this was something he couldn't do extremely well. But if he could preach now and have people listen, then he would probably get a bit better at it as time went on. With increasing confidence, he could introduce more humour, too.

A couple of years later, when Liddell visited the Central YMCA in London, again with the formidable, rugged-looking DP Thomson in tow, he was relaxed enough to open with a joke.

'I am Liddell,' he began. 'That thing in the corner is Thomson. To see us together you would think he was the athlete and that I was the writer.'

It was almost an invitation for the audience to laugh at both Eric and Thomson, who had by then edited several books on Scottish religious thought. Listeners chose to laugh with them during these ice-breaking moments instead. And right away, Eric had his audience in the palm of his hand.

Such light-hearted routines could be developed later. All that mattered for now was that the rookie speaker had faced down his terrible phobia.

It may not sound like much, a few score people listening to Liddell in a smoky old industrial backwater. But for Eric, those eighty-odd people were worth the forty thousand in Cardiff – and more. They may not have cheered him to the rafters, but they didn't leave either. They even seemed to like what he had to say. For Eric Liddell, this little event was life changing. He must have suspected, as he headed back to Edinburgh, that his ambition to become a missionary in China was finally a realistic possibility. The biggest barrier had been removed.

As Eric Liddell put it, 'In going forward the power was given me. Since then the consciousness of being an active member of the Kingdom of Heaven has been very real.'

As the athletic season opened in Scotland, you might have thought that Eric's release from his own self-doubt would have had spectacular effects on the track. And it would do so within a few short months. But that was something of a delayed reaction. Perhaps another dilemma was starting to play with his peace of mind instead: was he starting to wonder whether putting his body on the line in both rugby and athletics was unsustainable in the long run? Was he going to have to choose between the two before long? At any rate, his performance in the Scottish Amateur Athletic Championships in Glasgow hardly set the country alight. He won the 100 and 220 yards races in times that made him feel embarrassed to be considered for the 1923 AAAs down at Stamford Bridge in London.

What was the point of someone spending £5 to send him down to London, when that small fortune would only fund a sound beating? Liddell wasn't afraid of losing in the way Abrahams was. He just didn't see himself as a wise investment. Fortunately, he was going to be persuaded in time to take that train to the English capital. And although Harold Abrahams had never travelled north to watch Eric in Scotland as *Chariots of Fire* had us believe, the confident Cambridge man would certainly never forget Liddell's first foray onto his own territory.

On 16 June, Harold, still blissfully unaware of the storm that was coming down from Scotland, completed an encouraging hat-trick to win the 100 yards, 220 yards and long jump in the Midland Counties. Who cared that he had only been awarded a Third for Law at Cambridge? Athletics was his focus now. And there was to be no day of rest for religious reasons. He explained his decision to run on a "forbidden" day – just as Eric Liddell would one day explain his reason for not running.

A Jewish organisation called the Maccabeans held a dinner in honour of Abrahams in London's Holborn. Harold spoke about running on the Sabbath – which for Jews lasts from sunset on Friday to sunset on Saturday. Far from disowning his roots, Abrahams dared to claim that he was typical of young Jewry in his general outlook; and he was unwilling to sacrifice his athletic ambitions for the observance of strict religious laws. In fact he went so far as to say that to follow Jewish religious law would rule out athletic distinction. He pointed out that he had gained all his inter-varsity successes on a Saturday, and that it was necessary to travel to venues on the Sabbath. Furthermore, he claimed it was not possible to observe the Jewish dietary laws and still peak when it mattered. Harold's remarks were not designed to outrage or create conflict; rather to encourage members of the Jewish community to relax their laws sufficiently to take the opportunities that came their way, to embrace the equality they now enjoyed in English social life. And in order to emphasise that equality, Abrahams told a little white lie. He assured his audience that he had encountered 'very little antisemitism', even though the reality was that he had been hurt and even motivated by prejudice at Repton and to a lesser extent Cambridge. Perhaps he was conscious that many members of that audience had probably faced far worse treatment than anything he had known. With that in mind, Harold simply explained that antisemitism was 'foreign to all sportsmen and thinking people'. And so, he didn't see the need for Jewish public schools, as had been proposed. He gave the impression that life had been just fine for him at Repton. Abrahams took this conciliatory line, not just because he had embraced Christianity at university, something he wasn't anxious to share with the Maccabeans; more because he believed it to be in the best interests of the Jewish community to be flexible and open to the ways of others.

Did Abrahams later have an opinion on Eric Liddell's refusal to run on a Sunday? If he considered such a stubborn stand unnecessary in the general scheme of things, he kept such thoughts to himself. All he would ever say on the matter, when the time came, was that Eric's religious zeal and the passion of his running were inextricably linked. And he was about to witness Liddell's fiery passion first-hand.

### Chapter Sixteen:
# Liddell v Abrahams

The first meeting was less than a fortnight away; and three days after his speech to his Jewish audience, Harold won three more events. He romped through the 100 yards, 220 yards and long jump in the first English Closed Championships. These performances seemed to provide a perfect platform for success at the AAA championships at Stamford Bridge on July 6 and 7.

By then, however, people had begun to talk of a new talent, a human whirlwind from Scotland. Eric Liddell came south with a growing reputation, having won some big events north of the border. But Abrahams didn't think some stocky little newcomer could match his own class when the time came to cross swords. And the Englishman must have felt his AAAs championships were going to plan when he won his 220 yards heat in 22.4. Then he witnessed the Scottish storm – and saw what he perceived as an ugly brutality in all its force.

Harold recalled:

*The first time I ever set eyes upon Liddell was when I watched him in a heat of the 220 yards at the AAA Championships in 1923. No runner of his superb ability ever possessed a worse style. Liddell had a style which was a complete model of everything that should not be done. It was unorthodox in the extreme. Head back, arms all over the place, and an exaggerated knee drive. There was hardly anything about his knee movements that would commend itself to the experienced onlooker. Indeed, my reaction on seeing him perform for the first time was that I was witnessing the most misplaced direction of energy I had ever imagined possible. But my goodness for energy and determination he was second to none.*

Liddell used to make a joke about the origins of his whirlwind style. He used to point out that his Scottish ancestors had raided English-held lands with hit-and-run tactics. And when you were running away from scores of angry Englishman who were riding hard to cut you down, you weren't too bothered whether your style looked pretty or not, so long as you escaped with your life.

Aesthetically pleasing or not, there was more than determination at play in Eric's running. Though it was strange to see a man throw his head back so far as he ran, Abrahams may have been doing Liddell – the rival he somewhat disparagingly called 'the human spider' – a slight disservice. The 21-year-old Scotsman was deceptively compact, and his balance remained unaffected by his idiosyncratic running style – otherwise he would have found it impossible to run so fast.

One English reporter who witnessed the Scotsman's running at those Championships wasn't buying all the technical condemnation. And his remarks are particularly interesting in light of what was to unfold at the Olympics in Paris, 1924. The unknown scribe insisted:

*His style is splendid, for he is quick into his running, has a rare stride, and puts all his strength into the race. In the 220 yards he threw his head back in the last 60 yards, seemed to close his eyes, and yet ran as straight as a barrel, with unwavering resoluteness. There are those who thought that he wobbled, but he was in perfect alignment with his strings [lane].*

Eric himself, when asked how on earth he could see ahead while gazing at Heaven, replied: 'I knew where I was going, all right.'

And contrary to popular belief, the Scotsman had an excellent coach in Tom McKerchar, the printer from Edinburgh. Eric put much of his success down to the training regime his coach had devised. Whatever the imperfections of Liddell's style, it worked for him – and McKerchar already understood that.

⤝

Despite Liddell's brilliance, Abrahams remained confident that his own, more logical technique would carry the day against the Scottish upstart over any sprint distance. The semi-final of the 220 yards would give the Englishman the chance to establish his superiority, and expose Liddell's limitations.

When the race was done, one man's limitations had indeed been exposed; not Liddell's, though. Harold wrote:

*I realised his power to the full when I had a back view of him in the semi-final of that 220 later that same evening. I ran against him, was well and truly beaten up and did not reach the final.*

That simple account doesn't tell the full story of July 6, 1923. When Eric Liddell tore up the field and hit the tape in a record 21.6 seconds, Abrahams only clocked 22 dead. The Englishman was a good four yards behind the 'Flying Scotsman'. But a report in The Times the following day stated that Abrahams dead-heated with William Nichol as fastest loser. The pair would have had to agree to a run-off to decide who should compete in the final. Already 'beaten up' and probably facing another drubbing should he win through, Abrahams withdrew. He had no desire to be exposed to Liddell's searing pace again. Not at that distance anyway.

But could the next 24 hours bring Abrahams revenge over the Scot in the 100 yards? In a radio interview much later, Harold explained what happened – and, more to the point, what didn't happen:

*I never ran against Eric Liddell in a 100. I think I was a better sprinter than him actually, although he did win the AAA Championship in 1923 in 9.7! But so far as one can compare people . . . I didn't get in the final actually. I had a bad throat…by the time I'd run two rounds of the 100 and one of the 220 I'd sort of shaken off my bad throat and I long-jumped 23ft 8¾in. Much to my sadness I failed to beat the Championship best performance by less than an inch.*

Ah, the 'sore throat' again. Hadn't we heard that excuse a few months earlier, when Harold didn't feel as though he could face his responsibilities in the showdown against Oxford? He had complained of a 'ghastly sore throat', only to be told by his brother Adolphe that he had never been fitter in his life. Now Abrahams was effectively asking us to believe that his 'bad throat' caused him so much loss of form and speed that he failed to qualify for either sprint final, where Liddell would have been waiting. Then, miraculously, he shook off that sore throat so successfully that he suddenly found enough speed to make a British record-breaking leap into the long-jump pit.

A photograph shows Harold achieving an almost superhuman height as he flies through the air. The optical illusion sees his spikes hanging way above the sand-pit at the level of the judges' heads; and his head is up in the sky above the grandstand. You wonder how such athletic magnificence could have been achieved by a man who could barely swallow moments earlier.

High jump in the long-jump.

Mysterious indeed.

If he dared to watch the 100 yards final at 3.40 p.m., Harold probably did so with a blend of envy and relief. Had he been out on the track, he would surely have been burnt away by Liddell's pace in the hot sun. That winning time of 9.7sec gave Eric a new British record, which was to stand for thirty-five years. Abrahams never entirely believed what Eric had done.

Many years later, Harold wrote:

*I do not wish at this time to doubt the splendid ability of Eric as a sprinter, but quite frankly, I have always been a little sceptical about that British record. No reasonable criticism can be directed against the time-keeping, but both [his fellow finalists] Nichol and Matthewman were within striking distance of Liddell and must have done 9.8 performances themselves.*

Flying Scotsman: Eric stuns London.

*And they neither of them ever produced a performance really comparable before or after. Both these latter were good sprinters in their way, but they were never really in the front rank. Conditions that afternoon were exceptionally good and the record remains in the statute book. No one will begrudge Liddell his record, but I shall never believe he was a better sprinter than Willie Applegarth or Harry Edward.*

Mel Watman, doyen of athletics statisticians and a man who learned his trade directly from Abrahams, admired Harold but didn't agree with him on this one controversial issue. Watman explained, 'He never accepted Liddell's 9.7 and I think that was less than generous from Harold. My view is that it may have been a case of sour grapes on Harold's part, with Liddell stealing his thunder at the distance "HMA" regarded as his territory.'

The three official watches registered Liddell's time at 9.67, 9.65 and 9.65 – and were therefore all rounded up to 9.7 under the rules of the day. A fourth, unofficial watch showed 9.62 – just two hundredths of a second outside the world record of 9.6. According to John W. Keddie, one of Liddell's biographers, 'Harold Abrahams afterwards cast doubt on the performance on the grounds that the starting line had been largely obliterated by distance runners.'

Liddell explained his amazing breakthrough like this: 'The weather was perfect for short-distance running – very hot. Heat makes the muscles loose, so that there was no need for massage.'

The Scotsman's personal best for 100 yards before that day was 10.0sec – and he never broke ten seconds again. Then again, he didn't have many chances to do so, and British conditions were rarely if ever quite so inviting. Watman reflected, 'Progressing from 10 to 9.7 in one day is pretty remarkable, but then Liddell was running in good weather on a much better track than he was used to in Scotland.'

The conspiracy theory – that Abrahams had been running scared of Liddell at Stamford Bridge – was lightly aired in the Daily Telegraph just two weeks after the AAA meet. By then Abrahams had rediscovered his track form so convincingly that, 'one wonders how he came to fail in the AAA Championship. His own view may be that he met his master in the Scottish champion, E.H. Liddell, and that may be true, but on Saturday's running, he should have been fighting out the finish a fortnight earlier.'

Much later, largely because he had avoided meeting Liddell, Abrahams claimed again, 'At this long distance [of time] from the actual event I can perhaps say, without seeming too self-centred, that I believe I was, in fact, better than Eric over 100 metres.'

It was a brave opinion, and one that Lord Sebastian Coe and Lord David Puttnam were happy to contest in 2023, as we shall see later. The fans were denied the chance to find out for sure – and that certainly wasn't Eric Liddell's fault.

We can accuse Harold of losing his nerve in 1923 – or we can salute his tactical wisdom. By avoiding Liddell in the finals at the AAA Championship, Abrahams didn't lose face. He managed to steer clear of what would surely have constituted a psychologically damaging defeat. Fear may have motivated Harold on that English summer's day. But some would say there is nothing wrong with fear, if it helps common sense to prevail.

What times could Abrahams and Liddell have achieved, had they pushed each other in the 100 yards or 100 metres over two or three summers between 1923 and 1925? Could their rivalry have rewritten the record books further still? We will never know. After Eric's break-through summer south of the border, their paths didn't cross again for another year.

On July 14, there was a Triangular International at Stoke between England, Scotland and Ireland. Harold was rested so that he could be fully fit to run the following Saturday for Oxford and Cambridge against Harvard and Yale in London. In Stoke, Liddell won the 100, 220 yards and quarter mile. But it was the way in which he won the longer contest that became the stuff of legend. And what Eric did was arguably even more extraordinary than his 9.7 in London.

*The Scotsman* newspaper wrote:

*The circumstances in which he won the 440 event made it a performance bordering on the miraculous. Veterans, whose memories take them back thirty-five years, and in some cases even longer, in the history of athletics, were unanimous in the opinion that Liddell's win in the quarter mile was the greatest track performance they had ever seen. The runners were started on the bend, Liddell having the inside berth, but the Scot had only taken three strides when Gillis, England, crashed into him and knocked him off the track. He stumbled on the grass, and for a moment seemed half-inclined to give up. Then suddenly he sprang forward, and was after his opponents in a flash. By this time the leaders were twenty yards ahead, but Liddell gradually drew up on them, and by the time the home straight was reached he was running fourth. He would be about ten yards behind Gillis then. It seemed out of the question he would win, but he achieved the apparently impossible. Forty yards from home he was third and seemed on the point of collapsing, but pulling himself together he put in a desperate finish to win two yards from Gillis.*

He had won the 440 in 51.2sec after being knocked off the track. It was so remarkable that observers were convinced he had broken 49sec for the time he had spent actually running. This phenomenal run came at a cost, however. Eric passed out. Something had gone "bust" in his head, he later claimed, remembering the moment just before the darkness engulfed him. Eric Liddell was said to have been unconscious for half an hour after this race. When he finally began to show some signs of life, he was quickly offered a shot of brandy. True to form, Eric asked for a strong cup of tea instead.

The sheer inspirational wonder of this performance was superbly captured in *Chariots of Fire*.

The Flying Scotsman, who believed his qualities were God-given, seemed invincible. He was prepared to push the physical boundaries more than anyone else. It was as though Liddell simply trusted his fate to God. He could run so hard that his body cried out, and then he would just run harder. He'd push himself until he lost consciousness or worse. And if he dropped dead, so be it. A Christian had nothing to fear from death.

When Eric Liddell ran, it was almost as though he invited God to take him. He pushed his mortal body beyond normal limits of endurance because he had no fear. You could call it religious recklessness. His opponents just didn't have that.

CHAPTER SEVENTEEN:

# Seeking Something More

Eric Liddell's superhuman performances called for a swift reply from Harold Abrahams. His chance came the following weekend, by which time his batteries were fully recharged. The occasion would also provide an opportunity for revenge against Harvard and Yale, the American universities which had so outclassed their Oxbridge visitors two years earlier.

The venue in north-west London was new; it was called Wembley Stadium. The Duke of York – the future King George VI – was in an enthusiastic crowd of 10,000, which included many Americans. The stage was set and fit for a hero, though the English couldn't have felt excessively optimistic that he would emerge from their ranks. They hadn't won this contest since 1911.

Harold began his day by trying to win the 100 yards. His American opponents were 'the Yale crack', W.A. Comins, and E.J. Rusnak. In the opening phase of the race there was nothing to choose between the runners. But it was reported that a 'ghost of daylight' opened up between Harold and the rest of the field at 30 yards. His lead became more pronounced at 60 yards; and there was no way back for his rivals when he came 'whirling down the track like a human

Harold meets the Duke of York at Wembley.

windmill', as the *Daily News* put it. According to the *Daily Telegraph*, Abrahams 'ran at such a tremendous pace for the last half of the journey that he made the Americans, both credited with "evens" over the water, look like "platers". He won by three yards clear yards in 10.0 secs.

Later in the afternoon, Harold's problem was not so much the strength of his opponents as the impossibility of being in two places at the same time. His second event was the long jump; and the Americans seemed more than happy when the schedule was thrown into chaos. The allocated time for the 220 yards, the climax to the entire contest, was drawing near. An anxious Harold began to feel pulled in different directions. *The Times* reported, 'The long-jump was interrupted by various races, by photographs, by innocent bandsmen returning from a well-earned tea, by pole-jumpers who wanted to land almost on long-jumpers' toes. Abrahams looked restive and no wonder, with the 220 yards coming nearer and nearer. He deemed it wise to miss his last jump and have a little peace.'

Harold had already jumped 22ft 9¾in, a couple of inches better than W.A. Comins.

However, as the *Daily Telegraph* pointed out, missing his last jump was easier said than done. 'When he was retiring, someone insisted that an agreement had been come to that each man should have six jumps, and after some delay, a further round commenced.' This was the last thing Harold needed – which was probably why the Americans insisted upon it. Harold used his anger positively on the runway to launch himself with a vengeance. He produced a winning jump, as the report noted: 'The Cambridge man cleared 23ft 2¼in and then withdrew to the dressing room to prepare for the 220 yards .. . The rest continued, but Comins did not beat his earlier jump . . . I think conditions were against jumping, which made Abrahams' effort all the more remarkable.'

The match was a tie going into the final event. Everything depended upon who would hold his nerve and find his speed when it really mattered in the 220 yards. This was to be a straight run, starting just outside the stadium. The athletes were to pass immediately into a tunnel under the stands. And after 100 yards of secret warfare, they would burst out on to the main track and conclude their battle in front of the fans.

*The Times* set the scene nicely. 'Now came the tremendous moment when the four sprinters vanished into the tunnel for the start of the 220 yards. There was a dreadful pause, a muffled thud, and then – nothing. It was a false start.' With so much riding on the race and the crowd desperate to see the drama unfold, the tension only increased. 'Another pause and at last a loud bang, after what seemed almost an eternity to the waiting spectators.'

*The Times* writer Bernard Darwin captured the moment memorably: 'A moment's agony, and then there was Abrahams scudding along like some great bird, with a four-yard lead. He went further and further in front, running superbly.'

*The Morning Post* described the reaction of the crowd to this surreal moment. 'Abrahams came out fast, having apparently lost or mislaid his rivals . . . winning so easily that the race had a ludicrous aspect, and caused as much laughter as cheering . . . Eric Liddell, the Flying Scotchman, would have found him a very difficult proposition in the longer sprint had the twain met on Saturday afternoon.'

When Harold hit the tape in 21.6, upright but perfectly relaxed, he was so far ahead that the next best sprinter was barely in sight.

Since 1919, Harold Abrahams had been the leading light in Oxbridge athletics. Now, as one newspaper put it, this 'was a fitting farewell to a distinguished university career'. He could hardly have chosen a more dramatic way to leave his Cambridge days behind. For Harold, it was a sweet moment. 'We got our revenge against Harvard and Yale for the awful hiding they had given us two years earlier. We won by 6½ events to 5½ at Wembley.'

Harold soon received a royal seal of approval. One account described how 'everybody was pleased when the Duke of York called him out of his prompt retirement among the spectators to receive a warm handclasp and words of hearty congratulation.' Even the Americans joined in the ovation for the Cambridge hero.

Harold had matched Liddell's Stamford Bridge time of 21.6 in his final appearance of the year, though the Englishman hadn't been required to negotiate a bend. The Daily Telegraph could already see what such scintillating form might mean for Harold and his country the following summer. 'His achievement assures us of the promise, all being well, of a superb athlete in the English [sic] Olympic team in Paris next year.' Abrahams, however, was a perfectionist. And he knew there was much work to be done before he could consider himself a true contender for the Olympics.

*I realised about nine months before the Games that some effort such as I had never made before would be necessary if I was to do at all well in Paris. Before I had trained reasonably hard – as hard as most people, I think, but now we were up against a really tough proposition, and no stone must be left unturned which could in any way contribute to a success.*

Cambridge runner Arthur Marshall recalled:

*Liddell's achievement in winning the 1923 AAA 100 yards in the record time of 9.7 seconds was a devastating blow to Abrahams and shook him to the core. To date Abrahams had been a consistent ten seconds 100 yards winner but had only slightly broken 10 seconds on one or two occasions. He knew in the Olympics he would be up against overseas competition, particularly from the Americans, but this new and very serious opposition out of the blue and on his doorstep had come at a time when Harold had established his 100 yards supremacy in the UK.*

And there was something else about Eric Liddell that must have disturbed Harold Abrahams, knowing as we do just how insecure the Englishman was. Harold's former Cambridge colleagues were starting to love Liddell in a way they had never loved Abrahams. The sheer spirit and humility of the man was endearing. They took Eric under their wing, as though they owed Abrahams nothing at all in university loyalty.

Philip Noel-Baker was the most influential of the Cambridge set. He was ten years older than Harold and he had been President of the Cambridge University Athletic Club. More recently he had carried the

Union flag for the GB team at the Antwerp Olympics and he had won a silver medal in the 1500 metres there. He seems to have adored Liddell – and the feeling was reciprocated. Noel-Baker was a man of peace, like Liddell. In fact he had become a conscientious objector during the First World War, and had driven ambulances with considerable bravery to alleviate the suffering of the wounded. Noel-Baker certainly wouldn't have wanted to deliver a slap in the face to Abrahams. He wasn't interested in creating conflict. In fact he was to go on to win the Nobel Peace Prize in 1959. But it's hard to imagine that Harold's feathers weren't ruffled a little. Particularly when his Cambridge contemporaries such as Arthur Marshall, Douglas Lowe and Hyla "Henry" Stallard matched Noel-Baker's affection for Liddell with their own. Not only that; Liddell's coach, Tom McKerchar was friends with the Cambridge University coach, Alec Nelson. It seems that Eric was free to use the Cambridge University facilities whenever he liked. In short, Cambridge adopted Eric Liddell. And even though Harold Abrahams had been there for years, he never felt such warmth.

The relative proximity of Cambridge to the young lady Eric Liddell had taken to visiting in Harmer Green would have made the hospitality of the university's athletic community even more convenient for the Chinese Scot.

Eileen Soper and Eric Liddell seemed closer than ever. It appears that Eric might even have been weighing up whether Eileen would be suitable for the vital supportive role of preacher's wife in the wild and dangerous environment he would face before long in China. There can be little doubt that Eric had feelings for Eileen, and they enjoyed some kind of romantic intimacy, even if their relationship wasn't physical in the way we might assume nowadays. But Eileen was carving out a life as a celebrated artist. The idea of going to China for a life of hardship might have scared her.

Would it even have been fair of Eric to float such a suggestion, when he knew Eileen could have no idea of what she was letting herself in for? These were not considerations to be taken lightly. Life as a missionary's wife in China would be fiercely demanding – brutal, even. Eileen's early years in rural England and sophisticated London were no preparation for such rigours.

What we do know – or can at least feel safe in suggesting – is that Eileen Soper loved Eric Liddell beyond measure. Indeed, she loved him enough to want to be turned into Eileen Liddell one day. It appears that Eric and Eileen did talk about a life together during that happy summer of 1923. Only playfully perhaps, as young lovers sometimes do, exploring the boundaries and possibilities of what they have together. But Eileen took those conversations sufficiently to heart to write a poem about their June walks through the countryside, recalling moments when they carved their initials in wood.

Eileen Soper

If her poem is understood correctly, we can picture Eileen writing "E.S." and Eric writing "E.L." Eileen may have stated the obvious, that they shared the same first initial. And Eric may have replied that it was possible they might even share the same last initial one day, too. Whatever really took place, Eileen Soper was led to believe, perhaps through her own yearning, that she might also become "E.L." They seem to have exchanged letters on the same playful theme soon afterwards. If their love continued to grow, they speculated, they might end up with the same set of first and last initials. That was the theme. It was a dangerous idea to allow into the head of an impressionable young woman who was clearly in love, if Eric wasn't seriously considering a proposal. But then again, Liddell was new to all this as well. He probably thought he had done no more than casually test the water in a joyful moment, to see what her reaction would be.

Did Eileen overreact in the long run? There was almost certainly no proposal. And yet Eileen thought the moment important enough to capture it in a poem she diligently preserved, to be found after her death. The poem had a cleverly ambivalent title: "To E.L." Was she writing to Eric? Or to her imagined self, married to Eric, as she had clearly wanted to be? At any rate, the key lines tell the story in just nine words and two capital letters:

"You wrote that Time might spell
The letters E and L."

The word "might" in that top line remains key to defending Eric's honour. Much as the celebrated young artist felt close to securing her treasured international rugby star for life, it was a case of so near, yet so far. Those two lines tell us that Eric was in control of that situation; and he was offering no guarantees. A man of honour and a man of his word, Liddell would never have promised his hand in marriage and then withdrawn that hand. He could never become engaged, as Harold Abrahams had been, and then break off that engagement.

Liddell was still a free man, master of his own romantic destiny – and commanded only by his overwhelming love for Jesus Christ.

He did make one significant change to his life as Olympic year drew near, though. And it meant he was likely to become an even more devastating force the following year. Reluctantly, Eric came to a difficult decision regarding his rugby career. Difficult because he loved playing for Scotland. Harold Abrahams put it like this:

*He wisely abstained from playing Rugby Football during the winter of 1923-24 for fear of sustaining an injury, a very real possibility in the case of such a speedy performer.*

On Saturday, October 6, 1923, the *Illustrated Sporting and Dramatic News* made a big splash out of Eric's decision. Beneath a huge photographic portrait of the star, they wrote, "Mr Eric Liddell, the famous international wing three-quarter and champion sprinter, confirms the report that, in view of the Olympic Games of next summer, he will not be seen on the Rugby field this season. His loss will be greatly felt by the University and by Scotland, but all will applaud his self-sacrifice and devotion to the athletic interests of Great Britain."

The paper talked about "a season's rest." In fact, this was effectively rugby retirement at the age of twenty-one. Poor Eric had only played seven internationals for Scotland. He could have gone on to become an all-time great of that sport too. But when a hard decision had to be made, Eric Liddell wasn't afraid to make it. Perhaps he knew deep down where he would make the biggest sporting impact, and how he could use that impact for the common good. In truth, devotion to GB had little to do with it.

Abrahams wasn't overly patriotic either, in any sporting sense. He wanted to win for winning's sake. To show those who doubted and disliked him how it was done. To be the best.

With different motives, these stubborn men were starting to focus on the summer of 1924. A summer captured for all time in *Chariots of Fire*, and still relevant a hundred years later.

CHAPTER EIGHTEEN:

# The Big Shock

With Eric's sporting focus now exclusively on the track, Harold was going to have to do something dramatic to keep pace. There was an older man who was equally driven – a man Abrahams had known about for a very long time. Ambition told him what to do next.

Deep down, you suspect, he had always known.

It was no great surprise that Harold teamed up with Sam Mussabini, a man from a lower social class, in October 1923. It was more remarkable that they hadn't teamed up before. The way Cambridge University frowned upon professionalism may have been a factor. In *Chariots of Fire*, they unite during Harold's student days, to defy university traditionalists who still favour a more relaxed amateur ethos. In reality, Abrahams conformed slightly more to the Cambridge sporting philosophy than *Chariots* would have us believe. Though he had adopted an intensity of training that made fellow students feel uncomfortable, he didn't go so far as to employ a personal professional coach. Now that his Cambridge career was over, Harold felt free to take that final step. If Mussabini could give him the edge over Liddell and an outside chance against the brilliant Americans, the extra pain would be worth it.

Mussabini had spent most of his fifty-six years searching for perfection. Every aspect of athletics was given careful thought. But then attention to detail had always been important in his family. Mussabini's great-grandfather, a Syrian merchant from Damascus who traded with Trieste in Italy, had shown similar awareness. Seeking every possible advantage in a cut-throat world, he had decided to take the Italian-sounding Mussabini surname for commercial

Portrait of a genius: Sam Mussabini.

reasons. When you are prepared to break from the past and even change your identity to beat the competition, it says something about your will to win in life.

Born Scipio Arnaud Godolphin Mussabini, Harold's new coach had decided at some point to drop his two middle names and replace them with 'Africanus'. Then he simply used his latest initials to form the name "Sam".

Most of his school years were spent in France. But he returned to England in the 1880s and became interested in the professional athletes of the London League. Tom McNab, an ex-athlete, coach and long-time historian of the sport, said of Mussabini, 'He came from the traditions of professional running, the lore and mystique of the old "pro" racers of the nineteenth century. Much of what he had learned came from that era.'

Mussabini had also been a talented sprinter, footballer and cricketer. But his biggest talent lay in observing and improving upon the strengths and weaknesses in others. The mechanics of running fascinated Sam, and he began to develop training ideas based on the science of the body. Later he was almost apologetic about his brilliance and admitted:

*Quite possibly, I rely too much on what may be obtained by close obser-vance and experimentation with the main motive parts of the human engine. This, no doubt, is my own personal kink.*

Harold recalled, 'Mussabini was an absolute fanatic, a marvellous man. From the very first we plotted a plan of campaign. Sam told me that if I would put myself in his care and carry out his advice, he would make me an Olympic sprint champion. I laughed at the idea.'

But he was probably laughing a little less at how far-fetched it sounded when the Olympic schedules for Paris were released in early November. Those schedules would have profound consequences for his biggest British rival, though it took a while for most people to realise. Eric Liddell knew immediately. And his heart sank. The 100 metres heats were set for the first Sunday of the Olympic athletics programme. It was the same for the 4 x 100 metres relay and the 4 x 400 metres relay. Sitting in his hostel in George Street, Edinburgh, you could have forgiven Eric for a rare explosion of temper. Instead, he took the news quietly, except to say:

*I'm not running on a Sunday.*

He didn't utter those words in some defiant show of pique. It was a simple, measured statement of fact. Indeed, the hysteria didn't come from the athlete or his pals. It came from the newspaper men. They laid siege to George Street when they heard Liddell wouldn't run on a Sunday. It didn't matter to them that the 200 and 400 metres might still be an option for the devout Christian. Everyone wanted to see Liddell race in the blue riband event – and win the gold medal for his country. And when Eric ignored the reporters and their pleas for an audience, they grew frustrated and shouted 'traitor!' at the hostel windows. The coverage reflected their frustration. And so began a period of people pressurising Eric Liddell to change his mind.

By February 1924 however, there seemed to be a level of acceptance and respect for Eric's decision in some quarters, at least. The *Illustrated Sporting and Dramatic News*, having highlighted several sports stars who didn't play on a Sunday, came to Liddell's case in an almost matter-of-fact way. 'There is, for instance, Eric Liddell the Rugger international, who is to run in the Olympic games this year, but will not do so on Sundays even if, as seems probable, this regard for principles will keep the sprint champion from competing in his favourite event.'

In *Chariots of Fire*, Eric only hears about the schedule at the last moment, when he is boarding the boat for Paris. It's a clever dramatic device to condense the time frame, but it doesn't reflect the reality. Whatever people thought about his decision, Eric knew he had given fair warning. All he could do now was to control the controllables. And since his decision was final, he only trained for the events he could do – the 200m and 400m.

Looking back, Harold Abrahams hinted at a sense of relief when he realised that Eric Liddell's Sabbatarian beliefs had effectively removed a rival. Harold said:

*I was lucky in the sense that Eric Liddell, who had set up a British record the previous year, felt with his strong religious conviction that he oughtn't to run on a Sunday. The heats of the 100 metres in the Olympic Games were scheduled to take place on a Sunday and Liddell was always rigorously opposed to Sunday competition.*

With one rival removed by a cruel twist of fate, Abrahams knew there were at least two more who were just as dangerous. Somewhere across the Atlantic, two superstars would be turning their thoughts to Paris. And if these Americans were in their very best form, no one could realistically beat them.

CHAPTER NINETEEN:

## Harold and Sam

The Flying Scotsman was no longer a threat. But the "California Flash" and the "New York Thunderbolt" certainly were. Charley Paddock and Jackson Scholz were already successful Olympians – and they were still at the top of their game. Harold wanted gold badly; and he had to believe that Sam Mussabini could deliver on his promise. That meant Mussabini could enjoy Harold's undivided attention. Liddell might have ceased to keep Abrahams awake at night; but Paddock and Scholz had taken Eric's place.

There was no time for a personal life now. Abrahams was ready to make all the necessary sacrifices. 'In the winter I went through some hard, conscientious training,' he remembered.

Norris McWhirter wrote later of how 'he could be seen with Mussabini working on his start and finish at Paddington Recreation Ground, or for a change of scene at Queen's Club or the old White City track.'

Mussabini didn't bawl at his athlete like a sergeant major. Harold explained: 'He didn't motivate me, it was a very polite relationship. He always called me Mr Abrahams and seemed to have a great respect for me. He was a fanatic on arm action and I think he was right. We worked together a great deal.' When that work became tedious, Harold drove himself on. 'The really important factor is the will and determination to win – the power to stick to it when you are feeling like it and when you are not. This is the real essential for success.'

But Harold had to be careful. He was highly strung, and obsessive training risked sending him over the edge. By now Abrahams was living with his mother at 2, Hodford Road in Golders Green. His little back garden sometimes became his urban training ground. 'Occasionally, I would change and trot about my garden at home (which comprises a piece of grass about twelve yards square) simply because I was getting on edge and it was unwise to go to the track.'

Sometimes Mussabini needed the patience of a saint, as Harold challenged everything. 'I got a great deal of satisfaction from arguing with him, because I always believed and I say to people now: don't accept what a coach says because he is experienced…Every suggestion for improvement, every speculation as to what would be best, we argued out together, sometimes not without heat, but always with the best thought at our command. The part of a trainer should be to advise and correct. Any coach worthy of the name should be able to give reasons for everything he advises and suggests.'

It didn't take much debate for Sam and Harold to agree that all their focus should be placed on the 100 metres. It was a gamble they felt was worth taking. 'We believed that it would be unwise to train for 220 yards as well as 100 yards, considering that longer distance is apt to take the edge, which is so important, off the performances over the shorter distance.'

Before he could sharpen his competitive edge, Abrahams had to get his basic action right. And through the winter Mussabini used thousands of feet of cine-film to study that action in slow motion and improve it. Abrahams spent about six months, from October until March, trying to perfect the various components of his style. Two or three of these months were devoted to sharpening his reaction time to the starter's pistol – and finding the right body-shape to make his first, vital strides.

When Harold explained his painstaking routine, you wondered how it didn't drive him crazy:

*On a typical day's outing I made half a dozen starts from the holes, employing the 'slow cinematograph' method. By photographing movements at the rate of about 150 exposures per second, and throwing the film on to the screen at the normal rate of sixteen per second, we are enabled to see all movement analysed down to a series of primary actions. These actions as seen by the eye are not a series of jerks, but each action links up with the next, giving a harmonious, if uncanny whole.*

Smoky motivation!
Sam Mussabini fires his pistol and Harold Abrahams stays low.

Once Abrahams had studied his action carefully on screen, he applied the same slow-motion technique to his practical work. 'I tried to perform each movement of starting as slowly as possible. I moved not in a series of jerks, but performed the actions in the same way as I would when at full speed. I found that this enabled me to acquire the habit of good form, whereas if one always practises at full speed one is apt to acquire bad habits which are difficult to eradicate.'

It was, Harold admitted, 'a monotonous business', yet there were ways to fight the boredom and reduce lateral movement at the same time. He later talked of 'the importance in running of getting one's feet as near as possible one in front of the other – you can't do it actually, completely. I used to put bits of paper down on the track and pick them up with my spikes, but it was partly a gimmick to interest me.'

Harold knew he couldn't be wild-limbed and win, as he felt Liddell could. But at least there was some scope for personal choice in arm movement. He added:

One is driven to the belief that provided a style is not based on principles which are obviously contrary to the known laws of movement, it may well suit a particular individual, though it be recognised as unorthodox. I myself adopted a sprinting action which involved movement of the arms across the body. Most American coaches urge the cultivation of a piston-like arm movement. In the face of first-class exponents of both schools, it is absurd for anyone to protest that one is right and the other is wrong. Both styles possess very strong reasons for their adoption. Few people appreciate what an enormous part the arms play in sprinting.

Seb Coe knew this when it was his turn to shine on the Olympic stage. He explained, 'My father [Peter] took apart my arm action and put it back together again over a two-year period, during which he also put me in the sprints.' The result was gold in the 1500 metres at the 1980 and 1984 Olympics.

Long before Peter and Seb Coe, Harold Abrahams knew his biomechanics and the importance of arms just as well. He explained, 'They control the action of the legs. Try this experiment after your cold bath tomorrow morning. Walk along the road without using your arms at all. Suddenly bring the arms into play and increase the rapidity with which you move them. You will find it impossible to move the arms more rapidly without the legs following suit.'

Abrahams became a willing Mussabini disciple, partly because so many of his own ideas matched those of his teacher. Hard work didn't start or finish at the track, either. 'All this time I had been doing home exercises. Night and morning indoors.' And if he walked past a mirror, he used it. 'Exercises in front of a mirror are designed to produce improvement in form and in control at slow speed.' Escalators on the Tube suddenly had a new purpose. 'If the authorities in the Underground are not about, the pleasure of this exercise is considerably increased by running up the moving stairway which is descending. Nothing can be better than to ascend the moving stairway in this way, but you are particularly requested to avoid the rush-hours.'

Running dominated Harold's thoughts, whether at home, on the underground or out on the track. 'Regular visits to the dentist and lavatory' was another Abrahams rule. Everything was geared to racing, and it was a wonder he had time for any legal studies at all. Somehow, he managed to cope with reading for the Bar at the same time – and even worked in a solicitor's office to get some practical experience.

In addition to all this, Abrahams wrote to the BBC and said he would like to talk about athletics on air. His status as a top current athlete opened the door.

Harold's first broadcast for the BBC was on March 15, 1924, in the days when the corporation was based at Savoy Hill. The *Radio Times* scheduled fifteen minutes, between 9.45 and 10 p.m. under the title: "Harold Abrahams, the famous runner, on: Should sport be taken seriously?"

His conclusion, of course, was that it should. These fifteen minutes heralded a BBC career that would last an extraordinary fifty years.

CHAPTER TWENTY:

# Meet the Best

Eric Liddell didn't want to abandon the shortest sprint distances just yet. He was invited to join Oxford and Cambridge athletes at the University of Pennsylvania Relay Festival – known simply as the Penn Relays. Considering it a compliment to be made an honorary Oxbridge man, he gratefully accepted. The races were due to take place on April 25 and April 26, 1924.

Veteran athletics journalist Mel Watman claimed, 'The American races were sharpeners for Liddell. He knew he wouldn't be running 100 metres in Paris (nor either of the relays as the heats were also on a Sunday).'

Seasickness hit Liddell hard on the outward voyage, though he was able to make a good recovery in the team's comfortable base at the Pennsylvania Cricket Club. Soon he was ready for the 100 yards, which proved a close-run affair. Only inches separated the first four men. Chester Bowman from Syracuse broke the tape in 10.0. Unfortunately Liddell was fourth in an estimated 10.1. He did better in the 220 yards, but was beaten again – this time even more narrowly – by Louis Clarke of Johns Hopkins University in a time of 21.6.

These were still good performances, given the stresses of the voyage. Harold Abrahams wrote generously about Liddell's defeats at the time.

*If one considers that Liddell cannot have been able to do much sharpening up so early on, this augurs well for his performances in June and July.*

By his own admission, Eric Liddell hated losing. But he didn't let it bother him for long because he didn't have an oversized ego of the type Harold struggled with. And Eric took something valuable from this particular experience. Over the entrance of the University of Pennsylvania, he noticed the following words inscribed:

"In the dust of defeat as well as in the laurels of victory there is glory to be found if one has done his best."

Liddell took comfort from what he read. He made a note of the message; and thought it might suit more successful days too – if indeed winning were ever going to be possible against the brilliant Americans, that is. Standing there in the splendour of the University of Pennsylvania, that was by no means a given. After all, Chester Bowman and Louis Clarke weren't even the fastest Americans around. Charley Paddock and Jackson Scholz hadn't been racing, yet Liddell had still only finished fourth. It might have felt that little bit easier for Eric to follow his conscience after those results in Pennsylvania. And Liddell was in a light-hearted mood for the long voyage home.

Arthur Marshall, who would go on to become a Great Britain reserve at the 1924 Games, revealed:

*On the boat back, Eric and I became close friends. Eric was very strict about religion, but he was no prude and joined in all the fun and games on board, including the fancy dress dance. We played cards and mah-jong with two American sisters who were 'doing Europe' and going to the Olympic Games in Paris. Eric and I said, 'If we get into the team, we'll see you there.'*

The sisters were called Freddie and Edith; and by travelling alone, they displayed a spirit of adventure that even Eric must have found appealing. Marshall was a dashing character, and the two Brits made a formidable double act with their very different accents. Freddie and Edith made it clear they would take the boys up on their offer in Paris. And if this interaction told us anything, it was that Eric Liddell wasn't spending all his private moments thinking about Eileen Soper anymore. Not that any woman was a priority. Eric wanted to focus on the Olympics for the moment, and then devote himself to Christ.

Did Eileen lack the religious conviction that might have captured Eric's heart once and for all, and effectively booked her ticket to China? We can only speculate; but it's hard to believe that Eric Liddell, a man who lived by his principles, would have arranged a double date, however innocent, with a pair of attractive American ladies if he had still been in love with Eileen. Perhaps he had already realised that Eileen's initials were never destined to become "E.L." after all.

∼

Back in London, Harold's exam results were even less impressive than Eric's race results in America. On April 30, 1924 he received news of his legal qualification. He passed the Examination for Call to the Bar – but was placed 'in the Third Class'. Harold knew the legal certificate didn't spell disaster. He already had the right contacts to make a career in law; and now he had the basic qualification too. Best of all, he could forget legal matters for a while, and focus all his energies on his true passion – athletics. Training intensified. Harold recalled:

*The months of April, May and June were the months in which serious training was embarked upon. From April 1924 onwards I was training three times each week and competition itself began in the first week of May.*

New Zealand sprinter Arthur Porritt, another Olympic contender that year, felt that extra intensity left Harold ever further out of step with his peers. Porritt claimed:

*His training methods were way ahead of their time. They were absolutely unknown and I couldn't help admiring the way he trained, practised, dieted, did this, didn't do that, just to keep fit. This was entirely out of keeping with the spirit of the time. Harold was almost professional, though obviously not to the extent of receiving remuneration. For the rest of us, our training, by later standards, would make people laugh. A few hours on a Sunday morning, perhaps a few starts, a couple of hundred yards and some chatting. Harold was training long hours three or four times a week.*

Abrahams and Mussabini didn't care. They perfected a technique still used today by any sprinter hoping to steal a few inches at the tape. Harold claimed to be the first.

'I started the drop finish,' he maintained. He would dip down at the final stride, throwing his torso at the finishing line, his arms tucked straight behind him. To the uninitiated, it looked wholly unnatural. Surely a sprinter would lose speed by trying such a stunt? Abrahams and Mussabini begged to differ. They thought a properly executed dip finish could be worth up to eighteen inches.

They focused on generating extra speed by shortening stride length overall. Harold remembered how mathematics took over his life under Mussabini:

*In the first few days of May I ran a trial and measured every stride from start to finish. From a close study of the figures obtained, we decided to cut down my stride and, if possible, to get an additional stride into the 100 yards race, by increasing the rapidity with which strides were taken. I also aimed at increasing the length of the first few strides of the race. The result of about six weeks' training was that I covered nearly eighteen inches more in the first half a dozen strides, without lessening the rapidity with which these strides were taken. No runner attains his full stride until he has gone between thirty and forty yards.*

In the rest of the race Abrahams and Mussabini set about fitting in an extra stride. The overall benefit was mathematically indisputable. He explained:

*I take forty-five strides in, say, ten seconds. If I take an inch less at each stride I shall lose 3ft 9in. But if this enables me to put another stride into the same number of seconds of running, I gain 7ft 3½n [one stride], or a net gain of 3ft 6½in.*

Harold knew the technique required to find the extra stride. 'Avoid a high knee action ... the feet should always be as near the ground as possible.'

His body was serving basic scientific principles. This is why Harold was able to claim 'I was probably the first person who said that length of stride isn't speed; speed is length of stride multiplied by the rapidity with which you take them. It's an obvious truism but nobody had ever said it.'

Harold had all the mathematics worked out – including acceleration. He concluded: 'I find that I go on accelerating until the end of the seventh second.' That science would give him confidence if ever he were left slightly behind his competitors for the first half of a race. Abrahams didn't mind becoming a machine. A robotic approach helped him find the laser focus he needed. Human emotions weren't helpful. Not to someone as highly strung as Harold.

*A sprinter has to become an automaton. He must not worry about his opponents in a race. All he is concerned with is to listen for the gun and when he hears it run like hell until he reaches the tape. In fact, if sprinters could run in blinkers they might be able to keep their form better. Form is everything in sprinting.*

Harold Abrahams was almost a servant to time by now. Later in life, he remained a slave to the clock. He carried at least two stopwatches everywhere he went. He would time everything, from flights around the world to going to the toilet. Such intensive training with Mussabini may have scarred Harold for life.

Tony Abrahams was once asked whether his uncle's obsession with time as an older man was born partly of the pressure that he put himself under as a young man. He replied, 'Yes, I think so. I think it came in part from his relationship with Mussabini.'

Harold didn't seem to care about the price he might be paying for his athletic excellence. Looking back, he reflected simply, 'By 1924 I had learnt to be very good at sprinting. Nothing else mattered except the race against the clock.'

CHAPTER TWENTY-ONE:

# Time for Action

May was an important warm-up month for Eric Liddell and Harold Abrahams, as the countdown to Paris 24 began.

Abrahams had been itching to put theory into practice under genuine race conditions. He recalled, 'From 3 May, I had races every Saturday with two exceptions, up to the Olympic Games themselves.' He seemed to improve by the week.

Meanwhile Liddell had begun to focus on the 400 metres and 440 yards. Still relatively new to the longer distance, Eric opened up with

51.5sec on May 28, and improved on that time on May 31 with 51.2.

Without the unnerving distraction of Liddell at his shoulder, Abrahams was far more spectacular in his own races. And on June 7, 1924 at Woolwich, London, he did something which seemed even more extraordinary than Liddell's AAAs heroics the previous year. Harold was timed at a world record-equalling 9.6sec for the 100 yards. But he knew instantly that he couldn't genuinely claim to be in the same league as Charley Paddock, the fastest man on earth.

*At Woolwich on 7 June I won the 100 yards 'with a slight following wind' in 9.6sec. There were no wind gauges. When the timekeepers told me of the time, I asked how far Nichol was behind and was told 'one yard'. In that moment I knew I had not done a genuine 9.6. Therefore I queried the time and no application was ever made for a 'record'. As far as I remember in those days a sprinter was expected to ask for his record to be accepted.*

That didn't stop the *Morning Post* from describing Harold as 'an athlete evolved out of granite by the genius of Rodin – no stylist but with tremendous stride and grim determination.' And *Country Life* pointed out that 'nobody is ever recorded to have run faster. We seem this year to have a chance of making a fight of it even against the highly trained and "specialised" Americans.'

There can be no doubt that Abrahams generated some astonishing speed that day at Woolwich. He broke another record – and this one counted for a very long time indeed. Harold leaped 24ft 2½in (7.38m) in the long jump, and no one questioned the validity of that performance. Abrahams recalled proudly, 'It was my best jump ever, which was an English native record for over thirty years.'

Harold always called it as he saw it, seeking to be fair in his self-analysis. Whilst he admitted to being boastful on occasion, he was often just as dismissive of his own efforts. And his recollection of that day at Woolwich seemed to sum up his even-handedness perfectly. One record he had consigned to the trash can, the other he had gone to some pains to highlight. Of his long-jump feat he later confessed, 'Actually there had been no English native records before then, so I created them because I fancied a bit of recognition.'

If he had been forced to play second fiddle in British athletics the previous summer, he was now very much the star of the show. Not even the great Eric Liddell was making such seismic waves in the run-up to the Olympics. Harold's stunning new results set tongues wagging. Jealous traditionalists claimed privately that Harold had broken unspoken rules during the winter and spring by taking his training too seriously. Tony Abrahams acknowledged, 'It is perfectly true that Harold was criticised by the "Corinthians" of the day for employing a professional to train him. But he didn't care about that.'

At least his local paper was appreciative of his dedication. That June, the *Cambridge Daily News* wrote, 'There is no keener athlete in England than H.M. Abrahams and I think that most of the credit is due to the man himself. He has made athletics a religion – and a man who works at a pastime as he has done deserves all the success which comes his way.'

Harold didn't disagree. 'The sooner it is understood that to win an Olympic contest requires a good many months, nay, years of training, the better. This training is as much part of the game as the natural ability. The British public seem to regard this concentrated training as rather despicable.'

The culture clash sounded like something straight out of *Chariots of Fire*. And the two most exciting stars of the day both had their detractors. Some people still criticised Eric Liddell for refusing to run on a Sunday – as though they believed he should run every day. Others criticised Harold Abrahams for running every day – as though he should have a day of rest. Eric was called a traitor by the haters. Harold was called a cheat. Liddell and Abrahams shut out the noise and listened only to their coaches.

Eric Liddell was still using his own trusted coach, Tom McKerchar. Their partnership was paying off, too. On Saturday June 14, at Hampden Park, Glasgow, Liddell showed the Olympic Games what they would be missing. He won the Scottish 100 yards title in 10.0sec. This he did for fun or as another sharpener.

Liddell didn't stop at winning the 100 yards on that memorable Saturday at Hampden Park. He took the 220 in 22.6 and the 440 in 51.2, to become triple Scottish title-holder. It was a phenomenal display of running, and perfect preparation for the AAA championships in London the following weekend. Harold would also compete there, without having to dodge his former rival. All was well between them. In fact, the end to track hostilities could have led to friendship. Yet Harold and Eric were such different characters that no strong friendship ever developed. Tony Abrahams explained, 'I don't think Harold had a relationship with Liddell as such. He knew Liddell of course, and he very much admired the way he ran, but he wasn't a particular friend.' And Alan Abrahams echoed, 'I don't think my father and Liddell were friends or unfriendly. He never said he hated the man and I'm sure he didn't. They were polite to each other, I believe.'

As the biggest domestic event of the summer loomed, Harold didn't feel like being much more than polite to anyone. He tried to recharge his batteries, fearing burnout. Later he explained:

*I did not race between 7 June and 21 June – the second day of the AAA Championships. I was – in fact – very stale. The week before the AAA Championships was spent at Brighton with other athletes, and here we were out in the open air all day and actually on the track every morning and afternoon. A hot salt-water bath and a massage at the beginning of the week and an indoor sea-bathe every morning helped me to obtain looseness of muscle and limb.*

After lunch he went to bed for an hour every day. It was the calm before the storm.

Abrahams couldn't get away from the sense of anticipation created by his extraordinary performances at Woolwich. He imagined that the public would turn up at Stamford Bridge expecting even greater heroics. He would have to oblige, or else lose face in front of the people who thought he had crossed the line by training so hard with a professional coach. How they would laugh if he still didn't win! He had to come first in the big race. He just had to, or it would mean total humiliation.

Such thoughts kept returning at night. They put more and more pressure on him, until he was almost ready to crack. Harold explained later:

*Public opinion, however unjust, has great weight with us all. If we fail we are condemned unheard ... In 1924 the emotional state from which I suffered before the AAA Championships was appalling. The championships were on the 20th June. I was at the top of my form, and with a week at Brighton intervening, ought not to have had a care in the world. Yet three days before the race I suffered from "wind up" almost amounting to panic; couldn't sleep or get running out of my head. I was terrified of disappointing a crowd of twenty thousand people whom, I imagined, were all expecting me to win; terrified of being a failure.*

The atmosphere at the championships in London was enough to test the nerves of even the steeliest campaigner. Harold explained, 'There was a record crowd at Stamford Bridge . . . Many supporters came from Scotland to see Eric Liddell . . . I saw several Scotch enthusiasts outside who had walked all the way from Edinburgh, and were too tired to climb over to see the Sports'

If they had come to see Liddell take on Abrahams in the 100 yards, they would have been disappointed anyhow. Eric's absence from the big race left Harold clear favourite in front of a huge crowd. The obligation he felt to please many thousands of gathering spectators only intensified as the race drew near. And Liddell, the younger man who had dominated the 1923 Championships, would be still there, watching him.

Abrahams admitted later to being, 'so tense I was almost having a brain storm.' And without harmony between mind and body all was likely to be lost.

Harold himself had said: 'The truth is that perfection in any sport is the result of a perfect co-operation of mind and body and a beautiful synchronisation of the nervous system and the muscles.'

Harold's nervous system was shot to pieces, so how were his muscles supposed to perform adequately? There was no Sam Mussabini to hold his hand now. This was an amateur championship, and professional trainers had to keep their distance. Luckily Harold's brother Adolphe, a doctor with experience of psychiatric patients, was on hand – not for the first time – to bring some much-needed perspective to the moment.

Harold recalled, 'On this occasion, as in 1923 [at Queen's Club], I was so ill with excitement that I consulted a doctor, who informed me that I had never been fitter in my life.' Adolphe probably added one word to his 1923 diagnosis: 'You bloody fool, it's nerves – again!' Just as before, Adolphe's harshness helped his kid brother to snap out of it.

Slowly, the nervous energy he hadn't lost to sheer panic began to work in his favour once more. Soon he felt a little more like himself again. He decided to face the challenge in front of him. He had always loved running fast. That was all he had to do now, wasn't it? Tap into that love, which was almost innate.

'If the spirit moves you, all will be well,' Harold told himself. He probably still wished he could be blinkered from the many thousands of spectators banked high on terracing to his left, all the way down the straight. But he was almost ready for action.

Abrahams went into his pre-race routine, taking comfort from his trowel. Simple actions would help to banish wild thought. He crouched, waiting for the starter's pistol, hoping it would send him into his comfort zone. Would his training then kick in, or would he be left rooted to the spot? As soon as he heard that pistol, Harold sprang from his starting holes, staying low on the first stride. Adrenalin electrified him. Now the fear of failure could be used positively, his speed sharpened by the enormity of the occasion. He ran like the wind. The fans roared him on – a blurred, heaving mass which stretched from track to sky. It was Abrahams from start to finish. No one else stood a chance. His soaring spirit did not prevent Harold from staging the calculated finish he had learned from his coach. Not that Abrahams really needed to find a few extra inches on this particular day. For all his anxiety, he remained in a British league of his own when there was no Eric Liddell to race.

The joy of victory.

There is a marvellous picture of Harold breaking the tape with that famous drop finish, an expression of exhilaration on his face. 'It was the glorious thrill of winning,' he explained later. 'Relief as much as elation. 'The terror did not leave me until after I had won the 100 yards.'

The time – 9.9sec – was still a fifth of a second outside the AAA championship record set the previous year by Liddell. It was also ³/₁₀ of a second outside the so-called "world record" time he had notched on that Woolwich slope a fortnight earlier. But it was also a tenth of a second faster than the time Liddell had clocked north of the border the previous week.

Abrahams had recaptured the limelight. In truth, the time didn't matter. Victory at such a big event would give him confidence for the weeks ahead, and that was what he really needed. Somehow Harold had come through his personal crisis. But after the battle against himself, he felt totally drained.

'Then the reaction set in and I couldn't long-jump to save my life,' he admitted. 'On this occasion I performed none too well. I had become too excited.' *The Yorkshire Herald* concluded rather uncharitably,

'H.M. Abrahams had an "off day". He was a little stale and far from well. His sprinting lacked the usual fire whilst his final coordination, so vital to accurate long-jumping, was wanting. But such is the penalty of setting such a superlative standard.'

He still did the double. 'I managed to win the 100 yards in 9.9sec and the long jump with a miserable 22ft 6½in (6.87m),' Harold reflected.

Abrahams felt shattered – and the Olympic Games were just around the corner.

CHAPTER TWENTY-TWO:

# Preparing for Paris

Eric Liddell still seemed fresh. But then Eric's positive, almost self-less approach to running was so much more emotionally econom-ical than Harold's burdensome ego. The terror Abrahams felt at the mere prospect of losing face didn't exist anymore for his Scottish counterpart.

For Liddell, the race was a celebration of the ability God had given him. Why should there be any fear of failure? He felt a fierce determi-nation to serve his Maker by running as fast as he could on any given day. That would honour Him. When Liddell's inner fire resulted in him winning races, he was pleased. When it didn't, that was God's will and Liddell would try to do better next time.

'I hated losing,' Eric always admitted. But he didn't fear it.

The difference between the two men was as marked as the differ-ence between their respective environments. When Colin Welland visited Edinburgh many years later, in order to research for his screen-play for *Chariots of Fire*, he wrote to producer David Puttnam about Liddell's background.

*There is a Calvinistic simplicity about the man and his world that makes Abrahams' set-up look positively Baroque.*

Liddell took that valuable simplicity into all his races, wherever they were. And he was also successful at Stamford Bridge, winning the 440 yards final in 49.6sec. The time would not have struck fear into his Olympic rivals. Even so, when compared to those of the previous month, it represented considerable progress. So when he only came second to a South African called Howard Kinsman in the 220 yards, it wasn't the end of Eric's world. In fact the result guaranteed Liddell's Olympic selection at that distance too.

Though Eric wasn't the sort of man to look for excuses, the schedule at the AAA Championship had worked against him. And who was generous enough to point this out in print? Harold Abrahams, in the *Sunday Express* of June 29, 1924.

He wrote:

*Howard Kinsman, who has put up some fine performances in the Cape, beat Liddell, the holder of the furlong championship, in 21.7sec. In all fairness to Liddell, it must be said that he had run two 220s and two 440s on Friday evening, and was obviously suffering from the effort on Saturday. He managed to win the 440 in 49.6secs, and in this race he ran with great determination from start to finish. This time speaks volumes for his greatness as an athlete. People may shout their heads off about his appalling style. Well, let them. He gets there.*

Was it too late for Liddell to become a smoother runner? Harold observed:

*Liddell's style was quite the most unorthodox ever, with arms revolving like the sails of a windmill, head thrust back and an exaggerated knee lift. People are apt to ask whether he would not have been an even greater runner if he had possessed a more polished style. In theory the answer is 'yes', but often in trying to impose a style on a runner you ruin his individuality and spoil his performance. If you can teach a very young boy good style, it is well worthwhile, but you must study an athlete as an individual and not be too keen on 'orthodoxy'. I do not mean to suggest that good style is not a tremendous asset and if one had started when Liddell was very young, something advantageous might have resulted.*

It was a little early for Harold Abrahams to be patronising about Liddell's style. He and Eric might yet meet in the 200 metres at the Olympics, after all. But for both men that was a sideshow.

For most people, it was the 100 metres that captured the imagination. And it was the 100m that Harold had trained for above all other disciplines. Liddell no longer represented a threat to his self-esteem; and Harold felt he could say what he liked. For all that, there remained an element of rivalry between them – at least in Harold's head. It was something that went beyond their anticipated clash in the 200 metres in Paris. It was unspoken; and Harold felt it more than Eric. Who would hold centre stage and command the most limelight in Paris? Would it be Abrahams? Only if he could recover from the stresses of Stamford Bridge in time. Even then, it might yet be Liddell, if he adapted fully to the physical rigours of the 400 metres.

Two outstanding British athletes, each man destined to end their Olympic careers long before their natural time. One Olympic Games offered a chance of sporting glory. The big moments were fast approaching, to be seized or squandered. And yet all adrenalin appeared to have deserted Harold's body.

'I was dead stale,' he later admitted.

The fact that Liddell was flying and so full of energy probably didn't help Harold's mental state. To his credit, Abrahams prescribed the correct remedy:

*After the Championships I took five days of complete rest. Another weekend by the sea; a game of tennis or two and a couple of light outings on the track just to convince myself that I had not forgotten how to run.*

He spent part of his time trying to work out why he had come so close to a breakdown, so that he could avoid a similar scenario at the Olympic Games. In a *Sunday Express* article about 'Getting the Wind Up', Harold asked himself why any athlete would suffer so badly from nerves:

*There are two kinds. One form consists of a perfectly natural excitement – a suppressed tension to get at the foe. This is undoubtedly necessary and useful – it is nature's way of producing the best in an animal. But sometimes, coupled with this, is a kind of morbid anxiety – a fear of defeat, of disgrace, and of not doing one's best; often almost a moral certainty that one will not be able to move a muscle, and then, when the pistol goes, one will be glued to the ground unable to run. This morbid anxiety becomes less with experience, but it is always there.*

He read *An Introduction to Social Psychology*, William McDougall's ground-breaking book on such matters. Before long he was able to write, 'Analysis shows – if we are honest with ourselves – that we are afraid of doing badly before a crowd . . . It is the fear of shame which to my mind is such a strong factor in getting the "wind up"'.

When faced with the prospect of 'black failure', as Harold put it, he knew that he experienced a 'sinking feeling' far more acutely than most, and likened the rising tension to 'steam pressure in a boiler with no safety valve'. By now Abrahams had realised that the amount of pressure was proportionate to the size of an athlete's ego. He explained:

*If the person concerned has a very great opinion of himself, his qualms, when contemplating his failure and his anticipation of making a fool of himself, will be considerably greater than those of a man who realises after all that he is a very unimportant factor in the world . . .*

*How should this problem be tackled? First a man should try to realise that what really is of paramount importance is not the winning or losing of a race, but the amount of energy and effort that he has put into training.*

In short, it was about doing your very best, not making excuses if you lost or blowing your own trumpet if you won. Harold may have studied psychology more than Christianity, but he was gradually reaching the same conclusions as Eric Liddell. Eric had no ego; and he would never dream of boasting. Harold was prone to self-aggrandisement – and understood why:

Abrahams observed, 'Most boasting is caused by the individual feeling that in some way he is really rather inferior and is only another way of trying to force your own opinion of your worth (and even you yourself quite often don't really believe in it) on others.'

By the time he began to focus on the forthcoming Olympics, Harold had certainly learned how to play down his chances in order to reduce the pressure he felt. 'I am being completely honest when I write that I never seriously thought I had a chance of an Olympic medal,' he insisted later. It was a strange claim from a man who had trained all winter to give himself the best possible chance; but Harold said it consistently for the rest of his life.

'This wasn't mock modesty,' he insisted, 'for I always (according to my friends) had far too high an opinion of my ability. But the Americans appeared to me to be in a different class from myself.'

Such a belief suited him, for it helped him to recover mentally from the strains of Stamford Bridge. And if Abrahams really thought he had little chance of success in Paris, he believed many of his seventy-odd teammates had even less of a chance; and there were 'several whose chances appear to be as remote as the proverbial blue moon'. What's more, he said so in print. The article appeared in the *Daily Express* on June 25, 1924, written 'By a Famous International Athlete.'

Abrahams argued, 'The team is much larger than that sent to Antwerp four years ago, and it is to be hoped that the British Olympic Association have sufficient funds at their disposal to justify the inclusion of a good many athletes who must of necessity, from the point of view of Olympic achievement, be ranked as "also rans".'

Many fellow squad members must have known the author was Abrahams, since in April he had presented a similar argument under his own name:

*To send men hopelessly below [top six] standard is a waste of public money, and of time to the individual. Moreover, the inclusion of such men may well not only lower the tone, but also the morale and spirit of the team. Such members of the team as have a chance of gaining premier honours should be given every opportunity to enable them to produce their best form. Since funds are not unlimited, to take people who are not up to standard is to spend money on them which could be spent on others. Thus you are not giving your best performers all the attention that might be given.*

The British Olympic Committee had completely ignored his advice, and now Harold braced himself for the backlash when he met up with the squad. He could expect many a cold stare from less talented team-mates, only too aware of what he thought about their inclusion.

At least Abrahams had also argued against his own inclusion in one event. After the squad was announced, the unnamed 'Famous International Athlete' wrote, 'H.M. Abrahams is chosen for four events, which is unfortunate. From the point of view of the Olympic Games, this athlete should leave the long jump severely alone. The authorities surely do not imagine that he can perform at long jumping at two o'clock and running 200 metres at 2.30 on the same afternoon. Let us hope that Abrahams has been told by the authorities to concentrate his efforts on the 100 metres.'

This was a high-risk strategy; but it worked. The selectors duly approached Abrahams and offered to withdraw him from the long jump. For a man who didn't believe he was a serious medal prospect, Harold was making plenty of sacrifices to give himself the best possible chance in the sprints.

Training resumed and went well. Harold confirmed, 'I had redis-covered my form by the time we left for Paris on the Wednesday before the Games.'

In comparison to the domestic championship, Harold felt under no great pressure to succeed in Paris. He later explained, 'Fortunately in those days no one in England thought an awful lot about the Olympics, and few writers ever bothered to predict Olympic winners. In my view there is nothing worse than to be picked as the "favourite" for an Olympic title. Much much better to be an outsider as I surely was. I wasn't nervous for the very simple reason that I wasn't really bothered by what happened.'

That last remark might have been stretching credibility a little too far. But there was precious little star treatment for the athletes. Harold recalled, 'The British Olympic Team departed for France in their ill-fitting blazers made of shoddy material, almost without comment. For Paris we had ghastly team gear of white trousers, blazers and straw hats, we had a small union jack on our left breasts.'

Abrahams wasn't exaggerating about the uniforms. A photo from this time shows Harold wearing a jacket and a pair of trousers that look as though they have shrunk in the wash. Yet the careless approach of the Olympic officials didn't do Abrahams any harm. With his ego cut down to size, his nerves remained steady.

Only once was Harold given the sort of attention a departing Olympian expects nowadays. And even then, the brief media interest was enjoyed by the entire group – and not just the best athletes.

Harold in ill-fitting trousers and Olympic blazer.

## CHAPTER TWENTY-THREE:

# Last Advice in Paris

Harold's Caius colleague Henry Stallard, also a good friend of Eric Liddell, was chosen to compete in the 800 and 1500 metres. He recalled a commotion as the team received their send-off at Victoria railway station.

'On 2 July at 10 a.m. the Continental Departure Platform at Victoria witnessed a scene of hilarity. Some twenty-five staid and elderly gentlemen (officials of the AAA) were endeavouring to extricate seventy undisciplined youths from a melee of luggage and press photographers.' Abrahams claimed this media scrum was unusual because, 'The newspapers were interested only in Wimbledon and golf.'

There was no outcry when the Olympic team was sent from Victoria to Paris by the least comfortable route. Abrahams explained, 'I tell you in those days we went from Newhaven to Dieppe as a British team because it was the cheapest sea route, even though it was the longest.'

The official reason given was somewhat more fanciful; that the train from Dieppe came in at the right Paris station, 'allegedly because the Gare St Lazare in Paris was the nearest station to the "Hotel Moderne", where we were billeted,' Abrahams elaborated. 'We had a ghastly crossing: "Sea rough and a risk of thunderstorms." I spent the entire journey keeping my lunch down and my spirits up by singing Gilbert and Sullivan with Malcolm Nokes [hammer thrower] entirely disregarding the possible effect on my fellow athletes. I still have a very clear picture of Douglas Lowe, immaculately dressed (as ever), lying prostrate on the deck. Less than a week later he was 800-metre Olympic champion.'

The dramatic transformation in Lowe from sea-sick weakling to Olympic god would have seen him immortalised in *Chariots of Fire* along with Abrahams and Liddell, had he not turned down the opportunity. The expletive Lord Puttnam used in 2023 suggested his annoyance had survived the passing years.

The welcoming party for the travel-weary athletes, when they finally arrived at the Gare du Nord and not Gare St Lazare after all, consisted of Earl Cadogan and General Kentish from the British Olympic Committee, the British Ambassador, and several other dignitaries. But the Olympic team's afternoon soon took another turn for the worse when they were sent on to the Hotel Moderne in the Place de la Republique. The Hungarian team was also housed there. And the state of the hotel quickly removed any sense of importance the athletes might have gained from their welcome at the station.

Harold remembered, 'It was a miserable little hotel in one of the busiest centres of Paris. My room was on a corner and the high-pitched motor horns were not exactly conducive to sleep before the competitions. The Americans were in their own kind of village.'

At least Harold Abrahams was lucky enough to room with Philip Noel-Baker, the team captain and perhaps coolest head in the GB party. Given the more natural friendship they had formed, you might have thought Noel-Baker would room with Eric Liddell. The pairing with Harold may have been decided on the grounds of seniority, because both men had been to the Antwerp Olympics of 1920, where Noel-Baker had won a silver in the 1500 metres. But it's tempting to see this as a masterstroke of man-management from the future Nobel Peace Prize winner. Noel-Baker knew Liddell didn't need him. Eric had God to ease the pressure, such as it was for the 400 metre-runner. Harold, for all his outer bluster and arrogance, was far more vulnerable. The strains of competition had already been showing in Abrahams over the previous year or two. Harold needed Noel-Baker more, as the might of the Americans loomed on the horizon. Philip knew where an old head could have the most calming influence over a great British hope. He would be with Harold pretty much round the clock.

The USA team had endured a far longer sea route from New York; but they had done so in some luxury. The promenade deck on the chartered liner, the SS America, had even been fitted out with a 220-yard cork track, so that the athletes could train during the week-long trip.

These preparations befitted a group of men hailed by their chief coach Lawson Robertson as the greatest athletic force ever to leave the country.

Writer and television producer Neil Duncanson's description of the Americans' arrival in Paris made the British experience sound woeful by comparison. 'When they arrived in Paris they were greeted by thousands of cheering fans and boarded a convoy of seventy cars taking them to their own Olympic village, an estate outside the capital, once used as a stately home by one of Napoleon's marshals.'

The atmosphere in the French capital was beginning to build. Over three thousand competitors gathered in Paris. It was crowded; and each man wanted to familiarise himself with the most important place of all.

Harold noted, 'On Thursday and Friday a visit to the stadium – a couple of starts and one or two bursts. Incidentally a long jump (could not clear 21 feet).'

It is incredible to think that, after all his meticulous training, Harold did something as risky as attempt a long jump at full throttle, when there was no logical reason for doing so, other than to please a loitering group of cameramen. Perhaps there was some truth in his claim that 'I got to Paris in 1924 at the top of my form, but not bothering about the race too much.'

Luckily, he emerged unscathed from that moment of foolishness; though not entirely unscathed from his preparations in the crowded arena. Abrahams revealed, 'I bumped into another athlete while I was training and bruised a thigh.' Fortunately, there was time to recover; and on Saturday he took a complete rest.

There was no chance to benefit from a last get-together with Sam Mussabini. Harold's coach didn't even try to stay in the British Olympic team's hotel. He wasn't part of the official group and knew that he would not have been welcome.

Abrahams confirmed, 'Old Sam wasn't allowed to mix with the British team. He was not persona grata with the AAA.'

Nevertheless, Mussabini still found a way to take the tension out of the build-up, and instil belief into his athlete at the same time.

He penned a simple note, and made sure the tone was almost matter-of-fact. Sam sent it on the morning of 5 July 1924, from the Hotel Franklin, his frugal base on the Rue Bouffault. Handwritten in a barely legible scrawl, it read:

Dear Mr Abrahams,

You must please pardon my not coming to see you, much as I would like to do so.
However – I believe and hope you will win the 100 metres.
Go out determined to do your best and don't forget to go down at the first stride.
A sponge and some cold or preferably iced water used around the nape of the neck, under the ears and at the wrists and elbows will brace you up.
Get nicely warmed up and then react to the gun. I should use the springy old 6-spiked shoes.

All the best of luck from Yours Truly
S.A. Mussabini

P.S.
Please wish Fred Gaby [an ex-sprinter converted by Mussabini into Britain's best 120 yards hurdler] good luck from me.

Looking back at this note, Abrahams offered: 'A few words of explanation. "Go down at the first stride." I had practised for many months so that my first stride was as regular as clockwork, and I was not too upright. Many sprinters take too long a first stride and are in too upright a position.

The reference to spikes was advising me not to use a new pair I'd had made some weeks before the Games, but an old pair I had been using for a year or two.'

HOTEL FRANKLIN
RUE BOUFFAULT
PARIS

JULY 7th. 1924

DEAR MR. ABRAHAMS,

YOU MUST PLEASE PARDON MY NOT COMING TO SEE YOU, MUCH
AS I WOULD LIKE TO DO SO.

HOWEVER - I BELIEVE AND HOPE YOU WILL WIN THE 100 METRES.

GO OUT DETERMINED TO DO YOUR BEST AND DON'T FORGET TO
GO DOWN AT THE FIRST STRIDE.

A SPONGE AND SOME COLD OR PREFERABLY ICED WATER USED
AROUND THE NAPE OF THE NECK, XXX UNDER THE EARS AND AT THE WRISTS AND
ELBOWS WILL BRACE YOU UP.

GET NICELY WARMED UP AND THEN RE-ACT TO THE GUN.
I SHOULD USE THE SPRINGY OLD 6-SPIKED SHOES.

ALL THE BEST OF LUCK FROM
YOURS TRULY
S.A.MUSSABINI

P.S.

PLEASE WISH FRED GABY GOOD LUCK FROM ME.

Mussabini's handwritten letter and Harold's typed "translation."

Mussabini's message was wonderfully familiar, as if sent from a kindly uncle just before a village sports day in some picturesque corner of England. But Harold was preparing to run against rivals who came from the most prolific 100 metre breeding ground in the world. And it wasn't just the presence of the mighty Americans that added to the sense of occasion, as the teams prepared to march in full regalia despite sweltering heat.

Harold's GB and former Cambridge teammate, Henry Stallard gave a marvellous description of the Colombes Stadium and the pageantry as it unfolded on the opening day of those 1924 Games:

*The Arena is oval in shape, the green grass in the centre contrasting vividly with the red track and the white concrete stands, with their blue and gold-coloured iron framework . . .*

*At 10am on July 5th a most impressive service was given to the athletes of all nations in Notre Dame. At 3pm the Stadium was packed and ready to witness the march-past of the athletes. The day was perfect – a blazing sun in an azure sky.*

*An overture was sung by choirs of male voices. Then followed a deathly silence, broken a few minutes later by the sound of massed bands, the Marathon Gate was opened, and to the crashing of cymbals and the rolling of drums the South African team entered the Stadium, heading the parade. Those of us who had the good fortune to watch this spectacle will never again see anything to equal it in its splendour. Not even the most phlegmatic of us could fail to be thrilled at the sight of the wiriest and lithest bodies of the athletes of forty-five nations, clad each in their respective national uniforms, and marching with heads erect behind their flag-bearers.*

*Cheer after cheer went up as each column entered the Stadium, and, marching round the track, dipped its flag and saluted at the President's box. The Americans formed the largest detachment, being some 350 strong. Haiti and China were the smallest, and were represented by one standard bearer, one flag bearer and one rank and file. The national uniforms were splendid. The French deserve special mention for their smartness, and next to them the Turks, with uniforms of green sweater coats, white flannel trousers and crimson fezes.*

Enter Team GB.

Eric Liddell probably paid special attention to that tiny Chinese representation. China hadn't even been part of the Olympic movement when he had been born there twenty-two years earlier. Eric marched dutifully with the British, complete with their 'ghastly team gear of white trousers, blazers and straw hats', as Harold had put it. GB took their turn – and all went smoothly enough; but they won no prizes for style.

Nevertheless, Stallard continued patriotically, 'The demeanour of each nation was interesting to watch – the French with their characteristic alertness and vivacity; the Americans with their air of self-assurance; the Italians always demonstrative and emotional; and the stolid Britisher, displaying a calmness and a resoluteness of purpose in the face of odds.'

Stallard, who by the end of the games would be more admired by Eric Liddell than anyone else, was determined to savour every moment of this glorious occasion. Neither was he wrong about the Americans, or the bravery it would require just to dent that confidence.

In Harold's case, the odds against success seemed considerable. The "Cambridge Cannonball" was not widely tipped to defeat the "California Flash" or "New York Thunderbolt" when the world's press did its previews.

Abrahams acknowledged:

*The prospect of meeting the great Americans, Paddock, Scholz, Murchison and Bowman, put any ideas of supreme success out of my head. I didn't think about winning because one was so impressed about the Americans in those days.*

*I used to say, 'Britain is ahead of America in only one thing . . . five and a half hours.'*

*They had four of the world's best sprinters. So I was helped by a lack of intolerable pressure.*

In June, Charley Paddock, Jackson Scholz and Chester Bowman had all run 10.6sec at the US Olympic trials. There was no reason to suppose they wouldn't go even faster in Paris, once the adrenalin really started pumping. Loren Murchison had clocked a less impressive 10.8sec in that US trial; but he had been an Olympic finalist four years earlier and therefore had the experience to raise his game when it mattered.

Just as well for Harold that the US selectors had left black sprinter DeHart Hubbard out of their 100 metres squad, so that he could concentrate on the long jump – which he won. A few weeks after the Games, Hubbard clocked 9.6sec for the 100 yards. 'I always wondered how I would do against those boys [sic] from England,' he said later wistfully.

Harold hoped his Olympic experience in Antwerp might help him against the chosen American quartet. It wasn't much to rely on; but at least the magnitude of the Olympic stage might not be quite so daunting this time around. His Cambridge friend Stallard, on the other hand, still seemed in awe of the opening ceremony in Paris as he described its conclusion:

*When each nation had marched past and taken up its post in the centre of the ground facing the Presidential box, the flag-bearers advanced and formed a semi-circle around Andre (France), the chosen athlete, who, with his right forearm extended forwards and upwards, took the Olympic oath in these words: Nous Jurons, que nous nous presentons aux*

*Jeux Olympiques en concurrents loyaux, respectueux des reglements qui les regissent et desireux d'y participer dans un esprit chevaleresque pour l'honneur de nos pays et la gloire du sport. This oration was followed by a salvo of artillery and forty-five baskets full of pigeons were released. The massed bands struck up 'La Marche Heroique' and the teams marched out of the stadium.*

When they returned, the real action would begin – and we would see what Harold Abrahams and Eric Liddell were made of.

<br>

CHAPTER TWENTY-FOUR:

# Strychnine and Rivals

Stimulating as the spectacular nature of this Olympic gathering was, something else prepared Harold for the challenge ahead – strychnine.

People think of it as a murderous poison; and used in larger doses it could be. But used in the right amounts, strychnine was an effective and legal stimulant in 1924. Every athlete had his own little way of coaxing the best out of himself. Strychnine was Harold's little friend when he needed a tonic.

Half a century later, Harold explained, 'I concentrated on looking after my diet and my bowels. I took some tonic called Easton's Syrup which had some strychnine in it, so perhaps I would have been disqualified for taking "drugs" today.'

Had it been outlawed at those Paris Games, Harold wouldn't have taken it. He was no cheat. Sam Mussabini is believed to have favoured strychnine for athletes covering short distances – and may well have been the man behind this controversial habit. Easton's Syrup certainly wouldn't have been the brainchild of his brother Adolphe. As medical advisor to the British Olympic team, he wrote a few months later:

*The healthy sprinter needs no drugs of any description, and, unless he is actually ill, medicines of every kind should be avoided as poisons. Just as certain foodstuffs are invested with peculiar virtues, so we hear of 'nerve tonics' and 'strengthening medicines' to produce or increase athletic efficiency, extravagant claims which any reasonable person must dismiss as nonsense, but the keen athlete is only too prone to believe a lot of nonsense which he would like to believe.*

You can almost hear the resentment in Adolphe's tone, that responsibility for some of Harold's choices had been taken out of the elder brother's control. Did he dislike Mussabini? He must have known Old Sam was a fine coach. But a control freak hates a competitor for the influence he normally enjoys.

Despite his chosen "poison," Harold's Olympic Games started unspectacularly. There were no fewer than seventeen heats to accommodate eighty-two competitors in the 100 metres. Abrahams was in heat 14, along with "Slip" Carr from Australia. By the time Harold tried to focus, his four American rivals had already qualified, two of them clocking 10.8. Abrahams won his heat in 11.0sec, a time he described as 'slowish and not very encouraging'. He was even harder on himself when he added, 'I seemed to be moving like a dilapidated cab-horse.'

Fortunately, there were two hours before the second round, and Harold had a chance to talk to his amiable team captain, Philip Noel-Baker. Eric Liddell adored him, and Abrahams respected the skipper no less. A man who had reached two Olympic middle-distance finals at his peak was surely worth listening to.

Harold later revealed the key advice Noel-Baker gave him. 'He suggested that I had not limbered up enough before the event, and I certainly remedied this.' Abrahams didn't explain how the oversight had occurred, though. And old Sam Mussabini would have been horrified that his athlete hadn't been fully ready for action, after all their months of dedication. He had even reminded Abrahams to warm up properly in his last note. Thankfully, an attentive roommate had corrected the supposedly meticulous sprint star's pre-race routine in the most basic way.

The second round of the heats involved six races for a semi-final spot. Harold was in the fourth of the six, with the first two men set to go through to the semi-finals. The opening three heats, won by Murchison and Bowman (both USA) and Coaffee (Canada), had all been run in 10.8sec.

With Hester of Canada among the field in his heat, Abrahams couldn't afford to run like a dilapidated cab-horse again. Mercifully, he felt more fluent this time around, but was still astonished to hear that he had broken the tape in 10.6sec, which equalled the Olympic record. Further delight lay in the fact that none of his American rivals matched that time.

The Games record had been set by the great American, Donald Lippincott, in a 1912 heat back in Stockholm. Now, when he least expected it, Harold's name was also carved in Olympic history. And in that moment, he knew it was time to take his chances seriously.

'I didn't think I had any chance whatsoever of winning a gold medal (in fact one never thought of winning gold medals in those days as such) until 24 hours before the final. And that was the first time that I realised, "My Goodness! I'm not going to be outclassed, after all." I realised I had a chance of victory.'

Though Abrahams had hope, he quickly reminded himself that races were not won on paper, times could be deceptive, and expectation was his enemy.

*While happy with my effort, I was far too experienced to take too much notice of the fact that I was, on paper, ⅕ of a second faster than the other runners. I was sufficiently knowledgeable to appreciate that sprint times are completely fallacious. Timing at that date was by hand to ⅕ sec so that two runners given the same time could in fact be nearly two yards apart, whereas two runners given times on the watch a fifth of a second different could be only inches apart.*

The big boys were all through to the semi-finals. Could Harold really hold his own against the giants of his sport? The next day would bring all the answers. Amazingly, despite the enormity of the task ahead and those persistent Parisian car horns, he slept well.

If Harold had been given the chance to read some of the US newspaper reports on the morning of the semi-final and final, they would have fired him up in no time.

One read like this:

### SCHOLZ THE FAVORITE IN 100

*Jackson Scholz is the favorite among the majority of French newspapermen to win the final in the 100 metres dash today. Murchison, Bowman and Paddock, the other three members of America's famous quartet of sprinters, each turned in the time of 10 ⅘sec. It appeared from their races yesterday that any one of the four could have clipped off another fifth had he been pushed a bit harder. In the semi-finals and final Abrahams, the great English sprinter who made the only 10⅗ time yesterday, will furnish them with the necessary opposition.*

So now we knew. Abrahams was just there to make the Americans go faster – a pacemaker in the fastest discipline of all. And you could understand the American point of view, because no European had ever taken the 100 metres Olympic title.

The French had their own man in the first semi-final, an outsider who – judging by the American report quoted below – was rather too anxious to even up the odds:

*Colombes Stadium, Monday – Thirty thousand spectators turned out to the second day's competition in the track and field athletics of the Olympic Games at the Colombes Stadium this afternoon . . . The runners were manifestly nervous when they lined up for the first heat of the 100 metres semi-finals. The strain in the audience was great as the men got off to three false starts, Degrelle, of France, being the offender in each case. Scholz of America took the lead when the dash started and pulled away from the field, finishing in 10⅘sec, just ⅕sec above the Olympic record and ⅖sec above the world mark. Porritt, of New Zealand was second, and Murchison, of America, third.*

Harold had every reason to feel confident as he prepared for his own semi-final. The previous day's 100 metres times told him so. But it was what happened now that mattered. His Olympic record wouldn't mean much if he was edged out on the most important day of all.

Abrahams decided that adrenalin alone would suffice on such a big occasion – no magic potions necessary. The mere thought of facing Charley Paddock, "the world's fastest human," was enough to sharpen anyone. Harold was also up against the Canadian captain Cyril Coaffee, who had once clocked 9.6 for the 100 yards to become joint world record-holder alongside Paddock. Chester Bowman was there, buoyed by his 100 yards victory over "The Flying Scotsman" Eric Liddell in America that spring. The crack Australian, Edwin "Slip" Carr and Giovanni Frangipane of Italy completed the line-up.

Paddock and Coaffee were the most fearsome foe.

Even if he got off to a a perfect start, their speed promised to test Harold to the limit under pressure. This was a bizarre situation. In the space of a few frantic seconds, nine months of intensive training would either find its reward or be rendered futile. The start meant so much, and Abrahams was counting on Dr Moir to do his job well. But would he?

Charley Paddock, Harold's fearsome rival.

CHAPTER TWENTY-FIVE:

# Liddell Watches Near Disaster

D r Moir, the man with the pistol, probably didn't even realise the error he had made. He didn't see Australia's "Slip" Carr move before the gun – and leave Harold for dead.

Charley Paddock was already racing Chester Bowman, his fellow American. Carr and Coaffee were off to flyers too, and even Frangipane was briskly into his early strides. Harold only sprang into action after he had given all his rivals a couple of yards' start.

Faced with that alarming sight, not even the most fervent British optimist could believe Harold still had a chance of qualifying for the final.

'Go!!'

Belatedly Abrahams exploded out of his starting holes. The back walls held firm and did their job. With near-horizontal thrust, Harold executed a controlled 'fall' out of his holes, and he was into his first stride. He hit his mark, bringing his arms into play immediately. Under the circumstances, with his entire inner being in turmoil, this was a remarkable demonstration of self-control.

It is the first step that usually dictates the poise of a sprinter. The body position at the end of that first stride was the foundation on which Harold had to build. Still low, his torso began its steady journey towards a more upright position, just as Mussabini demanded. His 11st 10lb frame would soon be pumping forcefully. Yet his rivals were well on their way to completing this initial phase of the race. Harold always remembered how close he was to panic at the realisation:

*I got a shocking start and I was more than a yard behind in the first ten. My first inclination was to get into a panic and make a superhuman effort to catch up with the others as quickly as possible. Had I done this the result would have been a complete loss of form and bad running. Here I was in a desperate situation, and if I panicked I would not even reach the final. I almost shouted aloud, 'For goodness sake keep your form.' The only hope now is that by doing so you may qualify. Here I was in an Olympic semi-final, slow off the mark with five sprinters ahead of me in the first twenty-five yards. I was furious for three seconds.*

Negative thoughts were trying to take over his head. Why hadn't he just ignored Carr and gone like the rest? All that training, with Mussabini firing the starting pistol. All that work to shave precious fractions of a second off Harold's reaction time. All that personal sacrifice. How could he be so stupid, just when it mattered? Somehow he had allowed himself to be caught in two minds at the crucial moment. Insanely, he had tried to do the starter's job for him. It had never happened like this before. Why now? Harold dismissed such thoughts and held himself together. He recalled:

*The whole of my training came to my assistance and I realised the only way I could win was by not throwing all I'd learned in training myself to the winds. If a performer has done enough training, he can keep his head in a crisis. 'Don't panic,' said a small voice inside me. 'Keep those arms well down.' Now was the time to rely on my faith, to keep my form. 'Don't hurry too much.' By the mercy of heaven, my trainer and a little voice inside me, I did not panic.*

Harold could control his own emotions to an extent; but he couldn't control the rest of the field. And the calibre of that field didn't suggest a second chance for any straggler. Why should rivals let him back into the fray? It is kill-or-be-killed on the track, where only the ruthless belong.

Abrahams knew that; he also knew he had to be patient. Acceleration towards top speed has to be a smooth curve. No sudden jerking, jabbing or straining would help him find top gear more quickly. He had to let the familiar process run its course.

The good news was that Harold was into his seven foot three-and-a-half inch racing stride. That stride length had been chosen because it gave him more control than any other. With his torso angled over the advanced leg, he achieved a familiar sense of balance. With that balance came speed. Forty-five strides in ten seconds. That's all he needed.

He also knew that his arms, bent at the elbows, were as important as his legs. The propulsion of his arms was coming from his shoulders, so he kept those shoulders as loose as he could. However bad the crisis, he would only stand a chance through relaxation. Sure enough, there was rhythm in those arms as he moved them instinctively in what he described as a "criss-cross" action. His hands were tightly clenched as they flashed past each other. Everything was working in perfect harmony.

'Gradually I found myself closing that ghastly gap,' Harold recalled.

But at fifty metres, he was still one stride down. Abrahams stayed positive and kept pounding away as the clock ticked and his opponents neared safety. He tried not to look at them, though the temptation was great. One glance to the left or right might have upset his balance.

'Focus on yourself,' Mussabini always used to say.

By now Harold was moving at his maximum speed of thirty-six feet per second. But had he reached top gear too late to catch the rest? It seemed so.

Yet he felt speed in those twinkle-feet like never before – a searing pace that was eating up track and drawing his rivals towards him. The clock ticked some more. Three seconds, two . . . Harold would always remember these moments.

'Twenty yards from the tape I was almost on level terms.'

Two seconds, one . . . The roar of the crowd increased as the field raced for the tape. Harold's momentum was extraordinary. Then he swooped like a bird of prey.

'I thrust myself forward,' he recalled.

He dropped down for that tape, hoping not to lose power and rhythm. With his arms flung behind him, he executed the dip-finish he had practised on hundreds of occasions with Mussabini.

Time it right and you can steal a victory. Go too early and you lose speed at the vital moment.

Would he feel that precious tape? Or would his rivals burst through first and take the prospect of an Olympic final out of his reach?

Harold lunged with his torso. The crowd screamed. Abrahams heard nothing because his senses were focused on the tape alone.

*I felt a slight pressure against my chest. But I was too experienced not to know that to feel the tape does not necessarily mean that one has broken it. Often the tape is broken by another competitor, and as it breaks at its weakest part it does not necessarily break opposite to the winner. The second man may feel it on his chest when it has snapped elsewhere. I thought I felt it break. But experience told me that very often you can feel the tape and yet not have won.*

Half the field probably experienced the same sensation. Paddock was jumping at the tape and Bowman had already raised his hands as if to welcome it. Others were storming through in a blur. An American newspaper report described the finish.

'The audience waited breathless as the three first men dashed across the tape shoulder to shoulder. From the stands it was impossible to tell the winner.'

The race was over in an instant – and Harold's fate was sealed one way or another. It had all happened in roughly the time it takes to read the following stream of consciousness out loud.

*Bang! False start! No! Go! Don't panic, keep your form, arms low. Ghastly gap, halfway, getting closer, level, the tape! Have I won? Don't know.*

Optimism gave way to total confusion as the sprinters finally slowed to a standstill then turned. For some the quest to become the fastest man on earth was over. But whose dreams had been shattered? The outcome hung in the warm Parisian air. Harold waited ... Still nothing. In his own words:

*I walked disconsolately and almost despairingly back to the start. Had I won? Had I even qualified? An agonising few minutes which seemed like hours. At last, the French loud-speaker. 'Allo! Allo! Le cent metres, deuxieme demi-finale. Premier. Quatre cents dix neuf.' Four hundred and nineteen! My number! What a relief! 'Temps Dix, trois-cinquiemes. Record Olympique égalé!' I had qualified and equalled the Olympic record for the second time. The relief was tremendous. Fortunately I had just got home.*

He had done more than that. Officially Abrahams had equalled the record and that is what the history books still say. But in real terms he had smashed it, because he had started so late – well after the gun had set the clock ticking. As Norris McWhirter said later, 'This indicated that Abrahams was capable of covering 100 metres in 10.4 seconds.'

Philip Noel-Baker explained, 'The time was 10.6sec. But if you want his real time, you must deduct that yard and a half – or perhaps two yards – and that brings him to the Olympic records of [later Games].'

Harold gently rejected these theories, though perhaps he was being excessively modest. 'I still managed to win and many people think that was the best effort I ever made and they all tend to say, "Well, what would have happened if you hadn't been left at the start, wouldn't you have done a better time?" My answer is no, because I produced something that I never would have produced if I hadn't been left behind.'

His seemingly hopeless situation undoubtedly brought something special out of Harold. But the suspicion remains that, if someone had been able to time Harold Abrahams from the moment he finally sprang from his starting holes to the moment he hit the tape, he might have equalled the 100 metres world record. Incredibly, he had given the legendary Charley Paddock – the world record holder with 10.4 – a clear head start and still triumphed. Paddock came in second and Bowman third.

Looking back on that near-disastrous start, Abrahams reflected:

*I did a very stupid thing which nearly lost me the race. When the starter had told us to 'Get set' I saw the runner on my right move. The gun went. I thought the runner had beaten the pistol. But there was no recall. I had been left. I took my mind right off the work in hand, and started badly as a result, nearly two yards behind the others. I had nearly lost that very important race by allowing my attention and gaze to wander in the direction of my right-hand opponent. It is impossible properly to do two things at once. Keep your mind on the job in hand.*

When Harold returned to the dressing room, he encountered Eric Liddell. They had a short and fascinating exchange.

'You were badly away,' said Liddell simply.

There wouldn't have been a hint of a taunt in those four words. Eric didn't behave like that, even though he harboured opinions about Abrahams' overall style, and they weren't necessarily favourable. As one supreme athlete to another, they felt free to talk on a technical level. And above all, Eric would have been worried for his teammate, as the 100 metres final wasn't far away. Liddell was one of the few people in the world in that very moment who could truly understand the pressure Harold was under. He might also have been curious over what he had seen; and even hopeful of an explanation. He didn't get one.

'Don't talk about it,' Harold replied. 'I saw five in front of me.'

Harold knew what had happened and why. He didn't want to go through the reasons again with Liddell. Interestingly, however, he did want to share the moment of horror with Eric. The five backsides and the panic he had to suppress. What does that tell us? First and foremost, they were not enemies. He wouldn't have talked of the "five in front of him" if they were. And they weren't close friends either, a fact some people seem to struggle with. What they had was a respect for the passion and determination the other man brought to the party. Abrahams knew Liddell had driven him on to greater heights. And by pointing to Harold's poor start, Eric had the same effect on the biggest day of Harold's life. That's why the conversation wasn't over.

'But I won't be left again,' said Harold, concluding the exchange.

Lesser men than Liddell might have read that riposte as an arrogant rebuke to a man who had been a thorn in his side for two years. But Eric loved Harold's answer. It was just the bloody-mindedness he wanted to hear. Eric knew the rest of the team regarded Harold as a bighead. One of the few people who could see through that outer, protective shell was the magnificent Eric Liddell.

You had to be a top dog yourself to understand what this pair were going through. Perhaps only these two Brits felt the same, enormous weight of expectation on their shoulders at the Olympic Games in Paris during that summer of 1924. The expectation of their teammates, the administrators, royalty and the nation.

Eric felt it even more keenly, because he had refused to run on a Sunday and had still been pressured to do so, almost until the 100 metres heats were under way. Harold was under pressure because this was his whole life, and he knew some would be laughing if he failed and messed it all up. Not Eric Liddell. The Scotsman wanted his former rival to succeed. He was still defending the unpopular Abrahams as he recalled these key moments after the event.

Liddell could cope with all the pressure because the only thing that mattered to him was feeling God's pleasure through his choices, and through his speed on the track. Abrahams, he knew, required other qualities to help him handle the pressure. A siege mentality suited Harold because it helped him to summon the grit required. Especially now that he knew deep down what it took to protect his reputation. Indeed, Eric described Harold's promise not to be left again in the following, generous way:

*There spoke the match-winning temperament. It was not boastfulness at all. It was the conviction of a man who realised our hopes rested on him, and who intended to live up to them.*

Unsurprisingly, Eric Liddell had just summed up the confidence it took to rise to the occasion at the very top of sport. And they both knew that if Harold Abrahams made sure he wasn't 'left again,' he really could win gold. He had just proved it. That's why, even though Harold was angry with himself, he was also proud and confident like never before:

*That semi-final, when I was still a yard down at 50 metres, was my finest piece of sprinting,' he reflected later. 'The semi-final was really the most crucial race of my life, where I got left at the start and showed, if I may put it so, that the training I'd done and the determination which I believed I possessed came out at the critical moment. The semi-final of the 100 metres was the climax of my career. I broke the tape inches ahead of the Americans, Paddock and Bowman. That semi-final was the best piece of running I ever did.*

CHAPTER TWENTY-SIX:

# The Interminable Wait

Olympians are not supposed to produce their finest sprinting in the semi-finals. And semi-finals are not supposed to provide the climax to an athlete's career. Top sprinters are meant to save their best for the final itself. Peaking at the wrong time invites burnout at the worst possible moment. What had that semi-final crisis cost Abrahams in terms of nervous energy? The final was due to take place three hours later; and although Harold appeared to have tamed Paddock, the latter had qualified – and would be out for revenge.

For *The New York Times*, the obvious differences between the two men only added to the fascination.

'Their styles and build completely contrast, Paddock leaping forward with chest out, elbows in and knees up, while the Englishman, a lean figure, uses a tremendous stride and moves over the ground with arms flaying the air, his long legs stretched like a greyhound.'

Paddock loved the big occasion and often produced his very best in the final. Then there was the dynamic energy of Jackson Scholz – the "New York Thunderbolt." Add Bowman and Murchison, and you had an American quartet ready to overwhelm the upstart Englishman in any way they could.

Harold didn't know it at the time, but some of the Americans would soon be plotting against him. In a locker-room exchange which later caused huge controversy, Paddock allegedly wondered whether they might be able to use the false-start system to drive Abrahams half-crazy before the final; take it in turns to jump the gun, tear the Englishman's nerves to shreds. If the Americans could mess with his mind, Harold's body would be powerless to perform at the level he had just shown.

We shouldn't imagine that poor sportsmanship didn't exist in the *Chariots of Fire* era. The fact that Harold Abrahams and Eric Liddell were above such things is what made them extra special. It's why they should still be celebrated as the Olympic chariots return to Paris in 2024. But dirty games were afoot all over these 1924 Olympics, from rugby to boxing to fencing.

The only question was whether the four Americans would spread the skulduggery to the track.

Even without a Machiavellian plot to undermine him, it was asking a lot of Abrahams to repeat his heroics again so soon, despite his defiant pronouncement to Eric Liddell. A lot of mental energy had been expended to execute the comeback. To expect him to find more speed than he had summoned in the semi-final was probably unrealistic. These Americans probably thought one of them would win anyway. But with the right game plan, they could push Abrahams over the edge and make certain of victory.

'For the glory of sport,' the Olympic oath said. But if sportsmanship was important to the Americans, it didn't seem to show in those tense hours before the final.

The long wait for the big race had begun, and Harold tried to prepare body and mind for the supreme test. In truth, he had been preparing all his life. It didn't make the wait any easier, though. In fact, Harold described it as the worst of his life.

*I felt like a condemned man feels before going to the scaffold.*

There were hours of thinking time, even longer than the organisers had planned. Harold explained, 'The final was scheduled for 6.00 p.m. In fact, it was eventually to be run at five minutes past seven.'

Three and three-quarter hours; more than enough time for someone as highly strung as Harold to buckle under the pressure of being a serious contender now. The weight of expectation had caused near breakdown before the 100 yards final at Stamford Bridge earlier that summer. This race was going to be far bigger.

Thankfully, Sam Mussabini came to the rescue. He knew his mission; to ensure that Harold's demons did not take over. Old Sam hadn't been allowed near the British team hotel; but Abrahams was too intelligent to be foiled for long. He had taken the trouble to rent a small hut just outside the stadium. There he could benefit from Sam's wisdom when it really mattered. This was to be their rendezvous point before the final; the first time they had come face to face since arriving independently in the French capital.

Harold confirmed, 'I only saw Mussabini once in Paris before the 100m, for he kept well clear of the officials.'

In the sanctuary of that hut, Sam could help Abrahams keep things in perspective. And to further help defuse the tension, Harold made a smart move. He asked the other British Empire finalist, Arthur Porritt of New Zealand, to join them. It was just the sort of thing Eric Liddell would have done in similar circumstances. In colder conditions in the past, Eric had even been known to give his jacket to a rival before a race, preferring to shiver himself than watch another man suffer.

Mussabini later described his task, though he was careful not to name either Abrahams or Porritt. He didn't even mention the Olympics. Perhaps even then, Old Sam feared there might be reprisals from the authorities for the indirect involvement of a professional coach in a strictly amateur event.

He wrote, 'I can recall a hot summer's afternoon and a three-hours wait between the semi-final and final heats of a World's Championship sprint. It was my job to do the best I could for two of the leading candidates. As a believer in and a practical exponent of the many virtues derived from variety in this life of ours, my task really amounted to whiling the time away usefully yet pleasantly.'

Porritt was eternally grateful to Abrahams in particular:

*I thought this was a superb gesture, because here was a man who had devoted his whole life for a year to winning this race and it had now reached its most crucial stage, yet he was willing to take in somebody he only knew vaguely to let him share the peace and quiet of his hut at this very last stage. We mostly just lay on our backs, chatted a little, listened to Mussabini and had a rub down. It was very quiet and restful. I don't know what the Americans were doing but Harold and I were now in a totally different state of mind.*

It didn't all go quite as smoothly as Porritt would have us believe, though. Not at the beginning, anyway. And not if Eric Liddell's account is accurate. An argument broke out between the restless Abrahams and the insistent Mussabini, he claimed.

Liddell said of Harold:

*He had wanted to go around the outskirts of Colombes in a car – "just for a blow" as he put it. Mussabini knew his French taxi drivers and was not going to risk the fruits of a year of patient effort just to satisfy the passing whim of his charge. So he recalled the car just as it was about to start and made Abrahams sit down and sleep instead.*

It helped Harold to have Porritt there, particularly if he was really going to spend the best part of four hours in one confined space. His preferred antidote to cabin fever had apparently been denied him at the last moment. But did Liddell have his account exactly right? Harold claimed, 'You can imagine, we had four hours to wait for the final. I took a ride in a taxi. I went away from the ground, I spent all the time with old Sam Mussabini and Arthur Porritt, who'd also got to the final.'

That taxi ride may well have been far shorter than Harold cared to admit. But tales of longer rides emerged in the days, months and years after the 100 metres final. Abrahams' friend Norris McWhirter insisted the following:

*To kill time, Abrahams and his coach, Sam Mussabini, were reduced to long drives round the neighbouring suburbs. A car ride is not an ideal preparation for an Olympic final, but in this case keeping Harold's mind occupied took priority over keeping his legs from stiffening up.*

Had Mussabini compromised after all? If that seemed unlikely, subsequent stories of a legendary magical mystery tour were surely far-fetched. And they may have said more about Harold's playful mischievous side than what actually happened. At any rate, a BBC commentary colleague of Harold, Norman Cuddeford later made a startling claim: 'Harold explained to me that he had four hours to kill. This is what he told me: "I thought, what am I going to do? I wanted to fill in the time so I took a taxi and went up the Eiffel Tower." He didn't mention Mussabini or Porritt when he talked about this.'

A mad dash to the Eiffel Tower between the semi-final and final? The very idea of it made David Puttnam – producer of *Chariots of Fire* – smile. He confessed to having no knowledge of this twist to the sprinter's tale.

'I don't even remember that being in early script,' he smiled. 'It's a lovely story. Personally, I would not let it get away.'

But we probably ought to. If Harold had so much as dared to suggest climbing the hundreds of steps to the top of the Eiffel Tower, old Sam Mussabini would have had a fit.

Whatever the truth of claim and counterclaim, it was undoubtedly during the last hour before the big race that Sam Mussabini really earned his money. That's when Harold's dreaded nerves began to attack again, back at the Stade Colombes. Harold admitted:

*At six o'clock I was almost at breaking point, still with an hour to go.*

What could Mussabini do to keep his man from panic? He had enough experience to make his presence count – and lead by example. Sam explained:

*It is not by doing a spot of "backwash," talking or indulging in buffoonery that you take the minds of those due shortly to take part in contests where a World's Championship is at stake. Nor is there much consolation to be found in minutely detailing the essential racing points, as these should long before have been well digested and assimilated.*

*The coach's business in these somewhat nervy conditions is to be no less at his ease, with his thoughts intent upon the well-being of his charges, than on any ordinary day. He may exercise a trifle more care than during ordinary everyday associations with the track. You just rivet your attention upon personal and practical details. First comes the comfort, well-being and cool, calm state of the runner.*

But for all Mussabini's soothing expertise, Harold was not entirely calm. His mind had started to play numerical tricks as it searched for further reassurance. He revealed:

*It is curious how superstition creeps into one's mind before a race, however one may try to ridicule the possibility of good luck and bad luck. I was told some time ago by a palmist that my lucky number was 4. Well, this is the year 1924, which ends in 4 and is divisible by 4, and adds up to 16, which is the square of 4. That seemed a pretty good start. My number in the Games was 419, which adds up to 14. Our dressing room was number 4. The race was run on the seventh day of the seventh month – 14 again.*

At least these were positive thoughts; but they were becoming fanciful. Mussabini knew this dangerous overuse of the mind was Abrahams' Achilles heel. Old Sam also knew that it was his job to find a solution. Lt. Colonel F.A.M. Webster, the great British athletics authority of the day, wrote this of Mussabini: 'He had an analytical brain, the coaching eye and the genius of a scientist or psychiatrist for analysing what was going on in the body or brain of an athlete.'

Mussabini later explained how a lifetime in the game had taught him to keep things simple:

*One has to undergo the experience of being with Championship competitors right up to the last moment of their going into the arena for their contests to appreciate how a coach has to sink his own personality and try to infuse it with that of the athlete. His sole aim should be to take every precaution that will assist in bringing the very best out of the runner or hurdler. At the very last moment any particular failing – and there are*

*few runners who have not a weak spot somewhere in their technique –*
*may be recalled and be given as the final instruction.*

Harold's weak spot was that he thought too much. He was too intelligent for his own good sometimes. He complicated things. He anticipated
actions in others that didn't always come. That's why he had been left on
the blocks in the semi-final. Now he was trying to think too much again,
finding the figure four in every number he spotted. This was neurosis
at work. If Harold's only hope of reassuring himself came through
mathematical permutations, he was in trouble. Now was the time for
Mussabini to cut through all that superstition and take Abrahams right
back to basics. With the near-disaster of the semi-final in mind, Old
Sam came up with something so ridiculously simple that it was brilliant.

Harold revealed what Mussabini said:

*Before the final, my trainer said: 'Only think of two things – the report*
*of the pistol and the tape. When you hear the one, just run like hell until*
*you reach the other.'*

After nine months of scientific analysis and heated debate, this was
what it all boiled down to. This was what Harold needed to hear. The purity
of sprinting, distilled in a message that wiped away intellect and made
the challenge Pavlovian. Mussabini's basic instruction stayed in Harold's
mind as he and Porritt descended into the bowels of the stadium. Sam
wasn't allowed down there. It was a private underworld, where Abrahams
and Arthur would soon endure the rituals the occasion demanded.

Henry Stallard described what it was like for 1924 Olympic athletes
who gave themselves up too early to the tortuous stadium routine and
were lost to the long concrete corridor which connected some thirty
dressing rooms, showers and bathrooms. To listen to Stallard was to
understand why Mussabini had been wise to keep his highly-strung
sprinter out of dressing room number four for as long as possible:

*It would need an Edgar Allan Poe to do justice to the description of*
*those specific sensations experienced . . . There is an atmosphere of tension*

*in the changing room; the manager and captain are whispering into your ear those last few words of advice while a burly masseur is kneading your biceps femoris. The air is richly perfumed with the aroma of rubbing oils, and some cheery fellow remarks that it will all be over in half an hour.*

*One lapses into a reverie, only to be awakened rudely by the sharp crack of a pistol shot fired from outside. It is only the start of another race, and you express a desire to be one of those poor devils who have already got it over.*

Harold Abrahams didn't have to feel like a 'poor devil' awaiting his fate. There was only time for a swift, morale-boosting visit from royalty. Just before the race he and Porritt were taken to a holding room where the Prince of Wales, the future King Edward VIII, came down to see the two British athletes. Porritt recalled, 'He wished us well. It was quite a kick.'

In the American dressing room, meanwhile, there was no royalty; only an ambition which went way beyond the normal confines of sport. Harold later complained that Paddock had made an astonishing confession on American radio. He had apparently admitted to what Abrahams described as 'a dastardly plot by which I could be defeated in the 100 metres in Paris. He was declared to have said that a plan was discussed in the American dressing room by which the four Americans in the final should each arrange to get two false starts. Then it was figured I would be worn out by the time the fair start was obtained.'

Would the Americans put any part their plan into action? The time for combat had come. Soon after the Prince of Wales had left the Empire men in peace, they heard the shrill cries of the French official, whose job it was to summon athletes to their fate outside.

Stallard later described this process of being 'painfully disturbed by a maniac dashing down the corridor outside and bawling [your event details]. How one loathed that man! Somebody, kindly intentioned, thrusts a wet sponge into your face. Feverishly you collect your gear, and inserting your upper incisors into your lower lip, you advance to the fray.

'From the corridor, a subterranean tunnel labelled Entree de la Piste leads into the centre of the arena. The journey affords one a strange mingling of weird sensations. The earthy smell of this haunt is so comforting as one ponders on what is to be seen on ascending that last flight of stone steps leading up to the arena. Suddenly you emerge into a blaze of sunlight and, if you are a favourite, a roar of applause goes up, making you feel more unsteady than before.'

## CHAPTER TWENTY-SEVEN:
# The Start

By now Harold Abrahams was indeed one of the 100 metres race favourites, thanks to his amazing recovery in the semi-final. He could feel the pressure to satisfy the British elements in the crowd. He could hear their roars of recognition. But the British supporters were often drowned out by the more organised and vociferous yells of the American contingent. Perhaps that was a good thing.

Harold recalled, 'Just before the final I didn't really think much about the Americans. The crowd was about 10,000. I remember there was a kind of college yell from the Americans. "Rah, rah, rah, USA, America, A.M.E.R.I.C.A. Paddock, Scholz, Murchison, Bowman." But it didn't worry me.'

It didn't worry him, it merely strengthened his resolve. Somewhere in his subconscious, the persecution complex he had developed as a youngster went to work yet again. He used it to his advantage. We know what was going on inside his head, because when he reflected further on these vital pre-race moments, he made it clear.

*One of the reasons why I felt so determined and so alone was that there was some antisemitism in those days. At Repton it was there and at Cambridge. I may have exaggerated those things. Perhaps I found it when it wasn't really there. I didn't run for all the Jews. I ran for myself.*

Eric Liddell also ran for himself, far more than for any patriotic or nationalistic reasons. But when he ran for himself, he also ran for God. The only remotely negative thought in Eric's mind on a race day was that he hated losing.

Harold's idea of running for himself was very different. He had always thrived on the sense of isolation and injustice that antisemitism – imagined or otherwise – had given him at school and university. That was the anger he knew like a friend. It had always made him want to get even. So rather than feed off the British support in the crowd, he fed off American yells in support of his rivals. They may have been chanting the names of others; but it was almost as though they were calling him names. At best they were ignoring him; they were against him. And that was good, because Harold had a talent; and he had always used it to ensure that he could not be ignored.

Rejection was the source of the fire in Harold's belly. In those final pre-race moments, Abrahams felt rejected again by the majority. That's what he wanted. That's how the fire was lit again that evening in Paris.

The American quartet – Charley Paddock, Loren Murchison, Chester Bowman and Jackson Scholz – were doing their best to psyche out their opponents. Arthur Porritt recalled later that Scholz was more amiable than the others. But that wasn't saying much.

'Those four Americans were pretty aggressive,' Porritt explained. 'Jackson Scholz was a charming fellow. The other three had the idea they were the best in the world, and to hell with anyone else. The Americans were very over-keen on winning.'

So was Harold, though. And he was ready. The lane draw meant something to him, though he knew it shouldn't. Think only of the pistol and the tape, Old Sam had said. But Harold's lucky number was four. The officials had a little leather pouch full of ivory markers with numbers on. The numbers corresponded to the lanes. Abrahams drew out a number. He recalled:

*Strangest of all, I drew number 4.*

All the signs were good. And Harold Abrahams had reached the sanctuary of the pre-race rituals without suffering meltdown. Considering what had happened at Stamford Bridge a few weeks earlier, that was no mean achievement.

He limbered up, discarded his "warm-up suit," and set about digging holes in the cinders, just as he had for the semi-final. First Harold made sure his toes were touching the starting line. Then, staring at his feet, he took his trowel and sketched two grooves into the track at right angles to the start-line. If they continued on that same line towards him, they would pass through both his little toes. These lines gave Harold the correct alignment for his starting holes. Harold knew the importance of working out all the angles and measurements.

*If the holes are not dug square and the right leg is immediately behind the left, in the effort to swing the leg clear at the first stride, the body will become unbalanced and the first stride will be a crooked one. The result of digging the holes too closely to one another will be that the body will be too cramped and too uncertain in the "get set" position.*

Up in the press box, Freddie Dartnell of the *Daily News* was chattering with excitement and offering the wildest odds on an Abrahams victory. Word of this confidence later reached Harold, who reported, 'I think one British journalist said I was going to win it.'

In those final minutes before the race, it was what Harold thought and did that mattered, though.

Continuing his routine, he placed his left foot eight or nine inches behind the starting line. That was where the front hole would be created. He knelt down on his right knee, so it was laterally in line with the ball of his left foot. He moved his front foot an inch or two backward and forward until he was in a comfortable position. He adjusted his right knee accordingly, keeping it in line with his left foot. Now that he knew exactly where he would dig a home for his left, he checked to see where his back foot had come to rest. It always settled along the line of the original notch, the one he carved with the trowel by the little toe of his right foot.

Having marked the two spots, the serious excavation began. A steady hand was required as Harold started to use his trowel like a scalpel. His springy old spikes would find snug homes during the pressurised seconds before the pistol was fired. Within those spikes, his "twinkle" feet had been made equally welcome. For further comfort, Harold had had loops of broad elastic sewn into each shoe. When his feet passed through the loops and he felt the elastic caress the arches, he was buoyed by a happy sensation. His feet and his shoes effectively became one. Even his laces gave him an added sense of security, because he had followed Mussabini's pre-race instruction:

*Test the laces of both shoes so they will not burst at the critical moment.*

Harold could breathe easily until he heard the gun. Then breathing would become a mystery. He had never known nor cared to what extent he took in air as he flew down the track.

'Anyone who thinks about breathing in a sprint race is not concentrating properly on his running,' Harold had always said. Habit would take care of it. Besides, there would be time for calmer breathing at the end of this ordeal – and perhaps for a fuller life. What happened in the next few minutes would determine the nature of Abrahams' life, too.

A French newspaper described how, 'At exactly 7 p.m., a great silence descended on the stadium. Perhaps the best collection of sprinters ever seen together was ready to race the 100 metres.' They took their marks at 7.05 p.m. Abrahams was in his lucky lane four with Paddock, Scholz and Murchison inside him; Bowman was in five and finally, nearest the huge crowd and the press box, was Porritt in six, wearing the famous all-black of New Zealand.

One report observed, 'There were no signs of nerves among them, only a perfect calm, shared by the starter, a doctor who is used to delicate operations.'

In an old film of the race, Dr Moir can be seen ushering the athletes to the starting line in no-nonsense style. Had Moir found a way to relax better before the final too? He certainly seemed to be handling the competitors with more authority. Could the Manchester University man get it right this time? Surely lightning couldn't strike twice in the same place, and leave Abrahams for dead again?

Perhaps the behaviour of the crowd was helping Dr Moir to focus better this time around as well. While the loudspeaker had been forced to appeal for silence before each semi-final, no such plea was necessary before the biggest race of all. Everyone understood the importance of the occasion.

Webster, the most eminent British journalist, noted, 'The silence seemed electrical.'

Harold felt the back of his starting holes. Those launch-pads had served him well in the semi-final, even though lift-off had come dangerously late. This time there could be no distractions, whatever the rest of the field had planned. Harold knew how big this moment was, how potentially life changing. Unusually, he felt no fear. He knew what he had to do differently.

*I was determined that I would get a good start this time, and I felt that if I could give two Americans a start and still win, I was jolly well set to win without a handicap.*

It was one thing to feel confident, and quite another to convert that feeling into decisive action. The first fraction of the first second would be key – and Harold knew it.

*Ten seconds out of a lifetime! The smallest error – less than one per cent – and all would be lost!*

He longed for those ten seconds to begin.

Meanwhile Webster had just enough time to take his seat in the stand – a privileged one at that. He didn't want to be in the company of journalists for the moment of truth. Instead he sat with the man who best understood what Harold was going through in that precise moment in time – Eric Liddell. He was also the one man in the GB team who, on another day, could have ruined those long-held Abrahams ambitions.

Sitting on the other side was Philip Noel-Baker; and all three men very much wanted Harold to win this race.

Webster, still reflecting on Eric's refusal to run many years later, said:

*Nothing could shake [Liddell's] religious convictions. We sat together in the stadium stand and saw Abrahams.*

When he heard the word 'prêt', Harold raised his body slightly but menacingly, his spikes nestling against the back of his starting holes. He was among men who had agreed to do battle on a Sunday. And what a battle it would be. All Liddell could share now was the thick silence. Everyone felt the tension.

Down on the track, the silence was broken by the crack of the pistol being fired behind the row of runners. Had one of the Americans executed a deliberate false start, as previously planned? No. The first report of that pistol was the only one. What had happened in that American dressing room, once their darkest thoughts had been aired? Carefully coordinated plans to break the Englishman's will had been discarded.

Harold explained later, 'For some reason – Paddock said "American sportsmanship" – the plans never matured.'

And so Webster was soon able to tell how Moir 'got his field away to a perfect start at the first attempt. There was a great roar at that, followed by an even greater hush as the men sprang from their starting holes.'

In his rush to get away as quickly as the rest of the field, Harold made a different mistake to the basic error that almost destroyed him in the semi-final.

'Don't forget to stay down at the first stride,' Sam Mussabini had warned him. It was the final reminder to Abrahams to maintain forward movement off his launch pads. Stay low to eliminate unwanted upward movement – that was the idea. But the very fact that Old Sam felt it necessary to issue that final warning suggested that Harold must have been experiencing a problem with staying low at the first stride. He must have been standing up too soon in his starting sequence. Otherwise why would Mussabini have mentioned it? And now Harold stood up too soon once more. It was extraordinary. In the final, in the most important race of his life, he had let an old, bad habit creep back in.

Harold Abrahams stands up too soon in 1924 Olympic 100m final.

For a split second, as the Americans stayed low and burst forward, Abrahams went dangerously and prematurely vertical. For most athletes, this would have been fatal.

Sam Mussabini had tried to coach Harold to perfection. In this single component, contrary to popular belief, he had failed.

CHAPTER TWENTY-EIGHT:

# Recover for Glory

Was all lost, as Harold must have feared? Or could he stay calm yet again and adjust to the mistake he had made? Abrahams was blessed with such an exquisite physique that somehow he still managed to throw his balance forward with a thrust of his left knee and a high, angular left arm.

Harold recovers to find an exquisite body shape, with everything geared to forward motion.

To be able to adapt like this was instant brilliance. Abrahams had certainly defied the established slow-rise sequence of sprint racing.

'Usain Bolt used to take about thirty metres before he was fully up and into his running,' pointed out Lord Coe almost a hundred years later. And yet it almost didn't seem to matter what technical flaws Abrahams exhibited at this stage of his Olympic campaign. Like Bolt, he was taller than his rivals; and if he found a rhythm in the next few strides, he would be on his way.

In the mind of Harold Abrahams, none of these things happened, despite clear evidence from photographs and video footage. He wasn't being dishonest; he simply wouldn't have known; he was in a state of supreme concentration. Harold heard neither roar nor hush. The pistol and the tape; they were all that mattered. Unlike the semi-final, he was on the way to the tape with the others.

'The start was a perfect one,' he claimed. And compared to the semi-final, it really was. 'No false start this time. I made a very good start.'

A French reporter marvelled at the blanket reaction of six supremely focused men. 'The start was magnificent, the six men getting under way as one. They were quickly into action and already into their stride.'

For the first quarter of the race, nothing could separate their talent or desire. Webster observed, 'They seemed to hang together in a dead straight line until five and twenty of the 100 metres course had been covered. One could hardly breathe.'

And even at the halfway point, nothing could spoil that sweeping beauty, except that Porritt was half a yard behind. That was when Abrahams felt himself change gear. And he would never forget the moment for as long as he lived, though he didn't make a conscious effort to break free.

Harold put it like this:

*I had the supreme feeling of running just a tiny bit faster than the others, and, gradually, centimetre by centimetre, drawing away. I just found myself, a glorious feeling, just going a little bit faster.*

That sparked pandemonium in the crowd as each faction, previously struck dumb by the sheer speed, suddenly found its voice. Webster explained, 'One could have heard a pin drop until Abrahams broke clear and seemed about to forge right ahead. The Americans and English were roaring out encouragement but Scholz and Bowman came again and Porritt, although he looked beaten, was still to prove a danger.'

It was the moment of truth for Harold, as he sensed his rivals coming back at him. Many sprinters struggle to stay relaxed and keep their rhythm under such pressure. They try too hard and the magic deserts them in an instant. The temptation in Harold to strain those sinews just a little more was irresistible. Film footage shows those broad Abrahams shoulders tightening slightly, momentarily. Had he given in to that temptation for a split second longer, he might have dealt his hopes a fatal blow. He emphasised, 'The smallest error and all would be lost. What is the good of being second in an Olympic final? Forever one's name appears on the roll of Olympic champions, while the second man is soon forgotten. The winner gets all the flowers; it may not be justice, but it is life.'

Harold pushed such thoughts to the back of his mind. The report of the pistol, the tape; Mussabini was right. They were all that mattered. Abrahams had run like hell, as instructed. And now he was nearer the tape than the pistol. He relaxed back into the sheer simplicity of his mission. He did not want to be second. If there was anonymity to be inflicted, he would inflict it. He had not worked obsessively all winter just to falter at the death. He had not spent his life trying to better his brothers just to invite their sympathetic smiles when the race was done. With controlled passion, Harold's arms powered ever more quickly through the humid Parisian air. The engine had found the afterburners. A Parisian reporter wrote:

*Abrahams pumped his arms low in a brisk movement some thirty metres from the tape. He started doing it as sharply as it is possible to do.*

Harold suffered no loss of form or balance. His reward was speed.

When asked what he remembered of Abrahams during these defining moments in the race, Jackson Scholz later replied wryly, 'I remember his ass.'

Harold never forgot the feeling of satisfaction as he put daylight between his own body and those of Charley Paddock and Jackson Scholz.

'The best part of it was that I showed them the best part of my anatomy,' Abrahams echoed mischievously.

But pride often comes before a fall. And in those frantic fractions of a second, when victory seemed certain, it suddenly became clear that the race wasn't over. Porritt, the unfancied New Zealander who had prepared with Harold, found something special in the final metres. Where he had been struggling earlier in the race, now he was flying as fast as anyone – including Abrahams. Porritt tried to explain it.

'Then something, which I've never understood to this day, hit me and I just started getting into high gear and I could feel myself going through the whole crowd, passing one after the other. Had there been another five yards I'd have been second – I was catching up so fast.'

Webster, watching alongside Liddell, confirmed: 'Porritt passed Bowman in an astounding burst of speed.'

Still ahead, Harold held his form. Someone built on Bernard Darwin's unforgettable description of Abrahams from the previous year, and wrote that he was now 'scudding like some vast bird with outstretched wings, a spectacle positively appalling in its grandeur'.

At Wembley against the Americans of Harvard and Yale he had ruled supreme. This time the Americans were the best in the business, and yet Harold's flight looked even smoother.

As mere men jostled for position just behind him, the 'vast bird' refused to be drawn into a premature swoop for the tape. Porritt still felt ready to take Scholz with his late charge, but he was running out of race.

'They could not catch the Englishman, strive as they would,' Webster reported. A respectful Porritt admitted later, 'I'd never have caught Harold. He was a clear yard ahead.'

All that remained was for Abrahams to end it. Strange as it sounds, he took his time. 'I did not "dive" for the tape until I was within a couple of strides,' he said.

The French had a word for this move – "Flèche." It meant "Arrow." Harold's finish was suitably lethal. Like Liddell, Webster was sitting close enough to the finishing line to see the expression on Harold's face.

'I shall never forget his gritted teeth and the look of desperate determination on his set features as he staged his sensational stream-line finish,' the eloquent journalist said. The Arrow had found its mark. Abrahams recalled his relief.

*And through to the tape . . . The tape! It is over.*

A photograph from the side captured the split second in which Harold's grimace began to turn to joy, his 'thrusting chin and gritted teeth, a record of concentrated, dynamic energy', as the writer A.J. Wallis described it.

True Grit: Abrahams seals it like an arrow with his famous dip finish.

Throwing shapes! And Harold has that winning feeling.

There was an angular magnificence about his body-shape as he stretched the tape. His left knee pointed the way to glory, just as it had from his first meaningful stride. Meanwhile his sinuous left thigh rose at a perfect right-angle to his leaning torso. His strained face jutted as far as his leading leg, while both arms were tucked neatly behind him, like the folded wings of a hawk hitting prey. There is something almost mockingly logical about the winner's technique; for no one else in the picture is applying that logic. Harold's entire being is moving in one direction only at the vital moment – forward. Meanwhile Scholz looks right and flails, torn between the tape and his English conqueror. Porritt is bolt upright as he speeds towards the tape, the tension in his back betraying the realisation that first is impossible. And then there are the non-medal winners, the also-rans. Their faces are frozen in horror as their dreams are laid to waste. They slacken, knowing that all is lost. They are mere spectators to the drama exploding in front of them. Abrahams' face, where effort turns to ecstasy, is the focal point. Harold put it like this:

*This was the most exciting moment of my athletic career, In just over ten seconds I had achieved the ambition of a lifetime. What luck! Top of the world. And then it's fun.*

As Porritt observed later, 'Harold had to win that race – and win it he did.'

The margin of victory was put at two feet by Webster or, as a French reporter preferred it, 'By 50 centimetres, Abrahams won the most beautiful race I have ever seen, and one that will go down as one of the best in history.' Harold had left legends behind him. Scholz clocked 10.8sec and Porritt 10.9. Chester Bowman, who had beaten Eric Liddell in Pennsylvania that spring, didn't even get a medal. Paddock, reigning champion, and Murchison, another former record-holder, were fifth and sixth. Charley's famous jump finish looked redundant that day.

Abrahams didn't smash Paddock's world record. Given the effort required to stage his comeback in the semi-final just a few hours earlier, that was hardly surprising. However, Norris McWhirter explained how Harold's actual time was faster than many record books might indicate.

*A one-hundredth-second timer showed 10.52sec (worth faster than 9.7sec for 100 yards.)*

If that was the case, Abrahams had generated enough speed to have beaten Liddell the previous year. Unfortunately the rules stated that anything over 10.5sec should be moved up to 10.6sec. So he had to make do with equalling the Olympic record yet again.

Much later Harold confided to his friend Rosemary Warne, 'I was a bit better than that.'

Other factors had to be taken into account: the lack of proper starting blocks, the primitive track shoes and the crushed cinder-dirt tracks. Considering those disadvantages, he had clocked a wonderful time – one that stands proudly against the quicker times of the twenty-first century, generated as they are with the help of all the modern aids to sprinting technology. Harold's consistency was historic – he had succeeded in equalling the Olympic record for the third time in the space of twenty-six hours.

L.L. Owen – the latest correspondent from *The Times of London* to watch Abrahams in action, seemed less than impressed, though Harold wasn't bitter.

'He was not exactly one of my fans,' the champion suggested, remembering his critic's precise words:

*Abrahams again ran a fine race and was first to reach the tape – but could do no more than equal for the third time the Olympic record of 10⅗sec.*

This was a line Harold quoted for the rest of his life. He could do so and appear self-deprecating, while reminding his audience of his achievement.

Back in Paris, that achievement was appreciated instantly by those who were waiting at the finishing line. A.J. Wallis described the commotion.

'The finish is greeted with indescribable enthusiasm, and the British contingent goes mad with joy.'

Meanwhile another journalist, G. Ward Price, wrote, 'The crowd burst into loud cheers, which were renewed again and again, while Abrahams was kinematographed, photographed and shaken by the hand and clapped on the back by scores of fellow athletes.'

The home crowd were delighted that a European athlete had won the 100 metres title at last. More than that, they were thrilled that the Americans had lost. The Americans had saved the French during World War One, but that left an inferiority complex, aggravated by the USA's determination to meddle in post-war European politics. So in these glorious moments Harold Abrahams was France's hero too. He had put the Americans back in their place.

Harold recalled, 'I remember being surrounded by cameras, I remember clearly Paddock coming up to congratulate me.'

Haunted and relieved: there's more than joy after all the pressure.

Paddock, who minutes earlier had been plotting to drive Abrahams to distraction with a series of deliberate false starts. When Charley later let slip what he had contemplated, Harold initially refused to believe that the story was true. But not long afterwards, he had an opportunity to challenge Paddock on what he had said. Abrahams revealed:

*I discussed with Paddock the story he told over the wireless in America about the 100 metres at Paris 1924, when I was competing against four Americans, including Paddock. He said that the story as printed in America and other papers was garbled, and that he merely said in such a situation the difference between professionals and amateurs was that professionals might arrange for their four men deliberately to get false starts in order to put their chief opponents right off. He still maintains, much to my amazement, that it would be quite legitimate according to the rules, for a runner deliberately to try to beat the pistol. That is not the British idea of sportsmanship, nor does it represent the true American view.*

The aftermath of victory felt purer than that – though Paddock's post-race remarks sounded as though they were loaded with something more than simple congratulations.

'What a pity you're not American,' Paddock is reported to have told Abrahams after their race in the Stade Colombes. 'With our training you would certainly have broken the record.'

Was Charley reminding Harold who was historically faster on paper?

Abrahams could afford to let that remark go, even if he didn't agree with the sentiment in any shape or form.

'Where did you finish?' the victor asked his rival.

'Waal, I guess I was so far behind, the judges couldn't see me,' Charley replied.

For four years the "California Flash" had reserved the right to call himself the fastest man in the world. With a toothy grin, he now passed that title to Harold Abrahams. On behalf of the Americans, Paddock said soon afterwards:

*We think your Harold Abrahams is one of the most wonderful sprinters in history – in fact we have never seen a better man in action.*

The better part of Paddock's nature had prevailed. And in a fair race, without a succession of deliberate false starts, Abrahams had come out the clear winner.

Harold didn't celebrate wildly for the cameras, as so many of the modern-day Olympic champions do. But he did give off a glow of satisfaction.

Arthur Porritt recalled, 'Harold was obviously delighted, you could feel it. There was no arm-waving or great joy, he just smiled. On the other hand I could sense that all his tension had gone. He'd achieved what he'd set out to do. Harold did a lot after that race, but I think it was an apex in his life. The whole of his subsequent life depended on the fact that he'd won the Olympic 100 metres.'

And his performance in that final depended largely on the fact that he had taken so much confidence from the semi. He explained:

*It wasn't until the semi-final when I was left a yard-and-a-half down that I knew, absolutely knew, I could win. When I won my semi-final in*

*10⅗ seconds and Scholz won the other semi-final in 10⅘ seconds, I knew that I would certainly win the final. I knew at that moment I would win the Olympic final, and four hours later I was lucky enough to do so. I got much more satisfaction in retrospect from my running in the semi-final than I ever did in the final.*

## Chapter Twenty-Nine:

# Liddell's Verdict

Did Harold Abrahams miss his own victory ceremony? The one so famously depicted in *Chariots of Fire*?

What we know for sure was that he felt underwhelmed by what he saw and felt. In fact, Harold sounded a little like Eric Liddell when he said, 'I didn't have any feeling of patriotism, though I was pleased for Britain.' But his next claim was more startling:

*There wasn't any Union Jack. There was no victory ceremony, no prize-giving; no national anthem. Olympic champions of those days were not rated as highly as they were later. If they had been, perhaps I should have worried and not been one! There was no fuss. When I say fuss, I think some of these victory ceremonies are rather nice. I a bit regret that I didn't have one.*

It was a curious recollection, since many accounts of Paris '24 tell a different story.

One newspaper report emphasized, 'It was a proud moment for every Briton present at the stadium when H.M. Abrahams won the 100 metres sprint on Monday; the first time in the history of the Games that the event has been captured for Great Britain. One could have heard the cheering a mile off when the Union Jack was raised and the band played the British National Anthem.'

And A. J. Wallis had written, 'The cheering is renewed when the Union Jack is hoisted on a flagstaff of honour for the first time in the Games.'

F.A.M. Webster may have revealed the reason for Harold remaining unaware of his big moment:

*After his victory I met him on the way to cable his brothers, Sir Adolphe in England and Sir Sidney in East Africa.*

But Webster was wrong about one thing: Adolphe didn't require a telegram. His nephew Tony explained, 'Adolphe was in Paris! My father [Sidney] was in Africa; in '24 he was in Uganda I think.'

The third brother, Lionel, was probably waiting for a telegram back in England, too. And Harold couldn't wait to contact his family, wherever they were, so that he could tell them what he had achieved. He may have found the line was busy when he called his mother, though.

Harold always claimed, 'My mother had to wait for the nine o'clock news to know whether I'd won or not.'

But a British newspaper insisted they had spoken to Esther long before nine:

*Immediately the result was known, the Daily Express telephoned the news to Mr Abrahams' home in Golders Green. "It's fine, we are overjoyed!" was the response.*

It's extraordinary to think that Harold may have missed his own victory ceremony in all the confusion. And particularly ironic, given the huge emotional high point the ceremony creates in *Chariots of Fire*. It's only through the raising of the Union flag that Mussabini, stuck in his little hotel room outside the stadium, realises all his work has been worth it. His reaction in *Chariots* is priceless.

Wherever Mussabini was hiding in Harold's finest hour, he didn't feel it appropriate to be prominent. And there was no chance for the pair to celebrate together in the immediate aftermath of victory. Yet Harold Abrahams was fully aware of the debt he owed the older man.

'Please make it clear that the credit of my win is due to the coaching and genius of Mr Mussabini, the greatest trainer of sprinters in England,' he told reporters.

As an amateur athlete, he must have been fully aware that his tribute to a professional coach was controversial. He carried on regardless.

'Without our combined effort, the result accomplished would never have been achieved. He has encouraged me very much during the last six months and made me stick to it when I sometimes felt inclined to neglect serious efforts.'

That *Chariots of Fire* scene after Harold's victory is simply unforgettable. The Stade Colombes flagpole, just visible from Sam Mussabini's hotel window, tells the glorious story without words, as does the national anthem. The sight of Old Sam punching a hole in his hat in his little hotel room is surely one of the great moments in the movie. And it was appreciated by Sam Mussabini's daughter, Gladys.

The actor Ian Holm performed the Mussabini flagpole scene and all his others so beautifully that he won a BAFTA – and was nominated for an Oscar as Best Supporting Actor. Gladys was a great fan of Ian Holm's work – and sent him a heartfelt letter.

She said: 'I felt I had to write to you to tell you how delighted I was that you were to play the part, even before I saw the film. In spite of all the inaccuracies in the script, I left the Odeon Haymarket very proud and happy at the character you so sensitively brought to life...'

Ian Holm wrote back thanking Gladys for her 'sweet letter' and explaining that he hadn't known of any surviving relatives before playing the part – and had based much of his performance on 'a few photographs and of course your father's books, which were an enormous help.'

Holm concluded his apologetic letter with the following line: 'I'm glad despite all this, that you still managed to enjoy the film! And I conclude by sincerely hoping that my poor efforts were in no way offensive to you.'

We can be confident that both Harold Abrahams and Sam Mussabini would have loved that little exchange; and it was a fitting footnote to the victory ceremony the athlete may never have witnessed – the one Ian Holm immortalised.

~

Back in the Stade Colombes, Abrahams had climbed as high as any athlete can. He had received help along the way; but he alone had beaten the bigots, as though using their mixed-up heads as motivation.

'There was much more antisemitic feeling in those days and it provided me with the driving force to succeed in athletics,' he told David Emery of the *Daily Express* much later. Now he had enjoyed the last laugh over the Repton public school house which had refused him entry as a boy because his father was a moneylender.

'I just hope they were a bit peeved when I won my gold medal,' reflected Harold, looking his interviewer squarely in the eye as if to stress the seriousness of the point.

Harold didn't receive that gold medal while in Paris. It would take weeks to arrive at Hodford Road. Harold explained, 'Everything was so low-key that I had to wait before they mailed the medal to me. It got to me a month later and I tell people I even had to pay the postage.'

But he didn't need to see his medal immediately to appreciate the value of his victory on a personal level. Not only had he justified the sacrifices he had made; he had outshone his elder brothers.

'It gave Harold the final confidence over them,' Tony Abrahams explained. 'That may have mattered more than anything else. They could only dream about what it felt like to win an Olympic title; yet they were also part of his triumph.

Harold had seen his chance and seized the day. He explained: 'I think luck can play an important part in athletic success, though to be frank my definition of luck is a personal one. I believe that we all have opportunities, and it is the fortunate man who recognises the opportunity when it arises and has prepared himself to take advantage of it. Luck is no good if you don't see it; luck is no good if you see it but have not trained to take advantage of the fact.'

Harold Abrahams did both. And now he had his reward – sporting immortality. Yet even sporting immortals don't receive unqualified praise in their moment of elevation.

One critic began positively enough when he claimed, 'Abrahams owes much of his improvement to the more forward carriage of his body and head, and to keeping his arms in front of the body, so getting a forward balance. It is merely observing Sir Isaac Newton's teaching regarding the laws of gravity, and if other athletes will take note, they will profit.'

But then the critic added, 'Abrahams can still be greatly improved, as at present his lurching movement inwards with the shoulders is overdone, marring the rhythm and smooth carriage of his body, which is so desirable.'

Another critic, Hugh H. Baxter, of America, admitted, 'I felt sure his lurching style would lead to his defeat. He won in spite of it, which is a tribute to his great strength.'

And you have to say, when you study video footage of Abrahams, that the critics are right. He looks like a velociraptor, adopting an exaggerated lean forward as he strides out with predatory aggression. These aren't the movements of a natural human – and yet they worked when it mattered. Harold sealed the deal with a swoop that was undoubtedly his secret weapon – even though some observers didn't like that either.

Norris McWhirter said later, 'Abrahams' drop finish was much disliked by some critics, who said it broke rhythm.'

Even Eric Liddell, whose running style Harold had dismissed as 'the most misplaced direction of energy I had ever imagined possible,' was uncharacteristically critical of Abrahams' own basic running action. Comparing Harold's style to that of Scholz and Paddock, he did not rate the Englishman's aesthetic quality highly at all. Just as Abrahams had said of the Scot, Eric claimed it was Harold's fighting spirit that compensated for his technical imperfections. And it's amusing to think that heroes immortalized in *Chariots of Fire* held identical opinions of the other man when it came to sprinting strengths and weaknesses. Liddell said this of Abrahams, Scholz and Paddock:

*If you watch the trio in action, you will probably think that Abrahams is the more laboured of the three; he seems to expend more energy to get the desired result, yet this very fact only serves to confirm his real greatness... Scholz may have been a sweeter mover, with more rhythm and balance, and Paddock may have been more machine-like in his stride, but, when it came to a fight, Abrahams was supreme.*

Eric wasn't wrong. Somehow Harold had achieved a gliding grace while still retaining an almost imperceptible sideways sway in his shoulders. His style was one of laboured beauty, a strange contradiction in terms. But at this stage of the Olympics, he probably couldn't have cared less. Harold wasn't short of admirers, particularly among his hosts.

One observer remarked, 'Abrahams is beyond question the outstanding figure among the athletes of all nations. His performance of equalling the Olympic record three successive times has struck the French public imagination, and the press is generous in its admiration of him.'

Harold had identified the key moment on his way to glory.

*So what made me a world champion? More than anything else that lucky part of my character which did not panic in a crisis – coupled of course with months and months of hard, scientific, intelligent training. I sometimes wonder whether, if I had not had to face that crisis in the semi-final, my whole future life might have been different. Great opportunities came the way of world champions.*

It didn't take long for some of the most powerful spectators in Paris to raise a glass to the big hero of the hour. The British Olympic Association basked in the reflected glory of Harold's victory by holding a celebration dinner in Paris, with the Prince of Wales in the Chair. General Charles Sherrill, who was the US representative on the International Olympic Committee, was invited. He made a witty speech in recognition of the English sprinter's achievement. Sherrill said, 'America has every modern thing to help them win the 100 metres, but you in England went back to Abraham's day and you won.'

*The New York Times* busily prepared its report for the following day's paper under the headline: 'Sprint Upset Startles Americans'.

They had 'suffered an unexpected setback when Harold Abrahams, the Cambridge University star, outraced the four fleetest American sprinters and captured the 100 metres championship for Great Britain.'

Later the same paper described the hero as 'Harold Abrahams, the nemesis of American sprinters', and then as 'The English Wonder'.

The Americans had almost always won gold. Only in 1908 had they been denied glory, by Sam Mussabini's South African, Reggie Walker. Now they hailed "The Cambridge Cannonball," the man who had denied them once more. To beat the Americans, Harold must have seemed extraordinary in their eyes.

Unfortunately Abrahams had few close friends on the British team with whom he could share his supreme moment. How he must have wished he was loved like Eric Liddell.

*I wasn't very popular with the Cambridge crowd and the others in the British team. I didn't have much to do with Oxford and Cambridge athletes. I remember there was some clapping when I came into the dining room that night and I made a little speech and said I hoped they'd all do the same. Perhaps that wasn't very tactful.*

How it must have hurt to see his rival, Eric Liddell embraced so completely by his Cambridge contemporaries when he came south, and again when he had crossed the Atlantic before the Games. The Oxbridge set were still probably willing the "outsider" to outshine Abrahams. But could he? Could anyone?

CHAPTER THIRTY:

# Liddell v Abrahams: The Final Showdown

Many of the GB team knew they didn't have what it took to strike gold. But one man at least was good enough to take Harold's best wishes at face value – Eric Liddell. The Flying Scotsman would have his chance to compete with Abrahams soon enough. And that also meant Harold couldn't get drunk with Sam Mussabini in the way *Chariots of Fire* so comically and wonderfully imagined.

Abrahams emphasised, 'I didn't celebrate because I had to go out and run the 200 metres the next day. In my heat I beat Paddock in 22.2sec and in the second round another American B.M. [Bayes] Norton in 22.0.'

It begged one delicious question: could Abrahams pull off an impossible double? One journalist wrote, 'His victory by two feet over Paddock, the American champion, in the first heat of this same race on Tuesday encouraged British spectators to hope that Abrahams might add the 200 metres to the list of the triumphs of himself and of Britain.'

Liddell was showing slightly less promise in the same event. He won his first race in 22.2 but came in second to Australia's "Slip" Carr in the next round. Abrahams still looked the best British bet, though the opposition was flying.

Harold recalled, 'On the following day in the semi-final, I just managed to reach the final behind Scholz and George Hill (USA).' He did so in a personal best time of 21.9. Meanwhile Liddell was beaten in the other semi-final by Paddock, the man Abrahams had defeated in his first heat. If Harold could find something special again in the final, the gold medal was still there for the taking.

Controversially, he joined forces with Mussabini once more – to discuss what had happened in the semi-final and plan for his shot at the sprint double. Harold revealed, 'I had felt very tired and my trainer Sam Mussabini suggested that I had gone off a little too fast. Consequently I decided to start rather more slowly in the final, with the result that I lost whatever chance I had in the first 50 yards.'

This revelation is extraordinary, because it amounts to a confession that Abrahams and Mussabini, for all their combined experience and intelligence, got their calculations totally wrong for the 200 metres final. Without actually saying as much, Harold seemed to blame Mussabini's analysis of his semi-final start; either that or he blamed his own interpretation of Mussabini's observations. Whatever the reason for the error of judgement, Paddock compounded it by setting off at a frightening pace in the final. As they straightened after 100 metres, the American was still ahead. Meanwhile Abrahams was already so far behind the chasing group that he is obscured behind another American runner – George Hill – in a dramatic photograph taken from the stands.

Eric Liddell (second left) feels the heat in the 200m final.

One British writer observed, 'Abrahams left his dash and speed behind him on the 100 metres track, and, coming into the straight, he completely bogged down. There was astonishment in the press box as he fell further behind with each stale stride.'

Liddell suffered no such hangover, and another British scribe conveyed the excitement as the Scotsman 'made a great fight with the USA contingent, Charley Paddock, Jackson Scholz and Bayes Norton.'

Fight he did, though that same photograph shows Eric straining with tension at the end of the bend. Paddock and Scholz remain perfectly relaxed on either side of the whirlwind Scot. Liddell's arms aren't doing him any favours; they flail too far from his torso. The ultimate battle, you can already sense, will take place between Charley and Jackson.

As the runners approached the finish of the 200 metres, it looked as though Paddock still had the issue well in hand.

Perhaps the only genuine surviving photo of Eric Liddell racing Harold Abrahams. Harold is last and losing form. Eric (second left) is about to win bronze.

Harold's grimace is turning to despair. Liddell is obscured by winner Scholz. Paddock has cost himself victory.

But then he looked left, succumbing to the temptation to assess the extent of his lead. As if that lapse of focus wasn't dangerous enough, he also staged his usual sensational jump finish. Jackson Scholz, the "New York Thunderbolt", went past him with air-splitting rapidity in that very last second. He won by inches in 21.6sec. That equalled the Olympic record set up by Archie Hahn when he claimed the event in St Louis, 1904. Liddell, head and shoulders thrown right back, did superbly to finish third.

Jackson Scholz had triumphed at the age of twenty-seven – and it had been Harold's turn to view the American's backside from a distance. Later Scholz revealed that he had beaten Paddock – timed at 21.7sec on this occasion – in twelve of their fifteen career races. 'I was fast,' he said with quiet satisfaction. And what added to that satisfaction was the fact that Jackson wasn't very fond of Charley anyway. 'He never missed an opportunity to plug himself,' Scholz said of Paddock later.

Liddell clocked a creditable 21.9sec for his bronze.

That was no faster than Harold had gone in his semi-final. Yet, when it mattered Abrahams had been little more than a spectator; and he remembered sadly:

*When we entered the straight I was well down and I finished a very bad sixth. I have always regretted that I did not run better in that 200 metres. Naturally the reaction after the 100 metres was to be expected. I still believe that I was better over 200 than 100. If only I could run that 200 metres again! I have never ceased to blame myself for my indifferent running. I had a theory that I would reserve some of my speed for the last 100 yards, and I reserved so much that I finished up far down the course, with more than half my money to spend and the bar closed.*

The press were stunned and disappointed too. One reporter reflected, 'It must be seldom that H.M. Abrahams, the brilliant winner of the 100 metres on Monday, finishes last in a race . . . But he was clearly stale yesterday after his tremendous efforts of the previous three days.'

By the time F.A.M. Webster came to write a book called *Great Moments in Athletics*, he was quite brutal in his choice of words. 'The reaction upon a highly strung athlete, which Abrahams was, of a major victory, is, I think, noteworthy. Virtue seemed to go out of him.'

If there was any suggestion in the media that Abrahams had finally buckled under the pressure, because he was now expected to win the

200 metres too, Harold had an unlikely ally – Eric Liddell. Or perhaps we should have expected as much from the big-hearted bronze medallist. At any rate, Eric didn't want to hear so much as a hint that Harold had broken down psychologically when he was on the verge of a famous sprint double. Liddell put such rumours down to critics 'ignorant of the real facts.' The reason for Abrahams coming last was the more obvious and understandable one, Liddell insisted – 'he was quite run out.'

The two theories weren't necessarily mutually exclusive, of course. At any rate, this rare clash on the track was the last time Abrahams and Liddell ever met in competition. Many years later, Harold Abrahams looked back on his rivalry with the "Flying Scotsman." This time here are his words in full – and perhaps they weren't as generous as they should have been.

*I never ran against him in a 100. I ran against him in a 200 and he beat me. He beat me but I think I was a better sprinter than him, actually ... As for being sixth in the [Olympic] 200 I ran like a fool anyway because in the semi-final I'd only just qualified [having set off too fast] and [so] I started too slowly in the final. I was never in the race.*

It almost sounded as though Abrahams had decided in his own mind that Liddell's Olympic victory over him didn't count, because Harold had got his tactics wrong and therefore couldn't give the race his best shot. Meanwhile it didn't seem to matter that Harold had avoided Eric in the 100 yards the previous year. That didn't stop him from claiming superiority.

*At this long distance from the actual event I can perhaps say, without seeming self-centred, that I believe I was, in fact, better than Eric over 100 metres – though it is equally fair to say that on the only two occasions on which I ran against him (over 220 yards and 200 metres), he defeated me.*

When Abrahams talked about Liddell on a third occasion, he seemed to make a point of highlighting the fact that Liddell had been beaten in three of his four Olympic 200 metres outings:

*In the 200 metres in Paris, Eric won his first round tie in 22.2sec, and qualified for the final by running second to the Australian, Carr in the second round and to Charley Paddock in the semi-final. In the final he finished third behind Scholz and Paddock, beating two other Americans, G.L. Hill and B.M. Norton, in the process. Liddell was a pretty fair way ahead of me. I was last.*

Despite acknowledging the margin of Liddell's 200 metres victory over him, Harold was pointing to the Scotsman's indifferent progress through the competition. Abrahams, on the other hand, had remained undefeated on the way to 100 metres Olympic gold. In the king of all sprint events he had felt invincible. Therefore he had the superior Olympic sprint record and could claim to be the better sprinter.

Yet even someone as confident – some would say arrogant – as Harold harboured doubts. And he finally gave voice to those doubts many years later.

*I have often wondered whether I owe my Olympic success, at least in part, to Eric's religious beliefs. Had he run in that event, would he have defeated me and won that Olympic title?*

Seb Coe thinks so. 'Harold Abrahams was an outstanding athlete and the product of world class coaching, but the man with the innate ability, the more naturally raw talent was Eric Liddell, and I would go with him.'

Lord Puttnam smiled when asked the same question in 2023. 'The experts of the day thought Liddell would win,' he pointed out. And since David had already indicated that he much preferred Liddell as a human being, the thought of that scenario unfolding clearly pleased him.

But would Liddell have won? In 1923 there could have been little doubt. Eric had beaten Harold so severely in their 220 yards clash in London that Harold didn't even want to face him in the 100 yards. There was only going to be one winner.

Paris 1924 was different, however. Let's indulge Harold and discount his abysmal performance in the 200 metres, because he got his tactics wrong and was mentally shot after his 100 metres triumph. Let's agree that race with Liddell was never going to see the best of both men at play. And let's focus on the 100 metres Olympic final and imagine both Abrahams and Liddell in the race for gold. We should acknowledge that Abrahams was in the fighting form of his life. Even making mistakes at the start in the semi-final and final, he found that extra gear to beat the rest. But would he have been able to stay so relaxed against Liddell? That's the key to coming up with the probable result.

Our imagined scenario: Liddell beats Abrahams in the 100 metres.

It's logical to assume that Abrahams would have made another technical error at the start, since he did so twice in reality. Would he have adapted and recovered so swiftly? Looking at Liddell's bullet start in the Paris 400 metres final, it's equally logical to assume he would have got away slightly quicker than Harold in the 100 metres. So here's the big question: would Abrahams have stayed relaxed enough to reel Eric in towards the end of the contest?

Harold was never relaxed when he thought about Liddell. Eric had got into his head and made him doubt everything – his own ability and even the laws of physics. That torment lasted a lifetime. And so, it's hard to avoid the suspicion that Abrahams might have tightened under the pressure in the final. Would Liddell's erratic arm action have lost him the race anyway? As we shall see soon enough, it was not safe to conclude that Eric's arms always remained erratic in big moments. In summary, considering all the available evidence, and bearing in mind the fact that sprinting is so psychological, Eric's simple spirituality matters. He had the edge up top. That's why the mocked-up photo on the previous page shows him winning. Feel free to disagree – because we'll never know!

## CHAPTER THIRTY-ONE:
# Greatness and the Myth

At some point in proceedings at the Paris 1924 Olympics, Harold Abrahams took a photograph of Eric Liddell and his coach Tom McKerchar. Eric may even have borrowed Harold's cabin.

One assumes this moment came after Abrahams had completed his greatest challenges. Mussabini probably wouldn't have been keen for him to fraternise with Liddell while there was still important individual racing to be done. But Eric's finest hour may not yet have come, since McKerchar is pictured in a physio's white coat. He might have been ready to give a sports massage to his charge.

Tom smiles a smile that accentuates his fine bony cheeks. He looks friendly enough, but there is also just a hint of surprise in his eyes that such a spon-

Eric Liddell and Tom McKerchar – photographed by Harold Abrahams!

taneous little event has been sprung upon him. Eric's eyes are hard to read, because the harshness of the sunlight seems to have forced them to retreat deeply into their sockets. But he smiles obligingly and looks relaxed, striking a pose with his hands behind his back – just where he put them as a six-year-old, freshly arrived at the School for the Sons of Missionaries in south-east London.

The interesting thing is that the photograph is happening at all. You can't imagine Liddell ever being so keen to take a photograph of Abrahams. But Harold always did tend to worship other athletes. And as we have seen, Liddell dominated his thoughts at times, almost to the point of obsession. Harold probably didn't understand Eric as a man, any more than he understood his seemingly illogical sprinting style. But Abrahams certainly admired Liddell. This photograph is further proof of such esteem.

For all that, Eric Liddell hadn't yet set the world alight. Others were making all the headlines. His early progress through the 400 metres Olympic competition was unspectacular, though at least effective.

Harold Abrahams, always a great fan of records and statistics, wasn't slow to point out the way his British teammate was being overshadowed.

*Next day [Eric] ran in the preliminaries of the 400 metres. He won his heat in 50.2sec and easily got through the next round, running second to Paulen (the Dutchman). But the sensation of the second round was the Swiss, J. Imbach, who returned 48 sec for a new Olympic and world record. In 1916 the untouchable J.E. Meredith had run 440 yards in 47.4sec, but the world record for 400 metres still stood at 48.2sec.*

Yet Harold's boyish enthusiasm, as he recalled his own keen anticipation of Liddell's biggest races, was also rather endearing.

*When we went back to the hotel on the Thursday evening of July 10, 1924, we had hopes that Liddell might win the final on the morrow. But we had to confess that he had not to date done anything like 48.0sec for the distance. Indeed, his best was over a second slower.*

*At three o'clock the following day (July 11) the two semi-finals took place. In the first the American champion, H.M. Fitch, set up a new*

*Olympic and world record of 47.8sec, with Guy Butler second and D.M. Johnson (of Canada) third. In the second semi-final Eric won comfortably in 48.2sec, with Imbach second and the American, Taylor third.*

The final was to be run nearly three hours later.

Horatio Fitch was flying – and he was the new world record-holder. Imbach had broken the world record in the heats and now seemed to be saving himself somewhat for the big one. Everyone thought these two giants were the gold and silver medalists in waiting. It was only a question of which man would prevail when it mattered.

Eric Liddell? He was just the rabbit for the greyhounds to catch. And Fitch's coach assured him that the rabbit could not outlast him. Liddell would be caught and chewed up as he ran out of breath. Even more perfect for the main men was that Liddell had been drawn in the outside lane for the final. Ordinarily, that spelt death for the medal dreams of any athlete. You couldn't see your opponents until they flew past. You couldn't judge your own charge for the tape according to what was happening around you.

As the defining moment drew near, at least there was little chance of Eric Liddell being overcome by nerves. He had shaken off those episodes in his early running career, when the tension had made him so tight he could barely swallow. Now everything was positive in the mind of the underdog.

At this point the Cameron Highlanders struck up "Scotland The Brave" on the bagpipes. It was a patriotic gesture designed to stir Liddell's soul and inspire him to even greater heights. In that respect it failed because, as Liddell explained later, 'Don't forget, I was not running for Scotland. The Olympics are not like that. We've had enough of struggles between nations. They are individual events to find out who is the best in his particular event. I ran for myself...'

Like Harold Abrahams, Eric was no great fan of any overt nationalism in the post-war era. But there was one big difference. When Eric Liddell said he ran for himself, he meant he had his own spiritual motivation. And the religious passion that motivated Eric made him inspirational forever.

On the morning of the final, a British team masseur had handed Liddell a simple note. It wasn't American sprinter Jackson Scholtz and it didn't happen immediately before the race, although the *Chariots of Fire* version of events offered that delicious twist in the name of dramatic story-telling. Still, the gesture by the unnamed member of the backroom staff spoke to Eric's soul – and surely meant more to him than the pipes. The note read:

*In the old book it says: "He that honours me, I will honour." Wishing you the best of success always.*

It was an adaptation of a line in the Bible – 1 Samuel 2:30 – which says: 'Them that honour me I will honour.' And the meaning was clear. Eric always sought to honour God when he raced; now the Olympic final might show that God was on his side, too.

Among mere mortals, Eric certainly had a supporter in Harold Abrahams. And he was willing to pay a considerable amount of money to ensure that he could support from the best possible vantage point. Harold explained:

*I remember that as the seats allotted to Olympic competitors were in a very unfavourable position – at the start of the 100 metres – I paid my ten shillings to have a seat near the finish.*

Just as Liddell had watched Harold's 100 metres, so Abrahams returned the compliment. He shared the communal disappointment among the British at the lane draw, though.

*Liddell was drawn in the outside lane, the worst position since he was compelled to set his own pace the whole way and could not see any of his opponents. The 400 metres in Paris was run round two bends only; that is to say, there was a starting straight of, I should think, very nearly 200 yards. From the crack of the pistol Liddell ran like a man inspired.*

Eric was off like a bullet, just as he knew he had to be, if he were to stand a chance.

Eric (far left) executes a bullet start.

He was fully into his running before anyone else. The brilliant athletics writer, Peter Lovesey, described that style most memorably. 'Liddell, head towards Heaven, body almost in a backward lean.'

Abrahams admitted, 'He dashed off with all the frenzy of a sprinter. Indeed, the thought in my mind as he started off as if he were running 100 metres instead of 400 was "He can't possibly keep this up." He set off at a pace which looked so ludicrously fast that we expected him to crack when the home straight was reached. At half distance he was yards and yards ahead of all his rivals, and it seemed impossible that he should last the distance.'

A reporter from *The Scotsman* wrote: 'There was a gasp of astonishment when Eric Liddell, one of the most poplar athletes at Colombes, was seen to be a clear three yards ahead of the field at the half distance.' Eric had reached that point in 22.2 seconds. That was only 0.6 of a second slower than the time Jackson Scholz had run to win the 200 metres final; the difference was that Liddell had to do it all again. No wonder there were gasps and murmurs of discontent with the tactical naivety of it all.

But something else was astonishing. For all the previous criticism of Liddell's style, he was running beautifully. With his low centre of gravity, compact core and superb balance round the first bend, he looked sound. Only the slightest rocking from side to side robbed Liddell of technical excellence. But there was no evidence of 'windmill arms' or 'exaggerated knee lift' of the kind which had so offended the sensibilities of Harold

Abrahams when he had first seen the Scot run. Sure, Eric's head was tilted back somewhat illogically; but it didn't slow the momentum of a man the wonderful American reporter, Grantland Rice called 'the Scotch Meteor, flaming along.'

With a keen and winning eye for dramatic exaggeration, *Chariots of Fire* had taught Ian Charleson to run in such a way that couldn't possibly have generated high speed. But the real Liddell wasn't waving his limbs about wildly. His arms might have been pumping at a slightly lower height than would be deemed ideal, and they definitely weren't perfect; but they were working like piston engines all the same.

There was no 'misplaced use of energy' as Abrahams had noted previously. The worry for Liddell among spectators was the sheer speed being generated, and whether Liddell's heart could stand it. A reporter from the *Glasgow Herald* admitted, 'I feared that he would kill himself by the terrible speed that he had set up.'

Piston arms: Liddell (far left) is flowing.

But Liddell didn't fear death. And that was one advantage he had over his opponents. Eric would push himself way beyond the limits others set themselves. If God allowed it, so be it. If God took him there and then, he was happy to go. How do you race against that kind of willpower? The Americans decided you don't. You bide your time and wait for your opponent to blow up. They were convinced Liddell would lose his form in the second half of the race. As Eric explained later, his tactics were 'to run the first 200 metres as fast as I can. And then, with God's will, to run the second 200 metres even faster.'

Surely even Eric Liddell couldn't do that. The Americans were confident in the science of the human body. But they didn't understand Eric's relationship with his body – or the faith he had in its Maker. As Liddell fought off exhaustion on the final bend, something extraordinary happened – perhaps even miraculous. Liddell changed the habit of a lifetime. His arms became powerful allies. Did he even realise? For whatever reason, a bio-mechanical logic suddenly descended upon him, just when Eric so desperately needed to find another gear.

It's clear from old footage of the race, though no one ever seems to have highlighted the transformation. Perhaps people became too lost in the *Chariots of Fire* myth about the crazy flailing style of the eccentric Christian. And admittedly, that myth was founded in fact somewhere along the line. Eric's arms don't look too clever in those photos of the 200m final. And a technician as observant as Harold Abrahams would not have criticised Liddell's style quite so severely had something not been seriously awry in earlier races he had witnessed. But those accounts must have been exaggerated.

When it really mattered, a stunning change came over Liddell. A miracle happened and his arms did what they were supposed to do. We're able to see this at close quarters, because one of the cameras covering the race was perfectly positioned next to Eric's outside lane.

Strong arms.                    Liddell pumping.

Those famously unruly Liddell arms, criticized down the ages for their wild nature, take the Brit into overdrive. Eric pumps them higher than earlier in the race. They propel him like never before. The action is near-perfect, the fists very slightly across the chest at their most upward point. Those beautiful pumping arms take Eric Liddell into afterburner mode. The thrust is there. And after a career of apparently misplaced energy, you have to wonder where this perfection has come from. Some might be tempted to call it Divine Intervention.

The arms are superb; and Liddell's legs follow, just as Harold Abrahams had once explained they surely must. To watch the way Eric keeps his form – and with it the lead – is to destroy the myth that Liddell somehow ran the most important race of his life with his arms and legs thrashing about like a lunatic. It's the stuff of movies. It added a quirky charm to *Chariots of Fire*. But you can't win an Olympic Games by doing all the wrong things. You have to be doing at least most of the right things.

Harold had identified what good sprint technique was at least a year earlier.

*You avoid a high knee action and any kick-up behind. The feet should always be as near the ground as possible.*

And that's exactly where Eric's feet are. Firmly on the ground, as always. He isn't the tallest; but he makes that low centre of gravity work in his favour. There is no misplaced energy, contrary to the myth. Liddell's powerful thighs and rock-solid core work in perfect harmony. His relationship with the cinder surface is soft and intimate. His feet dance remorselessly towards the finish.

∼

Horatio Fitch tried desperately to get back at the front runner. With a hundred metres to go, he knew time was on his side. The earlier reassurance from his confident coach, and the well-known limitations of the human body told him so. But Liddell was tuned into a power that wasn't human. And every time Fitch thought he was eating up the distance between them, Eric responded and pulled away again. When you are running for God, reserves of energy and inspiration go deeper.

A staggered Abrahams observed it all like this:

*But he seemed to maintain it right to the finish. Every muscle in his body seemed to be working overtime in this wild rush to supreme victory.*

Nothing wild about it. The only time Eric Liddell let his arms flail was in the final two yards, when he knew he had won.

Liddell relaxes through the tape.

The American sportswriter, Grantland Rice suggested that all resistance to Eic Liddell's glorious, front-running charge was futile, because his rivals 'may as well have been chasing an antelope startled into high speed, or some high-powered motor driven by a Paris taxi-driver.' The true force behind the engine, he realised, was 'some divine power.' The result was simply stunning.

Harold continued to watch in amazement:

*Eric never seemed to slacken in his pace, though of course he must have slowed appreciably, and he won that glorious Olympic final by a good six yards in the new Olympic and world record time of 47.6sec. Fitch (USA) was second in 48.4sec and Guy Butler third in 48.6sec.*

A new world record, yet another! And no one was beating this one – not at the Paris Olympics of 1924. Liddell had done it. His radiant smile as he accepted the congratulations of others said everything. There was joy and even a little surprise in that smile. The run had surpassed even his own expectations. Those blue eyes blazed with satisfaction. But there was never arrogance in his demeanour, despite the understandable clamour around him.

Eric's new friend Arthur Marshall, with whom he had bonded on the boat back from Pennsylvania, described Liddell's achievement like this: 'The 400 metres provided the greatest thrill. It was thought Liddell had some chance of winning, but nobody thought Eric was capable of the amazing performance he achieved in the final…This was probably the greatest achievement of the VIIIth Olympiad, and superlatives were showered on Liddell by the press of the entire world.'

Whichever way anyone chose to describe it, Eric's brilliant victory at the Paris Olympiad would always remain a golden epic.

And it would always leave Harold in awe, because he could never quite understand it. Looking back he wrote, 'The outstanding memory is of somebody who was really regarding winning a race as a tremendous experience and putting the whole of his being into his running. He probably had the worst style of any great athlete that's ever been seen.'

Abrahams should have watched more carefully. That wounding technical assessment was past its sell-by date.

Courtesy of University of Edinburgh

Eric Liddell's gold medal.

CHAPTER THIRTY-TWO:

# The Unsung Hero

Eric Liddell wasn't interested in hero worship. He smiled modestly and shook hands with a couple of dignitaries, making sure to look them in the eye. Then he made himself scarce. There was work to do.

Reporters clamoured for a quote. Some of them had probably called Eric a traitor the previous autumn, when the news broke that he wouldn't be running on a Sunday. Liddell didn't think he owed them any favours – or would achieve much by making himself the centre of attention in these moments of euphoria and widespread astonishment.

If people wanted to understand what this victory meant to him, they could come and listen to his sermon on Sunday. That's what he was already working on, he let it be known in the aftermath of victory. The press could grow as impatient as they liked. Liddell didn't need an ego massage. Until he got up to speak in the Scots Kirk on the Rue Bayard, he would let his performance on the track do the talking for him. And if the press wanted a hero, they could look just beyond Eric; for he would always acknowledge his debt to Tom McKerchar, his trainer, for the quality of that performance.

What a run it had been! Shocking in its execution. Educational for the big-name Americans who had written him off. One observer wrote: 'I overheard two well-known American sportsmen prior to the race, discussing the chances of the contestants in the final, and they were just wondering by how much their representative would win, and whether he would surpass his previous day's performance. They never dreamt that defeat was in store for him. I saw them immediately after Liddell had breasted the tape, and their faces were a study.'

And so were the faces among the press pack. It's easy to picture them.

'Come on, he's got to speak to us!'

'Sorry. He's busy writing his sermon.'

Eric also had the ultimate satisfaction of sending a telegram to his family in China, letting them know that he had won the 400 metres at the Olympics. If any among them really had been worried about the time and energy Eric had spent focusing on running, their concern was surely now replaced by sheer joy that his efforts had paid off. Confident that he would know to do the right thing next and for the rest of his life, they could allow themselves to enjoy the moment.

The Liddell family's idea of doing the right thing may not have involved a spontaneous night out in Paris. But Eric allowed himself to be dragged downtown, because he had a promise to keep.

The evening's origins lay in that return voyage across the Atlantic from Pennsylvania a few months earlier, when Liddell and Arthur Marshall had teamed up with those adventurous American sisters, Freddie and Edith. The four of them had promised to meet up again in Paris. Eric and Arthur knew where the women were staying – and it wasn't hard to make contact. Perhaps the girls had been in the Stade Colombes to witness Eric's big moment.

Before long, the awesome foursome was dancing the tango on the Champs Elysees. Eric's fun and frivolous side, the part of his character that his wife Florence said she felt *Chariots* had slightly overlooked, was clearly at play here. And if there were any lingering doubts that Eric and Eileen Soper's time had passed, confirmation that he had moved on probably came in the way he celebrated his magnificent achievement in Paris. Did he throw his head back wildly as he danced the tango on the Champs Elysees, just as he had thrown it back to find glory on the track? Eric's interpretation of the

Handsome young man:
Eric Liddell in the first half of the 1920s.

tango might just have allowed for that gesture, though entangled limbs and dramatic cheek-to-cheek posturing weren't quite his style.

If Eric Liddell performed all those tango moves, you suspect his sense of humour came into play to prevent anything overtly sexual. Eric was determined to enjoy himself, and he could have chosen no better company than Arthur Marshall, Edith and Freddie. But there were limits, even after he had won an Olympic gold medal with one of the greatest courageous displays of running the world had ever seen. As Arthur and the women went on to a Parisian nightclub to party into the early hours, Liddell made his excuses and returned to the team hotel. He had celebrated in style, yet he had remained true to himself. Eric had done it his way. That's how he had won Olympic gold, too.

Harold never could fully comprehend Liddell's success; and that sometimes gave rise to a more grudging analysis of Eric's 400 metres record. On another occasion Harold pondered, 'I often wonder how Liddell would have fared against the great ones of 1936 – Brown, Roberts and Rampling – all of whom beat his times handsomely.'

Such comparisons pointed to Harold's underlying insecurity in relation to Liddell. He seemed to have an enduring complex about his Scottish rival. Eric's Olympic record held for twelve years before Britain's Godfrey Brown finally broke it in the Berlin Olympics of 1936. Those athletes ran in what amounted to a different era. Yet they never won individual gold like Eric Liddell.

Besides, there was no reason for Harold to have worried about Liddell's stature, because he was a sporting god himself. From the moment he hit the tape in the 100 metres, he became an icon. The hosts of the Games even printed a postcard of that moment, to reflect Harold's superstar status. Tony Abrahams revealed, 'Harold sent one to Derek, his brother Lionel's son. He was proud of the fact that he had won, after all that work.'

He remained proud; and there would always be one fellow competitor to help him relive that race annually. On July 7 at 7.00 p.m. for the rest of his life, Harold Abrahams met Arthur Porritt for dinner, in Paris if they could make it. For Porritt, who became Surgeon to the British Royal Family and Governor-General of his native New Zealand, it wasn't always easy to respect the arrangement. He did so in spite of his responsibilities; and they never tired of savouring those thrilling seconds when they both fulfilled their dreams.

Back in the Paris of 1924, there was one more dream left for Abrahams to chase. Having let his 100 metres success spoil his 200 metres chances, Harold was determined not to let his relay teammates down. 'By the end of the week my form had returned and I think I ran well in the relay,' he said with some understatement. He and his colleagues actually achieved a world record in the first heat of the 4 × 100 metres. Harold recalled, 'I ran the first leg. The others were Walter Rangeley, George (W.P.) Nichol and Lance Royle ... Sir Lancelot Royle as he became. We did 42 dead in the heat.'

That beat the existing world record by one fifth of a second. The British were jubilant, knowing they had made history. Ten minutes later the Dutch equalled that new world record. No matter, it still felt sweet to be a joint world-record holder. Twenty minutes later the joint record was smashed. The American quartet of Francis Hussey, Louis Clarke, Loren Murchison and Alfred Leconey set up a new record of 41.2sec.

Abrahams and his relay teammates equalled that time the following day. But the USA quartet ran even faster. They broke the world record again by clocking 41 dead. Harold remembered,

*In the final we ran the relay in the remarkable time of 41.2 but we were beaten by the Americans. We were second. Nobody remembers that I got a silver medal.*

It might even have been another gold. The British team ran their rivals desperately close, hampered only by the changeovers. One British writer observed, 'The event provided plenty of thrills, and whilst the British team is to be heartily congratulated on the effort it made to win the race, we feel compelled to point out that lack of practice handing over and receiving the baton may possibly have lost us the race.'

And how they could have benefited from the great Eric Liddell, who couldn't run in the heats of the 4 x 100 relays because they too fell on a Sunday. Imagine that British quartet with Liddell starting and Abrahams taking them home! If the Brits ran the Americans close anyway, how much of a difference could Eric have made? Everything points to gold. And that golden partnership could have made for a fitting end to *Chariots of Fire*. Two gold medals each for Abrahams and Liddell. Rivals for so long, then suddenly a combined world-beating force!

Even without Liddell, Abrahams and his friends had achieved a time so stunning that it remained a British record for 28 years. And it was typical Harold to ensure that his world record, however fleeting, was recognised forever. 'I've still got a world record plaque,' he pointed out many years later. 'I insisted on having it!'

A world record and Olympic silver to go with his gold; it was a wonderful way to conclude his French adventure. Unsurprisingly, Abrahams and Liddell were the great heroes of the hour.

But Eric would always proclaim the virtues of an unsung hero at the Games. And that said everything about the values he held dear in life – even at a time when he was worshipped for his own achievements.

The man he held in such high esteem was Henry Stallard, whose accounts of the pageantry at the Games had been so compelling. Though he hadn't won a gold medal like Abrahams and Liddell, Henry had shown as much character – if not more – than the others. The former Cambridge man and medical student had originally been favourite for the 800 metres. But he had suffered every athlete's nightmare – injury just before his big moment. In fact, poor Stallard had two problem areas – the arch of his foot and his ankle bone.

Fighting spirit could only get Stallard so far. And although he led the 800 metres final for the first lap, he began to break down when it really mattered. He probably knew he couldn't sustain his pace for two laps, but he could drag out the Americans and leave them vulnerable to attack from a fresher British rival. Seeing Douglas Lowe, the man who later rejected David Puttnam's *Chariots of Fire* offer, ready to strike for home, Stallard knew to give way. 'Go on, you can do it, go and win it,' he shouted without a thought for himself. And Lowe did just that, before Stallard finished an agonizing fourth. As Lowe took the glory, Henry hobbled away on a walking stick, his pain only eased by morphine.

Eric Liddell observed all this and concluded two things: Stallard had sacrificed himself so that Lowe could win, and now he would be unable to run the 1500 metres final, for which he had already qualified. Eric was probably right on the first point; but incredibly he was mistaken on the second. With another morphine injection and heavy bandaging, Stallard was determined to take part in that 1500 showpiece. Philip Noel-Baker asked Stallard to reconsider. He liked the young man too much to see him suffer for no reason. Paavo Nurmi, the "Flying Finn", was bound to win anyway. The amiable Stallard listened to his captain respectfully – and politely declined to take his advice.

Liddell watched as one of his favourite teammates tried out the heavily bound foot after the fresh shot of morphine. Either the drug hadn't kicked in yet, or the pain was too severe.

'Every time he put his foot down he was in agony,' Liddell remembered.

The GB team winced collectively, knowing the 1500 metres final was going to be painful to watch. But as the legendary Nurmi flowed almost effortlessly to fresh Olympic triumph, Henry's friends watched him suffer yet another injury. How cruel could this sport be? Undoubtedly compensating for the burning pain he was feeling in his foot with every stride, the injured athlete had put undue pressure on surrounding structures. The result was that Stallard felt a tendon go. It was the last thing he remembered about the race. Having blacked out, he was revived half an hour later with ice massage to the sides of his head. It was then that he was told the startling news. Hyla "Henry" Stallard had won a bronze medal after racing through the pain barrier and collapsing just beyond the finishing line. All he wanted to do, upon being revived, was apologise to Philip Noel-Baker for his antics. The GB captain shook his head with a smile and congratulated the medallist for his courage.

Eric Liddell saw it all. He was stunned and moved. Later he described Stallard's performance as 'one of the most heroic things in the history of athletics.' This from a man who was knocked off the track in Stoke and fought back to win from nowhere. Liddell, the man who would still try to race as an internee in a Japanese camp in his beloved China twenty years later, despite all the deprivations of life as a captive.

And when Eric gave talks in that camp to raise spirits, it was clear the man he admired most, when he looked back on 1924 was his friend Stallard. This was the athlete who inspired Eric above all others, for his selflessness and bravery.

Henry Stallard did appear in *Chariots of Fire*, played by Daniel Gerroll. But the full story was never told.

Did *Chariots of Fire* producer David Puttnam miss a trick by not including more of Stallard's courage, to impress upon us that wining wasn't everything? It seems churlish to suggest anything could have added much to a perfect film. But Stallard as a sportsman and a human being should not be forgotten.

CHAPTER THIRTY-THREE:

# Harold's Hidden Victory

Eric Liddell was never going to be blinded by the waves of hero-worship that came his way in the coming days. Neither did Abrahams require an immediate massage of his ego in the aftermath of his gold medal glory.

The crowds which pressed against the British team's train when it came to a halt at London's Victoria station carried Liddell shoulder high to a waiting taxi. But they didn't so much as catch a glimpse of Harold – because he wasn't there. His new friend Porritt, who travelled with the British as a Rhodes Scholar and member of the Empire, recalled: 'He didn't come home with us. I think he was just terribly emotional. He was just overcome by having achieved his objective, and also he was completely deflated mentally, worn out.'

Since there was no wife or fiancée waiting to hug Harold, there was no need to rush home. He had sacrificed the chance of marriage in pursuit of sporting glory. Now that the glory was his, he didn't know what to feel, and euphoria gradually gave way to an anticlimactic emptiness. Harold knew that public adoration couldn't fill the void. So he took a few days' vacation in Paris. Did he take the opportunity to have that famous drinking session with Sam Mussabini, the one depicted in *Chariots of Fire*, which allegedly left the pair so legless that they could hardly leave their restaurant? There is no evidence of such a session, and Harold wasn't a great drinker. Yet the chance was there to indulge freely without fear of discovery. Harold, like Mussabini, was able to slip back over the English Channel quietly on his own – with or without a hangover.

When he did finally reach London, Abrahams found that he was still the toast of Britain. He and Eric were both guests at a celebratory dinner in the House of Commons towards the end of July. A menu has survived down the ages, and carries the signatures of the many British Olympic athletes present, including the autographs of "H.M. Abrahams" and "E. Liddell."

Maybe, just maybe they talked that night about who would have won the 100 metres final had the heats not fallen on a Sunday. Liddell was too modest and principled a man to have staked any claim to Harold's crown, even in jest. But Abrahams probably knew deep down that Eric had pushed him as much as Sam Mussabini. Turning his thoughts to Old Sam, Abrahams decided that Mussabini deserved something more than payment for his work. 'When I got back to England I bought Old Sam a pair of starting pistols as a present and he was delighted,' Abrahams remembered.

~

The stars of Paris were the main attraction when an adoring British public flocked to see their heroes perform back home. Unfortunately, Abrahams' relay display in a post-Olympic showdown with the Americans at Stamford Bridge caused only embarrassment. Perhaps he suffered from the jitters again in front of a vast, expectant London crowd, which was estimated at between 30,000 and 40,000. At any rate, Harold felt obliged to explain the calamitous error he had made. He wrote:

*There have been many different descriptions about the 400 [4 × 100] yards relay which the Americans won in the world's record time of 37⅖ secs. The true facts are these: I ran the last stage, and owing to a big error of judgement on my part, did not start to run at the proper time, so that W.P. Nichol, who was handing over to me, had to slow down for fear of passing me. As he did not seem to be catching me I hesitated, and a man in two minds in a race of less than 100 yards is no good to anyone. When I did get the baton I was well behind Leconey. The error of judgement was due to lack of practice. The British Empire team had never once been together before. In a short relay like 4 × 100 yards the changeover is everything. And it takes a good deal of hard work to perfect this branch of athletics.*

In stark contrast, Eric Liddell's breathtaking relay display at "The Bridge" that day would go down in history. To hit yet another peak, less than a fortnight after his Paris heroics, was truly remarkable. This time Harold had nothing but praise for the passion Liddell showed in the 4 × 440 yards relay, so soon after his Olympic win. Abrahams recalled:

*Ten days later, before a record crowd at Stamford Bridge, he again showed an astonishing resolution when, as "anchor-man" and against Fitch, one of America's finest quarter-milers, he turned an appreciable deficiency into a three-yard victory. There is no man in the world other than Liddell who could give six yards to a crack American quarter-miler, who has recorded 48⅒, and beat him. The thunders of applause from a crowd of over 30,000 at Stamford Bridge as Liddell, his arms and legs working like some great helicopter, caught his man still sound in my ears whenever I hear the race. The excitement of the crowd as Liddell, with his arms radiating like an animated windmill and his head thrust right back, overhauled his American opponent at the last bend to win was tremendous. The applause they gave him was a combined acknowledgement for his magnificent win for Britain in Paris, his phenomenal victory that afternoon, and his popularity as a great sportsman. The relay meeting showed the British public first, how exciting relay racing can be, and second, how real is the friendship between the athletes of the British Empire and the United States. Liddell's quarter must have been something in the region of 48 seconds. It was his last race in England (though he did win three Scottish titles in 1925). It was the last time I ever saw him run. The following year he left for China to carry out his life-work as a missionary. No words can describe Liddell's running, and the passing years did not dim the picture of that indomitable courage.*

Had Eric's style gone wild again after his winning discipline in the Olympic final? It rather sounds like it – which makes what happened in Paris even more miraculous.

In that summer of 1924 there was no further chance to find out which sprinter was best, Abrahams or Liddell, because the post-Olympic roadshow lost Eric before it moved a mile or two across west London to the Queen's Club. There, the Achilles Club faced the British Dominions. Since Liddell was officially allied to neither, he headed home.

Harold's Paris sidekick, Arthur Porritt was at Queen's, though. Many expected the New Zealander to be the support act in this show too, just as he had been in the French capital. The Queen's Club had played host to Harold's first important triumph, the narrow victory over Bevil Rudd in the Inter-Varsity sports four years earlier. It had been a happy hunting ground ever since. Abrahams had every reason to feel confident. But he also felt the mounting pressure of living up to his new billing as Olympic champion. And as Harold explained on numerous occasions, he never did like the feeling of being the favourite for any race.

Porritt revealed what happened:

*I beat him on that occasion, within a fortnight of him getting a gold medal at the Olympics. It shows that he was tired out. I was on top of the world achieving what I did.*

A.J. Wallis explained what happened. 'The New Zealander, Porritt sprang a surprise by beating Abrahams in the 100 yards flat. Abrahams ran so poorly for him that he could do no better than finish third. The British runner was probably jaded after his exertions in the Paris Olympiad. His brother Dr A.A. Abrahams (as he then was) advised him not to run for a year.'

Coming from Adolphe, who had so often placed pressure on Harold to run at all costs, that advice seemed extraordinary. In fact there were rumours that Harold had suffered a complete mental breakdown, a full-blown manifestation of the anxieties that had plagued him for some time.

The speculation prompted Adolphe to speak publicly about his brother's predicament. He said, 'There has been a lot of rubbish talked about Harold's breakdown. There is no question of such a thing. He is simply acting on my advice that he has been tired out by his crowded programme of late and needs a rest.'

It was something of an understatement to describe that proposed break from racing as 'a rest'. Harold revealed later: 'After the 1924 Games at Paris I had resolved to give up sprinting, at any rate for a year or two, and to concentrate on long-jumping.'

But there was another battle to win that summer. Just a few weeks later, with the entire future of the Olympic Games under threat, Harold felt well enough to come out fighting, in print at least. And in that critical moment, he did as much to protect the future of the Olympic Games as any men alive at the time. Eric Liddell joined him in the fight.

The prognosis was not good. The 1924 Olympic rugby final had ended in a riot when the USA defeated favourites France. American players and fans were assaulted.

Even before the true extent of the violence was known across the Atlantic, one prominent newspaper expressed its indignation:

*The dispatches state that the American players were booed and hissed throughout the game, and that when the American flag was raised at the close of the game, the crowd went into a spasm of fury. The American flag was not received that way by Parisian crowds in 1917 and 1918.*

Another paper across the pond went further:

*If the team representing the Stars and Stripes is going to be hissed every time it wins an Olympic title, it would be better for the Americans to return home and concern themselves no longer with international athletics.*

Things only got worse. An Italian fencer called Oreste Pulitti had wounded a Hungarian judge named George de Kovacs in a duel, after Kovacs had disqualified the Italians for collusion. And a French middle-weight boxer called Roger Brousse was only belatedly disqualified for biting his British opponent Harry Mallin, when every English-speaking boxing nation threatened to withdraw from the Games in protest at Brousse's 'victory.'

On July 22, *The Times of London* published an alarming article under the headline:

**"OLYMPIC GAMES DOOMED – FAILURE OF THE IDEAL."**

A leader column supported this seemingly terminal conclusion under the headline:

**"NO MORE OLYMPIC GAMES."**

It added, "Unhappily the experiences of the present Olympiad have confirmed, with dreadful clearness, the long-felt misgiving that the tendency of these Games is to inflame international animosities rather than to allay them…"

At a public luncheon in Edinburgh, where Eric Liddell was being honoured, he gave his reply:

'In athletic circles, there was no trouble of any description,' Eric insisted.

And a newspaper soon reported his defence of the Games in more detail. "Mr Liddell said that there had been a good deal of discussion as to whether these Olympic Games really did any good to improve relations between the various countries. He would like to say that as far as pure athletics were concerned, there had been no trouble at all. They had seen statements that if a certain decision was not reversed, Great Britain and America would withdraw. He thought that could not possibly be true, for the definition of a sportsman was that he accepted the decision of the referee, whatever it might be."

That was an interesting rebuke for the British and American Olympic officials who had risked all with their threat at the boxing, to the possible detriment of every other competitor at the Games. For the Olympics to survive, Eric clearly believed, everyone had to keep cool heads when flashpoints occurred.

As Great Britain's star man in the most glamorous event in Paris, it also fell upon Harold Abrahams to defend the Olympic movement. He did so in some style, in the Sunday Express of August 3, 1924:

*A great deal has been written the past few days on 'Whether the Olympic Games are a good or bad thing'. Certainly no good can come of whitewashing the unpleasant incidents which undoubtedly did take place, but only harm can result from the attempt which has been made to suggest that these incidents are typical of the animosity which permeates the whole games.*

*Now, because 'unpleasant incidents' have occurred in three of the eighteen Olympic sports, it is suggested: 'The events have shown the world is not ripe for such a brotherhood' as Baron Pierre De Coubertin, who was responsible for the revival of the Olympic Games, anticipated.*

*Because the French nation, or a section of it, forgot themselves at a Rugby football match, because one or two fencers displayed lack of character and indulged in petulant and childish outbursts of anger, because a Frenchman confused boxing with biting, we are asked to endorse the suggestion that the Olympic Games are a bad thing, and that we should cease to take part in them.*

*I cannot speak with experience of any section of the Games but the purely athletic one, and here a whole week's programme was carried out with hardly a single minute of unpleasantness. There was stupidity over a walking race, but otherwise the spirit of true sportsmanship was wonderful. It would be a calamity if the athletic section of the Games – the pure Olympic Games – did not take place.*

The battle for the soul of the Games had begun. The fate of the Olympics was very much in the balance. And it is hard to underestimate just how influential the opinions of Harold Abrahams and Eric Liddell were in the summer of 1924. Their defence of the Games proved to be as successful as their performances on the track. As was so often the case, Liddell and Abrahams were at the forefront of the fight…and others followed.

# PART II:
# Love and War in London and China

*It is the spirit of the whole thing that matters.*

Eric Liddell on sport.

# CHAPTER ONE:

## The Power of Victory

'Mr Liddell, you have shown that none can pass you but the examiner.'

With that wonderful line, Edinburgh University's Principal, Sir Alfred Ewing, placed a laurel wreath on Eric's head and he graduated.

Eric wearing a laurel wreath is hoisted aloft by his fellow students.

The cheers were deafening. And as he left the ceremony, Liddell looked like a Roman emperor, worshipped as a demi-god by the heaving hordes. Normally, Eric carried crowds with him, thanks to his innate goodness and growing fame. This time the crowds carried him for the same reasons. His fellow students lifted him shoulder-high on what appeared to be a normal chair converted into a sedan for this very purpose. Not for the first time in 1924, Liddell was a sight to behold.

It wasn't Eric's final goodbye to Edinburgh academia. There was further serious studying to be done in the city soon enough. He was ready to embark on a year of training at the Scottish Congregational College, which would ultimately qualify and equip him for his future missionary work in China. But the aftermath of the graduation ceremony was memorable. It provided an iconic, enduring image of adulation – capturing forever the pure love that Eric Liddell and his lasting memory would be afforded in Scotland.

This scene would have gone against his instincts ordinarily. Yet here he was, smiling for the camera as he was carried through the university gates, the trademark dimple on his chin never more prominent. He seems to have surrendered to the moment quite happily. His fellow students had probably made it clear they weren't going to settle for any other kind of send-off.

In his own mind, however, Eric stayed grounded. It was God's power that was being celebrated. He was the source of the gifts Liddell had been given.

'When you speak of me, give the glory to my master, Jesus Christ,' Liddell always said.

Neither did Eric want anyone to think that his victory at the Olympic Games made him a better human being than anyone else. He remembered what he had seen above the entrance to the University of Pennsylvania. He had memorised the words; and he had promised himself to use them on a day of success. Treating those twin impostors, triumph and disaster, just the same – that was the idea. And what better time than this to show that honest efforts meant more than medals?

'In the dust of defeat as well as in the laurels of victory there is glory to be found if one has done his best,' Eric told his doting audience. 'I leave the track for four years,' he added.

Liddell knew the curtain was coming down on his athletics career for the foreseeable future. China beckoned. The Amsterdam Olympics of 1928 were not beyond the realms of possibility; but athletics wouldn't be the priority from now on. In truth, they never had been.

For the moment, however, Eric didn't mind using his Olympic celebrity to engage as many people as he could in religious contemplation. He still had a year before he left Britain.

Liddell wasn't the greatest public speaker, at least not as good as Ian Charleson's charismatic performance in *Chariots of Fire* would have us believe. But the massive demand to hear him speak publicly during that last year in Britain was going to keep him on his toes.

From around October 1924 to April 1925, Eric Liddell had a flavour of what it must feel like to tour as a modern-day rock star. He didn't just speak at churches and schools to spread the word of God. People also flocked to music halls and theatres in Scotland and England in a collective wave of love for Liddell. The big attendances reflected people's fervent desire to see their great sporting hero – and hear him speak about his Christian life. And there are contrasting accounts of how well Eric rose to the challenge as an orator. His great preacher-ally DP Thomson, perhaps unsurprisingly, suggested Eric had improved immeasurably from the raw recruit he took to Armadale. Others insisted he was no more eloquent or talented a speaker than he had ever been. Yet all agreed that Liddell found little ways to inspire, using simple examples in everyday life, and the values behind his sporting triumphs. He always held people's attention. Some gentle humour here; an intense gaze with those arresting blue eyes there. Eric maintained the momentum of the tour with what skills he had. He knew his celebrity was part of his appeal, and he saw nothing wrong with that. So long as he used his fame in the right way and allowed no one to use him, Liddell welcomed the widespread attention.

Then one day in 1925, presumably when the tour took him down to the London area, Eric was contacted by a young woman who knew the man behind the celebrity better than most.

Eileen Soper had dealt with considerable acclaim herself at a very young age. Even Queen Mary had become a fan and bought one of her pictures. She understood some of what Eric was going through, and he realised as much. A familiar voice from the recent past, someone he could now regard as a dear friend. This contact would have been welcome during these heady times. But even Eileen wanted a piece of Liddell in the form of a final favour. Everyone knew that time was running out – and Eileen was no different. She made her request while she still could. Would Eric sit patiently for a few hours, in whatever clothes he chose, so that she could capture him forever in a portrait?

The mere thought of this is poignant. She knew their own "forever" had passed them by; though perhaps there was a small part of the sensitive twenty-year-old that still hoped her beloved Eric might change his mind. Perhaps the turning point would be now, when he saw her again. And if he remained out of her reach then she could, at the very least, look at the painting. She would capture the man she loved using her brushstrokes, and have him there forever on canvass, even after he had departed for a new life on the other side of the world.

Eric wasn't one for vanity, so the idea would not have appealed to his ego. But perhaps he thought it would be unreasonable to shy away from such a request. Maybe he felt slightly guilty that the romance had been put to one side, a necessary casualty of his greater purpose. At any rate, Eric Liddell agreed to this favour for Eileen Soper, and she was given her big chance.

He arrived wearing a three-piece suit and posed holding some papers, perhaps designed to reflect the qualifications he was gaining north of the border. There's no hint of discomfort in Eric's face, though the intimacy only goes so far; and there is perhaps an air of neutrality in Eric, of the sort she might have dreaded seeing. Does his gaze go right past her?

Eric Liddell by Eileen Soper.

At least she captures his passionate eyes and almost cheeky, under-stated smile in the way she would have wanted to remember them. In truth, however, it's not the greatest likeness, other than the unmistakable dimple on that chin. And the sadness surrounding this picture is that of dying intimacy. Whatever exists in those final hours together, it's not something Eric will ever seek again.

Since this picture was found on display in Eileen's home after she passed away many decades later, we can assume that it meant everything to her. She never quite got over Eric – the one who got away. The poem, remembering the moment Eric somehow led her to believe she might become Eileen Liddell, was also discovered.

It seems unfair to blame Eric for this lasting heartbreak. He had explored the possibility of a union with Eileen, then realised at some point that it simply wouldn't work. He had then continued with his busy life. The fact that she apparently never found a way to move on roman-tically is not something that can ever justifiably be laid at Liddell's door. She did at least lead a fulfilling life in other ways, most famously as the illustrator of the charming and highly successful Enid Blyton books for children. And Eileen put her love and tenderness into many a picture capturing the beauty of nature, too. As she lived out her years, she probably heard about Eric's occasional visits home. And news of his eventual fate must have broken her heart all over again. But after that portrait was painted, their paths no longer crossed – even if he was often in her thoughts.

Eric had chosen China over Eileen Soper. It was probably as simple as that. He was destined to follow in the footsteps of his father. That was all he had ever wanted, though he might have wished once or twice in private that he had been blessed with natural public speaking ability to go with his calling.

~

His old rival Harold Abrahams knew he was a good public speaker. He didn't have Eric's passion for a cause, but he did have a quick wit and a commanding presence. Despite having been mentally and physically exhausted by the ups and downs of athletics, Harold still had the nerve to address large crowds before that summer was out. Liddell's religious conviction carried him through his public engagements. But it takes a certain self-assurance for a top sportsman to try to speak with authority about a subject which confounds so many great brains – politics.

Eric wouldn't have wanted that challenge. Abrahams gave it a go. When he made a major political speech at Spen Valley on August 21, 1924, the political situation was intriguing. The first Labour government had been formed in December of the previous year, by virtue of a hung parliament. The Liberal Party – which Harold supported – had effectively put Labour leader Ramsay MacDonald into power, even though Stanley Baldwin's Conservatives had won the most seats. The minority government was not popular, and the Liberals seemed to be on their last legs.

Responding to claims by the Conservative and Labour Parties that the Liberal Party was dead, Harold quipped that it must be extremely aggravating for the Labour Party to have to rely for their very existence on a corpse. If the Liberal Party were dead then they still had 4,000,000 very active ghosts who intended to do a good deal of ghost-walking during the next ten, fifteen, twenty or thirty years. The listening crowd laughed heartily, so Abrahams warmed to his theme and added that if the Liberal party was dead, death was a very pleasant thing, and he had no fear of it. The difference between life and death seemed to be somewhere in the region of 200,000 votes, he concluded, promising that the Liberals, having secured a budget to suit them, would continue to support their Labour friends until the next election – so long as their proposed measures benefited all classes.

It was a strong speech which went down well to cries of 'hear, hear' from the mostly Liberal gathering. But he was wrong on a number of points. First, the election came sooner than Harold thought – just two months later, in October 1924.

'I was "adopted" actually as a Liberal candidate for Walthamstow,' Harold recalled later.

This was all getting a little too serious. Harold liked making speeches and he enjoyed making people laugh, but was he passionate enough about politics to want to make a career out of it, to the exclusion of law and his beloved athletics? The ego trip which came with candidature was different to anything he had experienced before. But should he really allow himself to be seduced by the hope of power, when politics didn't burn in his soul like athletics did? Harold was intelligent enough to pull back before it was too late, though his withdrawal was embarrassing.

*I very quickly realised that it [my political conviction] wasn't genuine, that I was flattered. And I was adopted as a Liberal candidate. But I decided very quickly that I ought to go back [to law].*

As it turned out, the General Election was a disaster for the Liberals, both in the long-term and the short-term. Under Herbert Henry Asquith, they lost 118 of their 158 seats. Even Labour lost 40 seats, and Stanley Baldwin's Conservatives won by a landslide. It was the start of the two-party dynamic.

By the winter of 1924–25, therefore, Harold had reason to feel relieved that he had chosen law instead of politics; but he didn't feel all that passionate about law either. If he thrived in a legal arena, he felt he did so because the job required quick yet superficial thinking. Later he explained, 'I do work quickly, I can pick up a thing superficially very quickly indeed. I can pick up the thread of something while people are talking.' Even so, a part of him remained uncomfortable. 'It is all a little superficial, you see, that would be my criticism of it. But it was most entertaining. I was doing quite a lot of good work at the College Mission as a poor man's lawyer.'

But even Harold's colleagues saw him as an athlete at heart. He explained, 'I remember, when I was a barrister appearing in a case after the Olympics, Lord Justice Burke remarking "Mr Abrahams, as one would have expected, covered a great deal of ground in a short space of time." People knew about you.' A courtroom rival also once acknowledged, 'My friend goes in for swift settlements.'

Still searching for a purpose, Abrahams entered the secretive world of freemasonry. Harold was initiated into Oxford and Cambridge University Lodge Number 1118 on January 16, 1925. On March 20 he was Passed; and he was Raised on November 20. He went on to join the Athlon Lodge Number 4674 two years later.

But it seems that the more he wandered down fresh paths in his search for a sense of belonging, the more those paths led him back to where he had been before – the world of athletics. That was where he truly belonged – and always would.

Yet his days as an athlete were dangerously numbered.

CHAPTER TWO:

# The End and Beginning for Harold Abrahams

Burning ambition or obsessive-compulsive disorder? In the spring of 1925, Harold Abrahams was driven by a simple numbers game.

Every year since his adolescence at Repton, he had improved his long jump personal best to stay up with his age. Most recently he had managed to jump over 24 feet in 1924, aged 24. And with the arrival of 1925, there was only one target in his mind.

*I badly wanted to clear 25 feet, and believed that with hard work and specialised training I might do so. In those days, that was getting on for world record form. Long-jumping doesn't combine all that well with sprinting, so I didn't do much in 1924, but I determined that next year in 1925 I was going to concentrate on it.*

Harold didn't feel the need to make any radical changes to his action – even though he had seen the likes of Ed Gourdin achieve stunning success by kicking in mid-air. Abrahams insisted that any conscious attempt to try to copy this action would be counterproductive.

'Imagine the burden imposed on a brain (already fully occupied with the anxiety of the take-off) by the labour of carrying out elaborate reasoning,' he argued. 'How can a body in mid-air attain any additional impetus?'

With Mussabini, he embarked on one final mission: to find a way to jump further without resorting to the "kick" used by some of his rivals at the time. It didn't take long to come up with a solution, which was decided with Old Sam during the winter of '24.

*I did a lot of experimenting indoors at the Poly Gymnasium in Regent Street, chiefly with seeing how one could, with one's stomach muscles, hold the legs up during flight, so they didn't drop. But I wasn't doing any of those comic kicks in the air, I used to do a straightforward sail-tuck.*

A season or two of long-jumping and then back to sprinting; that was the plan. His brother Adolphe saw no reason why Harold could not hit new heights on the track in good time for the Amsterdam Games of 1928. When was a sprinter's peak?

The British Olympic doctor said: 'I am sure that twenty-four is much too young. I should place it at three or four years later . . . the optimum sprinting age is distinctly later than that popularly supposed.'

All Adolphe had to do was keep Harold away from women and any other distractions. Adolphe was good at that. Christina McLeod Innes had been eliminated as a threat to Harold's athletic excellence, and she had fallen in love all over again. This time she was formally engaged – to her cousin, an American called Francis Vigor Morley. One can only imagine Harold's feelings when his first love suddenly announced her engagement to her first cousin, a young man he had met on many occasions in Oxford, where Frank studied as a Rhodes Scholar. It was hard to take in. Their mothers were sisters, whose maiden name was Bird. Christina and Frank were to be married in May – and Harold was invited. How strange was that going to feel?

Harold tried to focus on what he felt he could control – breaking the 25-foot barrier. The first day of the 1925 season offered him the opportunity to do just that. Yet Harold soon had to record the moment like this.

'On May 6, 1925 – strangely enough the anniversary of the King's accession – I retired from active competition. I had been performing in a long-jump pit at the old Stamford Bridge track – as it developed, for the last time.'

In a match between Bedford County and the London Athletic Club, Harold finished in second place with a distance of 22 feet or 6.7 metres. That stark statistic masked a disaster caused by a combination of factors. In addition to his obsessive desire to jump 25 feet, there was the boyish impulse to play up to a posse of photographers.

Sue Pottle explained, 'Harold told me he damaged his leg by showing off for photographers doing the long jump.' Did he also want to arrive at Christina's wedding in Cambridge a hero once more, fresh from new, ground-breaking exploits in British track and field? A boost to his self-esteem would help him to handle an emotionally challenging day.

Whatever the undercurrents, there can be little doubt that Harold lacked focus as he sprinted towards take-off at Stamford Bridge. He may also have sensed, from his opening jump, that there was a problem with the board.

Harold revealed, 'The long-jump run-up at Stamford Bridge had been used a great deal of the day before by a lot of schoolboys, and the take-off was very badly worn. I ran up to the take-off board, I took off, and my take-off leg trailed instead of coming up to meet the other one. I think I must have twisted it.'

Harold would never forget the agony of these moments:

The end: Abrahams suffers his accident

*Anyway I went straight into the ground at about 15, 16 or 17 miles per hour with a straight leg. I heard a noise, rather like Smee tearing a bit of sail cloth in Peter Pan. I heard this, didn't realise that it belonged to me, and I passed out. The pain was so acute that I just passed out. I broke my leg, tore badly through a lot of muscles. My leg was nearly doubled up. When I got up my leg was all bent and I had to be carried. I think I was actually carried off the track to the dressing room on a hurdle.*

According to Rosemary Warne, the take-off board wasn't just worn – it was wobbly. She recalled, 'He was very upset about it because he said the take-off board was not fixed down properly. The board put him off balance. He didn't blame anybody.'

Had he not realised the danger after his first jump? Only the previous year he had advised athletes to examine carefully the pit sand, the board and surrounding area before committing themselves in a full-blown jump, emphasising the danger of 'the run-up immediately behind the take-off board being worn away, and the jumper, when taking off accurately with his toe well on the board, catching his heel on the sharp edge of the wood'.

In his early-season exuberance, Abrahams had broken his own rule and thrown caution to the wind. The consequences were devastating. Rex Alston, a fellow sprinter who later became Harold's co-commentator on athletics for the BBC, recalled:

*I had already run that afternoon and was getting changed in the dressing room when there was a great shout outside. A few minutes later the door opened and Harold was carried in by three ambulance men. He looked absolutely ghastly, as white as a sheet and only barely conscious from the pain. I had never seen a man look so ill or in such terrible pain. As he fell into the pit the momentum of his body tore all the muscles and the nerves of his leg.*

Despite his agony, Harold wouldn't let anyone touch him until his eldest brother arrived. Adolphe finally took him away, as carefully as he could, to what was described as a 'nursing home'. The next morning Adolphe returned to Harold's bedside, bringing with him one of London's leading surgeons. As he inspected the damage, even the surgeon looked mildly horrified.

'I can operate,' he explained. 'But if I do, there's a risk you'll lose your leg.'

That was not a risk Harold was prepared to take. And there had been so much collateral damage before the impact of his fall reached the bone. The initial reluctance of the bone to snap had caused devastation around it. 'I'd torn through everything without breaking the leg. If I'd broken my leg it would have been simpler. I'd taken all the strain on the muscles and nerves, torn everything I'd got. It was really a magnificent sight; it was purple from the ankle to the hip bone.'

'Such bad luck at the height of your career,' said the surgeon

Harold surprised himself with his own reaction.

*That was the end, so far as athletics was concerned. I'll be absolutely truthful, I laid back there and I said, "This is marvellous." I was very uncertain about what to do in athletics, and here I had no option, my mind had been made up for me. What did I think of it? Strangely, my first reaction was of relief, outweighing any disappointment. I was faced no more with any problem of when to retire.*

*The athlete's farewell to his speed is as embarrassing as the "positively last appearance" of an actor past his prime. Would I have gone downhill and tried to go on? That was the decision I never had to make. It was made for me. Rather painfully, but it was made. Now I could not be accused of retiring because I was afraid of being beaten – indeed, all sympathy was with me on my enforced departure.*

*I wonder, in a sense, if it was not another piece of good bad luck. It is difficult to climb to the top of the ladder in any sport, but so much more difficult to stay there. Of course, one shouldn't mind being beaten; many people, perhaps, do not. I did – which is why my retirement was such a relief. But I still feel sad that I never jumped 25 feet.*

Ex-athlete: Harold Abrahams in irritable recovery mode.

Above all, perhaps it was that fixation with numbers which had finally done for him. He was still bowing down to them years later, 'My age runs conveniently with the years, and I resolved that I would set my ambition as a long jumper to keep for as long as possible ahead in feet of the date. At 18, I jumped 20ft 5½in; at 19, 21ft 8in; and in 1920 I cleared 22ft 7in. By the end of 1921 I had reached 23ft 0½ in. In 1923 my best was 23ft 8¾in, and on one most fortunate occasion in 1924 I cleared 24ft 2½ in. Alas, with 1925 I had to abandon the task.'

Part of his relief may have lain in the mathematical inevitability of eventual defeat in this neurotic battle with time anyway. How could he ever have been expected to jump 30 feet at the age of thirty, for example? Now the pressure was off. But his long-term sprinting career had also been destroyed in an instant.

Evelyn Montague believed there would have been so much more still to come in both areas.

*It was cruel luck that in 1925, with the new style mastered and endless vistas opening up before him, his career should be brought to a sudden end. He tore clean through the nerves and muscles behind his right knee . . . If it had not happened, he would have gone on for many years, for his is the devouring keenness which never dreams of retiring discreetly in the moment of success . . . It would have been particularly interesting to see how his jumping developed, for he was the last great jumper who did not use the hitch-kick. He gained his distance by the old-fashioned virtues of speed, spring and float.*

But Montague knew that Harold's loss to sprinting was the greater sporting tragedy. 'In actual fact, he had only begun to realise his full capabilities. I firmly believe that, if he had not broken down, he would have won both the 100 and 200 metres at the 1928 Olympic Games, and would have proved himself one of the three or four greatest sprinters of all time.'

We will never know, and Harold liked it that way. 'I got every sympathy, with everyone saying "Marvellous, what would he only have done if he had gone on?" No question, I had to stop dead, more or less go out at the top. I was very relieved that it had happened.'

Relieved, and a little frightened. Rex Alston pointed out, 'For a while it was feared he would never walk again.'

Harold remembered the uncomfortable months of uncertainty. 'I didn't like the pain very much, and it was months before I got my leg to the ground.'

He gradually found that he could walk; but the limp made it painfully obvious that Harold's leg was 'permanently useless for strenuous athletics', as Montague put it.

'And that put an end to my career as an active athlete,' Harold concluded.

He couldn't take part anymore, but he would never desert athletics. He simply had to find a different role. 'It enabled me to do much more in athletic administration and I did quite a lot of lecturing in the early days, it was quite well paid.'

And he had always been more interested in sports journalism than law. Harold confirmed, 'I determined in the early days that I was going to write, because I didn't want to have all my financial eggs in one basket. That's why I wrote and broadcast, to have a second string all the way. If I'd been more courageous, naturally I'd have gone out for one thing. [But] I don't think I'd have been any happier.'

A new life as a famous ex-athlete was waiting – a life defined by ten seconds in Paris.

### Chapter Three:

# Goodbye 1924 ... Hello 2024

The sun came out and Eric Liddell put on his track shoes for a farewell tour. He won pretty much everywhere he went; and the biggest goodbye of all came at Hampden Park, Glasgow. This was the spectacular setting for the 1925 Scottish Amateur Athletic Association championships. The other victories on the farewell tour were nice enough, they gave the people what they wanted. But the SAAAs were always important to Liddell. Hampden was where Eric wanted to hit his peak; and it was almost as significant to him as the Olympic Games the previous year.

Eric Liddell wanted his athletics to be remembered as a testament to his love for God. He demonstrated that love in front of 12,000 souls at those Scottish championships. Eric equalled his record there of 10 seconds dead in the 100 yards. He had run faster down south in the past, but Scottish conditions were almost always more challenging. He clocked 22.2 seconds for the 220 yards, which was a new record at the championships. And Eric completed a glorious hat-trick when he took the 440 yards in 49.2. That new record was the first time anyone had run under 50 seconds in Scotland. And Liddell's time wasn't beaten until 1957! What a way to say goodbye, and how everyone would miss him.

It was also tempting to wonder what times he might have achieved had he continued to devote so much energy to athletics. Eric would surely have shaved many more fractions of a second off those sprint times each year. It was almost frightening to think what records he might have set over the next five or ten years. If he was already a legend, then unimaginable sporting greatness would have awaited him. But Liddell knew he had done enough for now. And his athletics future was not set in stone.

Contrary to what many believed and still believe, Eric was not going to give up running completely. It was part of him now. But he'd made his priorities crystal clear. And perhaps that's why this final athletics flourish brought a tear to many a Scottish eye.

Eric Liddell's first love was China – and the long journey home was about to begin. There was a huge throng to wave Eric off from the Congregational College, on route to Edinburgh's Waverley railway station. As usual, Liddell showed his class and treated everyone alike. A newspaper account described the scene like this:

*He shook hands with the Principal and then, seeing a group of servants of the College, he went over and bade them goodbye also. Attached to the cab were long drag ropes, which were held by male students, while behind the vehicle came a large following of women students.*

Asked to make a farewell speech at the other end of the short journey across the city, his efforts were reported like this:

*Liddell was obliged to say a few words in response to the great ovation, his words rising shrilly above the noise of the station. He said he was going out as an ambassador to another country in the great effort for the unification of the world. He hoped they at home would do their share. Their motto would always be "Christ for the World. For the World Needs Christ."*

'Jesus Shall Reign Where'er the Sun,' Eric sang as his train departed, and the crowd dutifully joined in with the hymn, to show their respect for the choices he had made.

Almost from the moment he reached China, Eric was trying to spread God's word – combining his passions for the country and its people.

Courtesy of Eric Liddell Community

Eric and Bible class – Tientsin 1925.

There were soon new female admirers too – and plenty of them. Would he ever marry? Anyone who loved Liddell and wanted to share his life would have to understand what that involved. They would have to share him with Jesus and China. They might even have to settle for the bronze medal on that podium of priorities. Romantic considerations were for the future, though. For now, Eric could renew family bonds in private moments. After the way he had been left to his education as a child, you could argue there was a lot of catching up to do.

Liddelll family in Beidaihe – 1925.

Back in England, Harold Abrahams was also still single – and would remain so for many years. Anyone who loved Harold would have to share him with athletics. And he was still so devoted to his sport that his lack of a meaningful personal life didn't seem to matter to him either. But did Harold have a clear vision and purpose like Eric?

Abrahams didn't consciously embark on a lifelong mission to make millions of people love track and field as much as he did. It just turned out that way – and his energy seemed endless. Norris McWhirter, who later created *The Guinness Book of Records*, was able to declare, 'Harold Abrahams raised athletics from a minor to a major national sport.'

From June 1925, he began contributing to the *Sunday Times*. Abrahams soon became a permanent fixture at the newspaper, generating more support for his chosen field. To have any real influence over the direction of athletics, however, he had to join the administrators. Ten weeks after he left the Stamford Bridge stage in agony, he returned with a clipboard to officiate as a field judge at the AAA Championships.

Peter Lovesey, respected writer and athletics historian, plotted Harold's early rise through the administrative ranks. 'He became Hon. Treasurer of the Middlesex AAA; served on the Southern Committee and, from 1926, the General Committee of the AAA. Not one of these enterprises was skimped. He worked at them as he had worked at winning a gold medal.'

The irony was that, by his own admission, Harold's motives were not altruistic or clearly defined. He said much later:

*I wish I could feel honestly that one's inclination to take part in athletic administration was a sort of virtuous response to all one owed to athletics. I would be dishonest if I said that. I have always liked administration. I have liked more than anything else using my knowledge in negotiation in getting things straightened out, untangling problems. And of course there is a certain amount of power complex involved because I like helping to direct things. But my biggest urge is that I hate more than anything else quarrelling. I've done my share of it.*

Harold knew he was clever with words. That would help with administration; and it also made him the ideal man to experiment in a new journalistic field – live radio sports commentary. He was like a test pilot, making the airwaves safe and slick for the 24/7 live outside broadcasts of the twenty-first century. But back in the 1920s, the newspapers were understandably terrified that their reports would be rendered outdated and pointless; and there was much negotiation behind the scenes before any sport on the radio was broadcast.

Harold remembered those pioneering times and explained, 'I think I must have given the first athletics commentary. We did some trials. Originally they weren't allowed to do running commentaries, because of the press. So there was a lot of practising.'

On March 26, 1927, Harold Abrahams broadcast live to the nation from the Varsity sports between Oxford and Cambridge at the Queen's Club. It blazed the trail for so much of what we take for granted today. Harold's rich tones on the radio would soon become the recognisable voice of athletics.

Broadcast pioneer: Harold in the commentary box.

As Norris McWhirter put it half a century later, 'Harold possessed one of the finest speaking voices in the country. Those wonderful articulated and modulated words of his and his meticulous statistical preparation set a standard and comprised a whole technique of live commentary and summary on which the BBC reputation as the world's premier sports service can justly be said to have been founded.'

Meanwhile Harold continued to establish himself as part of the British athletics administrative team, devoting himself to a variety of roles. Abrahams was Press Steward at the AAA Championships in 1926 and Official Recorder in 1927. Unspectacular titles, but his influence was growing all the time.

Sometimes he risked slipping back down the ladder; for example, when he launched a withering attack on the International Olympic Committee in 1927.

'The composition of this autocratic body, the IOC, has always been veiled in obscurity. Membership seems to consist of those who are invited by the body itself to join,' he complained controversially.

Harold had spent enough time in the company of that formidable outcast, Sam Mussabini to know that "the establishment" had left plenty of room for improvement in athletics administration at home and abroad. Abrahams would try to bring about change from the inside. But Mussabini couldn't inspire from the sidelines anymore

On June 27, 1927 Old Sam died on a French train while on his way back to London. He was 64 years old – and still held the post of coach to the Polytechnic Harriers when he passed away. Among his possessions, they found a photo of Abrahams breaking the tape in the Olympic 100 metres in Paris. It carried the inscription 'To S.A.M., in memory of nine months together.' Harold's long jump injury might just have broken his former trainer's heart. But Old Sam would have been proud of the way Abrahams continued the fight to introduce common sense into athletics. The chaos had gone on long enough.

Slowly but surely, Harold began to shape athletics events in a way that would lead to the prospect of a smooth-running Paris 2024 Olympics. Norris McWhirter explained, 'His drafting ability enabled him to transform the rules of competition – making sensible changes which are today taken for granted but which were revolutionary in the mid-1920s.'

This process had started during the summer of 1924, when Abrahams had complained about the unlimited numbers of entrants at the AAA Championships. Overcrowding had made a mockery of serious competition, he claimed. Harold had drawn attention to the plight of his great rival for public affection, Eric Liddell. He still saw Eric's treatment as the most scandalous example of administration gone mad.

*The whole programme is full of absurdities on account of this unlimited entry. E.H. Liddell had to run three 220s and three 440s in less than 24 hours ...And the long and high jumpers could have almost gone to sleep between the times they were called upon to perform . . . The running of three quarter-miles in the space of under twenty-four hours is no light task for any man.*

Abrahams wanted seeding – and byes to the second round for those of known AAA standard. He wanted harmony between track and field. He pushed for all the things that ensure the success of major championships these days.

The common-sense continuity we enjoy today is partly down to Harold Abrahams' belligerent attitude the best part of a century ago. We could look forward to sensible scheduling at Paris 2024 thanks to the changes he initiated. Mercifully, the chaos Eric Liddell endured a hundred summers ago was unlikely to be echoed at these Olympics.

Chapter Four:

# Liddell and Abrahams – Bigger than Amsterdam

The Amsterdam Olympics of 1928 offered a tempting stage for the enduring brilliance of Eric Liddell. Were those Olympics on his mind at the turn of the year? Away from the limelight, we know that Eric was enjoying more time with his family. But calls for his athletic return reached him in his far-flung corner the world.

It would be untrue to suggest that deep down Liddell no longer loved the feeling of running fast. He trained regularly in China and beat anyone who dared to challenge him at the Anglo-Chinese college in Tientsin, even after giving them a healthy head start. Eric had helped design the Min Yuan stadium, built in 1926 with a nod to the set-up at Stamford Bridge. He had won and had fun there too. Although details are sketchy, Liddell seems to have clocked some decent times over the next year or two.

No wonder there had been attempts by his supporters to persuade the British Olympic Association to consider making special arrangements for Liddell's return to the fold from the Far East, or at least to encourage that return. Sadly, since Eric hadn't raced competitively in Europe for so

*Courtesy of Eric Liddell Community*

Liddell family in China 1927.

long, the powers that be felt that any plans to reserve Liddell a place in the GB team for Amsterdam were inappropriate.

Whether Eric picked up on such indifference at the highest level is hard to say, but his mind was made up by the time spring came to Europe. He wrote to his trusty old trainer, Tom McKerchar, to give him the bad news. Much as Eric would love another Olympic adventure, he couldn't abandon the college where he worked just to go in search of more personal glory.

Disappointed but hardly surprised, Tom let an Edinburgh newspaper know, thus ending any wider speculation once and for all.

A press cutting from April 19, 1928 confirmed:

*Mr McKerchar, his former trainer, has received word from "the Flying Scotsman," to the effect that his duties render it impossible for him to come home this year; much as Liddell would wish, for from several newspapers received from China it is apparent that Liddell has not forsaken his running path and has retained his old-time pace. His absence has been a great loss to Scottish athletics, and it will be many a long year before we see a worthy successor to him.*

London papers picked up the story the very next day, and one ran the headline:

**FAMOUS SCOT NOT FOR THE OLYMPIC GAMES**

*Eric H. Liddell, the Olympic Games 400 metres champion of 1924, who went out on missionary work to China some time ago, has written to friends in Edinburgh to the effect that it will be impossible for him to come home during the summer, and the hope entertained that he would run in Amsterdam is abandoned by the Scottish Amateur Athletic Association.*

Anticipating this outcome, another paper had already reflected that it was a 'tragedy' how British athletics had lost both Harold Abrahams and Eric Liddell before the Amsterdam Games. But Harold hadn't faded from the scene. He wasn't going to miss the Olympics entirely, even if he couldn't compete. In April 1928, just as Liddell ruled himself out, Abrahams was made Captain of the GB athletics team for the forthcoming Amsterdam Olympics. The BOA wanted to salute Abrahams for his achievement at the previous Olympics, and to recognise how, despite his injury, he had retained his status as a national hero and athletics figurehead.

Behind the scenes, Harold was also still helping people less fortunate than himself. Perhaps he had never been more popular. His friend Walter Ashley wrote that year, 'Through it all, Harold has maintained his eagerness to help the underdog. He has lectured regularly to working boys and working men. I have never known him refuse a request to help a good cause. It is these qualities of character and leadership, even more than his own athletic record, which so well qualify him for his important task in Amsterdam.'

But Harold's big mouth always risked throwing a spanner in the works. His twin roles as Team Captain and media commentator collided in the build-up to Amsterdam '28. Not for the first time, Abrahams wasn't very complimentary about his own athletes.

'Our ten representatives in the field events have no possible winners and only a couple of possible finalists,' he stated somewhat brutally.

He wasn't wrong; but his team members wouldn't have wanted to hear such bleak realism just before they embarked on their Olympic adventure.

Mercifully, there was more reason for optimism around the British track athletes.

Harold recalled, 'I left London with the British team on Wednesday, July 25, and sailed from Harwich to Flushing. The competitions began on Sunday, July 29, and Lord Burghley was the first athlete to break a tape at the ninth Olympiad, for he easily won [his] 400 metres hurdles [heat], and the next day we yelled ourselves hoarse when he ran magnificently to win the final in record time. He had enormous courage when he wasn't 100 per cent fit.'

Harold soon had something else to shout about. 'The other victory which fell to Great Britain was in the 800 metres, which Douglas Lowe won for the second time by nearly 10 yards in 1 min 51.8sec – a new Olympic record. He dominated the entire field.'

Perhaps such old-school success explained why Abrahams no longer expected others to train as intensively as he had done for Olympic victory. He wrote, 'One American trainer asked me how many coaches we had got for our gallant little team. I replied, "Oh, we have two – motor-coaches".'

Winning the Olympics had felt like a matter of life or death to Harold four years earlier. The Games had almost broken him; and afterwards he had needed a few days alone, just to get over the ordeal. Now he no longer saw the point in young men almost destroying themselves in pursuit of glory. Coaches were suddenly almost surplus to requirements in his mind.

And there was another issue he was keen to brush aside because it didn't fit his way of thinking: why on earth would anyone risk their health by using illegal chemicals to improve their chances of victory? As British captain, he was asked to comment on an IAAF resolution in Amsterdam which recognised the existence of doping – and provided for 'the exclusions of persons who knowingly dope from places where IAAF rules prevail.' He thought people were fretting over nothing.

*I myself have never come across a case of doping, and, further, from conversations I have had with medical men on the subject, I have been unable to discover that there is any drug that would be of assistance. The first thing that has to be decided is: 'What is doping?' Most of us use sugar between the heats and the finals. Would that be considered doping? Also, what about any tonic taken for health purposes? To imply that people would inject a drug with a hypodermic syringe would be nonsense. Supposing it were discovered that the taking of cocaine or opium would assist runners, how could this question be tackled if athletes consumed foods containing those things? Altogether, I think the problem much too fantastic to tackle.*

For a man who saw and shaped the future in so many ways, this view was extraordinarily naïve and short-sighted. Time would see doping become a monumental problem – one that would threaten to ruin Harold's beloved sport completely. For now, however, he was happy to ride the joyously amateur Olympic wave and embrace his enduring fame, free from unwanted complications.

Athletics writer Tony Ward later described the British team's homecoming. 'A great crowd assembled at Liverpool Street on the team's return to England, and, in scenes reminiscent of four years earlier, rushed the train as it arrived. Their cries of "Burghley!" and "Abrahams!" were followed by cheers. He [Harold] was still a celebrity.'

∼

Although Eric Liddell hadn't been in Amsterdam, he was still a celebrity too – and he wanted to test himself athletically against all-comers to his part of the world. When he heard that some of the French and Japanese Olympians were coming to compete in the South Manchurian Games, Eric couldn't resist a fresh challenge. He dusted off his track shoes and entered a couple of events.

'And it happened, somehow, that I won the 200 and 400 metres,' he told a journalist a few years later.

More than that, his times compared favourably to the Olympic gold medal times in Amsterdam. With similar training to 1924, there was little doubt that Eric could have dominated yet again in 1928. Liddell had proved a point – and now he was ready to return to his part of China. But as he neared the boat that was due to take him there, he noticed it was already edging away from the quayside. Straight away, Eric knew what to do. He hastily threw his bags onto the boat, summoning the athleticism to join them. A journalist who spoke to witnesses reported what happened next. '[Eric] leaped what witnesses say was more than fifteen feet across the water onto the deck of the boat.'

The headline was straightforward. 'Flying Scotsman Leaps Fifteen Feet.' If locals didn't already know why Liddell was called the Flying Scotsman, they realised after that extraordinary stunt. And another great athletic challenge was waiting for him the following year.

CHAPTER FIVE:

# The Price of Liddell's Sacrifice

Eric Liddell knew all about a legendary German called Otto Peltzer. And after what he had heard, the chance to race Peltzer in a fascinating Tientsin showdown proved completely irresistible.

Otto was a world record-holder who had always been very unlucky where the Olympics were concerned. For a start, he had been born German in 1900. That ruled him out of the 1920 Olympics in Antwerp, where the rest of the world was trying to heal after the horrors of the Great War. It was the same story at Paris 1924, because the Germans still weren't invited. When they were finally brought back into the fold for Amsterdam 1928, Peltzer suffered a foot injury while playing handball. That meant he couldn't perform to the best of his ability at the Olympics – and failed to reach the final in his strongest event, the 800 metres.

Even without a history of Olympic heroism and medals galore, Otto Peltzer was still a legend. In 1926 he had beaten the Olympic champion of Paris, Douglas Lowe over 880 yards in his own backyard. Then, even more impressively, he defeated the seemingly unbeatable Paavo Nurmi over 1500 metres. In that Berlin showdown, he even shattered Nurmi's world record, taking it down from 3:52.6 to 3.51.0. That's why Peltzer's poor condition in Amsterdam had been such a disappointment to everyone – not least the Brit who respected him most and had relished the challenge of racing against him once more. Douglas Lowe still felt the need to do something on his rival's behalf. On Lowe's suggestion, the British team sent Peltzer a letter congratulating him on his courage and commiserating with the German on his bad luck with injury at the Games. But Lowe made an even more extraordinary offer in private – one that his friend Eric Liddell found deeply impressive when he heard about it over in China.

Eric summed up his friend Lowe's qualities like this:

*Generosity was another element. In 1928 Douglas Lowe decided to leave the track after running in the Olympic Games, but he felt that Dr Peltzer was not in his best form during that time, and so he kept in training for a little longer so that he might give Dr Peltzer a chance of beating him. That was sportsmanship, but it was a far greater quality than courage. Sportsmanship had reached its height when it could do that.*

Eighteen days after the Games, at the big Berlin Grunewald track, Peltzer sent the home crowd wild when he passed Lowe on the home straight of their 800 metres showdown. But the Englishman wasn't done, and he hit back just in time to reach the tape first. In doing so, he avenged his defeat of two years earlier. In Eric Liddell's eyes, however, it didn't matter who had won. The fact that the race had taken place at all, thanks to Lowe's generosity, was the only important thing. And when the opportunity arose, the Flying Scotsman also intended to give the great Peltzer a chance to beat him.

A man who loved to travel almost as much as he loved to run, Peltzer reached China in 1929 – and threw down the gauntlet to Eric Liddell. They would race twice in Tientsin; a straight head-to-head over 400 metres and then again over 800 metres.

How joyful Liddell must have felt, as he too rediscovered the thrill of running fast against a world-renowned opponent. Adrenalin produced an extra competitive edge. Eric flew round that Chinese track as though it were 1924 in the Stade Colombes all over again. Astonishingly, Liddell managed to beat the great Peltzer with some ease over Eric's favourite distance of 400 metres

In the second race, Liddell wasn't expected to live with a man who had beaten the great Douglas Lowe. How could Eric, who only ever ran flat out, avoid blowing up long before the finishing line in the 800m? To everyone's amazement, Eric Liddell did not fade. The man who had defeated the magnificent Paavo Nurmi was suddenly under threat. Untrained and yet bubbling with spirit and talent, Liddell pushed Peltzer all the way and nearly beat him. A fraction of a second separated the two men at the end. Otto had restored his pride; but that didn't mean much to such a fine human being. And instead of basking in the glory of a revenge victory, he simply set about trying to persuade Eric to make a proper comeback.

The German knew he would be well past his own peak by the time the Olympics reached Los Angeles in 1932. (As it turned out, he was Germany's team captain for that event.) But Liddell was a different proposition entirely. He would be thirty years old for Los Angeles; and that was no obstacle to success. Too old for the sprints, perhaps, but Eric could make a longer distance his own. Based on what he had just seen, Peltzer had already made up his mind. If Eric Liddell trained regularly for the next three years, he would be the fastest 800 metres runner in the world come LA '32.

Peltzer delivered his verdict – and waited for Liddell's reaction. His attempt to inspire Eric didn't receive the response he had hoped for, though. Flattered as Eric must have been, training for Los Angeles simply wasn't the way he intended to spend his next three years. It meant far more to Liddell to continue the work that his ailing father had begun. To follow in James Liddell's footsteps and serve the Lord among their people in China. That was the only target Eric wanted to meet.

Liddell did enjoy another important athletic occasion the year after that Peltzer showdown, though. 'I believe I won the North China Championship in 1930, but that was all,' reflected Eric casually and modestly, when asked a couple of years later whether he had run again. But in 1932, one last Olympic Games was still within his reach – theoretically at least.

Portrait of Liddell in late
1920s or early 1930s.

Before any British athlete could make a final decision on Los Angeles, however, the very future of Great Britain as an Olympic entity seemed to be under threat. In 1931, Abrahams teamed up with Paris and Amsterdam gold medallist Douglas Lowe to restore order to British athletics. Some of its national associations were pushing for individual representation on the International Amateur Athletic Federation.

Peter Lovesey said of Abrahams, 'His ability to present a case persuasively came to the rescue of British athletics. With another able lawyer, Douglas Lowe, he resolved the crisis over the United Kingdom representation on the IAAF by negotiating the formation of the International Board, known later as the BAAB [British Amateur Athletic Board].'

Would the British authorities reward Harold for protecting the future of "Team GB" by giving him a role at the Los Angeles Olympics? The silence was deafening.

Meanwhile some were still urging a Liddell comeback in time for those 1932 Games. Tantalisingly, Eric did return to Britain; and he did hope to do some running. The main purpose of his trip, however, was not to train for the Olympics. His aim, as always, was to spread God's word on a preaching tour.

At one stage he took the opportunity to stop off at his old school, Eltham College. Rather than run, he watched others express themselves on the track. The next generation were coming through.

This return to the UK would have happened a year earlier, had tragedy not struck very close to home in his native China. A colleague had been murdered by Chinese bandits. One dispatch said of Liddell:

*He pays a fine and fitting tribute to his former colleague, Mr Eric Scarlett, whose untimely death at the hands of brigands determined him to remain in China for the present at least. Mr Scarlett's death has increased both [Liddell's] work and responsibility at the Anglo-Chinese College in Tientsin ...*

Eric had been given no option but to remain at his post until a replacement could be found. And the tragedy was a reminder of the lurking danger when travelling beyond the confines of the Anglo-Chinese College community. Potential perils could never deter someone as fearless as Eric Liddell, of course. And when he was safely back in Britain for a while, he explained the rewards awaiting a missionary who kept an open heart and mind in his dealings with the local inhabitants. Speaking in the most beautiful terms of how faith could be used to bring the world closer together, Eric said:

Eric Liddell hosted back at Eltham College.

*In China the evangelists are going out amongst the people. They are going into their homes. They are sleeping in places just the same as the Chinese themselves. They are trying to understand the problems those people have to face, and to look at them from their point of view. One of the greatest challenges to every Christian person asks for no great courage but asks for patience and sympathy that we will be able to sit beside those whose opinions are different from our own and try to enter into their problems and see them from their point of view.*

For a man who wasn't supposed to be very good at public speaking, he seemed more than capable of inspiring his audience. He also knew the kind of amusing detail that might grab their attention. One correspondent's account of an evening listening to Liddell revealed:

*Particularly interesting was his story of the fondness of the Chinese for birds. So affectionate were they for their feathered pets that they took their birds for walks in the morning and evening, just as dogs are in this country.*

Beyond such eccentricities, Eric knew there was more to the missionary challenge than often met the eye. The same British report laid out Liddell's understanding of a much uglier reality beneath the surface in China. And yet he was still determined to help make everything right:

*China and the Chinese were fascinating, but below that there was a darkness greater than in this country, the darkness of ignorance, poverty, sin and filth. But because of the beautiful thing they could make of China, they engaged in their missionary work there.*

It sounded like mission impossible. And in the final analysis, it was. Yet in Eric's mind, his formidable task wasn't fundamentally different to that of any Christian:

*We are all missionaries. We carry our religion with us, or we allow our religion to carry us. Wherever we go, we either bring people nearer to Christ, or we repel them from Christ.*

Liddell was getting better at bringing people nearer to Christ. And that left little time for anything else – least of all athletics. It was soon clear that Eric was not going to follow Otto Peltzer's advice and make the journey to the Games in Los Angeles in 1932. His year back in the western world for his furlough might have allowed for it. But the logistical demands of the preaching tour had consumed him.

On June 05, 1932, a newspaper article announced:

*Eric Liddell, the famous Olympic runner and Rugby international, who is now on leave from the mission fields of China, has decided not to run again, as he is returning to China almost immediately…It seems hard to believe that we have seen the last of one of the greatest sprinters of modern times and a most magnetic personality. The reason why*

Olympic year but Eric is with family in Carcant, Scotland.

*Liddell did not run as he intended during his present visit to England is because he found it impossible to train properly while moving about the country addressing missionary and other religious gatherings.*

At least he could spend precious time with family, before he embraced the dangers of life back in China once more.

Meanwhile Harold Abrahams had ample time to go to the Olympics – but not the cash to travel under his own steam. And despite the notable firefighting he had done the year before to protect GB's Olympic identity, no one saw fit to send Abrahams to LA. He explained a few years later, 'I hadn't the money to get to Los Angeles in 1932. I had no means to get there. I stayed up till two o'clock every morning eagerly watching the tape machine as it ticked out the results.'

Harold couldn't help but spare a thought for his old GB colleague, Eric Liddell as he monitored the latest Olympic action from a London newspaper office.

*Eight years after Liddell's triumph in Paris, an American [Bill Carr] was to win the title at Los Angeles in [a world record] 46.2. I wish Liddell could have been present on that Californian path!*

Los Angeles '32 never knew what it had missed due to Eric Liddell's decision to stay away. We can only guess at the 800m drama he might have created. But Eric did cross the Atlantic that year, to visit Canada. He was so close to the last Olympics that were ever realistically available to him as a runner – and yet he still didn't go. What was he thinking?

Towards the end of 1932, when those Games had come and gone, Liddell had a fascinating exchange with a Canadian journalist called R.E. Knowles.

The interviewer asked him an alarmingly honest question – and Liddell answered in kind. The exchange went like this:

*Reporter: Are you glad you gave your life to missionary work? Don't you miss the limelight, the rush, the frenzy; the cheers, the rich red wine of victory?*

*Liddell: Oh well of course, it's natural for a chap to think over all that sometimes. But I'm glad I'm at the work I'm engaged in now. A fellow's life counts far more for this than the other. Not a corruptible crown, but an incorruptible one, you know.*

This exchange tells us so much about Eric as an ordinary human being. A myth persists that he left for China and never thought about athletics again. Not true. He not only thought plenty about athletics; he kept fit and kept racing in the Far East for a good while. He could have won another 400 metres gold in Amsterdam 1928; and he could have won the 800 metres gold at Los Angeles in 1932. The fact that Eric missed out on two more wonderful world gatherings – when he knew he could still have made his mark – must have hurt him. He was admitting as much to the reporter. Eric Liddell had his wistful moments. 'Of course, it's natural for a chap to think over all that sometimes.'

You can only truly appreciate the man if you realise that he had natural desires, temptations and weaknesses just like the rest of us. He simply overcame them.

That distinction spoke to the soul of the *Chariots of Fire* producer, David Puttnam, who probably had a better understanding of Liddell than most. Puttnam once revealed his favourite line in the movie. It came when Eric Liddell was sitting in the stand with his trainer "Sandy," watching Harold Abrahams in the 100m Olympic final in Paris.

Sandy asks Liddell: 'Any regrets, Eric? That you're not down there with them?'

'Regrets, sure,' says Liddell. 'No doubts, though.'

It's perfect. Liddell is admitting to the human cost of his decision to stick to his guns. Just as he hinted at that cost to the Canadian reporter in real life. And, naturally enough for a devout Christian, he had paraphrased something from the Bible to explain his motivations.

1 Corinthians 9:25 says the following (using the King James Version 1900):

*And every man that striveth for the mastery is temperate in all things. Now they do it to obtain a corruptible crown; but we an incorruptible.*

The New Living Translation has it like this:

*All athletes are disciplined in their training. They do it for a prize that will fade away, but we do it for an eternal prize.*

A prize that will fade away; and it's true – they nearly always do – even in the case of the most celebrated and universally adored champions!

It was fascinating to observe the great Usain Bolt in Greece at the precise moment he realised his prize would fade away. It was September 12, 2009 – at the height of his fame. You could see the alarm on his face when he realised that he might one day become an unknown among sports fans. He might even become an unknown among future sprint champions. How did he learn this? Through his own poor grasp of sprint history. He had never heard of Harold Abrahams. He had never heard of *Chariots of Fire*, either.

'What year was that?' he asked.

When he was told we were going back to 1924, he seemed relieved at first. Then you could almost see him calculating how long it might take for his own achievements to disappear from human consciousness. Soon after this exchange, he began to contemplate retirement – and what life might look like beyond the "corruptible glory" of his career.

Yes, the prize always fades away sooner or later. That's why Eric Liddell had no doubt whatsoever that he was doing the right thing by sacrificing his chances of more Olympic gold medals. But because he was only human, that sacrifice still hurt. Even so, the pain and frustration were worth it to him. The irony is that, while *Chariots of Fire* remains in our consciousness, the memory of Eric Liddell's Olympic prize will not fade. In that sense, his life as an athlete has been immortalised on the silver screen. But it wouldn't have happened had he not refused to run on a Sunday. And even then, it wouldn't have happened had he failed to win the 400 metres in Paris.

Puttnam was once asked that specific question: would he have made *Chariots* if Liddell had only won silver?

'No,' he said simply.

That wasn't because he would have valued Liddell any less; but because he knew the movie industry – and he knew how hard it had been to get his movie made, even when Liddell and Abrahams had won gold.

∽

While Eric Liddell rose above athletic glory during Los Angeles 1932, Harold Abrahams was distraught at not being there to watch the drama unfold. He had never missed an Olympic Games in his adult lifetime. And he vowed never to miss another Olympics as long as he lived. It was a promise to himself that he was destined to keep – at considerable personal risk.

Harold and Los Angeles presented a further irony. Abrahams died just before the best version of himself lit up that city in a film that captured the imagination of Tinsel Town and London alike. It was the early 1980s by the time *Chariots of Fire* took Hollywood and the rest of America by storm. Back in 1932, he wasn't even a spectator in LA, let alone a star. And he was determined to ensure the Olympic movement would never pass him by again.

Eric Liddell willingly let the Olympics continue without him. And the following year, he received news that only served to reinforce the decision he had made to pursue preaching over further Olympic stardom. James Liddell, who had already returned to Britain in 1929 due to his failing health, finally passed away. Though Eric couldn't have been surprised, the news must still have hit him hard; for his father had always been his hero. Eric would continue the great man's work, as he had already begun to do.

James Liddell had shaped and inspired Eric from the start. And it's no exaggeration to say that James Liddell shaped *Chariots of Fire* in one fundamental way, too. He was the earthly force behind Eric's decision not to run on a Sunday. Without James, we can safely say there would have been no *Chariots of Fire*. Now the man who had shaped Eric Liddell's beliefs was gone.

For the men destined to be immortalised in the movie, life went on. And in one sense, the lives of both Eric Liddell and Harold Abrahams were about to become more complete. Romance was in the air. And it had been a long wait.

## CHAPTER SIX:

# Harold and the Opera Singer

Harold Abrahams was setting his journalistic sights on the next Olympic Games in Berlin when he was distracted by an opera singer called Sybil Evers. She invited Abrahams over to her table at the Grosvenor hotel early in 1934. That marked the start of a great love story – and the end of at least a decade of Harold's life without a serious romance.

The simple truth was that Harold had a fear of commitment – except to athletics. But now there would be two loves to contend with. Athletics would never have to give way; but it would occasionally share the top step. To those who knew Harold Abrahams, such a change was scarcely imaginable; yet it happened.

Sybil Evers – beautiful on the outside and inside.

Like Harold, Sybil had grown up at a boy's public school – her father Claude was a housemaster at Rugby. Asked once by a radio interviewer whether she was an athletics expert, she replied, 'No I'm afraid I'm not. I was born and brought up at Rugby with boys and used to watch the sport there. But I'm very far from being an expert. I can't manage to keep the times in my head.'

Music was her absolute passion. Sybil's artistic leanings came from her mother, Jessie, who was a talented water-colourist. In a book called *Butterflies in Camphor*, a relative called Elliot Evers confirmed:

*Sybil's great interest was in the stage, and particularly in musical comedy. As a child she had produced playlets and composed tunes. She sang well and was pretty, though petite. She was extremely attractive, full of gaiety and able to take things as they came with a smile. She studied at the college of music and then achieved her ambition of a stage career. She acted in The Beggar's Opera, was the Lily Maid in the opera of that name, and was in the D'Oyly Carte Opera Company which suited her perfectly as she loved the operas and relished every moment of them. Her charm as one of the three pretty maids from school in The Mikado is still remembered. She had many other singing parts on the stage and on the radio.*

The book also revealed that 'Sybil had a youthful serious illness and operation, [which meant she] could have no children.' Her adopted daughter Sue Pottle confirmed, 'She had suffered from TB of the uterus.' Sybil married Noel Brack, an Old Haileyburian, but the marriage quickly fell apart, and they were divorced.

When Sybil was asked to look back on her life before she met Harold, she airbrushed Brack right out of it. 'Well, I was a singer. I trained at the Royal College of Music. I used to sing in light opera. In fact, I was employed by the BBC for some time, second soprano of the Wireless Singers before the war; that was in the old Savoy Hill days. And then after that I used to work fairly often for their music production department, which gave performances of light operas.'

She had played a number of supporting roles while performing in the D'Oyly Carte Opera Company from March 1930 to September 1931.

Then in January 1934, Sybil appeared in a children's play called *Ever So Long Ago* at the Cambridge Theatre in London. It was reportedly the first play attended by Princess Elizabeth, the future Queen.

At around this time, fate took a hand and put Sybil in the same room as Harold.

'I met him at an old school dance,' Sybil explained simply. It was the first time they had talked together, though not the first time Abrahams had laid eyes on the alluring Miss Evers. By then she had finished her spell with the D'Oyly Carte – and was alternating between the Webber-Douglas and the Chanticleer opera companies. 'I think he had actually seen her performing,' his nephew Tony explained. And a singer friend called Julia once wrote to remind Sybil, 'Do you remember telling me about your [first] meeting with Harold, when we were doing Figaro?'

In *The Marriage of Figaro*, Sybil usually played the part of Susanna (Maid to the Countess). The *Figaro* plot saw Sybil spurning the advances of the Count who, tired of his wife, pursues her maid Susanna. Sybil's character is about to marry Figaro, which explains her unwillingness to do the Count's bidding. It is a lovely role; and one critic described what Sybil brought to the part: 'Figaro being what it is, a combination of "opera buffa" and sophisticated comedy of manners, those who perform it must be able not only to sing well but also to act well . . . For Susanna we have Miss Sybil Evers and she is entrancing. She also knows a thing or two about acting and oh, the difference to us!'

We can picture Harold gazing at the stage, similarly entranced, just as *Chariots of Fire* portrays him. On stage, Sybil was playing hard to get in scenes alongside Count Almaviva. Off stage, Harold would soon see whether she still played so hard to get. Sue Pottle set the scene for that first meeting.

'It was a party for old girls from Wycombe Abbey [a top private school]. It was held at the Grosvenor and each group of old girls had their own guests sitting at their respective tables. As far as I understand it, dad was at one table and my mother was at another. And I have been told that it was my mother, or at least those on her table, who invited my father to come over and join them at some point in the evening.'

Even in the mid-1930s, Harold remained something of a celebrity. Most people knew about his Olympic win in Paris back in 1924. Sybil might even have been able to tell Harold where she had been on his big day; because July 7, 1924 had been unforgettable for her too. At 3 p.m., just as Harold was preparing to run his epic semi-final in Paris, Sybil had begun to perform over in London – 'in the presence of Her Majesty the Queen', as the theatre programme put it. The occasion was a private dress rehearsal of *Hugh the Drover*, a romantic ballad opera in two acts, at the Parry Opera Theatre. Queen Mary was invited to attend. Sybil played Susan, hardly the leading role; but it wasn't every day you performed for the Queen. It wasn't every day you won gold at the Olympic Games either.

Since Harold and Sybil were both accustomed to holding centre stage, onlookers must have been fascinated to see how their egos would interact at the Grosvenor. Instead of clashing, they fed off each other comfortably. What started as a daring, fun flirtation in front of Sybil's friends became something more. It isn't hard to imagine Harold plucking up the courage to ask Sybil to dance, even though by his own admission he was a hopeless dancer at the time. Sybil clearly didn't hold that against him, because they agreed to meet again. Perhaps Harold was invited to see *Figaro* a second time. And there would be more opportunities for Sybil to mesmerise her suitor.

When Sybil performed in Milton's *Comus*, at the Open Air Theatre in London's Regent's Park that summer, a reviewer in *The Times* purred, 'The appeal for indulgence on behalf of Miss Sybil Evers, who had taken up at short notice the part of the Lady, was quite unnecessary; she was the very incarnation of Milton's idea of the queen-hood of innocence, and her first entrance onto an empty stage was pure beauty.'

If hardened critics were so touched, it is easy to see why Harold was completely captivated. Sybil, with her background in light opera, seemed almost made for him. She had made a career of bringing passion to the kind of music that already left Harold spellbound.

That she was equally enchanting off stage touched Harold more deeply than he had thought possible. And although she had suffered an unhappy marriage, she couldn't prevent herself from falling in love with him either.

'It was a whirlwind affair,' Sybil admitted a few years later.

There have been claims that Harold converted to Catholicism in 1934, but there is nothing in Catholic Church records to that effect. Perhaps there was talk of it during this heady time. The depth of Harold's feelings was never in doubt. And that intensity sparked moments of extreme crisis in the early years of their relationship, as we shall see.

Harold once said, 'I am much too terrified of putting all my eggs in one basket and doing one thing, getting involved in one thing, then it being lost. I dare say a Freudian analysis would suggest that someone took something away from me as a kid that I liked very much; it could be as simple as that. But certainly the pattern is there.'

Perhaps for that very reason, Harold had seen fit to put some distance between Sybil and himself by September 1935. This move seems to have caused her some anxiety. On September 1, she wrote a mock-formal letter to him – her own little protest at the lack of contact between them – and put an unspecified little present in the envelope:

*Miss Evers presents her compliments to Mr Abrahams, and trusts he is in good health and has enjoyed a pleasant week out of Town. She begs to inform him that to her the week has seemed endless – and hopes he will take an early opportunity of acquainting her of his safe return. She further begs that he will accept the enclosed as a very small token of her affection and esteem, and desires to remain only ever his faithfully.*

On September 3, Sybil showered Harold with love in the form of a poem called *Gifts*, which talked of a permanence which Harold didn't feel he could promise.

I would give you Beauty
Were Beauty mine to give,
And all the happy things of Life
As long as you may live.
The glory of the sunlight,
The laughing summer hours –
The wonder lying 'neath the scent
Of hay, and sun-warmed flowers.

And you should hear the music
Of softly-falling rain,
And watch the ever-changing light
And shadow on the plain.
And I would give you starlight,
With the pale moon above,
And gentle peace, and quietness –
And love.

This created anything but a sense of peace in Harold. The poem was beautiful, but love terrified him. He wondered whether any two people could love each other for ever. His parents hadn't. Sybil and her first husband hadn't. Harold and his first fiancée hadn't either.

Abrahams wrote from personal experience when he later voiced his concerns to Sybil:

*God, suppose our love, my love just peters out like that? You know that hopeless feeling that you can't prevent love just vanishing.*

Harold felt ill-equipped to deal with romantic intensity. Memories of the impermanence of his love for Christina came flooding back. Harold and Sybil had also begun to talk about marriage; but deep down the idea made Harold want to run for the hills – or even Nazi Germany.

Yes, his determination to reach the 1936 Olympics in Nazi-run Berlin was absolute. He had missed Los Angeles; and he wasn't going to miss another Games.

Professional and personal pressures were growing by the day. Something had to give.

CHAPTER SEVEN:

# The BBC Turns on its Jew

Harold Abrahams thought the Olympic movement could persuade Adolf Hitler to tone down Nazi Germany.

It sounds ridiculous now. But back in 1935, no one was quite sure how evil Hitler was. By then, however, he had already been in power for two-and-a-half years, and the Dachau concentration camp was already open. Jews and any other groups who disagreed with the Nazi regime were being hit hard. And even though the Holocaust was still a few years away, the climate in Germany was disturbing.

Nevertheless, Harold argued his case to his bosses in British athletics, as though there were a realistic prospect of taming Hitler by letter. Writing to appeal for reason in the run-up to the Olympics; that was the way to achieve meaningful diplomacy, he decided.

*I fully appreciate the very natural reluctance which athletic bodies feel in 'meddling with politics' as it is sometimes put. But I believe that the more liberal elements in Germany would greatly welcome an opportunity of reversing the present policy of oppression, and I think it would provide an attractive weapon for the present regime to be able to mitigate the present extremity without the appearance of climbing down. To be able to give as a reason for generosity the upholding of the Olympic ideal, would provide a world-wide gesture which might very well appeal to those in authority. And of course if Herr Hitler was able to make some concession, the effect in Europe would be tremendous. I don't want to exaggerate, but such a gesture might literally result in more genuine co-operation with Germany in disarmament and allied problems.*

*I know full well that it is said that the Olympic Games should keep clear of politics, but if I rightly understand the fundamental principles which underlie our enthusiasm for international sport, it is that we have here a means of emphasising the similarities between nations, and we are, I think, shutting our eyes to reality, if we believe that the mere organisation and support of such institutions as the Olympic Games, constitutes the end of our duty in this matter. Quite legitimately the common bond of sport can be used to ameliorate international relationships, and unless all our profession that the Olympic Games are a good thing is so much eyewash, a body such as the British Olympic Association can legitimately regard it as within its provinces to point out that racial and religious prejudices such as exist in Germany today tends [sic] to undermine the good which sport hopes to achieve.*

*I naturally feel very strongly that the total negation of all liberty in Germany is a deplorable thing, and I believe that a dignified appeal to Herr Hitler, taking the form of a request and not a protest, would tend to do much more good than many people imagine or even hope.*

*If such a request could come from the I.O.C. [International Olympic Committee] representing all nations, it would of course be far better than one from the B.O.A. [British Olympic Association], but I hope that the Council will feel it right and desirable to do something.*

Everyone was weighing up how to deal with Berlin 1936. The BBC knew it would be no simple task, ethically or logistically, to mount their first ever outside broadcast of an Olympic Games from Nazi Germany. That is why they had started planning almost a year early, with Abrahams soon prominent in their considerations. The question was this: who would be the main British voice of the Games, the man with the microphone for the showpiece track and field events? In early September 1935, it was clear that Harold Abrahams was the favourite, though even he had expressed the fear that his Jewish heritage might complicate matters in Nazi Germany.

Looking ahead to the following year's Olympics, Seymour Joly de Lotbiniere, the BBC's Outside Broadcast Director, advised the organisation's Foreign Director:

*We shall probably want a number of afternoon running commentaries, beginning on Monday, August 3, and ending on Friday, August 7. They would be quite short, and we should want Harold Abrahams to do them. In any event he will almost certainly be going over for the Games, but he feels that for racial reasons he might be able to get better facilities if he were recognised as our representative and not as a mere private spectator. I gather that I can reassure him as to any possible victimisation, although perhaps you would explore a little in the meantime to make certain as to this.*

Beneath this typed memo was a note, handwritten after a meeting of the BBC's Programme Board. It read rather more ominously, 'Prog. Board decided better to leave the Abrahams question until we were justified in predicting what the situation would be next August.'

But there was no doubting his quality. And in November 1935, he seemed to be winning the BBC executives over.

'By the way. we have a record of Abrahams doing a commentary at the White City. He is very good,' one told Lotbiniere in a memo – as if Harold's boss didn't know it already. The word 'very' was underlined.

But there was a wider question being debated at the time: should the British and American Olympic teams go to the Berlin Games at all? Many in the free world already felt that collaboration with the Nazi regime would do far more harm than good. Across the Atlantic, such feelings were running particularly high.

On December 3, 1935, Madison Square Garden played host to strong protest at American participation in the Berlin Games. Hitting back at those who insisted the Olympic ideal was noble and untouchable, the American Federation of Labor had stated:

'There is nothing noble in the persecution by sixty million Germans of six hundred thousand Jews.'

Sadly, it wasn't just Hitler who was beginning to see the Jews as a problem.

On December 6, 1935, Cecil Graves, the BBC Programme Controller, wrote the following extraordinary memo:

*The point about this is, of course, that Abrahams is a Jew. He is our best commentator on athletics. Apparently if we are prepared to come out into the open and label him the BBC commentator for the Olympic Games, he is quite ready to go to Germany. The question arises as to whether we should do this. We all regard the German action against the Jews as quite irrational and intolerable and on that score we ought not to hesitate, but should we, as between one broadcaster and another, put aside all views of this kind and take the line that however irrational we regard another country's attitude to be, it would be discourteous to send a Jewish commentator to a country where Jews are taboo?*

With breathtaking nonchalance, it was decided to hand over the entire question of Harold Abrahams' presence at the Berlin Olympics to the Nazis. If Hitler's regime said that Abrahams the Jew was welcome as the BBC's official man, then all would be well. If the Germans didn't approve, then the BBC were not going to cause a controversy. After all, Cecil Graves reasoned, it simply wouldn't do to offend the hosts on a point of principle.

Six days later, on December 12, a seemingly jubilant Harold wrote to his BBC boss to make it perfectly clear that no such offence would be caused, and there was no element of risk in sending him officially. The way Abrahams had secured this confirmation seems truly extraordinary even today.

My dear de Lotbiniere,

It will interest you to know that last week I had an interview of nearly half an hour with Herr von Tschammer und Osten, and among other things he gave me his personal assurance that I would be welcome in Berlin next year at the Olympic Games. I gave him my personal undertaking that I would not disclose to the Press the fact of our interview, so that you will appreciate that the information given to you is confidential !!!!!!

Yours ever,

Harold M. Abrahams.

Hans von Tschammer und Osten was Hitler's Reich Sports Führer, whose organisation of gymnastic displays at Nazi rallies promoted Aryan superiority. This was the man who went on record saying, 'Sport is a way to weed out the weak, the Jewish and any other undesirables.' He also played a major role in excluding non-Aryan competitors from the German team for the Olympic Games.

It seems amazing that Harold could be so blinkered, so focused on his own ambition to get to the Games, that he would see fit to associate with such a man. Though the Holocaust hadn't begun, the writing was on the wall – quite literally – for German Jews, whose shops were already being boycotted and vandalised. It was no secret in England that the Jewish community in Germany was already being persecuted.

The idea that Abrahams wished to appease such an individual and give him any kind of 'personal undertaking' seems distasteful in hindsight. And it was only a measure of the Nazi desire to project a positive image abroad that von Tschammer und Osten was prepared to give a Jew so much time.

But before we condemn Harold outright, it should be acknowledged that he had also sought advice at the highest level of the British Government. 'I had met Sir Robert Vansittart, who was head of the Foreign Office, at Sir John Simon's house, and I asked if I could go and see him and talk about it at the Foreign Office and he advised me that the right thing to do was go [to Berlin].'

On December 16, Stephen Tallents, the BBC's first Director of Public Relations came out strongly against sending Abrahams to the Games:

*I am inclined to think it would be wise not to send Abrahams to the Olympic Games. I noticed the other day that the American Games authorities had only by a small margin agreed to participate in the Games at all – as a result, I imagine, of the restrictions alleged to be imposed in Germany upon the training and entry of German athletes, a question which was dealt with a week or two ago in two long articles in the Manchester Guardian.*

The paper argued that, since Jewish athletes were being denied the same opportunities as their Aryan counterparts, participation 'means endorsement of all the injustices, discrimination and tyranny under which German sport now suffers and which is directly opposed to the Olympic ideal.'

By sending Harold, a man of Jewish origin, the BBC was going to cause itself trouble. Either he would fall foul of antisemitism, or be manipulated for the purposes of Nazi propaganda. Tallents added: 'There are so many possibilities of friction in the situation that I feel it would be wiser to avoid the risk. There is even the minor danger that if Abrahams went, and were courteously received, the Germans would make capital out of their courtesy, as showing that their ways with the Jews were misrepresented.'

By New Year's Eve, Harold's hopes of going as the official BBC man had been all but dashed. Graves wrote: 'I brought this up at Control Board this morning and it was very generally felt that we should not send Abrahams out as our commentator to the Olympic Games. The name of Rudd was suggested instead.'

Nearly sixteen years after they had first met on the track for Oxford and Cambridge at the Queen's Club, it seemed that Bevil Rudd and Harold Abrahams were still competing for the big prize. Not for the first time, Rudd had taken a commanding lead.

CHAPTER EIGHT:

## Breakdown on the Road to Berlin

Realising that the mood had changed among his BBC superiors, it didn't take Seymour Joly de Lotbiniere long to start dancing to the official tune. He swiftly informed his bosses that he too had changed his mind on the thorny issue of Harold Abrahams.

*I have had the opportunity of talking unofficially with someone closely connected with the German Embassy. He was reluctant for me to pass on anything that he said, but I think you should know that his opinion about Abrahams and the Olympic Games was that it would be definitely impolitic for us to send Abrahams as our official commentator, but that there would be nothing unwise in using him if he was out there.*

Some will say that Abrahams should never have considered putting himself up for Berlin; that he should have taken a stand on behalf of his fellow Jews instead. The fact was, however, that Harold didn't consider himself to be a Jew anymore – only a person of Jewish origin. Abrahams had become a Christian; and even if he wasn't a devout Christian either, people were missing the point. He didn't want to be restricted by his roots, or by any kind of racial or religious stereotyping. He was Harold Abrahams; unique and irrepressible. And he was going to Germany.

He quickly approached the British Olympic Association, to ensure that he could travel to Berlin as an assistant manager to the team. That guarantee would keep alive his hopes of broadcasting from Berlin as a 'guest expert'. Yet everywhere he looked, in his personal life and career, there was confusion and frustration.

Whether the discouraging news from the BBC laid him low, or whether the acute anxieties of his on-off relationship with Sybil finally got the better of him, poor Harold was admitted to hospital. And his health problems, seemingly more mental than physical, brought matters to a head in his personal life. In a make-or-break moment, Harold and Sybil realised they faced a straight choice: either they would have to put their faith in each other or go their separate ways. Living in limbo wasn't doing either of them any good. Harold would have to overcome his aversion to commitment, grasp the nettle and pop the question; or else risk living the life of a bachelor forever, with the very real possibility that he would die a lonely old man.

For the second time in his life, Harold proposed to the woman he loved. For the second time, that woman accepted. This time it was going to be different – or at least Harold hoped so.

As for Sybil, she was happy from the moment she left the hospital, engaged to be married. In fact, she was hardly home before she sent him a typically upbeat note.

It was short and to the point and read quite simply:

*7.30.*

*Feeling energetic I walked here from Hampstead Hospital. Hope you've had a good afternoon, darling, and will sleep well. I'm feeling grand!*

*S.*

On February 19, 1936, mindful that Harold's doctors had advised the couple to tone down their romance, Sybil wrote the following amusing note to Abrahams from her West London base. Harold was out of hospital by now, because the letter was addressed to 'Harold Abrahams Esq, 29 Abercom Place, N.W.8'. Sybil had clearly broken the news of their engagement to her parents a few days earlier.

*Wednesday. 19.2.36 Watcher, Mate.*

*Hope you're feeling better? I heard from my Mamma this morning – a bit cold and cautious, but otherwise all right. She expanded rather more in a letter to Mary! [Sybil's sister]*

*Hope this finds you as it leaves me – in the pink.*

*Bless You. S*

On the very same day, Sybil's father wrote to Harold with more warmth than her mother was initially willing to show, giving the engagement his blessing. Now it was official.

Under these new and seemingly definitive circumstances, it was time for Harold to try to put his psychological problems behind him. There was a future with Sybil to fight for; and there was an Olympic Games to prepare for. He still had to satisfy himself that he would be doing the right thing by going to Nazi Germany. But he had a point to prove, a last laugh to enjoy over anyone who treated Jews shabbily. It had been that way since Repton. And even though he didn't identify as a Jew anymore, he had never forgotten his family roots. How could he forget, when he had never quite shaken off the inferiority complex that antisemitism had given him as a youngster? But he wasn't ashamed of his Jewish origins, far from it. By doing things well – better than anyone else – he usually found the perfect answer to the bigots.

It had worked until now, so why should the Berlin Olympics be different? The problem was that antisemitism in 1936 Nazi Germany was far crueller than anything Harold had experienced or could even imagine.

Organisations with links to the political left were the first to condemn Hitler's Fascists. Pretty soon the entire free world condemned the Führer's persecution of the Jews. But what should the free world do about it?

There was organised opposition to the idea of sending a British team to the Berlin Games. G.H. Elvin of the National Workers' Sports Association moved the following resolution: 'The AGM of the AAA is of the opinion that the spirit which prompted the organisation of the Olympic Games cannot be forwarded by participation in the 1936 Olympic Games in Berlin, and instructs the Association to withdraw its support, and withhold the necessary permission for a permit to participate.'

Harold argued against this, though he acknowledged that the matter had given him no little concern. He approached it, he said, as an Englishman who had been fortunate enough to represent his country at two Olympic Games, as a man who had enjoyed working with his athletic colleagues for over ten years on the AAA, and 'as a man of Jewish origin'. He argued the case for Olympic participation like this:

*I know there is not a single person in this room who does not deplore the conditions in Germany today: but in spite of these conditions, I ask myself whether it is ultimately in the best interests of world sport and better world relationships that the AAA should pass the resolution and withdraw from the Games. We must remember that the International Olympic Committee, the body solely responsible for the Games, has, rightly or wrongly, decided that it is still the right thing to hold the Games in Germany. This body is entrusted with the observance of the Olympic Charter. We must remember that the British Olympic Association, the body responsible for Olympic matters in this country, has decided to support the Games. I have no delusions about the situation in Germany today; and if I had been born in Germany, knowing myself as I do, I doubt if I should be alive today.*

With these words, Harold was admitting that he was so opinionated and outspoken that he would have found it impossible to stay silent as a persecuted German Jew. His objection to the Nazi regime would probably have resulted in his death. However, this dramatic admission didn't change his position on the Berlin Games:

*I still think the right thing is for us to show the German people what Great Britain believes to be real sport. After all, in my opinion, to isolate an individual because his behaviour does not meet with your approval never ultimately achieves anything. Countries are only collections of individuals and to isolate Germany will never achieve what we ultimately want, namely, the furtherance of these ideals in sport – absolute freedom for all to participate – in which we all believe.*

*With most of the facts which Mr Elvin has put forward in support of his proposition we must all agree, but I nevertheless do not believe that any real good will come if this resolution is adopted; on the contrary, I believe that it will do harm.*

Seeing the way the wind was blowing, Mr Elvin sought support elsewhere, and held a meeting at Shoreditch Town Hall in the East End of London under the auspices of the Workers' Circle Friendly Society. Over 2,000 people turned up, and the meeting 'unanimously adopted a resolution declaring that no time was to be lost for the cause of peace and progress if the entire annihilation of the Jews in Germany was to be prevented'.

History, of course, lends more weight to Mr Elvin's argument than that of Harold Abrahams. And the idea that the health of world sport was more important than the health of millions of Jews under Nazi rule seems ridiculous now. Yet Abrahams was adamant that he was doing the right thing, even when he was asked by the *Jewish Chronicle* to defend his decision to fraternise with Hitler's Minister of Sport.

Abrahams admitted that he had shaken hands with von Tschammer und Osten, and insisted he was not ashamed of it. He didn't think boycotts ever did any good, but he was deeply uncomfortable with the idea that people thought he was being treacherous, or that he was wilfully causing hurt to Britain's Jewish community. That was the last thing he wanted. He had been invited to accompany the British team to Berlin and he had accepted the invitation. If, however, he could be convinced that such action would do more harm than good to German Jewry, he insisted he would not go. And he gave that assurance in all seriousness, he said.

Yet no one ever could persuade him that going to Berlin would harm the cause of German Jews. He remained determined to go, even when it emerged that he would not be the BBC's official commentator. His private misgivings were not enough to change his mind. He admitted later that he had viewed the prospect of Berlin 'with a good deal of misapprehension, unhappy about it really, because that was the height of antisemitism in Germany; when I say "the height", that's not a very good description because it became much worse. And although I hadn't been a practising Jew for years, I was very uneasy about going at all.'

Not uneasy enough to pull out, though.

Later he reflected, 'I took [the Foreign Office] advice and was subjected to a lot of criticism, which I absolutely understand. Whether anybody could have had any effect on the Nazis, one doesn't know. I mean, if the world had been courageous enough to say "no Olympics," would it have had any effect on the political situation?'

The compromise that Abrahams made with his conscience was this: he promised himself that, while in Berlin, he would make some kind of personal protest against Hitler's Nazi regime. He didn't know precisely what he was going to do; it might be something quite small, or something more widely noticeable. But one way or other, he planned to make a stand.

He told his fiancée Sybil of his intentions, and this worried her greatly. Sybil soon wrote to him about a confidential chat she'd had with a friend who had just been to Berlin and felt that she understood the psyche of the average German.

*She gave it as her opinion that a protest such as you have considered would make no impression at all. The answer would simply be 'You cannot possibly appreciate our difficulties.' She also said that the people themselves were not inimical – and could not be held responsible for what their leaders did.*

Sybil knew just how fragile Harold was; and she wanted him to focus on their wedding. The stability of marriage would surely be more beneficial than some hair-brained showdown with one of the world's worst tyrants. She hoped to marry Harold quietly and spontaneously somewhere, perhaps even before the Berlin Olympics.

*My lovely "wedding dress" has at last arrived from Rugby, so now I really am complete, and can be ready to come off at a moment's notice! If possible, I should prefer the "moment" to be 48 hours – or 24 would do! – as I should like to get my hair done.*

Harold was torn between a desire to please Sybil and an urge to displease Hitler.

When a Special General Meeting of the Amateur Athletic Association was called to discuss further the possibility of pulling Britain out of the Olympics. Abrahams made himself absent. It was decided to go – in the vague hope that someone might talk some sense into the Nazi regime while the sporting world was Hitler's guest.

## CHAPTER NINE:
# Harold's Chance to Shoot Hitler

Harold and Sybil couldn't be happy together or apart. It was enough to send anyone to the edge of madness. Yet Harold would soon have to cope with Nazi Germany too. He was to travel as a freelance journalist, with a vague managerial role for the British Olympic team when time allowed. He was confident that he would be accredited by the Germans; but there was no guarantee he would be respected or left alone by the Jew-haters.

On July 2, 1936, the servile BBC gave their German hosts the names of the men they had chosen for staff duty in Berlin. They were Mr Alan Wells, a member of the News Department, and Tommy Woodroofe of Outside Broadcasts. Woodroofe was to be in charge of the pioneering "live" Olympic commentaries – and pick commentators as he saw fit. It might help if they weren't Jewish, he must have sensed.

Sybil accepted a late invitation to travel to neighbouring Austria with opera friends. They would stay at a lakeside hotel just outside Salzburg and go into town for the music festival. Hitler's shadow stretched to his native Austria too, as Sybil would soon find out.

It was a heavy-hearted Harold Abrahams who boarded a train bound for Berlin with his good friend Evelyn Montague, former Oxford rival and GB team-mate from the 1924 Olympics. Harold wouldn't see his beloved Sybil for weeks; and he didn't know what awaited him at the end of his journey. Still aware of his own mental fragility, he was pleasantly surprised by the way he adapted. He wrote to Sybil, 'After a good dinner and a lot of athletic chat with Monty practically all signs of gloom dispelled.'

Sybil.

Sybil had bought him a ring, as though he were now her property. You can almost feel his anxiety as he wrote, 'My love, I do like the ring. Honest. I never thought I should. Of course for a day or two it will feel unfamiliar.'

All the underlying tension probably brought on Harold's somewhat hysterical reaction to what he saw when he reached the German border. He wrote to Sybil:

*The train rolled into Germany and there are literally hundreds of Swastika flags about. I was particularly amused at the railway engines and their tenders. The tender has five Olympic circles painted – the engine a huge Swastika. I don't expect the Germans would appreciate the humour. Many people have suggested that the Olympic Games are being exploited by Germany to political ends, and the idea of Nazism dragging the Olympics after itself rather tickled me.*

It may have looked absurd, but the significance of the sinister symbolism couldn't have escaped Harold. Perhaps he and Montague preferred to poke fun at Hitler's regime, because they didn't want to consider the more serious implications of what they were seeing. These Olympics were to be nationalistic like no other. But as they reached Berlin, Abrahams couldn't deny that the German talent for organisation already pointed to a spectacular event. He added:

*We saw the Stadium from the train – most impressive – surrounded by trees. Gosh, we shan't be able to do the Games as magnificently in London, if we get them in 1940 – a matter which is most wisely not to be announced until these Games are over . . . Darling I'm going to make this job one of the best I have ever done. Curious, all the mental conflict about coming at all – I mean apart from our own problems – and once the decision is made all is relatively peaceful.*

At least there could be no confusion now. He was in Nazi Germany; there was no turning back. For her part, Sybil kept her correspondence supportive and light-hearted, knowing the pressures her partner would face. 'I am so glad you really like the ring,' she wrote merrily. And, reacting to his account of his journey, she added, 'Your descriptions of bits of it are excellent . . . Am so very glad that you will be seeing much that is new and interesting.'

Some of Harold's observations would prove portentous. On July 30, soon after arriving in the German capital, he wrote, 'We eventually got our press passes and Monty's seat is next to mine. From [the Press Bureau] we were taken by coach to the Olympic village where our team and the 5,000-odd other competitors are housed. It is incredibly well done and will doubtless serve easily for quarters for troops hereafter.'

Harold was soon very busy – and that made him feel strong, independent and happy. 'We've been hard at it all day and it completely puts London and even you right out of my mind. Six months ago the ability to live my own existence would have profoundly disturbed me. Now, thank heaven, it doesn't.'

Harold was among his own people – the world athletics community. And as a former Olympic champion, he could spot a man with even greater ability. He already suspected that no member of the Aryan race had as much athletic talent as the African-American sprinter Jesse Owens. He made a point of meeting Owens and being photographed alongside him in Berlin's Olympic village.

Olympic legends:
Harold Abrahams and Jesse Owens.

And Harold later explained why he considered Jesse to be extra-special: 'In the year previously, the incomparable Jesse Owens had, in the course of an hour, set up world records for 100 yards, 220 yards, 220 yards hurdles and long jump – the latter went with a leap of 26ft 8¼in which remained for 25 years.'

Now he could watch the great man go through his paces at close quarters. 'Owens was lovely to watch,' he added. 'Jesse just seemed to float down the track.' Having met Owens and confirmed he was in perfect mental and physical shape for the challenge ahead, Abrahams must have sensed what would unfold when the Games got under way. And he couldn't wait to see Hitler's face when it did. He would be close enough to do so. And Harold already realised just how sinister Nazi intentions were at these Games, and how badly the impact of Owens was needed. Later he explained:

*The atmosphere at the Berlin Olympic Games was something new and unpleasant. It was the determination to win, the determination that Germany should come out of the Games as the conqueror, which spoilt the fun in Berlin in 1936. It was quite obvious from the moment one arrived in Germany, that Germany considered 1936 an occasion to advertise herself. In Antwerp, in Amsterdam, in Los Angeles, in Paris, there was no sense of national arrogance but only of honour being paid to the Olympic Games themselves. Germany seemed to leave this honour on one side and claim the Games as a national occasion.*

The Nazis had hijacked the Olympics with their swastikas. Hitler's presence whipped the vast crowds into a frenzy.

Later Abrahams wrote, 'Hitler attended the Games several times and made it obvious to everyone that he was only interested in Germans winning.' At the time, under scrutiny of censors in Berlin on the first day of competition, Harold described the German wins like this: 'The German crowd were roused to the height of enthusiasm when in the presence of Herr Hitler they gained two Olympic victories . . . And for quite three minutes thousands of Germans present yelled with unrestrained enthusiasm . . . The Stadium was packed; the track is obviously in wonderful condition, and the presentation of the events was carried out with great showmanship.'

Had Abrahams unwittingly become part of Hitler's monstrous propaganda machine, or was he simply reporting the facts? Any criticism of the Nazi regime could have rebounded on him while he was still in Germany, and he knew it. That was enough to keep his tone positive, though there is also a suspicion that part of him – the boyish sports fan – really was swept up in the sheer drama of it all.

Yet something continued to prick his conscience, even while he acknowledged the great theatrical aspect to the Games. He would later express his regret at not confronting Hitler. And from what he told his nephew Tony, he certainly had the chance because they sat only yards apart.

*Harold used to say to me that he was as close to Hitler as from here to there. He regretted not killing him. He used to say, 'What a difference it would have made if I had.' In reality though, he wouldn't have been allowed to do it even if he had tried.*

Sue Pottle confirmed that the idea had crossed her father's mind. 'He told me, "I wish I had shot Hitler." Judging by the number of times he used to say he could have shot him, I think he really felt he could or should have done something.'

Alan Abrahams, the boy Harold and Sybil later adopted, said that his father had discussed a different method of assassination, 'He told me that he wished he had a bomb in Berlin, to chuck over the railings at Hitler.'

Tony Abrahams, who did become a war hero, took it all with a pinch of salt. He observed, 'I can't see Harold shooting anybody really. Harold couldn't have killed Hitler anyway.'

Maybe Harold couldn't have killed Hitler; but there were still opportunities for others to undermine the Führer's belief in Aryan superiority. Several of those opportunities fell to Jesse Owens. And fortunately he wasn't intimidated by Hitler or the fanatical German spectators. If only his sprints could have lasted longer, to make Hitler's humiliation slower and more painful. At the time, his graceful glide through the preliminary heats came and went in the blink of an eye.

Harold wrote, 'The only trouble is to watch so many magnificent achievements at the same time, which is rather exhausting. Indeed, when Jesse Owens is in action, if one looks away for a few seconds he's gone. It's a case of "That's Owens – that was".'

To the connoisseur, Owens was already standing head and shoulders above everyone else. And there was no greater connoisseur of sprinting than Abrahams. Harold was beautifully honest in his appraisal. Watching Owens sail through the heats, he wrote:

*I thanked my lucky stars this morning, and again this afternoon, that I was not born twelve years later. If I had been I certainly would never have had the proud distinction of winning an Olympic event.*

Imagining Eric Liddell as a 100m Olympic rival had created doubts in Harold about what the outcome would have been. In the case of Jesse Owens, there were no doubts – just feelings of inferiority and wonder.

He described Jesse as 'certainly the most beautiful moving human being I have ever seen tearing down a sprint track…He seems to float along in effortless precision.' He referred to 'the glorious speed with which the modest whirlwind traverses the cinder path.'

But would Abrahams be allowed to use his eloquence to describe his new friend Jesse to a BBC radio audience during the final?

## Chapter Ten:
# Creating the Future of Commentary

The BBC's decision to silence its Jew for his own specialist event represented the ultimate humiliation; a hideous conclusion to the discrimination they had exercised by not making him their official man for the Olympics.

Tommy Woodroofe's patronising account of how Harold performed in Berlin – and how the 100 metres commentary selection was made – was priceless. He described the most experienced athletics commentator in the business like this:

*Abrahams was very good, keen and always ready to learn. Husing and Henry of C.B.S. were only too ready to help (not unnaturally) and they were useful for filling in on occasions … I chose Husing for the 100 metres because I considered that he would be able to follow the race better than Abrahams. Abrahams agreed that he might have been inadequate on this occasion.*

It is hard to believe that Harold would have thought himself anything but equal to the task. He had been born for such moments – and he was in his element. His beautiful description of Jesse Owens for the readers of his newspaper would not have been so very hard to reproduce on air. Such was Owens' dominance of the event from start to finish – he won the final in 10.3 – that it wouldn't have provided the greatest observational challenge for a commentator.

Abrahams kept a recording of the 100 metres commentary from the 1936 Games. His American replacement's attempt to capture the moment was less than impressive. At one point the commentator's voice fades into crowd noise completely. It sounds as if he has forgotten to direct his words into the microphone. When a commentary is barely ten seconds long, there is no time for such an oversight. Of course, it should be remembered that these were pioneering days, and any audible commentary was something to appreciate. But would Harold have done better? Almost certainly.

What mattered to history was the offence Owens' victory caused Hitler. Albert Speer, Hitler's architect and future Armaments Minister, said his boss was 'highly annoyed', blaming Owens' 'primitive jungle antecedents' for his superior strength over 'civilised white men'.

And the Führer was further infuriated by what he saw at the long-jump pit the following day. A German jumper called Luz Long showed friendship towards Jesse Owens, even advising him on technique during competition. A grateful Owens promptly beat his rival into second place, though later praised his sportsmanship. Owens ended up with four gold medals in Berlin – he added the 200 metres and 4 × 100 metres relay to his collection. It was one more than Abrahams had predicted.

Denied his right to make a mark with the microphone as Owens stunned the world, Harold probably felt deflated. But then he was handed the opportunity to commentate on a young friend – the highly-strung New Zealander, Jack Lovelock in the 1500 metres. From the moment Lovelock had arrived at Oxford as a Rhodes Scholar in 1931, Harold had tried to help him channel his nervous energies positively. And after all the trials and tribulations Abrahams had been through thanks to his own unpredictable temperament, there was probably no better man on earth to have as your track mentor. Now here Jack was, standing on the verge of greatness; and Harold would be there to describe it all when the big moment came. Immediately, Harold was aware that he might let his emotions run away with him.

On a postcard to Sybil, by now in Salzburg, he wrote, 'Jack Lovelock got through to the final all right [and] I have every hope that he will win. If he does, I think I'll burst the microphone.'

Adolf Hitler came to the stadium especially to see the race. And among the finalists was a Nazi favourite called Fritz Schaumburg, one of the Reich's big hopes on the track. Another German called Werner Bottcher would compete to spur Schaumberg on. The scene was set as 100,000 packed the arena. It was Harold's pal Jack against the Aryan supermen and the best milers of recent years. Abrahams wouldn't have missed this for the world. In another letter to Sybil, he described the build-up to the big race that Thursday.

'I went to my broadcast pitch about 5 and at 5.10 started to give information about the 12 runners. I wonder if you heard the effort?'

She didn't, but millions of others did. One newspaper went on to describe Harold's commentary as 'the most human and dramatic broadcast ever sent out by the B.B.C.' The report added, 'For the first three laps he gave a clear description of the race, but on the fourth lap excitement got the better of him and all he could do was to cheer on Lovelock against his American rival, [Glenn] Cunningham.'

Abrahams seemed to have completely forgotten that there was a British runner out there too – Jerry Cornes. Lovelock had started slowly, and it was Cornes who led the field around the second bend. Then there was a huge cheer as Bottcher came through, setting up an inviting platform for Schaumburg. Cornes raised British hopes once more when he regained the lead after 400 metres.

A lap later, Cunningham had surged into the lead, but then the American stumbled and almost fell. He recovered and did battle with the Swede, Eric Ny. To Harold's inner delight, the Germans soon began to go backwards, destroyed by the early pace. Cunningham looked to be the chief threat to the steadily advancing Lovelock. He was a formidable opponent, yet Jack seemed focused and fearless. As the duel developed, the excitement up in the broadcasting position reached fever pitch. A transcript of Harold's commentary hardly does it justice, because it was the wild emotion behind the words that made them so unique. This is what Abrahams said as battle was joined during that final, frenetic lap.

*Lovelock's running beautifully, in perfect position . . . Lovelock's running perfectly now . . . come on Jack! Lovelock's up to second position*
*. . . Lovelock leads, 300 metres to go . . . Lovelock, come on Jack! . . . Cunningham's leading . . . no, no, Lovelock leads by three yards . . . Lovelock leads by four yards . . . Cunningham's fighting hard, Lovelock leads, Lovelock!*

By now Harold was shouting hysterically and he didn't seem to care. Back in Britain, where suppression of emotion was still regarded as a virtue, listeners to the broadcast could hardly believe their ears. But people became caught up in the excitement, hanging on Harold's every word. Abrahams brought his glorious 1500 metres commentary to a climax like this:

*Lovelock! Come on Jack, only 100 yards to go! Come on Jack, my God, he's done it! Jack, come on! Lovelock wins! Five yards to go, he wins, he's won! Hooray!*

It wasn't complicated or poetic; but it was liberating. Back in London, the BBC didn't know quite what had hit it. Where had the British runner finished? No one seemed to care anymore, but the answer was sixth. The Germans had flopped horribly in front of Hitler, Schaumburg tenth and Bottcher last. It only added to the joy. Lovelock had broken the world record to win gold in 3:47.8. That was a full second faster than the previous world record set by Bill Bonthron of America. Cunningham had come in second and an Italian called Luigi Beccali had to settle for bronze.

Harold only cared about Lovelock; and even then he was too over-come to put across all the relevant information. The listeners only cared that Jack had won – because he was the commentator's favourite. The broadcast was over.

A few moments later a dry, formal BBC voice said, 'We are now back in the studio . . . the next part of our programme is a selection of gramophone records.' The juxtaposition was priceless.

Harold had made broadcasting history with his unbridled enthusiasm. He had emerged a winner, just like his young friend. He rushed down to trackside to congratulate Jack personally. He wrote to Sybil, 'I saw him immediately after the race, gave him your love and said I knew you would be as delighted as I was.'

Had Hitler been close enough to Abrahams during that commentary to have heard the joy in the British Jew's booming voice as the Nazi favourites were humiliated? In his book *The Olympians*, Lord [Seb] Coe described Harold's extraordinary moment on air as, 'the least objective athletics commentary by an Englishman that can ever have been recorded for posterity'.

If that ecstatic, triumphant screaming was heard by Hitler and his friends as the German crowd fell silent, perhaps Abrahams had been justified in going to Berlin after all. He had allowed his soul to dance, in an era when it was still unusual to show much emotion in public. He had celebrated his humanity and individuality in a stadium built for mass-produced Aryan super-humans. That was his own little slap in the face for the Nazis. And it felt good.

It was that sheer passion for athletics drama, the driving force deep in the soul of Harold Abrahams, that helped carry the Olympic movement through its darkest times. It also brought sports commentary into a shining new era, and created a style that still captivates Olympic audiences to this day. A *Chariots of Fire* hero had found new ways to help save the soul of the Olympic Games in a year when all seemed lost.

When Harold was asked to pick the most exciting moment of his broadcasting career, it was no surprise when he picked 'Jack Lovelock winning the 1500 metres in that Berlin Stadium, where I disgraced myself as a commentator. I was doing a commentary. I spent most of the last lap shouting, "Come on Jack, come on, come on, by golly he's done it." . . . And of course, the thing one really enjoys is where one's got a particularly personal interest, and my wife and I knew Jack frightfully well, and all he'd done towards training. And of course, one really almost shares in him winning.'

It was no accident that he changed 'My God' to 'by golly' in his recollection on air. At the time of the original commentary, some listeners complained to the BBC that he had blasphemed in his excitement. On another occasion Harold admitted, 'I got into awful trouble with that broadcast because people wrote in and said how profane it was, because I said, "My God, he's done it."'

But it wasn't such a sin to be deliriously happy for another human being. You get the feeling that Eric Liddell would have forgiven his old GB teammate for what was essentially an expression of love.

When he was a guest on the iconic radio show, *Desert Island Discs* later in life, Harold revealed to the presenter, Roy Plomley why he hated the idea of being shipwrecked alone. 'I think it's ghastly. It fills me with horror, because I essentially love people. I don't like my own company very much.'

He loved his fellow athletes and he loved the next generation. And in return, Britain had loved Harold's company in those immortal seconds from Berlin. And for Abrahams, the euphoria didn't just go away straight after Jack Lovelock's race. In the early hours – at 1.50 a.m. to be precise – Harold wrote to Sybil:

*Darling, it is quite impossible to go to bed. Monty and I are so excited over Jack's win that although it happened nearly nine hours ago we have not yet recovered and the best and happiest thing is to write to my love.*

*What a day! After Jack's running yesterday we felt confident he would win. I think we have been the only two who have backed him all along . . . Jack's run was unbelievable, I forgot everything and everybody in a delirium of joy.*

Sadly Sybil had missed the iconic broadcast. 'You can imagine my

frantic efforts to get you – turning of knobs, and making awful noises!'
she wrote. But when the news of Lovelock's victory reached her in
Austria, she shared Harold's elation. 'I sent Jack a wire, and hope he got
it in time. We nearly went mad here – with excitement and delight on
hearing that he had won! Please give him my very heartiest congratulations. You must be simply delighted. I am so glad.'

## CHAPTER ELEVEN:
# Adolf, Sybil and the Wedding Day

What would Eric Liddell have thought about someone cheering
the sporting misfortune of another human being at an Olympic
Games? It's hard to imagine that Liddell would have approved, whatever
the provocation.

Maybe you had to be in Berlin in 1936. Maybe you had to be of
Jewish origin to fully understand what happened next.

If the wild jubilation of Harold's Lovelock commentary was partly a
form of protest at the oppressive nationalism of the Games, then an even
more blatant rejection of all this mechanical German posturing was just
around the corner.

A relay race at the Berlin Olympics caused a much stranger elation
in Abrahams, just before it was time to come home. Something had
been building up inside him; a disgust for the Nazi philosophy that had
polluted the Games.

Harold recalled:

*The atmosphere was extraordinary and very uncomfortable. It had a
queer effect on me. I remember myself cheering when a German girl in a
relay race, which the German team were winning, dropped the baton. I
cheered loudly, though I felt ashamed of myself and frightened too.*

We will never know how close Harold came to being hauled away for a beating. No doubt the Germans within earshot would have loved to see it happen; but with that one defiant cheer, Abrahams the Jew had made an unequivocal personal statement against Hitler's murderous regime.

The young woman whose error caused the commotion was 24-year-old Ilse Dorffeldt; and ordinarily Harold would have felt sorry for her. But he explained later, 'Of course one gets to the stage where there is hatred. One longed to see the Nazi athletes beaten in Berlin. Which is human but not very healthy.'

It was also human for Harold to stay high on the adrenalin of his personal success. He told Sybil, 'Well, this Olympic Games is nearly over. I don't remember ever such a hectic time, though I've really enjoyed it ... *The Daily Sketch* say my articles have been good and the broadcast about Jack's race seems to have created no little excitement. I was told today that John Snagge who runs part of the broadcasting of running commentaries. . . said it was the best thing he had ever heard.'

Harold's sister Dorothy had also written to tell Harold that their mother had heard the broadcast and 'was thrilled almost to tears'. And Abrahams had made good money as a freelance in Berlin. 'Please feel that you can spend a bit more than you otherwise would,' he told Sybil. 'I really would have done it for no pay at all. It is a compliment dearest to have the job of all jobs – and certainly that running commentary on Jack will be remembered always, simply because it expressed all that personal emotion.' Harold was typically immodest in his self-appraisal; but he was also right about his own impact.

He had enjoyed the Games, just as much as he had abhorred the distasteful undercurrent in Berlin. He couldn't wait to express some of his deeper concerns, and finally felt able to do that by writing to Sybil while taking the train out of Germany:

*We are now about 1½ hours from the frontier and I shall breathe a sigh of satisfaction when we get over it. Dearest, I suppose I am biased; and I'll tell you lots when we meet that will take too long to write and which in any event I deliberately refrained from writing in Germany, as most letters are opened if not all.*

Harold had looked further into Nazi Germany than most journalists in Berlin that summer dared to. He made it his business to do so just before leaving, and told Sybil:

*This morning I went on a two hours' tour of Berlin with that Jewish lawyer I met in London, and whose flat I was at one time anxious to rent for the fortnight. He is of course unable to earn a living and lives with his mother aged 65 – Heaven knows on what . . . Darling, such a refined, cultured and gentle woman, who could not be capable of any unkindness I'm sure. Lived in Berlin all her life and so proud of all it really should stand for. Talked halting English with a very pleasant accent. She told me how lucky I was to be born in England where everyone is free to say and think what we like. The iniquity of persecuting any human being like that!! Did you know the shops in Berlin had got out the flags of every nation except Deutschland? Jews not being Nationals are not allowed to fly the German flag.*

*Well dearest, I'm glad to be out of it. I've not felt really depressed because I have in the most part had so much to do – but every time people said 'auf wiedersehen' I felt 'you won't see me again while this regime lasts.'*

Sybil replied with a warning from Salzburg: 'I can understand what you must have been feeling. Letters to Austria are opened too, so be discreet, darling. One from my mother arrived opened the other day.'

~

The persecution of Jews disgusted Harold; but it did not make him feel any more fervently Jewish. In reply to a letter from a man writing a book about Jewish runners, Abrahams was quite firm in his refusal to be categorised exclusively in this way. He explained, 'With regard to Jewish National Sport, that is the "Maccabi", I am not a supporter thereof, believing that people of Jewish origin who are British subjects should play their part in British National Athletics, and not encourage a separatist movement.'

Harold had played his part in British athletics more passionately than most; and having been to Nazi Germany, there was only one thing about his sprinting career that he would have changed if he could. 'I would do it all again except that I would love to have won gold at the Berlin Olympics in 1936.' His Jewish roots were surely speaking for him there. How Harold envied Jesse Owens, for his ability to show the German people that the Aryan race was not superior after all. Abrahams would dearly have loved to illustrate that truth himself.

But could he really have challenged Jesse for gold, had they raced each other? Philip Noel-Baker, Harold's 1924 Olympic captain, thought so:

*I have always believed that Harold Abrahams was the only European sprinter who could have run with Jesse Owens, Ralph Metcalfe, and the other great sprinters from the US. He was in their class, not only because of natural gifts – his magnificent physique, his splendid racing temperament, his flair for the big occasion; but because he understood athletics – and had given more brainpower and more willpower to the subject than any other runner of his day.*

As honest as ever in his self-appraisal, Harold couldn't go along with that claim. Even in the 1970s he reflected, 'Many are the arguments as to who is the greatest sprinter of all time . . . If I had to plump for one man, it would be Jesse Owens . . . If it were possible to line up those who could claim to be the world's greatest, Jesse Owens should win. No sprinter I have ever seen was such a delight to watch.'

The task of shattering Hitler's delusions – temporarily at least – had fallen to Owens; and he had exposed German limitations beautifully. Harold observed later, 'You can't sprint straight with the weight of the Swastika on your shoulders.'

Jesse Owens had made a mockery of the Nazi philosophy – and Harold loved him for it. They struck up a friendship that stood the test of time. Tony Abrahams recalled. 'Harold was fond of Jesse Owens and they kept up the relationship even after the ['36] Games.' Abrahams bumped into

Owens occasionally, when the former Olympic champions were working at track and field meetings. The two men always enjoyed an easy rapport.

However, despite the privilege of witnessing the magic of Owens firsthand in Berlin in 1936, Abrahams made a startling confession in his old age:

*I'm inclined to think that if I could put the clock back and decide that again, I wouldn't go.*

That may have been how he felt when elderly; but it's hard to imagine a 36-year-old Abrahams – so ambitious and passionate about athletics – ever refusing to go. Nor did he favour any other boycott for the rest of his life – no matter how compelling the case. He never stopped believing in the power of sport to provide common ground for very different people.

With Berlin left behind, and Harold having shown the courage to express himself freely in an intimidating atmosphere, he returned home to contemplate one burning question: did he have the courage to get married?

Just when it seemed he was brave enough to face anything, Harold's phobia of marriage returned. He was hit by a new crisis of confidence, sparked by the separation of close married friends.

'They were so much in love – so sure,' he told Sybil, admitting that 'such a thing is apt to frighten me if I let it.'

In turmoil, Abrahams sought fresh psychiatric help. 'I am writing by this mail to Dr Suttie to resume treatment on Tuesday.'

But he remained in a state of despair about the collapse of his friends' marriage, partly because he had been best man at their wedding and was godfather to their children. He wrote to Sybil from Loughborough, where he was lecturing on the Berlin Games, and poured out his fear and confusion.

*What did disturb me was that the attraction which undoubtedly did exist has entirely gone and the thought crossed my mind, "Heavens can* that attraction absolutely go so that physical contact would be repulsive? Could it ever happen that I shouldn't be thrilled at having my little tuppence in my arms? And what then?"

Harold's wild mood swings were perfectly illustrated by the way he signed off this deeply serious letter with the following postscript:

Darling, I've lost my heart to a lovely golden-haired . . . RETRIEVER – aged ten weeks.

In a thoughtful reply from Austria, Sybil wrote:

I do know and understand how very upsetting it must be for you. I long to be with you, to talk about things sanely and sensibly, and feel most horribly far away out here. It is wretched that it should have happened when you were feeling tired and low – but I do believe that when you are less tired you will reason it out fairly, and not take so much to heart.

As to 'being so sure' and 'so much in love' at first, I have lately come to the conclusion that those who are not sure, and not too blinded by love in the beginning are 100% more likely to be successful in married life. Looking round among my friends, too, I really believe that this is so.

There is everything, darling, in being prepared to give, to work, and to wait for happiness – and in having real friendship and understanding for one's patience.

One thing, to me, is a never-ending source of wonder and joy – and that is the way in which we seem to bring out the best in each other, even in the most trying circumstances! This alone fills me with confidence – so, beloved, here's hoping!

Bless you, my dear, dear love. May you feel better – with each succeeding day, and come back feeling really fit and happy to

Your own loving Sybil

It was a wonderful letter to a troubled man, and exactly what Harold needed to hear. All the psychotherapy in the world wasn't worth a few home truths from Sybil Evers, opera singer, beauty and, it seems, dream partner for a man she brought back from the brink.

'What a perfectly precious darling you are!' wrote Harold by way of reply. 'Your complete understanding – and our knowledge that each of us wants always to give of our best and to try and work with the other – is so comforting.'

It was time for the fretting to stop and the loving to be rewarded. Harold could only achieve this if things were done spontaneously, and almost secretly – which was exactly what Sybil wanted too.

She revealed what happened next to a *Daily Mirror* reporter a few weeks later when it was too late for the press to spoil the big day.

*It was so quiet that nobody knew about it. I came back from Glasgow, where I had been singing, and Mr Abrahams met me with, 'What about getting married in two days' time?'*

*I replied, 'What about it?' – and we arranged it. Not a single member of either family was told. We had been engaged for some ten months.*

Harold Maurice Abrahams and Sybil Marjorie Evers were married on December 22, 1936 at Hammersmith Registry Office. Sybil was living in nearby Brook Green; so Hammersmith Registry Office was the logical place for a divorced woman to marry afresh. Perhaps it wasn't the most romantic wedding London has ever seen, because Harold's new wife had to be recorded on the marriage certificate as 'Sybil Marjorie Brack, formerly Evers'. While Harold could happily record that he was a 'Bachelor', Sybil had to explain that she was 'Formerly the wife of Noel Douglas John Brack, from whom she obtained a divorce.'

But there was still a strangely romantic strand to the wedding, revealed by the daughter Harold and Sybil later adopted.

Sue Pottle explained, 'My mother always told me that her wedding ring was made of gold clippings taken from my father's Olympic winner's medal.'

That might not have been every woman's idea of a romantic gesture, but Sybil knew what it meant; how Harold was still trying to give her the very best of himself.

No one could spoil the wedding day – the simple climax to a very complicated courtship. Only the fridge in their new home tried.

Sybil explained, 'The only celebration we fixed was a bottle of champagne at lunch, alone together, at our flat. When we got there, after our wedding, we found the wine had frozen solid. It had been put in the refrigerator the night before. So we thawed it – and celebrated.'

The story broke in the *Daily Mirror* of Tuesday, January 12, 1937, under the headline, 'Olympic Runner Wed Secretly to Opera Singer'. There had been no honeymoon at that stage because, as the paper pointed out, 'Miss Evers is playing the leading part in *The Lily Maid*, the new opera by Rutland Boughton which opens at the Winter Garden Theatre tonight.'

Later they honeymooned in Finland – around one of Harold's athletics meetings. That's when the long-suffering Sybil must have realised that she would always have to share Harold Abrahams. But there was never a dull moment in their life together. The irrational fears of one very highly strung former Olympic athlete proved groundless. Their love did not die. Harold and Sybil remained happily married – until death did them part.

CHAPTER TWELVE:

# Marriage and Machine Guns

Eric Liddell had beaten Harold Abrahams to it. As on the track, so in matrimony. And as with Harold, it had been a long and tricky journey to the altar.

Eric had met and even taught a girl called Florence Mackenzie at Sunday school in Tsientsin, China back in 1926. Florence was from a respected Winnipeg family. She was the daughter of Mr and Mrs Hugh Mackenzie, who were based at the Honan China Mission of the United Church of Canada. They lived in Tientsin too, where Mr Mackenzie was also treasurer of the United Church Mission. There was no question of Eric ever offending such respected people or abusing his position.

Gradually, Eric had watched Florence blossom into an attractive young woman. By the time she was seventeen, Eric's feelings towards her had begun to change. By then she was helping the younger ones at Sunday school, playing the organ and piano, quietly becoming a central pillar of his existence. Before long, Eric realised he had fallen in love, though Florence famously claimed that she had never even known they were courting, so careful was he not to cross the line.

Liddell was ten years older than Flo. When he asked her to marry him, she had to check whether he was serious. And one of her first thoughts was of the many women she knew of a much closer age to Eric's, who had expressed deep admiration for him, and would now hate her with a passion for effectively taking him beyond their reach.

Eric didn't care what other women thought. He had met the person he wanted to spend the rest of his life with. Unlike his tentative time with Eileen Soper, this courtship of Florence Mackenzie had left him in no doubt whatsoever of his feelings.

There's a glorious and joyful photograph of Eric and Florence at what looks for all the world like their own wedding. In fact, they're

Handsome couple: Eric and Florence –
best man and bridesmaid at a 1930 wedding.

acting as best man and bridesmaid to friends. But it might just be the happiest Eric Liddell ever looks on camera in his entire life. And young Flo seems swept away by the romance and magnificence of the occasion. Love and excitement are in the air – you can feel it down the ages. Eric is immaculate and elegant, holding a top hat in his right hand. Florence is glamorous and statuesque, her poise just perfect in a beautiful, flowing dress and extravagant hat.

Their own engagement was announced in the first week of July 1930. But it would be several years before they were married. At first, Florence's chosen professional path was the priority. She returned to her family's native Canada to train as a nurse. But Eric was not about to let continents come between them. He sailed to Canada during that furlough between 1931 and 1932. His break from Asia would otherwise have been spent entirely in Britain. But the voyages to North America were worth it. Their love was renewed; their bonds remained strong. Eric and Flo may only have seen each other twice between mid-1930 and early 1934, but their love wouldn't die.

Florence returned to China and married Eric Liddell at Tientsin's Union Church on March 27, 1934 – the same year Harold Abrahams met his Sybil back in London.

Time was precious. Time was also short – particularly for Eric. There was barely a decade left for him on God's earth. Florence would go on to live a long and happy life, though sometimes bitter-sweet. This was the woman who, almost half a century later, would tell David Puttnam what she liked and found less pleasing about his iconic movie, *Chariots of Fire*. She would also turn to Ben Cross, the actor who played Harold Abrahams, and tell him: 'My husband talked a lot about you.'

Abrahams would have liked that. And you could almost imagine Harold and Eric meeting somewhere in London in the late 1930s, each man asking the other how married life was treating them. The golden heroes could even have shared a few jokes about how much time they had taken to get hitched. Sadly, that reunion of two Paris greats probably

Courtesy of Eric Liddell Community

Their turn: Eric and Florence get married.

never happened. But make no mistake, Abrahams and Liddell had both undoubtedly met the right person and chosen well.

Florence faced more hardship than Sybil in her married life. She settled down with Eric in China and they had a couple of children, Patricia and Heather. But war had swept across the Far East long before tragedy began to unfold in Europe. Japan had invaded China – and now they took Tientsin. Mercifully, Liddell's family were staying in the slightly safer Peitaiho when that happened. Eric had gone even further afield to work as a missionary in the increasingly perilous Siaochang, basing himself at the hospital where his brother Rob had been working.

Liddell was brought into the hospital community at Siaochang in a way its administrators hoped would attract the least attention. Frances McAll, whose husband Kenneth was the main western doctor there, knew Liddell's purpose and how his arrival was camouflaged.

She wrote: 'At this time Eric Liddell, the famous Olympic runner, had come to Siaochang to help with the evangelistic work. As this side of the Mission work was not appreciated by either the Japanese or the

Communists, Eric was given the title of hospital business manager and in fact, did help Ken with this side of his work as well as doing his own – and shared a house with Ken.'

Ideally, Liddell wanted to be sharing a house with his wife. Neither Eric nor Florence were the type to be consumed by fear, despite the increasing violence all over China. Indeed, the strength of Flo's character for one so young was undoubtedly a major reason why Eric had fallen in love and decided to marry her. It was no surprise that Florence wanted to join her husband in Siaochang. She was only thwarted when the London Missionary Society, effectively Eric's employer, instructed her to stay put because travel carried too many risks.

These were dark times; and there was much testing work for Eric and those around him to do beyond familiar boundaries. The hospital, for example, was the only one practising western medicine in an area the size of Wales, with a population of about ten million to serve. Liddell relished the challenge of being somewhere he could make a difference and make himself heard.

'At no time have we had such a great opportunity as we have now. Every home is open to us, the people feel that we are working with them, that we are helping them, and they will listen to our message anywhere,' he reasoned.

A photo survives of the two Liddell brothers out in the field in China during the turbulent late 1930s. If they look as though they have seen too much, it's because they have. And there were moments when Eric must have wondered if he would ever see his wife again.

Courtesy of Eric Liddell Community

Rob and Eric unshaven – Siaochang 1938.

Liddell's most perilous challenges seem to have been faced with another accomplice, though. Ken McAll possessed a bravery bordering on the reckless; and he often seemed to require Eric by his side. They would leave the protective environment of their living quarters, and find the danger that lurked in the open countryside. There was an unfortunate encounter with children who had grown old before their time in the chaos of Japan's invasion of China. Kenneth and Frances McAll both told the story of how close Ken and Eric came to being mown down by child soldiers:

Frances explained: 'Eric Liddell, the famous Olympic runner had left his teaching job to work as an evangelist in Siaochang. He joined Ken, the only doctor, in going out after a battle to look for any wounded there might be.'

Ken added: 'I thought something was wrong. The Japanese seemed to have disappeared. They had come from the fighting area towards us. They were carrying all their wounded on carts at a walking pace going south.

'I thought that I should go seek the wounded. I asked Eric Liddell, who was a manager of the hospital, if he would come with me. We loaded our bicycles with Red Cross stuff and set off...'

Frances explained, 'They used bicycles to travel on unmade roads and across fields. Eric was ahead when Ken had the sudden thought to get off his bike.'

Ken recalled, 'We had gone probably ten miles, and maybe I was feeling weary, pushing against the mud. I thought that we should go a little slower. I shouted to Eric, who was in front, "Let's go slowly!" He was athletic, as you know, and he was once a famous runner... So we both slowed down, and exactly at that moment there was a burst of machine gun fire that went right between our bicycles.'

Frances described what happened as her husband dismounted. 'As he did so, a hail of machine gun bullets passed between him and Eric. Neither was hit.'

A natural impulse when you come under heavy fire is to run. And Eric Liddell was a world-beater when it came to running. But as with

Sundays in Paris, this was another day in his life when Liddell chose not to run. And for the second time in less than twenty years, that decision eventually worked in his favour.

Their attackers were not experienced military campaigners from Japan; they were Chinese resistance fighters. They were jumpy and trigger-happy, and they would surely have shot Eric and Ken had the British pair tried to run off. Ken remembered these life-or-death moments vividly.

*We got off and put our hands up and some little boys came rushing across, trembling and fearful; they didn't know who we were. They each had pistols. Far behind them was this little mound with their machine gun. They then led us off further in the direction that we were going.*

Frances added, 'As often happened, they were taken off to the guerilla headquarters but this time, instead of being interrogated, they were welcomed for their help and the medical supplies they had brought.'

❧

Eric Liddell would sometimes see tangible results in return for this kind of heroism. A Buddhist temple twenty miles away was harbouring a badly wounded Chinese soldier. When Eric reached the location, a remarkable man helped him prepare the stricken patient for the return journey to the hospital. Almost as seriously wounded, this second individual had been the victim of a botched Japanese beheading.

Frances McAll knew what had happened. 'One man, Lee, was brought in, with his head partially severed from his body, on a springless mule cart. Lee, press-ganged on his way home to join the guerillas, found himself with his unit who had been hiding in a bunker, surrounded by Japanese. They were all lined up to be executed after digging their own grave. But Lee, at the end of the line, refused to kneel. The Japanese took an only partially successful swipe at his neck...'

Thanks to Liddell's mercy mission, Frances explained, 'Lee was able to live a productive life before making a bid for freedom. Lee took refuge in Ken's house, where he did odd jobs, painted beautiful pictures and acted as language teacher. When Siaochang was evacuated, Lee travelled as one of the servants with the departing missionaries, and escaped undetected by Chinese communists or Japanese whom he feared equally.'

Liddell had saved the artist's life, and it was typical that Eric had put the safety of others before his own. On this occasion there was an unexpected reward for that unselfishness. And one Scottish newspaper reporter soon heard Eric speaking about this incident first-hand:

> *Mr Liddell told how [the] severely wounded Chinese soldier whose life he had saved sought to express gratitude by painting a number of pictures which he gave to him. The hope of this man was that these pictures might be sold to friends of the cause in Britain, and so help the work of the society to which he owed so much. Through these pictures, Mr Liddell went on to state, he expected to raise £200 for the work.*

Despite some notable, morale-boosting successes, the violence in China was only getting worse. And while he remained in the thick of it, even Eric was on edge at times. When the intrepid Liddell and McAll were next set to leave on a death-defying rescue mission, Kenneth was offered a pistol before departure. McAll decided that if he was armed, he might at least feel he had some sort of protection against potential killers. The well-meaning donor was only trying to help; and McAll was ready to accept the weapon gratefully.

'Don't touch it!' said Eric Liddell, who had witnessed this offer and was appalled by the idea. 'If you have that in your pocket, you will depend on it rather than God and I would refuse to travel with you.'

This was the first of only two occasions when Ken McAll saw Eric Liddell annoyed about anything. Liddell wasn't afraid to die. But if he was going to die, he wanted to be doing God's work when death came. He didn't want to be caught up in some exchange of fire involving someone from his own side. If they were meant to live, it was because God would protect them – not a pistol.

~

Yet the world had become such a dark place by the end of the decade that not even Eric Liddell felt he could remain a man of peace in the face of such evil. In September 1939, Britain went to war with Germany. Eric Liddell was due a furlough and sailed for Scotland, while Florence took the children to Canada. By the time Liddell reached British shores in November, recruitment for the armed forces was in full swing.

Eric had recently rejected a gun in favour of the power of persuasion. But as Harold Abrahams had taken rather too long to realise, there was no persuading Adolf Hitler. Like most people, Eric saw this European war as a straight battle between good and evil. He went directly to an RAF recruiting office and tried to join up.

Liddell was asked what experience he had as a pilot. He had to admit he had none whatsoever. The painful irony was that Liddell's great friend from the 1924 Olympic Games, Arthur Marshall, could and would have trained him for just such a role. The Marshall Flying Schools had been established before the war and were playing a vital role by now. They trained around 20,000 pilots and instructors to take the fight to Hitler in the air. When planes were damaged, Arthur even had his own repair centre at his aerodrome near Cambridge. Around 5,000 aircraft were nursed back to health in this way during the Second World War.

Since Eric lacked the pilot skills his old friend could have given him, and his offer to become a crew member in some other capacity fell on deaf ears, this visit to the recruitment office was to prove futile. Eric had to give his age as 37, which was regarded as middle-aged back then. The recruiting officer may have recognized the legendary Liddell and thought he could become a useful propaganda tool for the RAF. At any rate, he suggested that Eric could best serve his country from behind a desk. Although Liddell probably chose his words carefully, the RAF was firmly advised where they could put their desk job. He had already been through untold dangers in the violent outpost of Siaochang; and he certainly wasn't going to see out the war in an office. China beckoned once more. If Liddell wasn't to be allowed to fight an evil regime in the air, he felt he could put his fearlessness to better use as a force for good in his missionary role back home – despite the increasing dangers associated with the Japanese invasion.

Eric must have been confident there were still parts of China where his family could live relatively safely. On that basis, he was reunited with Florence and the children, after they braved a risky Atlantic crossing from Canada. Another hazardous voyage from England to China awaited the Liddell family. It would be the last great journey Eric would ever to make from the west to his beloved Far East – if the British convoy managed to dodge enemy submarines and warships.

CHAPTER THIRTEEN:

# Propaganda and Puttnam

For a man as addicted to athletics as Harold Abrahams, the war was going to cause severe withdrawal symptoms. His recent appointment as Assistant Honorary Secretary to the British Amateur Athletic Board was rendered largely irrelevant. The thrills and spills of racing were over for the foreseeable future. But there were other uses for a stopwatch. And in a letter to his old BBC boss Seymour Joly de Lotbiniere, Harold displayed a delightful sense of humour in the face of adversity. He wrote:

My dear Lobbie,

I am at present awaiting some indication from the Central Register people as to my War Work and biding my time with the A.R.P. [Air Raid Precautions].

I have to use my stopwatch, and you will be glad to hear that my time from bed on hearing the siren to the Post, including dressing and 1¼ miles by car is 5min. 20.4sec. I expect to knock a lot off this as I had to return for my false teeth, seeing that I cannot blow the whistle without them.

All the best, Yours ever,
Harold M. Abrahams

Knowing that his permanent limp ruled him out of combat, Harold was determined to undermine Hitler in any way he could. He and Sybil had already fostered a German Jewish boy, Kurt Katzenstein. He became Ken Gardner, and soon began to thrive in England under the guidance of Mr and Mrs Abrahams.

But Harold still wanted to be able to say he had done something useful for the British war machine:

*I eventually got into the Ministry of Economic Warfare, where I started a thing called the Enemy Exports Committee, which is the opposite of contraband. With contraband you automatically stop things going into a country but with this you captured things coming out from a country.*

Before long another idea came to Abrahams; a way to rally the troops. He would use his experience of Berlin 1936 to belittle Hitler in lectures he could give to British Armed Forces abroad. The aim was to highlight the sporting victories that undermined the Fuhrer at his own Games, thus boosting British morale. And so, in January 1940, having used his political contacts to secure authorisation, Harold headed for Hendon. From there he would be flown over to France to give a series of lectures, illustrated by lantern slides, to Royal Air Force units still stationed there:

*We left in a six-seater plane at 11.15 a.m. We flew into thick fog about five miles from the French coast. Eventually the pilot got his bearings, though we had to fly very low indeed. We were on occasions actually lower than the cliffs. I set off for Amiens with an RAF padre driving a Renault car. Being driven at between 80 and 90 kilometres an hour by a very indifferent performer on what seemed all the while to be the wrong side of the road, was far more frightening than flying . . . I eventually arrived at my destination . . . The audience was composed of officers and men from squadrons stationed in the vicinity . . . A picture of Hitler in the Olympic Stadium met with the kind of catcalls to be heard when the villain comes on to the stage in a pantomime.*

The overall message to the British Expeditionary Force was not lost; the Germans were far from invincible, as Jesse Owens had shown to devastating effect in Berlin four years earlier. Unfortunately, within a few months the British Expeditionary Force – including no doubt the men Harold had visited and entertained with his morale-boosting talk – were forced to retreat in desperation to Dunkirk in the face of a huge German onslaught. It would be a good many years before Harold Abrahams could venture onto the Continent again. But a brave young photographer called Leonard Puttnam did just that.

The carnage and terror of Dunkirk was enough to test the resolve of anyone – and that made Puttnam's actions even more remarkable. His efforts weren't initially appreciated, though. Winston Churchill wasn't keen on photographic evidence of chaos and death at the hands of ruthless German pilots. What he wanted captured on camera was the heroic, never-say-die heroism of the British rescue effort. This was made possible by a flotilla of small boats that headed for Dunkirk from the southern harbours of England. Those civilian boatmen were ready to risk death to get their soldiers off the Dunkirk beaches. And Leonard Puttnam was willing to take the same risk again to get the photographic record Churchill demanded.

To work skilfully with a camera in that horrific environment required nerve. Yet the best words to go with Puttnam's morale-boosting photos were crafted by a man who wasn't even there. Evelyn Montague – whose letters home from the 1924 Olympics would one day provide so much magnificent material for *Chariots of Fire* – was a phenomenal wordsmith. Harold's friend and companion for Berlin 1936 wrote this of Dunkirk:

*In the grey chill of dawn today in a south-eastern port, war corre-*
*spondents watched with incredulous joy the happening of a miracle. By*
*every canon of military science the B.E.F. has been doomed for the last*
*four or five days. Completely out-numbered, out-gunned, out-planed, all*
*but surrounded, it had seemed certain to be cut off from its last channel*
*of escape. Yet for several hours this morning we saw ship after ship come*
*into harbour and discharge thousands of British soldiers safe and sound*
*on British soil. What will happen to the rearguard is uncertain, but it is*
*certain already that the majority of the Force will be saved.*

Mercifully Leonard Puttnam, the courageous captain-photographer who had witnessed Dunkirk with his own eyes, also returned in one piece. He fell gleefully into his wife's arms, having probably wondered a few hours earlier whether he would ever see her again. What happened next led to movie history.

CHAPTER FOURTEEN:

# War Babies

E ric Liddell and Harold Abrahams agreed on one thing during World War Two: whenever possible, children had to come first.

Having fostered "Ken", Harold and Sybil also took in an Austrian Jewish refugee called "Minka". They were all living in Rickmansworth in a house called 'Whiteladies', situated near the local golf course. Unfortunately, an important building belonging to the Admiralty also stood close by, and the Germans were trying to flatten it. In September Sybil wrote to her father describing what life was like:

*We've been having nightly air raids for a week now, and two or three*
*each day as well ...The regularity with which the German planes come*
*over is quite astonishing. The warning now goes about 9.30 p.m. and after*

*half an hour we have them coming over, usually one at a time, and flying very high and out of reach of the searchlights. One night they came over exactly sixteen minutes apart . . . Then at 3.30, approximately, they finish and at 4 o'clock punctually the "All Clear" goes.*

You can just imagine Harold sitting there with his stopwatch, a part of him grudgingly admiring the discipline of the German Luftwaffe's time management. But this was a cruel kind of sport, a game that could easily end in death for those below. Sybil and Harold suffered some early near misses, as she explained:

*We've had some excitements, the worst being when a salvo of bombs was dropped on the golf course, exactly opposite our house, five hundred yards away! Luckily they were small ones – 110 pounds – and fell on soft ground, so all we heard was the rattling of doors and windows, and the sound of eight rather large fireworks, and we saw a blinding yellow flash like sheet-lightning!*

The nearest air raid shelter didn't tempt them. Sybil went on, 'Harold says nothing will induce him to leave his bed and seems to sleep very well. I couldn't sleep at first when these wretched planes came over and found the sound even penetrated cotton wool in the ears, so that, try as I would, I lay tense, listening for them. However, since Wednesday night we've been getting used to them; and their astonishing regularity seems to make sleep easier!'

~

Leaving the aerial onslaught behind, the Liddells set sail from Liverpool in August 1940 as part of a huge naval convoy. The Olympic champion and his family arrived safely in China a few weeks later. Except that nothing was safe about China anymore – and conditions were set to deteriorate further still. Within months, Eric's work in Siaochang had become impossible. Japanese attitudes towards a western presence turned from disapproving to threatening. In February 1941, Liddell was forced to return to Tientsin, along with the other missionaries. At least that meant more precious moments of comfort and togetherness for Eric and Florence; and it wasn't very long before Flo was pregnant again.

~

Across the world in London, Sybil was charged with a task that would have tested the mettle of many a man. 'I was sent out to look for an unexploded bomb which was thought to have fallen on the golf course between us and the road to the Club House. I didn't feel very brave but managed to search pretty thoroughly and found nothing, so presumably it was a mistake.'

Such were the increased responsibilities handed to women in wartime. Back in 1936, Sybil had admitted to feeling unnerved by cockroaches in Austria. Now she was steeling herself to seek out bombs on her doorstep. But Rickmansworth was still safer than central London, where Harold had been a lawyer before the war. Sybil told her father:

*You have probably heard that there have been a number of bombs on the Temple? Harold's Chambers in Elm Court have been completely demolished by a land-mine, and all his books, law notes, and some athletic records, furniture and other possessions including a stop-watch are lost. The only remaining possession is his name, still clearly visible on the door! How lucky that it happened at night, when nobody was there . . . but the law notes and records are, alas, irreplaceable.*

Harold's precious possessions were gone. Would Harold himself be next? By 5 February, 1941, the big picture looked bleak. Despite victory in the Battle of Britain the previous autumn, Harold had warned his family to prepare for the worst again. Sybil wrote to her father with a casually disturbing question:

*What do you think about the impending invasion of this country? I gather from Harold that it is thought officially to be imminent any time this month, in fact. Then, presumably, we shall be under martial law, and have to "stay put" for an indefinite and unpleasant period. It won't be nice but we shall have to try not to worry about one another, shan't we?*

Either Sybil was trying to block out the obvious implications of invasion for a man called Abrahams, or she really didn't comprehend the

inevitable consequences. Her husband was already on a list of prominent British Jews, who would be swiftly rounded up in the event of a
Nazi invasion. Rosemary Warne, Harold's friend later in life, revealed,
'He told me on more than one occasion that the Nazis had put him on
a list of British Jews to be dealt with if they invaded. He was under no
illusions about what would have happened had they invaded, because he
always said he wouldn't be here now if it had happened.'

Tony Abrahams, Harold's nephew, believes the information about
the death list was uncovered by Solly after the war. Tony said, 'My
father showed me lists of British people who had been identified by the
Germans. The Nazis had cobbled together a series of lists, not just one,
and Harold's name was there.'

For Harold, 'staying put' for any 'indefinite and unpleasant period',
as Sybil put it, would have involved a grim term in a concentration camp
before extermination.

Leonard Puttnam and his wife Marie Beatrix, whose maiden name
was Goldman, would also have had their world destroyed had Hitler
invaded. It wasn't the most stable situation for anyone to handle – let
alone a new-born baby. But later in that month of February 1941,
*Chariots of Fire* director David Puttnam arrived anyway. He noted
decades later:

*I was born exactly nine months after my father returned from Dunkirk,*
*My mother must have been pleased to see him!*

Sadly for young David, his father was not to feature in the first five
years of his childhood. The war and its immediate aftermath had to take
priority for an army photographer.

～

Later in 1941, the threat of invasion began to ease. But it was only replaced
by more intensive bombing. One of the worst-hit cities was Liverpool,
where a young boy called Colin Welland was more excited than afraid.
Welland would be the man to write the screenplay for *Chariots of Fire*
nearly forty years later. But in 1941, there was no guarantee he would live

to tell the tale of Liddell and Abrahams – or even his own childhood. He adapted to his precarious routine remarkably well, though. Nights in the shelter, mornings to assess the damage. That's how it worked.

He remembered, 'I can hear the planes now…It was all a thrill for us kids…Every morning we'd get up and see whose house had gone.'

~

For parents, the war was more frightening. Over in China, Eric Liddell was responsible for two children already; and now Florence was pregnant again. What if the Japanese tried to hurt them? His own capacity for violence was not something he wished to explore as a missionary in China. He had always controlled his temper so well, often in the face of fierce provocation. But that had been when he was the one in danger. If his wife and children were threatened, there was no telling what he might do to defend them.

'He was worried that if they took us hostage, he wouldn't be able to trust himself,' Florence explained later.

The best protection he could provide for his family – and for the integrity of the life he had chosen in China – was to ensure that his loved ones had a safer future in Toronto, Canada. He hoped he would be able to join them in time. Surely all westerners would be ordered out of China before long? Surely the London Missionary Society would make the right decision for brave men like Eric, so they could live to save souls another day? There was no guarantee. But Eric and Flo both understood what had to happen next, reluctant as she was to leave him.

Florence always insisted:

*I wouldn't have gone if it wasn't for the children. It was a very difficult decision. I didn't want to leave at all. But we were sure Japan was going to come into the Second World War. Eric could have come with us, but he didn't feel he should. I never felt his work came first. It wasn't like that at all. He just felt others were staying and he ought to as well.*

This points to how severely Eric was torn between loyalty to his family, and his sense of obligation to the local community as a missionary with medical knowledge. He knew his strength would be needed in all the suffering that was to come. His wife and children numbered four, including the unborn baby. If he stayed, he might be able to help four hundred or four thousand. Yet he was only human; and a big part of him – Eric the husband and father – just wanted to leave all the chaos behind and start over.

His sense of duty carried the day. Duty to the vulnerable; and duty to God. Patricia would always recall his final words to her:

*I remember as if it happened yesterday, my father coming with us to the dockside to see us off. I was six and Heather was four. He took me aside and said 'Patricia, I want you to be a good girl and promise me you will look after your mother and help her with the baby until I return.'*

Then Eric watched in anguish from the quayside, as his pregnant wife and two daughters sailed away. Ironically, they did so on a Japanese ship, because that was the safest way to get across the Pacific. It spoke of the shift in power and aggression during those troubled times. There was less of a threat to his family if they stuck with the invaders, because the Japanese navy wouldn't sink a Japanese ship.

Sure enough, Flo and the kids arrived safely in a saner world.

As for Eric, he was about to be caught off his guard in the most unexpected of places.

CHAPTER FIFTEEN:

# Bald Heads and Jellyfish

In August 1941, Eric Liddell took a rare moment away from the chaos to relax in the sea at Beidaihe (Peitaiho). The resort served the luckier among the population of what is now called Beijing. Missionaries also liked to gather there for a social swim. And with the women and children mostly sent to safety by now, there was increasing testosterone at play, even among the holy men. They were able to let off steam away from the pressures of their very dangerous everyday lives; and they did not hold back.

Eric enjoyed the camaraderie of these occasions as much as anyone. Having played rugby for Scotland and been to the Olympics with Great Britain, the team spirit was probably what he missed most. Splashing about in the waves with the other men was just another form of bonding. And being a such fearless, sporty individual, Eric would dive down into the cool sea and swim underwater for long periods, too.

There was only one drawback to these communal swims. Huge jellyfish seemed to enjoy these waters every bit as much as the missionaries. To avoid a nasty sting, some of these men of God armed themselves for the water. They carried sturdy wooden sticks to batter the jellyfish into submission if they came too close. Only a mighty blow from a solid plank seemed to deter these creatures. Such a whack also helped the disrupted water to carry them away.

Eric Liddell didn't seem to mind that he had lost most of his hair. Occasionally, his children had gently teased him about how his hairline had receded between reunions. He would laugh along with them perfectly happily. Baldness was generally harmless. It even made him more aquadynamic. But the way Eric's baldness was perceived on this fateful day was a different matter entirely.

As the top of his head occasionally broke the surface, Eric didn't consider what it might resemble from above or from the side. An anxious fellow missionary might have poor eyesight; and his fear could get the better of him. The unrestrained wildness of their mood in the water could tempt a younger man to dispose of any perceived threat indiscriminately. You could understand it if there was a certain ruthlessness at play. Even these days, Chinese citizens are regularly stung and hospitalized on this very stretch of water, with fatalities due to allergic reactions not unknown. Jellyfish are the enemy now – and they were the enemy in 1941. And unfortunately, Eric Liddell's

Bald head and bathing gear: Eric and Jenny in the Beidaihe resort some years before the incident. And Eric almost completely bald in 1940.

bald head bobbing in the water resembled the dreadful dome of a poisonous jellyfish.

The unsuspecting Liddell hadn't prepared for the possibility that anyone could bring a heavy wooden stick down on his crown with a swing so vicious that it might do him serious damage. Sadly, it seems that Liddell was just surfacing when the blow was struck, because it was said to have bruised his head visibly. When he came to his senses, Eric flew into a rare temper and confronted the culprit – a young man called Alex Baxter.

It may be that Liddell already found Baxters hard to like. This one had followed in the footsteps of his father – also called Alexander – to become a missionary in the land of his birth. Eric and Alex junior had that much in common. Unlike Eric's father James, however, Alexander A. Baxter had not been universally loved in China – quite the reverse. And Eric was probably aware of this, if he'd done his homework.

In his first stint in the country, as Vice-Provost of Lingnan College, Alex Baxter had refused to condemn the massacre of over a hundred protesting Chinese youths, including some of his students. A group of American faculty members urged the United States to support China's struggle against imperialism. Baxter went to Hong Kong to express the opposing view. Lingnan students found out – and accused Baxter of being anti-Chinese. He was forced to leave the college for good. Many colleagues were relieved.

In a talk he gave back in Britain a few years later, Baxter called the Chinese 'a very backward race.'

When Eric Liddell talked of underdevelopment in China, he was careful to counterbalance such remarks with love, understanding and optimism for the future. The elder Alexander Baxter showed few signs of being capable of such warmth.

That didn't prevent the experienced and fearsome Reverend Baxter from being offered – and accepting – the influential position of Chief Secretary to the China Council of the London Missionary Society in November 1933. Did he later influence the decision of the LMS to keep their missionaries in China too long, despite the Japanese entering the Second World War? It was just the sort of stubborn, intransigent position Baxter liked to adopt in a career blighted by a spectacular failure to understand changing times.

However, if Baxter did indeed lead the resistance to moving these vulnerable LMS missionaries to a place of safety, it meant he was prepared to endanger his own son, who had been ordained and sent to Northern China to work alongside Liddell in Siaochang.

So, what sort of a man was Alexander M. Baxter, who had just dealt such a forceful blow to Eric Liddell's head? At his ordination back in Cambridge, it had been suggested that 'the long, faithful and devoted service of his parents in China will afford much guidance and help him in his work.' The son of the infamous father agreed, acknowledging his 'indebtedness to his parents and teachers, who had influenced his life.' And he looked forward to what he called 'the thrill' of missionary service.

Perhaps the younger Baxter had inherited his father's air of anti-Chinese superiority – then added the thrill of the chase to his own dubious motivations. If so, this was a dangerous cocktail for Eric Liddell to be around. We must accept that Alex Baxter only accidentally assaulted Eric. But there's a sense that the inner "safety catch" – the one that prevents more mature human beings from doing such things – was not yet in his make-up. We can assume that he was guilty of careless-ness rather than any malicious intent. Nevertheless, the effects of Baxter junior's rash behaviour were grave. And poor Eric seemed to realise that something very serious had happened to his unprotected head.

'Don't you ever do that again!' Liddell yelled. 'You jolly well nearly killed me!'

At least Eric was conscious and able to shout at his fellow missionary. Observers were relieved to see he was still apparently in possession of his faculties. Yet they knew that losing his temper was something Eric rarely did in any situation, however much danger he was in.

Ken McAll said, 'It was the only time I ever saw Eric really angry.'*

McAll had literally dodged a hail of bullets with Eric Liddell a few years earlier, when their bike ride had been interrupted by machine gun fire. Ken had been told off by his friend for wanting to carry the gun he had been offered for self-defence. But he had never seen Liddell react like this.

Wisely, Baxter didn't try to argue back or excuse his actions. He was described as 'startled' during the verbal onslaught. He was also probably mortified the moment he realised his terrible mistake. Eric being Eric, he quickly forgave young Alex, who had at least tried to do some good in Siaochang. But was that the end of the matter?

Much has been made in a previous biography of Liddell's collision with a Tientsin photographer – an incident which must have taken place about a decade earlier.**

It happened on the athletics track, after a photographer from the local Tientsin newspaper attempted to get a head-on shot of the sprinter running ferociously towards his camera and tripod.

The photographer lingered longer than he should have done. The collision involved a painful clash of heads; and Eric was knocked uncon-scious. He recovered quickly enough and dismissed the incident. Were there long-term repercussions? It seems unlikely, given the many years that passed before Eric's brain took on its fatal changes.

* Page 103-104, "ERIC LIDDELL: Complete Surrender" – by Julian Wilson.
** Page 193 "FOR THE GLORY" – by Duncan Hamilton.

But Baxter's brief and brutal attack in the water may have been a different matter. It occurred just three-and-a-half years before Eric died.

Did Baxter set off a chain of events in Eric's brain that led to his deterioration? Tumours can take years to grow into something that will do visible harm, create behavioural changes and diminish physical capacity.

A case of blunt trauma to the head little more than three years before Eric's death? You do have to wonder.

A medical study in 2023 suggested we are *four* times more likely to develop a brain tumour after being hit heavily about the head. Medical researchers at the University College of London Cancer Institute, UCL Laboratory for Molecular Cell Biology and UCL Institute for Health Informatics teamed up to reach some startling conclusions, helped by external collaborators from Imperial College London. Their new look at the molecular make-up of brain cells led them to conclude that injuries to the head could cause a brain tumour called glioma.

Two years earlier, the *Journal of Inflammation Research* had also produced a paper on "The Promoting Effect of Traumatic Brain Injury on the Incidence and Progression of Glioma."

The medical profession hasn't entirely embraced these findings; and the evidence isn't universally regarded as conclusive. The human brain is the part of the body hiding more mysteries than any other. And as the 2021 study readily pointed out, many of us have taken heavy blows to the head in our lifetime without developing a tumour on the brain.

It's almost preferable to think that Eric's demise was due to a combination of bad luck and his brave decision to endure the deprivations of a Japanese internment camp. Stress, overwork and a poor diet could have contributed to Liddell's downfall once there. The idea that Eric Liddell might have died so young because his bald head looked like a jellyfish is almost too much to take. But the possibility can't be ignored.

~

Before that pivotal year of 1941 was out, the prospect of internment became practically inevitable for Eric Liddell. All that could save him from a loss of liberty would be his own escape to safety – which would mean deserting his post. He was never going to do that. Otherwise, it would take a compassionate decision by the London Missionary Society to withdraw their vulnerable people from China while they still could – and that was never going to happen either. What sealed Liddell's fate, while he tried to spread peace and love in China? Japan hit the American Naval base at Pearl Harbor, in Honolulu, Hawaii. The sheer scale of this attack is sometimes overlooked. As the base was taken by surprise that morning, the huge human cost – sustained by a nation not at war – was extraordinary. Over 2,400 people were killed – and nearly 1200 more wounded. The material damage done was also considerable. Four battleships were sunk and over 180 aircraft were destroyed. There was no way this act could be misinterpreted by the Americans, any more than there could have been any doubt about the consequences.

Eric and Florence Liddell had been right in their earlier assessment. Japan had indeed entered the Second World War, bringing the Americans in with them.

From that moment, it was clear the Japanese would make life even more unbearable for westerners in China. They would regard men like Liddell as an unnecessary inconvenience. Eric must have known his days as a free man were numbered. Within weeks, he was under house arrest.

Horrors would lie ahead; but his work on behalf of Jesus Christ was far from over. He sensed that his biggest test was yet to come. And he intended to be ready for whatever was thrown at him. Eric had already achieved something that represented the fulfilment of a dream. The Chinese had taken to calling him Li Mu Shi, which effectively meant "Pastor Liddell." Li Mu Shi was

Eric Liddell in the early years of WW2.

what the local population had also called James Liddell.

To walk in his father's footsteps was all Eric Liddell had ever wanted, from his earliest days at Eltham College. This simple mark of Chinese respect was confirmation that he had achieved his life's ambition.

He was about to pay a terrible price for turning that childhood dream into reality. But all his fury had been spent on Alex Baxter. Eric would endure the suffering ahead uncomplainingly.

CHAPTER SIXTEEN:

# When Children Mattered More

After careful consideration, Harold and Sybil Abrahams came to a decision which took them way beyond their early successes as foster parents. In 1942, they formally adopted a baby boy called Alan. He later explained the strength of the bond. 'I was adopted when I was only eight weeks old, so effectively there was no period of time in my early life when I wasn't with them.'

Harold, Sybil and Alan.

Over in China, Eric Liddell was about to take hundreds of children under his wing. And he would give them his love for as long as he was able. House arrest had been relatively easy; but now he had been sent to Weihsien internment camp – and that meant a whole new level of deprivation. His life would be at stake. He knew it, and yet he was ready to give everything he had for others.

Lord David Puttnam explained: 'Eric's generation understood the concept of sacrifice. They'd lost people. Sacrifice to Eric had a precise, visceral meaning. I have no doubt he was prepared for what was coming in the camp and he was quite able to get his mind around it and deal with it.'

The Japanese crammed about two thousand prisoners into a space of only 150 yards by 200 yards at Weihsien "Civilian Assembly Centre."

Hunger was the norm, and tragedy was never far away. One boy died touching the electric perimeter fence as a dare. That was what boredom did to children in places like this. Tempers were short as the interned western population grew weak and desperate. For nearly two years, Eric Liddell was a tower of strength and comfort for his fellow campmates. From the start, he always put others before himself.

"Official" jobs allocated to Eric were those of camp science teacher, sports coordinator and roll call warden for some of the accommodation blocks. The wider role Liddell adopted was to care for the camp's children, who took to calling him "Uncle Eric."

He was the man who refereed sports matches between the children. Basketball, hockey and rounders were among their favourite games. Liddell always made sure that fairness and order were observed in these matches, so they could be enjoyed to the full by all the kids. He knew these games were a vital outlet from the daily frustrations and deprivations of life in the camp. He was the perfect referee, because he was naturally firm, fair and compassionate towards those with lesser ability. But the man who had refused to run on a Sunday in 1924 also refused to referee on a Sunday in 1943. He hadn't been through so many tests of character just to abandon his Sabbatarian principles now. This time, however, he found there were consequences to his refusal to take part; a disorder that made him feel uncomfortable.

The children began to set up their own games on a Sunday, and Eric didn't feel he could deny them their only real pleasure in what was, after all, a living nightmare. To his alarm, Liddell heard that the kids often fought in his absence. Inevitably, when there was no adult in charge, bullying reared its ugly head. When tribal rivalry and a primitive desire to be dominant took over from decency, it created anarchy.

Eric Liddell reflected on all this. Was he making the right call by obeying God's will and insisting that Sunday should be his day of rest? It was one thing not to run on peacetime Sundays at an Olympic Games. The person he most hurt through his adherence to that basic Christian belief was himself.

How should this rule be applied to children, though? That was the question. An early scene in *Chariots of Fire* has Eric Liddell almost bumping into a boy playing football on a Sunday. He asks the lad what day it is – and promises to play with him the following day. The youngster realises his error – and follows the moral guidance he has been given.

But here in the camp, things were different. The children were playing on a Sunday because they needed to play on a Sunday – for their emotional well-being. By sticking to his principles and refusing to referee these Sunday matches, Eric risked causing chaos for the very people he was trying to protect and develop. What would God really want him to do, in this case? Should he follow to the letter what the Bible decreed? Or should he listen to his heart and consider what it really meant to be a Christian in these dreadful circumstances?

It is a measure of the man that he didn't fear the loss of face that a climbdown might entail. For Eric Liddell, a moral stand was never about personal pride or pomposity. It was simply about choosing the right thing to do. After deep thought, "Uncle Eric" did the right thing once more. He abandoned the habit of a lifetime – and refereed on Sundays. There was no betrayal of his beliefs. He simply loved the children enough to change his ways for them. He showed them the love God would have wanted him to show. No one ever said being a Christian was simple. But sometimes the best Christians are the flexible, practical Christians. They adapt for the greater good. And that's why Eric Liddell put the children before his own strict code in 1943 and 1944.

CHAPTER SEVENTEEN:

# The Death of Eric Liddell

In time, the slow deterioration of Eric's body and mind would make it difficult to referee matches. Finally, an irreversible process would render it impossible. What caused that tragic decline? The lack of food and medicine took their toll on everyone. In another camp, his colleague Ken McAll's weight had dropped from twelve stone to just eight stone by the time American forces arrived to liberate him. But something else was happening to poor Eric Liddell. And although liberation was now just months away, it would come too late for him. Even prolonged speech and clear, coherent thought were difficult for Eric towards the end. And no one understood the reason why.

Eric's athletic power had already waned. At first, he had given Japanese guards head starts in races, and won to earn more food for others. Then he had raced pacey fellow inmates too. Liddell had always beaten all-comers until, in his final year, a rival prisoner's superior physical condition carried the day. Eric offered his sporting conqueror hearty congratulations, probably knowing he would have won their race easily, if only he had been well.

What no one knew, including Liddell, was the sad reality that he was terminally ill by then.

Perhaps he had always been destined to die this way, slowly and with no hope of a cure – even if he had remained free all his life. The same deterioration could have taken place in the western world, albeit better managed. We will never know for sure.

Three years earlier, before she had set sail with the children, Florence had tentatively planned a new life with Eric in Canada, where they had thought of setting up a Home Mission. But that dream had depended on the London Missionary Society finally ordering Eric's evacuation from China – the order that never came.

In the camp, he had often thought of his wife and children, and worried about everyone but himself. He had done chores for others almost from the moment he woke to the moment he slept. He had carried the weight of that insular world on his shoulders. When he finally buckled, he was annoyed with himself. He felt he should have passed more of the burden onto his Lord Jesus Christ and remembered that he himself was only human.

As he neared the end, Eric was hospitalised and he sent a Red Cross letter to his beloved Florence:

*Was carrying too much responsibility. Slight nervous breakdown. Am much better after month in hospital.*

He had no idea that a brain tumour had debilitated him more surely than any miscalculation of his own capacity for helping others.

Eric hoped to ease himself back to mental and physical health by taking a break from teaching and games. But soon it became clear that he wasn't regaining his strength. Although many refused to believe it, Liddell was starting to slip away.

Worried friends sang his favourite hymn outside his hospital room. It was called "Be still my soul," and sung to the tune "Finlandia." This beautiful music was composed by Jean Sibelius. It's easy to imagine what comfort it brought to Eric Liddell. The theme is about surrendering to God and bearing short-term pain, because a glorious reward is coming:

"Be still my soul, the Lord is on my side;
Bear patiently the cross of grief or pain;
Leave to thy God to order and provide;
In every change He faithful will remain.
Be still, my soul: thy best, thy Heavenly Friend;
Through thorny ways leads to a joyful end...

"Be still my soul, the hour is hastening on;
When we shall be forever with the Lord;
When disappointment, grief and fear are gone;
Sorrow forgot, love's purest joys restored.

Be still my soul: when change and tears are past;
All safe and blessed we shall meet at last."

Eric rallied just enough to receive a visitor for some religious discussion. His final words before he slipped into a coma and passed away were said to have been 'complete surrender'.

Under house arrest in 1942 he had written *Manual for the Christian Disciple*. One passage seemed poignant:

*Let us put ourselves before ourselves and look at ourselves. The bravest moment in a man's life is the moment he looks at himself objectively without wincing, without complaining. Self-examination which does not result in action is dangerous. What am I going to do about what I see? The action called for is surrender to God.*

Eric Liddell spent his entire life showing, through action, that he had surrendered to God. He demonstrated complete surrender – and he asked others to do the same. In his last moments, he must have known there was no more complete a surrender than acknowledging that his fight for life on earth was over, and all that remained was to present himself to Jesus Christ his Saviour. Eric died on February 21, 1945.

The camp mourned like never before. Its shocked inhabitants knew just how lovingly Eric had supported them. They came out as one big family for his funeral. As the coffin passed, lines of children paid their respects. Their tears said everything about the love they felt for Uncle Eric. And it wasn't just the children who were inconsolable.

One internee, Norman Cliff, described Liddell as 'the finest Christian gentleman it has been my pleasure to meet. In all my time in the camp, I never heard him say a bad word about anybody.' Another prisoner called Mary Taylor Previte, who was still a child when he died, called Eric 'Jesus in running shoes.'

His family in Canada didn't know what had happened for some time. When they heard the news, they could scarcely believe it. For many years, there were conflicting emotions as they came to terms with the tragedy. Eric's eldest daughter, Patricia later spoke movingly about her father's contribution in the camp, and wondered whether his life might have been saved with a loving family around him. She said, 'I used to ask myself: "How would things have turned out if the three of us and our mother had been in the camp with him?" Then I understood my father would have spent less time with the other youngsters, which could have deprived them of so much.'

Eric would surely have been proud of those words.

Maureen, the daughter he never met, overcame early feelings of resentment at having her father taken away. In time, she too came to terms with what had happened, and was at peace with how events unfolded. After a visit to China in his memory, she said, 'It all made sense. What happened allowed him to touch so many lives as a consequence.'

Again, you sense Liddell would have admired that understanding from the daughter he had longed to know.

The camp survivors were aware they had been in the presence of someone special. One Christian called Langdon Gilkey reflected, 'It is rare indeed that a person has the good fortune to meet a saint, but he came as close to it as anyone I have ever known.'

Similarly Reverend Dr Arnold Bryson, a senior missionary who spoke at the funeral, revealed what someone had told him the day before: 'Of all the men I have known, Eric Liddell was the one in whose character and life the spirit of Jesus Christ was pre-eminently manifested.'

And Eric really shouldn't have been ashamed of the breakdown he suffered under the strain of his decline. The post-mortem revealed the source of the problem – and it certainly wasn't weakness of character. A tumour had developed on the left side of his brain; perhaps due to a blow on the head, perhaps not. Stress and malnutrition could have played their part. And sometimes there's just no logical explanation for such things.

With his fate sealed, Eric Liddell had remained extraordinarily strong and resolute. He had been a total inspiration to others for as long as he could walk and talk.

They didn't just mourn Eric's passing in the Weihsien Camp. They mourned in the other camps too. Frances McAll remembered what it was like in the Pootung camp to the south. She wrote,

*... In the spring we had heard of the death of Eric Liddell in Weihsien camp. Many of us had known him well and had looked forward to meeting up with him again after the war. We thought of his wife, Flo and their three children, the youngest of which he had never seen. He was also known, of course, by many others as one of our greatest athletes and a large number came to the memorial service that we held for him.*

In his own camp, Eric left a simple legacy that made it easier for the next man; it said so much about his character. A fellow inmate explained how it was his 'privilege to follow Eric Liddell in 1945 as the Warden for Blocks 23 and 24 ... Liddell had clearly made a good impression on the guards, and so Rollcall always went smoothly ...'

∽

D.P. Thomson, who had cured Eric's phobia of public speaking, led the tributes in Scotland. At a memorial service at Dundas Street Congregational Church in Glasgow, Thomson said it was fitting they were gathered where Eric had begun his first evangelical tour 21 years earlier.

'He hated praise and shunned publicity,' DP added, 'yet he was worthy of praise.'

That was an understatement. And Duncan McLeod Wright, who was a teammate of Eric's in the Paris Olympics of 1924, went much further. He said, 'A picture of him should be hung in every youth club and sports pavilion in the country, with the title "Eric Liddell – a Christian sportsman" on it.'

The night before they gathered in Glasgow, both these men had led similar tributes in the Morningside Congregational Church in Edinburgh, which was packed to the rafters. Also present was George Robertson, Eric's old headmaster at Eltham College. He remembered the timid boy who faced his fears to become a man, and who never showed a trace of arrogance, even when his sporting talent began to astonish everyone.

Down in London, Harold Abrahams penned a simple account of his fearsome rival's demise. 'He so tragically lost his life in the Far East,' Harold wrote. It was Liddell's work as a missionary in China that had 'led to his untimely end,' news that would 'cause deep feelings of regret to his many admirers and friends,' not least because Liddell 'was a man whose intense spiritual convictions contributed largely to his athletic triumphs.'

Liddell's name among the WW2 fallen and commemorated at Eltham College.

Those convictions would never be forgotten. One hundred years after Eric Liddell refused to run on a Sunday – and won the 400 metres instead with a stunning display of raw athletic courage – he'd be back in everyone's thoughts. Paris 2024 was going to show that the memory of Eric Liddell lived on.

Perhaps Eric Liddell's legend has been enhanced in some way by the fact that the world never saw him grow old. On one of his trips back to Scotland in the 1930s, Liddell had given prizes to young rugby players. And a newspaper reporter picked up on his humorous reluctance to embrace the advancing years.

*It was, in some ways, he said, rather a doubtful honour to be presenting a cup. When he was on the running track, and used to go from meeting to meeting, it was interesting to be introduced to officials. One would always find, however, that it was the largest and fattest who would come up and say, "Let me introduce myself. I used to be a 100 yards sprinter." He felt that when a person had come to the stage when he was presenting prizes, he had reached the sere and yellow leaf, and was becoming old and decrepit, and perhaps stouter.*

That never happened to Eric Liddell. His race was run early.

For Harold Abrahams, athletics official, old age would come. But first there was much to do.

# Part III:
# Saving the Soul of the Games

*I would arrange for different events to take place in different cities – possibly in the same country but perhaps even different countries.*

Harold Abrahams on the future of the Olympic Games.

## CHAPTER ONE:

# The Fight for London '48

In order to protect his beloved Olympic Games from extinction, Harold Abrahams went on air in Britain to make one of the most important broadcasts of his entire life. It was 1945, and the war in the Far East was not yet over.

*There has been considerable discussion lately in America and at home about the future of the Olympic Games; and the opinion has been expressed that they are not wanted for at least ten years after the termination of hostilities. It has also been said that the Olympic spirit is dead. My colleagues on the International Olympic Committee and I are satisfied that the Games could be staged in London with even greater efficiency, and with far wider facilities, than would have been possible before the war. We are confident that the Games could be celebrated in the true spirit of sportsmanship – avoiding the nationalistic twist which the Nazi government gave to the 1936 festival.*

In a few confident sentences, Abrahams had countered those who were conspiring to bring down the Olympic movement completely, and had restored the authority of the IOC. More importantly from a British point of view, he had prepared the ground for London 1948. In order to eliminate any lingering fear that the Olympic stage might be hijacked once again by warlike countries, Harold emphasised:

*There is no question that Germany and Japan, when defeated, could be readmitted to the comity of nations, before they have proved themselves fit to participate in the true spirit of sport.*

*... The Olympic Games can and must play an important part in building a structure of friendship and understanding between peoples of different nations. It is totally wrong to say they breed ill-feeling.*

*... There is no doubt that a friendship built up in sport is an enduring one, and the opportunity which international competitions provide for people to get to know one another is of very real value to the future peace of the world. Sport is one human activity of universal appeal, and we should surely cultivate to the utmost any activity which can so readily be shared by men and women of every nation and creed.*

*Let us hope therefore that all that the Olympic ideal stands for – the ideal of the common humanity of all men – can be revived as soon as is practicable. It is what we have been fighting for, for over five long years. It would indeed be most fitting that London, the centre of the British Empire which stood almost alone at one period of the war, should be the first city to celebrate the revived Olympic Games.*

It was Abrahams at his most eloquent, using his legal brain to mount one argument after another in favour of an Olympic Games in London in 1948. These arguments proved conclusive.

London had earned the right to take the Olympic movement forward. It was generally accepted that the English capital was best disposed to provide the facilities and stability required. Meanwhile Harold's new home was best disposed to provide facilities and stability for another young child.

Sue Pottle explained, 'Harold and Sybil had moved to "Great Jenkins" from "Whiteladies" in Rickmansworth in 1945. My natural mother, Florence Hodge, had come to work for them there, and I'm told she wanted to emigrate. But she couldn't do so if her child did not have its father's name on its birth certificate. So Harold and Sybil adopted me in 1946, when I was nearly three.'

Alan remembered his new sister's arrival. 'The maid, her mother, came in with her and left. And Sue stayed behind.' Heartbreaking as that must have been for Sue at the time, her new surroundings were at least stimulating and spectacular. She explained, 'Great Jenkins was a large, rambling Tudor farmhouse, with half-moat. We kept chickens in the stables and had lots of cats.'

These idyllic scenes were exceptional in a nation still generally trying to heal itself. Millions of families were searching for a semblance of normality after all the confusion and pain to which they had been subjected. It was a strange environment in which to plan for an Olympic Games. Yet life had to go on; and Harold Abrahams believed the London Olympics could be part of the healing process. But he knew the tone for the Games had to be judged perfectly. Harold explained:

*How to combine world record achievements with the spirit of amateurism is a problem which becomes more and more acute each year. We have a grand opportunity to make the first post-war Olympic meeting the starting point for something really worthwhile.*

Eric Liddell, you sense, would have approved. Sportsmanship would be more important than ever, something Harold was able to convey to British athletes from the moment he was appointed as one of their Assistant Team Managers. In return, he ensured the athletes were going to be provided with everything they needed. It was their party, after all.

In January 1947, Abrahams wrote, 'As a former competitor, I'm delighted above all to see that every consideration is promised to the needs of competitors. They are after all the most important people at the Games – and too often in the past they have had just complaints against the arrangements made for them.'

London '48 would showcase the best starting blocks yet, of a quality that would propel Olympic sprinting into the modern era. The days of digging holes with trowels were over. Now athletes could slide their launch-pads back and forth, so that each individual could settle into their most comfortable and effective position, ready for an explosive start.

The technology was ready. Now the athletes were invited to put the horrors of war behind them – and start serious preparation for the great sporting spectacle. There were pre-Olympic trials for the

GB team at the White City in August 1947. They took the form of a match between the Combined Services and the British Amateur Athletic Board. Harold looked smart enough as he did the announcing in his jacket and tie. But as the midday rays began burning into his bald head, he protected himself with an outrageous floral sunhat. It was so floppy and incongruous that photographers forgot the track action and began to photo-

Harold Abrahams looking less formal than usual at the trials.

graph Abrahams, the Assistant Honorary Secretary of the BAAB, in his strange attire.

Picking up her newspaper the next day, Christina McLeod Innes – or Christina Morley as she had been known for the past twenty-two years – was amused to see her old flame looking so comical. Highly strung as a young man at Cambridge, he had only rarely relaxed enough to let people laugh at him. Even then it had required something irresistible to make him swallow his pride – the opportunity to perform a Gilbert and Sullivan song on stage, for example. Now he didn't seem to care how bizarre he looked in public. Christina, who had spent the war as a nurse on the other side of the Atlantic, cut the photograph out of the newspaper and kept it. One day, she sensed, she would see Harold again.

CHAPTER TWO:

# David Puttnam's First Olympics

In June 1948, Harold Abrahams spoke about the dangers of becoming too obsessed with Olympic victory. Yes Harold, the man who had been totally obsessed with Olympic victory in 1924!

He hinted at the mental problems such pressures had caused him. Victory – and sometimes even defeat – often came at a price. Harold reminded his audience that a healthy perspective was essential for London's Olympians, especially with the Games coming so soon after the war. It was all about getting the balance right. Again, Eric Liddell would have been proud of him.

*I should be the first to recognise that the modern trend of intensive specialisation contains dangers and problems; but it is much wiser to acknowledge and solve these than to condemn or ignore them. How can we, with such a prize at stake, still retain our sense of proportion? How can we strive to win without minding too much when we lose? If we solve that problem, we gain all that is best in international competition . . . What does matter is that those participating and watching should unstintingly appreciate the brilliance of achievement, no matter from what country the performer comes.*

Alan Abrahams once said of his father:

*The film Chariots of Fire was very accurate in terms of what it said about the kind of person my father was when he was younger. Later in life he wasn't like that at all. Somewhere along the line there was quite a sea-change of personality.*

Perhaps the sea change in Harold came in the run-up to London '48. Drawing on his pre-war and post-war perspective of the Olympic movement, Abrahams knew just what had to be done differently this time around. Winning should never again matter as much as it did to the

Germans on a nationalistic level in Berlin; or, for that matter, as much as it had to him on a personal level in Paris. Excessive sporting ambition without balance was dangerous, both individually and collectively. With the right spirit, however, this Olympic gathering would be very special indeed.

Lord Burghley captured the mood when, as Chairman of the Organising Committee, he made a wonderful speech at the Opening Ceremony, setting out the significance and objectives of the Games. Addressing a packed Wembley Stadium and King George VI, Burghley said:

*Your Majesty, the hour has struck. A visionary dream has today become a glorious reality. At the end of the worldwide struggle in 1945, many institutions and associations were found to have withered and only the strongest had survived. How, many wondered, had the great Olympic Movement prospered? In 1946, the clarion call went forth to the athletes of the world bidding them to gather here in London to celebrate the XIV Olympiad. Here today, in this vast arena are assembled 6,000 competitors, the cream of the youth of the world drawn from sixty-one nations, who have answered this call. This is the answer to that question, and here is the proof of the inherent strength and vitality of the movement.*

As he asked the King to formerly open the Games, he reminded his sovereign, 'You are kindling a torch, the light from which will travel to the uttermost corners of the earth; a torch of that ageless and heartfelt prayer of mankind throughout the world for peace and goodwill amongst men.'

Harold Abrahams witnessed the scene and sensed the enormity of the moment. He wrote, 'After long years of almost unending national and international strain and stress, here was the light of a flame which crossed a continent without hindrance, caused frontiers to disappear, gathered unprecedented crowds, and lit the path to a brighter future for the youth of the world.'

It didn't matter that the stars of the Games weren't destined to be British – just that the Games had some stars.

The seven-year-old David Puttnam was in a perfect position to watch those stars rise, thanks to his father Leonard. The photographer had come home at the end of the war to get to know his son properly, making up for so much lost time. And Leonard had lived up to the hero young David had created in his head. Always loving, here was yet another example of his thoughtfulness. Lord Puttnam explained: 'My father, who by that time was picture editor at Associated Press, organised (as I understand was quite normal at the time) the whole pool of photographers at the Games.' With such a position came the perks of having access to the odd extra ticket. That's why young David was now present and ready to enjoy the action. And this was the start of something special. An Olympic love affair, leading to *Chariots of Fire* and beyond, with the right values cherished and protected all the way to Paris 2024.

Even in 2023, Puttnam knew the significance of 1948:

*It was the creation of what you could call an umbilical chord between the Olympics and me, because from that moment I felt an emotional tie to the Olympic movement that never really left me.*

The occasion demanded exceptional characters. Strangely, what captured Lord Puttnam's imagination, at the age of seven, was not the athletic power and prowess of youthful bodies in their prime. A woman who must have seemed to a little boy to be nothing short of middle-aged was showing the youngsters how it was done. What extraordinary scenes were these? Sport was to be enjoyed by everyone – men, women, young and old. There were no barriers.

Three-quarters of a century later, Puttnam was still amazed by what he had witnessed. He remembered:

*I have a clear memory of Fanny Blankers-Koen and Emil Zatopek, (who between them won five gold medals), because they seemed to me to be about the same age as my parents, and I remember that a lot was made of the fact that Fanny BK was a Dutch mum and a housewife.*

Lord Puttnam's memory did not fail him. She was known as the "Flying Housewife" and was a mother of two when she competed in the London Olympics at the age of 30. She won four gold medals – and was the most successful athlete at the Games.

The studious Harold Abrahams already knew her backstory:

*In track and field events there is almost always at least one compet-itor whose performances are automatically brought to mind whenever the particular Games is mentioned. For example Paavo Nurmi in 1924 and Jesse Owens in 1936. Without doubt Fanny Blankers-Koen of the Netherlands, the 30-year-old, is the headline for 1948. She had competed in the 1936 Olympics at the age of 18, and in 1938 had equalled the world's 100 yards record. During the war in occupied Holland, she set up world records for the 100 yards, high and long jumps and equalled that for the 80 metres hurdles, while in June 1948 she added the world's 100 metres record to her quiver. At Wembley, she broke the tape 11 times (including a heat and final in sprint relay), her victories in the two sprints being clear, her only struggles being in the 80 metres hurdles and the relay.*

Had Blankers-Koen entered the long jump – won with a leap which fell almost two feet short of her world record – she would almost certainly have claimed gold there too. And she had begun to change Harold's mind about women's athletics, for which he had previously shown no great respect or affection. Of the eighth day of London '48, Harold wrote, 'In the women's sprint relay Fanny Blankers-Koen brought her total medals up to four by a brilliant "anchor" run which brought victory for her country over Australia almost with her last stride.'

Britain was still searching for her first gold, and it seemed tantalis-ingly close later that evening, in what Abrahams described as 'one of the most thrilling duels imaginable'.

He explained, 'Most of the crowd stayed to watch 28-year-old Dorothy Tyler of Great Britain in what seemed an endless duel against an American high jumper, Alice Coachman. Twelve years previously Dorothy, a 16-year-old schoolgirl, had gained second place in the Berlin

Olympics . . . [With the bar set at] 5ft 6¼in Alice Coachman took several minutes to make her first effort and then cleared it first time. Dorothy Tyler failed, but got over second time. Neither could clear 5ft 7in. Miss Coachman won because she cleared the height at her first effort.'

The very idea that women could be the greatest stars of an Olympic Games would have sounded nothing less than outrageous twenty-four years earlier.

As Lord Puttnam recalled, however, there was at least one man who stood out at London '48. And although he probably looked considerably older than Leonard Puttnam, due to his receding hairline, Emile Zatopek was only 26 in 1948. The "Czech Locomotive" won gold in the 10,000 metres and silver in the 5,000. Four years later he would become a living legend by winning three golds in Helsinki, including the marathon. But young David Puttnam was impressed enough by his exploits in 1948. And his parents probably didn't seem so very old after all, if people like Zatopek could achieve so much glory.

Of the fifty or so countries taking part in the track and field events, thirteen had winners. Great Britain was not one of them. Yet the true triumph of London 1948 was that GB – and not least Harold Abrahams – had ensured the survival of the Olympic movement by striking the right note.

Of the sportsmanship on show, Harold was able to write, 'I am sure that the XIVth Olympiad can fairly be regarded as a model for all time.'

He couldn't have known that the Games had just sparked David Puttnam's love for the Olympics, a flame destined to burn so bright that it would end in the celebration of Harold's own story in an Oscar-winning film. For now, the ever-protective Abrahams was concerned about any backlash the Olympic movement might suffer from a British public still on their knees after WW2.

Financially the Games were a success, which was almost as important as anything that took place on the track. Any obvious loss would have caused an outcry among the suffering British population. And the fear of financial loss – or at least lack of tangible reward – prevents many cities from bidding to hold the Olympic Games in the 21st Century. Abrahams was way ahead of his time in realising the significance of the bottom line.

In 1948 Harold assured Londoners:

*Despite the enormous difficulties produced by shortage of mate-rials, rationing and so on, the organisation met with universal approval. Improvisation was the order of the day – a special track was laid at Wembley stadium for the athletics . . . Expenditure [for the Games] amounted to under £600,000 which included something in the range of £200,000 for temporary work at Wembley and other venues and services provided by Government Departments. The income provided from 'gates' – on many occasions there were over 80,000 spectators at Wembley – meant that overall there was an excess of income over expenditure of between £10,000 and £20,000.*

No wonder Harold Abrahams had now been promoted to Honorary Treasurer of the British Amateur Athletic Board. He was also elected a Vice President of the Amateur Athletic Association that same year. These honours justly reflected the role he played in reigniting the Olympic flame.

Having worked so hard, perhaps he was entitled to one care-less moment. Looking back on his life speaking into a microphone, Abrahams reflected, 'I never had a real disaster – except in the Olympics in 1948, when I said there was a hold-up because the girls were taking their shorts off, when I meant tracksuits.'

Back in 1948, that was not an acceptable image to evoke – but he got away with it. And since he had been commissioned to add commentary to the official film of the Games, he was able to redeem himself, and help shape the way they would be viewed in retrospect.

Many others were credited with the organisation and success of the 1948 Olympics. But who best personified the spirit of the Games, and helped to take athletics to new audiences at home and abroad? Harold Abrahams.

CHAPTER THREE:

# Groundbreakers!
# Harold Abrahams and Roger Bannister

R oger Bannister was about to spark a national obsession with the stopwatch. The popularity of athletics was going through the roof. But sometimes the organisation of events – and the recording of their outcomes – still lacked precision.

Such problems could be fixed – with hard work and common sense. As soon as the Games had finished, Harold Abrahams began re-writing the athletics rulebook, a process which took three long years. Finally, in 1951 he was able to announce that, 'after a great deal of coming and going and very much burning of midnight oil, the task is done and the new rule book will in due course see the light of day'.

The process of starting a race – something close to Harold's heart – had been changed. He explained:

*Much bad starting has in the past been due to raggedness, caused, I believe, by the irregularity with which runners 'get to their marks.' A new rule states that in all races up to the half-mile there shall be an 'assembly line' 10 feet behind the starting line and that from this line the starter will tell the competitors to 'get to their marks.'*

*... At the other end of the race, it has been strongly recommended that the "photo-finish" camera should be in use, and, along the same line of thinking, electric timekeeping is now to be 'officially recognised.' Experiments have shown that human timekeeping on the whole favours the runner, so we may expect that, in sprints particularly, records in future will be harder to beat.*

Later that year, he put further pressure on his IAAF colleagues by asking publicly, 'Ought we not to time more scientifically with electrical timekeeping always in use?'

No wonder Harold Abrahams was described by the athletics historian Peter Lovesey as 'the architect of the modern laws of athletics.'

And yet electronic timekeeping wasn't in use for arguably the most famous race against time ever undertaken. More remarkably, Harold Abrahams and his stopwatch were to be caught out of position.

~

There's a wonderful photograph of a young man stripped to the waist and riding a motorbike towards the camera on a sunny summer's day. It is a snapshot of someone clearly pleased to be able to do something fun and just a little dangerous without fear of recrimination. He is getting away from the pressures of competitive athletics, and his name is Roger Bannister.

The 'L-Plate' on the motorbike suggests that he is a novice. Indeed, Sir Roger admitted in 2010, 'I hardly ever rode a motorbike. It is definitely me in the picture, but I cannot remember exactly where or when. The only time I remember riding a motorbike was later in the Royal Army Medical Corps; but on that occasion the weather was far too cold to be stripped to the waist like that.'

The photograph is taken either on the country roads around Great Jenkins, or on holiday with the Abrahams family in Cornwall. The history of athletics might have been very different had Roger's lack of experience led him into trouble on that motorbike. Such concerns don't appear to be worrying the young Bannister as he rides towards the camera; he looks as though he is having the time of his life.

A young Roger Bannister risking his limbs on a motorbike.

Of course, Harold still had to write objectively about his young friend Roger in the newspapers after track races. And he wouldn't spare Bannister from criticism if he felt it necessary to point out a few home truths. The key was this: his criticism was always constructive, something greatly appreciated by Roger's father. On August 7, 1951, Ralph Bannister wrote to Harold to thank him for getting tickets for an athletics meeting at the White City stadium in London. He ended the letter by saying, 'We take this opportunity of thanking you also for the encouragement and advice which you have given to Roger. We have detected your keener critical faculty on occasions passed unnoticed by other observers.'

The mentoring seemed to be working. Harold remembered, 'By this time people were beginning to tip Bannister as a probable winner of the Olympic 1500 metres at Helsinki in 1952. It was obvious that in so far as anyone can be said to have a chance of winning an Olympic title, Bannister had that chance.'

But journalists wanted to know what Roger was going to do in order to build up his competitive strength for the Olympics. They weren't furnished with a satisfactory answer. Perhaps they didn't understand Roger's shyness – or his stubborn streak when it came to training schedules.

Harold explained:

*Unfortunately, his very personal methods of training, his refusal to accept any 'official' coaching, and his deliberate policy of avoiding publicity, led to much criticism from the British press. But Roger, though extremely sensitive to criticism, particularly when he felt it was so unjust, deliberately followed his own policy and prepared for the 1500 metres. He planned to be at his peak in Helsinki, and consequently refused to race week after week against strong opponents as many other great middle-distance runners do.*

There was little Harold could do but help to choose Roger's key races. Then came the bombshell. Bannister had dreamed of emulating Lovelock by winning the 1500 metres gold medal at the next Olympics in 1952. Previously, the heats had been scheduled to allow a day or two's rest before the final. 'That was what I was planning for and I could have coped with it,' insisted Sir Roger later. But just three weeks before the Olympics, the technical director in Helsinki decided that Bannister and his rivals would have to race on three successive days.

'It was said afterwards that there had been a rather deliberate attempt to change the programme because I was the favourite,' Bannister recalled.

Asked whether he had been 'nobbled', Sir Roger replied, 'I can't make that claim, but what happened favoured one of the other competitors, Josy Barthel, who was a hard racer trained by Woldemar Gerschler.'

Abrahams explained, 'Bannister had planned his peak for a heat and a final at Helsinki with one day's rest in between. Unfortunately the organisers – in my view quite unnecessarily – inserted an extra round, which meant three days racing in succession.'

Sir Roger picked over these words many decades later and concluded, 'Harold understood why I was dismayed at the change in the programme, with the extra race introduced.'

Harold Abrahams said of Bannister during these difficult pre-race days, 'He was like an actor who had thoroughly worked himself into a part, only to be faced on the opening night with an extra scene which he hadn't rehearsed at all.'

Sir Roger didn't dispute that analogy. 'By the third day of these successive races, I knew in my heart that it was a virtually impossible task for me. And it all went disastrously wrong when I came fourth instead of winning. There were no British track and field gold medals in Helsinki.'

As supportive as ever, Harold said, 'That he finished fourth and himself beat Lovelock's Olympic record by two seconds, was a great achievement. And to me, knowing intimately just how seriously the extra race had worried him, it was proof positive that he was, potentially, the greatest runner in the world at one mile.'

Even so, it was Barthel who collected gold.

Yet in some ways it was a blessing in disguise, because Bannister often said he would have retired had he returned with Olympic gold. As it was, there was unfinished business. Roger licked his wounds and vowed to come back even more determined. Sure enough, within a year, he was beginning to build towards something that became even more historic than an Olympic triumph.

To run a mile in under four minutes was the "Everest of Athletics" in the 1950s. But could anyone do it? And if they could, who would be the first? Harold Abrahams set the scene like this:

*Will 1953 produce the first four-minute mile? That possibility is brought a little nearer by Saturday's performance of Roger Bannister in shattering the British record with a time of 4:03.6. Earlier in the year, unaided by any real opposition, John Landy, of Australia, had run the mile in 4:02.1...*

It didn't happen for either man in 1953; but Bannister chose May 6, 1954 and Oxford University's Iffley Road as the time and place to try to conquer Everest. The weather wasn't kind. The men who intended to act as hares to the hound, Chris Brasher and Chris Chataway, persuaded the highly-strung Roger to make his assault on the summit. Halfway round the third lap, Brasher began to gulp like a goldfish and Chataway took the strain, moving from third to first while Bannister stayed second. Halfway round the final lap it was Chataway flagging, and Roger realised he would have to hit the front and do the rest on his own. He was a long way out; but it was now or never. How much did he want his place in history? Like Eric Liddell thirty years earlier, he put everything he had into his race to the tape – more than any man had ever done. When he hit that tape, in his own words he felt like 'an exploded flashbulb with no will to live.'

Norris McWhirter, who later starred in the hit TV series *Record Breakers*, finally announced the result to a crowd that could no longer stand the tension. McWhirter seemed to delight in prolonging the drama:

*Ladies and gentlemen, here is the result of event number nine, the One Mile. First, number 41, R.G. Bannister of the Amateur Athletic Association, formerly of Exeter and Merton Colleges, with a time which is a new meeting and track record, and which, subject to ratification, will be a new English native, British national, British all-comers, European, British Empire and World's Record. The time ... three minutes...*

Very few heard the next words, which were 'fifty-nine point four seconds...' He had done it. And the ratification duly came, even though one of the timekeepers – a certain Harold Abrahams – was incorrectly positioned a few yards away from the finishing line.

Bannister breaks the 4-minute barrier –
but official timer Abrahams (far left) is not where he should be.

Abrahams may not have been where an official timekeeper should have been; but more than a quarter of a century of expertise apparently helped him to press down on that button at the right moment. 'All the times were identical' emphasised Sir Roger in 2010, when it was explained to him that doubts had recently been expressed about Harold's positioning.

In the immediate aftermath of Roger Bannister's sub-four-minute mile, even that veteran observer of great athletic moments, Harold Abrahams was overcome.

## International Amateur Athletic Federation

Founded in 1912

*President :* THE LORD BURGHLEY, K.C.M.G.

*Honorary Secretary-Treasurer :* D. T. P. PAIN.

### APPLICATION FOR A *WORLD/OLYMPIC/EUROPEAN RECORD.

*(Cross out the words which are not applicable)

To : THE HONORARY SECRETARY OF THE I.A.A.F.

Application is hereby made for a + WORLD AND EUROPEAN ........ Record, in
support of which, the following information is submitted :—

+State the nature of the application—World, Olympic or European)

Reference should be made to Rule 24 I.A.A.F. Competition Rules.

1. Event ......... *One Mile* ......... Men/Women

2. Record claimed (time, distance, height, palm) ... *3min 59·4sec.*

3. Date and hour ... *6 p.m. Thurs. 6–5–1954*

4. Where held (Ground, Place, Country) ... *Oxford, England.*

5. Condition of track, runway or circle ... *Firm.*

6. Level or gradient of track, runway or circle ... *level. NOT furlong.*

7. Weight, measurement and material of implements ... *—*

8. State of weather ... *Gusty wind. Rain.*

9. Force and direction of wind ... *Gusty wind.*

10. Name of Competitor, Club and Country ... *ROGER GILBERT BANNISTER*
   (Surname) (Christian names)

   *ACHILLES CLUB , GREAT BRITAIN* ... Born *MORTIMER. IRELAND*

   (*In relay events, the full names of the competitors should be stated*)

*K.S. Duncan* ... *95 Mount St, London, W.1.*
   (Signature of Referee) (Address)

### TIMEKEEPERS' CERTIFICATES

I, the undersigned official timekeeper, of the event above-mentioned, do hereby certify that the time set
opposite my signature was the exact time recorded by my watch, and that the watch used by me has been certified
and approved by my National Association (Refer to Rule 9.)

Time *3 min 59·4sec* (Signature of Timekeeper) ... (Address)

Time *3 min 59·4 sec* (Signature of Timekeeper) ... (Address)

Time *3 min 59·4 sec* (Signature of Timekeeper) ... (Address)

I confirm that the above Timekeepers exhibited their watches to me and that the times as stated are correct.

(Signature of Referee or Chief Timekeeper)

### STARTER'S CERTIFICATE

I hereby certify that I was the starter for the event above-mentioned, that it was a fair start and no advantage
was given to or taken by the claimant. (Refer to Rules 10 and 27.)

(Signature of Starter) ... (Address)

---

*PROGRAMME* ............ *PRICE* 6d.

## O. U. A. C.

*v.*

## AMATEUR ATHLETIC ASSOCIATION

(UNDER A.A.A. LAWS)

at

IFFLEY ROAD ATHLETIC GROUND

THURSDAY, MAY 6th, 1954, at 5.0 p.m.

### OFFICIALS

*Referees:*

THE RIGHT WORSHIPFUL THE MAYOR OF OXFORD, A. B. BROWN, B.C.L., M.A.
K. S. DUNCAN, M.B.E.

*President O.U.A.C.:* G. H. JEFFRIES (Magdalen)

Hon. Secretary O.U.A.C.: D. I. N. JOHNSON (Lincoln)

Hon. Treasurer O.U.A.C.: A. W. SELWYN, M.A. (B.N.C.)

A.A.A. Hon. Team Manager: L. R. TRUELOVE

A.A.A. Hon. Masseur: G. W. MAYS

*JUDGES*

| *Track:* | *Field:* |
|---|---|
| K. S. DUNCAN, M.B.E. | A. W. SELWYN |
| E. TOMLINSON | A. GOLD |
| B. BASHFORD | W. W. PLUMBRIDGE |
| REV. C. J. TUCKER | L. P. H. BROWN |

*Timekeepers:*

W. C. A. FINDLAY, C. S. HILL, R. G. HUDSON, L. R. RICHARDS, W. J. BURFITT

*Starter:* R. C. BARKWAY

*Clerk of Course:* A. J. VINCENT

*Recorder:* D. I. WEEKES

Harold Abrahams is listed as one of three official
timekeepers for Roger Bannister's historic record.

Harold Abrahams is not originally listed
among the officials for the event.

'The record caused me more emotional disturbance than any event I have ever seen in nearly forty years' association with athletics,' Abrahams confessed.

Bannister was thrilled to receive Harold's Omega Chronometer, stopped at 3 minutes, 59.4 seconds, as a gift from the man who had guided him. By way of reply, Roger penned the following note from his Harrow home.

My dear Harold,

Your wonderful surprise arrived this morning and I quite literally don't know how to thank you. (I can hear you saying 'Don't try!') You have played such a large part in any success I have achieved – as my guide, philosopher and friend – that it is difficult for me to say enough of what I feel. All I can hope is that we can continue to remain as close when my running days are over! My father will be using the new watch this afternoon – though at the moment I think he feels it's too precious to touch. I expect I shall see you before you read this but I wanted to write immediately to say how much I was thrilled by your present.

Yours ever, Roger

After hearing that letter read back to him, Sir Roger acknowledged, 'I was extremely moved that he gave me the stopwatch – that was the one from the four-minute mile. It was a very generous gesture. I think my letter reflects my gratitude and was a gesture of friendship in return for his gesture of friendship.'

It hadn't been an Olympic event; so, what was the significance of Bannister's four-minute mile, and the role Harold Abrahams played in developing and promoting this young superstar's profile? How did it impact on the health and survival of the Olympic movement between 1924 and 2024?

Athletics has always been the heart and soul of the Olympics. And in a changing world, athletics demanded a happy, dramatic story to capture the imagination. Bannister's stunning success was a shot in the arm for the Olympic movement, even though Roger conquered the Everest of Athletics away from the Olympic arena. People had rarely if ever been more passionate about running. And despite an increasingly political backdrop to athletics, Bannister had run his race for the sheer joy and the love of going fast. Just like Eric Liddell, he retired early. Roger regarded a career in medicine as more important than athletics – just as missionary work was more important to Eric. They shone and were gone in the blink of an eye. And they were among the very best of British athletes.

CHAPTER FOUR:

# Perspectives of a Lord and a Prince

'Harold actually became the living embodiment of the things he had fought in the 1920s,' Lord Puttnam – producer of *Chariots of Fire* – pointed out. 'There is quite a rich vein for you there, if I may say so.'

You ignore David Puttnam at your peril. But it wasn't always a bad thing when Harold championed a cause he had previously undermined.

In 1928 Abrahams had written, 'I do not consider that women are built for really violent exercise of the kind that is the essence of competition. One only has to see them practising to realise how awkward they are on the running track.'

Just before World War Two he added, 'I confess to a deep-seated opposition to women's athletics'.

Fanny Blankers-Koen had changed all that at the London Olympics of 1948. By March 1955, Harold was writing in *World Sports* 'as a sporting suffragist.' The journal even carried a cartoon of Harold holding a placard which read, 'Equal Rights for Women.'

Abrahams genuinely wanted that. He even served as the Women's Amateur Athletic Association's legal advisor.

What sparked such an emphatic defence of women in the 1950s, apart from the Olympic debt owed to Blankers-Koen, was a claim by a group of Belgian doctors that the "fairer sex" should no longer take part in competitive sport.

Harold replied:

*I write as one who used to have considerable doubts on the subject – pretty forcibly expressed, too, a quarter of a century ago. It is nonsense to suggest that women shouldn't take part in competitive sport, and I challenge the Belgian doctors, or other medical men, to produce any real evidence to support this contention . . . Competitive sport for women has come to stay, and it will need something more impressive than a few pompous utterances to stop it. Some of the most charming women I know are first-class athletes.*

One of the women Harold surely had in mind was an athlete called Valerie Ball, whom he described as 'one of the best middle-distance runners Britain has had – and a most attractive personality both on and off the track'.

Valerie once told a funny story about an official athletics gender test she had to undergo, which was supposed to involve a full medical examination. 'I had to go to a doctor to get a certificate to say I was a woman,' she said. 'He just looked at me and signed it.'

Harold tried to offer Valerie Ball coaching advice, but she wasn't the most dedicated of pupils. She admitted, 'I was young and I was already winning just about every 440 race I ran. I don't think I appreciated how clever he was, or the fact that he wanted to help me. He was fascinated by the clock. The stopwatch was his god.'

It was understandable if she lacked extra motivation. When it came to the big Olympic stage, Valerie Ball was excluded due to her gender. As Roger Bannister, Chris Chataway and the rest headed for Helsinki in 1952, Valerie Ball was left at home. Her favoured 400m and 800m events were not open to women at the Olympic Games. The "fairer sex" had been banned from running anything further than sprint distances.

'I'd have liked to have been in the Olympics, I must admit,' she said wistfully in 2010. 'It's difficult to explain to people. They come and say, "You were in the Olympics, weren't you?" I say, "Not exactly." I'd have loved to run in the Olympics; but I didn't protest or complain – I just took it. This all went back to 1928 when the women ran the 800 at the Amsterdam Olympics and collapsed at the end. That's why it was no longer included.'

In the summer of 1952, Valerie was powerless to do much more than follow Harold's reports on the British Olympic team's indifferent progress. But all the time something was building inside her. On the evening of September 17, 1952, the moment came to unleash it. Valerie was racing under floodlights in west London, which always put her in the mood.

'Floodlights were fun,' she recalled, 'it gave an athletics meeting an exciting air.' She was ready for two laps like never before. And little over two minutes later, barefoot by then and wrapped in a blanket, a beaming Valerie knew she had made history.

One report announced, 'Valerie Ball, 23-year-old daughter of Sir Nigel Ball, set up a new world record of 2:14.5 for the women's 880 yards run during last night's floodlit international athletics meeting at White City, London. After the race Miss Ball said: "I was most surprised by my performance; I had no thoughts of a world record attempt either before or during the race."'

The injustice of Valerie's Olympic exclusion while still in her prime stayed with Harold somehow. By early 1957 the former male chauvinist was really getting somewhere in his fight for women's equality in athletics. He wrote proudly:

*European Championships have been extended from five days to six, and a women's 400m race is to be added to events. The International Olympic Committee is to be asked to include an 800m for women and a women's pentathlon in the 1960 Games.*

The likes of Dame Kelly Holmes, Jessica Ennis, Denise Lewis and Katarina Johnson-Thompson would have reason to be grateful for the pioneering pressure Harold Abrahams exerted on their behalf back in the 1950s.

Yet the male athletes were furious with him during that same decade and beyond. They blamed him for slowing the march towards professionalism. And his stubborn fight to prevent the inevitable is interesting, if only because it seemed to contradict the younger Harold so comprehensively.

Lord Puttnam seemed saddened by the way Abrahams changed.

*My interpretation is that ironically Harold became the mirror image of the very things he had once opposed. He became the establishment; he became the person who blocked advances in training, in what he termed as professionalism.*

Tom McNab, who trained the actors and worked as a historical consultant on *Chariots of Fire* shared that view. 'Abrahams was a poacher turned gamekeeper. In his athletic days he had a professional coach and often went against the mainstream of athletics thinking. But when he became part of the establishment, he undermined professional coaching and became reactionary.'

Had he really become the mirror image of what he had once been? The truth isn't quite as simple as Puttnam's conclusion suggests. Sir Roger Bannister, who knew Abrahams so well, understood his motivations better than most. 'Harold felt that coaches were becoming too big for their boots. He felt there was a danger they were becoming too dictatorial. He felt that the athletes' personality had to be protected and respected.'

Harold tried to remind everyone that his own involvement with a coach had never compromised his independence:

*I was not just being trained; I was being helped with my training, which is a vastly different thing. Well, a lot of these modern people regard a coach as a wet nurse or a Svengali. I didn't. I thought for myself. I argued with Sam Mussabini. If I differed with him I said so.*

*If he recommended something I almost invariably asked 'why?'. . .*
*I think a lot of the modern coaches are just hangers on, frankly. I don't*
*think they know much about it and you can be over-coached.*

The battle over coaching in the UK caused ill feeling for years. During
the mid-1950s, two camps were close to war. On one side were Harold
and his British Amateur Athletic Board colleague, Jack Crump, who acted
like officers. On the other side was Geoffrey Dyson, more of a sergeant
major in his ways. Dyson had been appointed AAA chief coach in 1947;
and it was Dyson who enjoyed the support of most of the top athletes.

At times the President of the British Amateur Athletic Board, HRH
Prince Philip, The Duke of Edinburgh must have wondered what kind
of civil war he had walked into. He could act as a confidant but had no
real power. Queen Elizabeth II's husband explained in 2011:

*I came to know Harold Abrahams when I was invited to become*
*President of the British Amateur Athletic Board in 1952. He served as both*
*Chairman and Treasurer of the Board between 1946 and 1975. I never*
*played an "executive" part in the activities of the Board, but I had many*
*discussions with Harold Abrahams about the state of British athletics and*
*the many hideous problems involved in trying to administer such a diffuse*
*collection of fiercely independent athletic disciplines.*

Sometimes Harold just left enemies like Dyson out of the loop.
Tensions rose when Harold and Crump took a British athletics team
on a ground-breaking trip to Trinidad and Jamaica without a coach in
February 1956. The move was considered provocative and they were
criticised for it, because Crump's wife and Sybil went too. Harold and
Sybil both worked hard on the trip, which was paid for by Simon Vos of
the Regent Oil Company, then British-owned. Sybil worked for Trinidad
radio while out in the Caribbean, while Abrahams encouraged a passion
for athletics locally. Harold explained:

*Soon after our arrival in Trinidad we were all hard at it, for the basic*
*idea behind the trip was not so much the actual competition as the general*

*encouragement to athletics which the visit of some of our leading competitors could give. [They] gave a series of 'clinics', or coaching sessions, which were tremendously popular. Jack Crump showed a number of films, and I gave a talk, illustrated by slides of most of the leading past and present performers, to an audience of about 200 . . . A particularly fine slide of Jesse Owens had a tremendous reception. I talked for the best part of an hour and then came many and various questions . . . One of my audience asked me whether, when running, you should breathe through your nose ... I pointed out that the mouth is a much more rapid source of supply. I added, rather hesitatingly, that you should keep your mouth shut when you have won – and was most relieved when they were on to it like a shot!*

Reunited: Harold and the great Jesse Owens.

Harold concluded, 'The trip was thoroughly worthwhile, and I hope it may be repeated in the not-too-distant future . . . There is great enthusiasm and much hidden talent in the West Indies.'

Abrahams wasn't wrong, as the world knows after adoring Usain Bolt's Olympic contributions and those of many other Caribbean athletes in the early 21st century alone. Yet this innovative trip attracted condemnation for its alleged opportunism.

Tensions escalated further still towards the end of the year when John Disley, who had been the 1952 Olympic steeplechase bronze medallist, led protests against the lack of coaches with the British Olympic party at Melbourne '56. Harold was there as assistant manager and found himself in the firing line. Disley wrote, 'We could see that where other teams had half a dozen coaches to cast a critical eye over training workouts, the British only had one, supplemented by the willing but uninformed assistant team manager.'

Disley added, 'We were not receiving the unofficial daily cash allowance enjoyed by many other teams. After agitation we were given limited free postal facilities, but this measure did little to restore our pride. It appeared that the Swedes, who had started a fund for the hapless Hungarians, were even contemplating doing something for the "poor" British!'

It seemed so wrong, because back in 1948 Abrahams had used an IAAF Congress to try to end such resentment once and for all. 'The British proposal advanced the suggestion that no athlete should be prevented by any financial embarrassment from representing his country in international competition, and a man's governing body should be allowed, in proved and suitable cases, to see that he suffers no financial loss from international selection.'

Abrahams had also been the brains behind a British Amateur Athletic Board presentation to that same IAAF Congress, showing how it would be possible to redraft the rulebook without using the word 'amateur'. But that didn't mean Harold wanted the sport to turn professional; he simply preferred the term 'non-professional'. He also despised any rule-bending practice which smacked of professionalism – the sort of underhand compromise the national boards of some other countries often indulged in quite unashamedly.

The late Prince Philip, The Duke of Edinburgh, understood perfectly well the pressures and complexities Harold faced:

*The period in history during which Harold Abrahams was involved in British athletics, both as a highly successful competitor and as an administrator, covered the evolution of both national and international athletic competition. The pioneers were amateurs, but the growing popularity of athletics, both as a sport and as a spectator event, created massive strains for the administrators as they endeavoured to cope with the transition from amateur status to "assisted competitor" status which allowed all talented athletes to compete on equal terms.*

Harold had done more than any man alive to grow that popularity. Now he was paying the price. Money had entered athletics. And it wasn't leaving.

CHAPTER FIVE:

# Fighting Professionalism

Harold's own earnings from the sport hardly strengthened his case as he fought to hold back the tide of professionalism. An athlete called Derek Johnson won the 1956 Olympic 800m silver medal in Melbourne. That didn't quite give him the platform Harold Abrahams enjoyed after 1924. But Johnson was powerful enough as he pointed to the alleged hypocrisy:

*According to I.A.A.F. and AAA laws an athlete must obtain permission if he wishes to ask payment for writing an article in a newspaper or magazine, or for taking part in a television or radio broadcast. Permission is invariably withheld if the subject of the article or broadcast is directly connected with athletics, unless the athlete can show that writing is an integral part of his livelihood . . . But many of these officials, among them Jack Crump and Harold Abrahams, write or broadcast regularly.*

*This cynical attitude towards professionalism is, in my opinion, the biggest single cause for the bad feeling that has so long disgraced our sport; and until we have one law that applies equally to everybody – whether it allows or prevents us all from writing or broadcasting for payment – I can see nothing of real value being achieved towards healing the breach.*

It was a persuasive argument. And Harold's privileged position in journalism had already aroused the wrath of the unions. The National Union of Journalists had long argued that Abrahams should be banned from writing for newspapers. He was not a full-time, trained journalist – and not a union cardholder either. Besides, as an athletics administrator he was operating from an insider's position of unfair advantage. On one occasion, Harold even broke a press embargo, writing in detail about a freshly selected British athletics team on a Monday, when the news was not meant to come out until Tuesday. On more than one occasion union members refused to handle his copy in newspaper offices.

But Harold wasn't going to give up writing or broadcasting for anyone – not for the unions or the athletes. He defended himself against Johnson's attack with a hint of irony:

*The growth of athletics in popularity since 1946, a progressive trend which occurred doubtless in spite of the officials, has led inevitably to the sport becoming "news" . . . The real question is not, so it seems to me, 'Should officials write for payment?' but rather: 'Should those who write for payment be appointed as officials?' It is apparently forgotten that officials cannot obtain their appointments except by favour of those who have the power to appoint . . .The problems to be solved require the best combined efforts of athletes and officials; there is really no time for either party to add to these problems.*

Unfortunately, the ill feeling was hard to eliminate when the man most British athletes looked up to, coach Geoff Dyson, was being treated so shabbily in their view. In 1957, for example, during an end-of-season, two-match tour to Poland and West Germany, Dyson travelled as GB team coach; but by the time he arrived, Crump and Abrahams had already picked the team. It was a similar story when a replacement had to be found quickly for an injured relay runner. This time Crump made the decision unilaterally. A furious Dyson asked to be flown home. Harold acted as peacemaker.

Even so, Abrahams didn't seem to care very much about coaches or medals anymore. 'In the Olympics, I feel that the important thing is not so much to win as to take part,' he kept insisting. 'This is the ideal behind the Olympics, and is still common sense.'

It was also the complete opposite of Abrahams' attitude towards the Paris Olympics, for which he had seen fit to be coached intensively for nine months. Remember, according to bronze medallist Porritt, Harold felt he 'simply had to win the final and win it he did.' Now he was denying the latest generation of athletes the chance to satisfy similar ambitions, and the opportunity to benefit from a similar intensity of professional coaching. Now he valued the amateur ethos above all – and seemed to be advocating the same, relaxed attitude to athletics that he had criticised as a younger man. This is why Lord Puttnam talked about mirror images, and Harold as the living embodiment of all he had fought.

Two things had changed. First of all, having suffered too much as a young man because of his sporting ambition, Abrahams now had the wisdom of an older man's perspective. Secondly, there was now a more general threat to the competitive purity of athletics, one which hadn't existed in his day. The latest crop of athletes seemed to want payment for their competitive efforts. Rightly or wrongly, Harold saw Dyson as part of the new, infected way of thinking.

The AAA soon decided to scrap the differential in salary between the Chief Coach and the other national coaches. This, apparently, was the final straw. Dyson left. Many still believe that represented a severe loss to British athletics. And Dyson soon proved his value on the other side of the Atlantic. First he wrote a brilliant and definitive work on training and coaching called *The Mechanics of Athletics*. Then from his new base in Canada, he influenced some of the top figures in North American athletics. And when Carl Lewis won four gold medals at the 1984 Olympics in Los Angeles, his coach Tom Tellez waved Dyson's book at reporters.

'This is my Bible,' he explained. 'I owe it all to him.'

Harold Abrahams may well have underestimated Dyson's value to British athletics. Peter Radford, a British sprinter who became 200 metres world record holder in 1960, revealed, 'Geoff saw him as an obstacle, a man who couldn't see sense. I was on Geoff's side, on the side of the future, whilst Harold was fighting for the past of the sport. Geoff saw Harold as a man who was not at all interested in the future of the sport.'

But on that last point Dyson couldn't have been more wrong. Harold was desperately worried about the future of the sport, and determined to ensure that it remained pure. He was fearful of what professionalism might mean for the integrity of his beloved sport, and he reacted accordingly. Sometimes he was right, sometimes he was wrong.

Most people change as they grow older. Lord Puttnam once analysed his own journey through life, using Abrahams and Liddell, the central characters in *Chariots of Fire*. 'For the first twenty-five years of my career – certainly until I left the film industry, really – there was more Harold than Eric about me. And I sincerely believe or hope that since then there has been more Eric than Harold.'

In Puttnam's mind, Abrahams still seemed to stand for selfishness and naked ambition, Liddell for altruism. The real Harold Abrahams was slightly different, and he too tried to make the trek from one pole to the other. Even so, had Puttnam's film covered Harold's entire life, you suspect Abrahams would not have come out favourably.

'Did she marry someone nicer than Harold?' Puttnam asked hopefully when he was told the story of Christina McLeod Innes.

Abrahams could be extremely nice. To protect the ethos and spirit of the sport, however, he could also be ruthless as he tried to crush rebellion or even mere dissent.

Lord Sebastian Coe, "Mr London 2012", was a fan of both Harold Abrahams and Eric Liddell – in different ways.

He was fascinating as he explained how a leader's natural desire to be liked cannot always be allowed to prevail – especially when there is only a limited amount of time to ensure that important things are done his or her way.

Seb explained, 'Harold Abrahams left no one in doubt over who was in charge. But one of the qualities of leadership is that sometimes the decisions you make are not particularly popular, not with everybody. It's a question of finding a route through – because no one gets everything entirely right. The main thing is to make sure that you are shaping events, rather than the other way round.'

Abrahams habitually shaped events and refused to be shaped by them. As we have seen, he even went a long way towards shaping Paris 2024 – through his exploits on the track, as captured in the glorious *Chariots of Fire*; and through his clever revision

Lord Coe with the statue of Eric Liddell at Eltham College.

of rules and schedules. Keeping things as pure and simple as he could in a complicated world was his life's work. That led to an unfortunate disrespect for the new generation of coaches, and understandable allegations of hypocrisy. Love him or hate him, Harold did it his way. But if we see sporting purity and effortless simplicity at Paris 2024, we should think of Harold Abrahams every bit as much as Eric Liddell.

CHAPTER SIX:

# Paris 24: Relive and Reshape

Harold Abrahams suddenly became a picture of concentration in the Stade Colombes, Paris.

Oblivious to the crowd, which was filling the arena in anticipation of the main action, Abrahams saw his chance.

Timing was everything to the tall Englishman. Sam Mussabini had taught him patience, too. In the Colombes, Harold was used to being kept waiting. But after thirty-four years, the moment had arrived. Abrahams was focused on two things only: the report of the pistol and the tape. When he heard the one, he would head for the other.

No one else heard the pistol or saw the tape. But Harold did. This was 1958 – but in Harold's mind, it was 1924.

Peter Radford witnessed these priceless seconds. 'It was an international meeting between Great Britain and France. It wasn't during the height of competition; the crowd was still coming in. Harold had gone to the start of the 100 metres. To me he was already an old man. He looked down his lane, standing quietly. No one was talking to him.'

Had they tried, Harold probably wouldn't have heard them. The pistol, the tape. Shut out everything else. Shut out time itself. Harold heard the pistol and reacted.

Radford said, 'Slowly, steadily, he began to move.'

Harold didn't try to sprint. He didn't need to. Even in his prime, Abrahams had been a master of slow motion, until he perfected the right steps and body-shapes. That's how he had honed his technique under Mussabini's guidance. They had even used slow-motion film to analyse everything.

In 1958, Abrahams was in no hurry. He already had that supreme feeling of moving just a little faster than the others.

Radford added, 'He walked the lane very deliberately, all the way to the end.'

Lane Four. Reliving every inch of the race, he could probably hear the crowd's roar all over again, as his rivalry with the "California Flash", Charley Paddock and the "New York Thunderbolt", Jackson Scholz reached its climax.

*How close are they? Don't look. You know what to do.*

Radford, the up-and-coming teenager, watched transfixed.

*I sensed that, as he neared where the tape would have been, there was a slight, almost imperceptible dip of the shoulders. It happened on his final stride . . . then he walked away.*

Harold Abrahams had just won the 1924 Olympic final all over again with his trademark "arrow" finish...Or had he?

This might equally have been an action replay of the finest piece of running he ever did – to come back from the dead in the semi-final.

～

There was a lot more to Harold Abrahams than met the eye. He wasn't just the man who shaped modern athletics. He helped shape the way we view and use the very best of the British landscape. Throughout the 1950s and early 1960s, the beauty of Britain provided the perfect escape from the ugliness of athletics politics. Harold Abrahams played a leading role in the setting up of Britain's National Parks. And that meant he left his country yet another precious legacy.

Curiously, the National Parks project was something he fell into by chance. Harold seemed to have a commendable sense of the absurd as he recalled how his post-war path was determined by a typically British combination of daft bureaucracy and old school tie. Legal eagle Abrahams wanted to go back to the Bar; but the Civil Service wouldn't release him; and they offered him a job at the Ministry of Town and Country Planning instead. Harold declined initially, but then remembered that he knew the Establishment Officer in that department. For this trivial reason, he reconsidered.

With a chuckle he explained, 'I went there initially to help out with an Act of Parliament, which I never in fact did help out with, and I liked it there and stayed on.'

After a year representing the Ministry in his beloved Cambridge, he became Secretary of a new body called the National Parks Commission. It was the perfect opportunity to preserve what was best about his native landscape.

'The British Isles were the best in the world for him,' said his daughter, Sue Pottle. 'He was absolutely patriotic, all for king and country.'

Harold once summarised his task like this:

*The National Parks Commission was set up primarily to designate National Parks. We've got ten of them. Lake District, Peak District, Pembrokeshire Coast, Dartmoor, Exmoor, Northumberland and so on, with the idea that those are areas where the public can enjoy beautiful scenery and get sufficient recreation. It is a frightfully lucky job to have because it brings one into contact with so many people. Local authorities manage the Parks. I go down to Park meetings and help with problems. You've got a great conflict. You've got a limited amount of land in this country. How is it to be used? Are you to have recreation or are you to have a power station? I am essentially a person who believes that the only way in life is compromise. It doesn't mean giving way on things that really matter. There are precious few things that you can be absolutely certain about. I enjoy enormously trying to bring together two conflicting interests and trying to sort it out . . . and get those people thoroughly dissatisfied with the result!*

Harold could afford to joke, because his negotiation skills brought stunning results and new National Parks. 'I would say the Cornish Coastal Park was ninety-nine per cent down to Harold,' his daughter claimed.

The job brought out the best in him. Rosemary Warne, his last close companion, explained:

*He had a superb way of dealing with people, a charm about him and a lovely laugh that made you feel relaxed. He saw the ridiculous not only in others but in himself, which made you feel good because he wasn't too pompous. He would have been incisive about what he wanted to do in the National Parks and he loved his team and the people he worked with. That came over hugely in his recollections of that phase in his life. He set up the Lake District, I think, and a difficult one on Dartmoor where he crossed swords with a Lady Sayers but charmed her. He negotiated land from owners and things like that.*

Harold knew how lucky he was, and after around a decade in the role, he enthused, 'I've got a lovely job, one of the nicest jobs I could ever have run into . . . I've seen more of England in the last ten years than I saw in the first fifty.'

The reward for his good work was announced on the BBC in 1957: 'Among those made Commanders of the Order of the British Empire was Mr Stanley Matthews, who was honoured for services to Association Football. Other CBEs include Mr Harold Abrahams, Secretary of the National Parks Commission, and a well-known sporting commentator and journalist.'

Harold Abrahams, CBE. It had a ring to it; but with brothers called Sir Adolphe and Sir Sidney, Harold hadn't quite kept up this time.

He continued to give everything he could to athletics, both nationally and internationally. To an extent he applied the same principles as he did in the National Parks. Sir Roger Bannister readily acknowledged, 'Harold was highly intelligent and he was a lawyer who understood how to coordinate meetings. He was able to steer his colleagues towards making difficult decisions in a diplomatic way.'

He had become Chairman of the IAAF Technical Committee in 1956, a post he was to hold for twelve years, patiently chipping away each year until the IAAF listened to and implemented what he wanted.

Harold explained, 'In 1956 we proposed – I did most of the advocacy – that the Olympics had become so large that there should be what was called a qualifying standard, and which is now rightly called an entry standard.' The IAAF procrastinated and delayed. But in 1959 Harold was able to announce on radio, 'What they're doing now is they're allowing one entry from each country, and two more if they reach a certain standard.'

There had been chaos at the start of the 800 metres with jostling and casualties. Harold was the man who persuaded the powers that be to introduce lanes. At first the IAAF ruled that the first 300 metres of the race should be in lanes. Later that became 100 metres in major championships.

Sebastian Coe – now Lord Coe – thought he probably benefited from the new ruling.

*Putting in lanes was certainly the right thing to do, because it protects people from being bundled off the track. Probably on balance, with the kind of style I had, that was a good thing for me, though personally I was never worried about mixing it in a race.*

Harold had made the race fairer – pure and simple. Abrahams virtually wrote the IAAF rulebook, using the abiding principle of common sense. He explained:

*Time and again one is apt to get bogged down in words, unless one stops to inquire 'What are the rules trying to achieve?' Rules are made not to hamper competition, but to ensure that it takes place on a fair basis. Many officials are influenced too much by the actual wording of the rules instead of trying to understand the reasons for them. They seem to think they are considering an Act of Parliament. How often is a perfectly wise rule abused by a pernickety official!*

With all this in mind, it's little wonder the late Prince Philip, The Duke of Edinburgh called Abrahams 'one of the most influential figures in the creation and development of athletic competition as we know it today.'

<br>

CHAPTER SEVEN:

# The Geek Who Saw the Future

Harold Abrahams was addicted to numbers.

The older and more eccentric he became, the more obsessive he grew. Eventually his love affair with numbers bordered on an illness, though he insisted they had healing powers.

'Well, they don't mean a lot to me emotionally,' he once said, almost defensively. 'It is a bit of a narcotic, this record business. When I'm tired and depressed – and quite frankly I'm not often tired and depressed – I find it helps to do a sort of mechanical thing.'

It was an asset to his athletics broadcasting, particularly in an Olympic year, when he would prepare a list of the best performances of British athletes ever in the Games.

*It delights me to be able to throw away a line and then for people to say, 'Good Lord, how did he know that, doesn't he know his athletics well?' One's got it all in front of one.*

Harold's obsession with time, distance, speed – and just about anything quantifiable – had begun in his childhood. There was the compulsion to jump further in feet than his age; then there was an account Abrahams gave of his voyage to the USA while at university. He wrote, 'The journey took six days, nine hours and 48 minutes. The most we ever went in one day was 542 miles, the least 454 miles. The average speed was about 24 miles per hour.'

And all this was before Sam Mussabini educated him on the exact number of strides he should take, the length of stride, maximum speed and the time it took to reach maximum speed.. Numbers were everything to Harold Abrahams – and it stayed that way. In 1935 he described statistics as 'my pet lunacy'. He collated them during the war at his Ministry; he carried on in peacetime.

People were baffled as Harold took his love of statistics into the wider world. Instead of telling one astonished interviewer about the highlights of a round-the-world trip he had just completed with Sybil, Harold revealed, 'The last lap from New York yesterday took nine hours, 23 minutes, 57 seconds. I took all the timings – from take-off to landing – throughout the 45 days of the trip. And we've done 21,900 miles in the air, 77 hours and 49 minutes, 49 seconds.'

'I'm afraid he is maddening!' admitted Sybil, perhaps only half-joking.

Harold freely admitted to his addiction:

*I time almost everything. Speeches at dinners, going upstairs, overs at a Test Match, the number of rallies at Wimbledon. It amuses me, but I think there's more than that in it. I once handed my stopwatch to a dentist, when I was going to have my tooth out, and I said, 'Would you mind?' Because I had tried to time having a tooth out before from start to finish and I had unfortunately gone under before I could. And this time he did it and when I woke up, I asked how long it had taken, and he said, 'Four minutes and eight seconds', and I said, 'Oh, world record!' I think again this is a pattern. The statistics are solid and unemotional.*

Rosemary Warne, Harold's companion towards the end of his life, admitted, 'I did find the timekeeping thing infuriating. It did used to jar on me at times, when I found it unnecessary. It was all part of his psyche; the obsession with time was just part of him. I remember him saying, "I just did a minute pee," and I thought, "So what? You're getting a bit desperate if you're timing that."'

Rosemary and Harold's nephew Tony agreed that nine months of time-intensive work with Sam Mussabini might have left lasting scars on Harold. Was this a mild form of Post Traumatic Stress Disorder?

'Could be,' said Tony. 'He was obsessed with time. He always wore two watches – one stopwatch. He timed going to the loo and going out for a walk.'

He would infuriate people by taking off his watch and putting it in front of them, especially if he suspected they were going to be long-winded. Then he would punish them with statistics afterwards.

Tony recalled, 'Some politician made a speech which went on and on. "Do you know how long you spoke for?" demanded an irritated Harold. "About five minutes," came the reply. "You spoke for the amount of time it took Zatopek to win the 10,000 metres," Harold told him.'

Abrahams also became obsessive about the precise location of tube exits on platforms. Tony recalled, 'He wrote something to show which carriage stopped opposite the exit at any station he used from Edgware to Morden or Camden Town. It's all detail. In sprinting, time is all detail.' Some might say these were further symptoms of a form of post-traumatic stress, after all his painstaking preparations as an athlete and the mental anguish on race days. By the time he stopped running, he had almost tried to turn himself into a machine. There were bound to be repercussions, and sometimes he sounded like an overloaded computer.

Harold stayed sane despite his obsession, because he loved people as much as he loved numbers. He loved athletes and wanted them to help him unite the world in a common love of sport, and not become poisoned by money. He was an idealist; he saw athletics as a wonderful agent for peace and harmony. He had a vision for an Olympic medal ceremony that would prevent countries from using his beloved Games as a vehicle for nationalism. He wanted the Olympic theme played instead of the national anthem, and the Olympic flag flown above that of the winning country. The gold medal winner would be introduced as 'Your Olympic Champion' and his nationality mentioned only coincidentally. If scores of different countries won a medal each, that was Harold's idea of Utopia.

Later in his life, Abrahams went even further. He made the following simple statement – the words of a visionary:

*I would arrange that different events took place in different cities – possibly in the same country but perhaps even in different countries.*

Incredibly, some insiders believe that, three or four Games from now, we will see the Olympics simultaneously staged in different countries – perhaps even different continents!

These organisational innovations will come, partly due to the huge financial commitment that single cities or countries are now required to make in order to stage an Olympic Games. The commitment is daunting – and one that single-host bidders are reluctant to make. The push to take the Olympics to new territories will only hasten the expansive trend, the one Harold foresaw.

Lord Coe, an International Olympic Committee member, sees Harold's vision becoming a reality at some point in the not-too-distant future. Coe explained:

*It's certainly technically possible thanks to the advances made in TV technology – and we've seen something similar happen in football. There's talk of the Gulf region potentially staging a future Olympic Games, not just across different cities and countries, but different continents.*

Harold Abrahams was way ahead of his time. Did he ever meet John Lennon? He certainly sounded like him sometimes, almost imagining no countries. Abrahams added:

*I believe that any common experience that can be shared, which doesn't depend on nationality or language or anything else, is something to be encouraged. I mean the obvious thing to speak of is music. You don't bother about the nationality of a composer unless you are an expert musician; you just enjoy the music. And I would like to feel that one can enjoy the athletic performance of a great athlete not thinking about where he is from. I don't think that one thought during a race that Nurmi was a Finn.*

These remarks echoed what Eric Liddell had said about his motivations in Paris. 'Don't forget, I was not running for Scotland. The Olympics are not like that. We've had enough of struggles between nations.' And when Eric Liddell left Scotland for China, he said he was going out as an ambassador 'in the great effort for the unification of the world.' Eric wanted to achieve that through Christ. Not sharing the same religious conviction, Harold felt it could best be done through sport. *Chariots of Fire* might lead us to assume that Eric Liddell and Harold Abrahams were opposites. In fact, they both wanted exactly the same thing – world peace and unity.

Whether he was writing the rulebook, recording statistics, looking at the past or the future, it was his love of the world athletics community that gave Harold Abrahams such energy. His influence was founded on that love, and he gave more to athletics than he received. Considering the way he protected and resurrected the Olympic movement at various critical moments in its history, you could argue that there has never been a greater British Olympian.

'He is right up there,' said Lord Coe. 'Certainly up there.'

CHAPTER EIGHT:

# Tragedy Strikes

Harold loved every moment of his life with Sybil. She was kind, funny, talented and beautiful. He knew he had been lucky to find her.

He played a cameo in her productions when she let him. He would meet each artistic challenge as best he could, given his lack of artistic talent. Abrahams freely admitted that his enthusiasm for his wife's world far surpassed his ability.

*I love Gilbert and Sullivan. My wife was in D'Oyly Carte; I've taken part in amateur productions. Not leading parts, unless you call the Executioner in the Yeoman a leading part. I was jolly good as the Executioner – I brought the axe down exactly at the right moment on the right note. I took the part of Mr Bunthorne's solicitor, and I sing in choruses. I never know quite what my voice is, nor does anybody else, and I dropped a fan at the critical moment in The Mikado.*

His own musical limitations helped Harold to appreciate his wife's talent even more. On *Desert Island Discs* he complained to Roy Plomley, 'Well, you told me I would be unable to take a record of my wife singing. I should love to have done that...'

The last thing Harold wanted was to be without Sybil; especially after they had worked so hard to conquer his demons in the mid-1930s. That personal victory had won them many years of happiness.

By the early 1960s Harold and Sybil were friends to the stars, too. Sue Pottle recalled, 'Harold was friends with [the famous comedian] Norman Wisdom – he came to White City sometimes. Sybil would get people like Diana Dors to come and open fêtes. He knew the footballer Billy Wright, and his singer girlfriend Joy Beverley [the Posh and Becks of their day] too.'

It was a lovely life and Harold lived it to the full. His nephew Tony Abrahams remembered one strange occasion involving a celebrity at the

Garrick Club, where the rule was that you had to converse with your neighbour at the dining table. Some made more effort than others. Tony recalled:

*Harold was with Alec Guinness and me. Sitting next to us was an old chap, a master in lunacy at the High Court. Harold was asking Guinness which film he most enjoyed playing in and Guinness thought for a moment and said, 'Kind Hearts and Coronets because I played several members of the same family, including one woman.' At this point the dear old thing on his right, who was taking his soup, looked up and said, 'Are you a civil servant?' and Guinness said, 'No, I'm not actually.' The chap just went back to his soup. He had respected the rules.*

No famous acquaintance meant as much to Harold as Sybil Evers, the woman who had made him complete at a time when meaningful relationships had seemed beyond him. By the time they celebrated their 25th wedding anniversary in late 1961, they had taken to calling each other "Mr and Mrs Punk" – a daft but endearing family nickname. Harold recorded a mock radio broadcast to mark the anniversary. There was a drum-roll, and then the pips you normally heard before the top of the hour, the news headlines or a major announcement. Harold's voice was heard next, playing the role of an excited broadcaster battling to keep his tone within the confines of BBC formality:

'This is the BBC Home Service. Here is the news. Today, Friday December 22, is the 25th anniversary of the wedding of Mr and Mrs Punk.' The announcement was accompanied by a fanfare of trumpets playing "The Wedding March". Then he went on, 'We offer them our affectionate greetings on this historic occasion. We should like particularly to congratulate Mrs Punk on her remarkable tolerance and stamina. For 9,131 days, she tolerated Mr Punk. For 219,144 hours, or if you preferred it, 78, 891,830 seconds, she's put up with all his faults. Mr Punk has asked us to say – without prejudice – that he's a jolly lucky chap. Hail, Punks!' The broadcast ended with a further trumpet fanfare.

There were those statistics again, the ones Sybil found so maddening. It was hardly the most romantically worded tribute ever composed by a husband to his long-suffering wife. Yet the message was brilliantly delivered and still sounded funny half a century later. It was full of love and driven by a frivolity worthy of a man forty years younger. Sybil had to love him for that. And everyone knew just how fortunate Harold was to be loved by her.

Then, in the summer of 1963, tragedy struck. Sybil thought she was suffering from mild food poisoning, and in a telephone conversation with her daughter Sue, she put her 'tummy upset' down to a meal they had eaten in a local restaurant together the previous day. What had really happened was that a poisonous virus from garden manure had entered her bloodstream. The doctors later said there was nothing they could have done to save her by that stage, even if they had known the precise nature of the problem.

Bravely, Sybil got up the next day to fulfil her obligations. It was mid-June and she was producing the local village play – *A Midsummer Night's Dream*. Her son Alan remembered painfully, 'I was there. It was extraordinary; we were in "Vicarage Garden" in Great Amwell. They had been rehearsing something in the church. We were having drinks, almost a cocktail party kind of thing, and it was very dramatic. She keeled over, fell to the ground and that was it. She had something. I don't know what it was. My mother's death had a devastating impact on my father.'

As Harold had said on *Desert Island Discs*, 'I don't like my own company very much. In fact whenever I am alone I indulge in athletics statistics, so that I'm not at all happy at the prospect of you marooning me.'

But Sybil's death had indeed marooned Harold, and in some ways he never recovered. All his life he had feared putting 'all his eggs in one basket' in case he lost the thing he loved most. He thought that someone had probably taken something away from him as a child, something he liked very much, and that his fears had spun out of control from there. Now someone – perhaps God – had taken Sybil away; and it left him feeling afraid and childlike all over again.

Harold had expected more time with Sybil. As their daughter Sue put it, 'They had twenty-nine years together in all, which many people these days would regard as a long time. But in those days most marriages lasted even longer, and their time was cut short. It is a long time if you look at marriages that have broken down, but if you look at marriages that haven't broken down then it isn't, because a lot of them go on for fifty or sixty years.'

Harold knew that to be alone would destroy him. Norris McWhirter later revealed that Sybil's loss 'tested his fortitude to the uttermost'. Tony Abrahams helped Harold emotionally and practically in his hour of need. He explained, 'After Sybil's death he came to live with us for a while on the top floor of the Goldsmith Building in Temple, central London.'

In a relatively short space of time, Harold did feel he could carry on – perhaps because he felt he had to. He returned to what remained of his normal world as quickly as possible – and took over the running of British athletics. Sybil had always known she could do no more than share Harold with his first love, athletics. And his love for the Olympic Games still burned bright.

The Tokyo Olympics of 1964 partially healed him. The Games brought Harold closer to joy than he had been for a year, because a British protégé of his struck gold. He had watched Lynn Davies jump 25 feet – the barrier Harold was never able to smash – when the young Welshman had competed as a youngster in Brighton. Davies, the man Harold described as 'Britain's finest long-jumper ever', took the Olympic title in Japan with a leap of 26ft 5¾in. A few years later, Lynn wrote to Harold acknowledging his contribution. Davies wrote, 'As one long-jumper of bygone years to another, may I thank you for your help and encouragement during the last decade.'

Abrahams sounded euphoric after Tokyo. He said, 'This has been the finest Games ever in every way. The superlative character of the arrangements rather terrifies me. I don't see how any country in the future can possibly live up to the standard which has been achieved here.' The damage the Japanese had done to Harold's old sprint rival, Eric Liddell seemed to have been lost in this wave of enthusiasm for his beloved Olympics. Later Harold added, without a hint of prejudice, 'Tokyo was the best organised Games, with Berlin '36 a close second. The Tokyo Games were much more human because the Nazis were trying to prove their regime during the 1936 Games.'

For Harold, any time he reflected on the 1936 Games also served as a reminder of a time when he and Sybil had been trying to prove they could make it as a couple, while their future hung in the balance. Now Sybil was gone; but Harold was determined not to let her memory die. Each year from 1964 onwards, the Duke of Edinburgh, President of the British Amateur Athletic Board, kindly agreed to present a cup called The Sybil Abrahams Memorial Trophy to the best British woman athlete at Buckingham Palace. The first winner of Sybil's cup was Mary Rand, who had also won long-jump gold at those Tokyo Olympics, silver in the pentathlon and bronze in the 4 × 100 metres.

Meanwhile Harold set up a trust so that another award could be created, something closer to his wife's heart: the Sybil Abrahams Memorial Prize for Singing. It was a cash prize awarded to the best female singer in her last year at the Webber Douglas School of Singing and Dramatic Art. The prize was first awarded in 1965; and the practice continued all the way through to 1995. Every year for the rest of his life, Harold went to see a production of *A Midsummer Night's Dream* at the Open Air Theatre in London's Regents Park. It was one of the places where Sybil had most enjoyed performing; and of course, the production was always a poignant reminder of how she had lived – and how she had also died.

CHAPTER NINE:

# Seeing Past the Medals

B y the late 1960s, Harold's love affair with the Olympics was losing its sparkle. In fact, Abrahams had begun to worry that he had helped to create a monster.

That was a dramatic change of heart in the space of just four years. Or had his Tokyo euphoria been born of necessity, because without it his grief over Sybil might simply have overwhelmed him?

In 1968, just before he left for the Mexico Games, Harold sounded weary. He explained, 'I'm seventy next year, I'm setting out for the Olympics and this will be my tenth (I missed Los Angeles in 1932). It has become much more important to people since 1936 in Berlin; and then of course from 1952 onwards, television has played its part. The whole aspect of the significance of the Olympics has changed so much that I wonder whether dear old Baron De Coubertin would recognise it at all.'

Behind the scenes, drug cheats were already starting to undermine the integrity of the Olympics in a way Harold had simply refused to imagine possible back in 1928.

Add to that the increasing commercialism and nationalism creeping in, and something insidious was growing that needed a counterbalance. An urgent dose of athletic purity was required. But where was that going to come from? Abrahams had spent his life loving and defending the Olympics. Now he was wavering.

Harold was asked if he would miss the Olympics if they didn't exist. For one who had served the movement almost all his life, Abrahams gave a poignant answer:

*Well, I think you are absolutely laying my soul bare, aren't you . . . If you said to me, "Would the world suffer if there weren't the Olympics?" The way they are going, I'm not sure.*

Just as well something incredible happened at those Mexico Olympics. It was enough to rekindle the flame in any athletics lover. An American long jumper called Bob Beamon had only qualified for the final with the last of three attempts. Harold could scarcely believe what he saw next: 'He sailed into the stratosphere with his first jump of 8.90 metres or 29ft 2½in. In doing so he added 55 centimetres or 21¾ inches to the previous world record. He won the competition by a margin of 71 centimetres or 28 inches, easily the biggest margin ever. The long jump of Bob Beamon was almost literally out of this world'. As the 1964 winner of the Olympic long-jump title Lynn Davies observed: 'How can one compete against a man who goes into orbit?'

On December 21 of that Olympic year, Harold received a further boost to his morale. He was given a fitting reward for his lifelong commitment to his sport when he became Chairman of the British Amateur Athletics Board. The Guardian claimed his appointment proved 'that he is almost as durable as General de Gaulle'. He was almost as prickly too. When asked how the BAAB – which was in debt at the time – proposed to pay for a certain item, Abrahams replied, 'By cheque.'

He did not intend to lose a single verbal skirmish, however minor, now that he was in full control. He did not intend to deny himself the various joys of life, either.

One of Harold's closest friends in the final years of his life was a woman almost half a century younger than he was. Abrahams first met a vivacious 23-year-old teacher called Rosemary Warne in 1969, when she picked him up at Felixstowe station as a favour to a friend.

'He is a BBC broadcaster and he lost his wife a few years ago, have you heard of him?' asked Elsie Eaton, a fellow singer in the Felixstowe Amateur Operatic Society. Rosemary admitted that she had not, though the gentleman who introduced himself at the station cut a striking figure. Rosemary described him in the following glowing terms:

*This very tall, balding man – like Mr Pickwick stretched – with very bright blue eyes which seemed to sparkle. He wore a light blue shirt, bright*

*blue blazer and similar bright blue trousers with brown shoes which I*
*thought were most incongruous.*

*We had a very entertaining lunch. He was funny, a good raconteur,*
*very amusing. I laughed a lot, I can remember, and so did Elsie and her*
*husband Will. Harold was a very likeable, easy person. We both adored*
*Gilbert and Sullivan, and from the age of ten I had been a member of the*
*D'Oyly Carte Trust. I had all the magazines, and when he told me his wife*
*had been second soprano that was it – smitten.*

Harold Abrahams with his last companion, Rosemary Warne.

They developed a close but platonic relationship, and there were
times when both would need comfort. In Harold's case, a depressing
moment came in early 1970. His Olympic 100 metres gold medal had
been mounted in a frame and surrounded by the signatures of his fellow
1924 finalists. *The Daily Telegraph* of March 3, 1970 carried a headline:
'GOLD MEDAL STOLEN'.

'Harold Abrahams, the only British athlete to win 100 metres in an
Olympic Games, has had his gold medal stolen, in a weekend raid on his
London home.'

It wasn't so much a raid as an inside job. Harold's sister Dorothy had
married a man who turned out to be unfaithful. He had a child by their
maid, and Dorothy bravely agreed to adopt the baby. The boy was called
Kim, and he turned out to be even worse than his father. He began to

steal from the family whenever he could. 'At some stage "Cousin Kim" went round and stole the medal from my father's house,' said Sue Pottle. 'I think there were even fingerprints and a confession.'

His administrative colleague Arthur Gold had another Olympic medal made for Harold, a commemorative one which was also engraved. But of course, it could never replace the original, complete with all the signatures of his fellow competitors. Thankfully there were other young Brits for Harold to focus on. Young men who dreamed of winning an Olympic medal, just as Harold had done in 1924.

Later in 1970, the GB team landed in Zurich for an athletics meeting, with Harold Abrahams managing the group. Abrahams saw the most junior athlete sitting directly behind him and as he got up, Harold said: 'Would you mind carrying my bags?'

It wasn't that Abrahams was so physically weak by then that he couldn't comfortably deal with his travel bag himself. Just that it would be more convenient if the youngster did it for him; and the "request" asserted a sort of order in the general scheme of things. Harold Abrahams was at the top of the food chain – and the newest member of the team was at the bottom. Carrying his bag was probably the sort of thing Harold Abrahams thought newcomers should do. Sure enough, the young man did as he was told. His name was Brendan Foster.

'Harold Abrahams was my first team manager,' he said. 'It was going to be my first time running for Great Britain. When we landed in Zurich, he asked me to carry his bags. I didn't mind. The athletic administrators were stiff old bastards in those days; but I quite liked Harold Abrahams.'

In the funniest moment of a 2023 interview with Lord Coe, Seb responded to that story quick as a flash: 'Ah, I didn't know that. It's joining up a few dots for me now. I often wondered why for my first five or six years I had to carry Brendan Foster's bags.'

Mercifully Seb Coe never had to go through what Harold and Brendan experienced together – the trauma of 1972. Eleven Israeli athletes were murdered at the Munich Olympics in a terrorist attack that shocked the world. Some felt the Olympics should be cancelled there and then, out of respect for those who had lost their lives. Harold felt that to abandon the Olympics Games almost before they had begun would play into the hands of those behind the atrocity. It was typical Abrahams to argue that the Olympic show must go on. But what did the athletes think?

Brendan Foster recalled:

*Munich promised to be such fun and full of wonderful memories. It was my first of three Olympics – and I was so excited by everything associated with the Games. But all that changed with the attack on the Israeli athletes in the Olympic village.*

*We knew something terrible was unfolding but we were unaware of what was happening. It was devastating when we finally discovered the extent of the tragic circumstances, everyone was shocked and there was talk of taking the team home. They didn't understand we wanted to stay on and show the world the Olympics could not be beaten by terrorists. It's up to others to decide whether their continuation was a good or a bad thing – that's for history to decide. It was a hugely significant event and a savage massacre. But if the Games hadn't gone on it could have been the end of the Olympic movement.*

Foster and Abrahams, from very different generations, were of the same mind, then. The show must go on. The Olympic movement had be saved.

They stayed, and Brendan Foster had the opportunity to try and win an Olympic medal despite the tragedy. It wasn't to be in '72, but he did equal a British record on his way to reaching his first Olympic final. No one in the history of athletics was ever more excited for young athletes when they showed clear signs of progress than Harold Abrahams. The world had seen that in the cases of Jack Lovelock and Roger Bannister; and we saw the same warmth at work again with Brendan Foster.

The Olympic Games had lost their innocence forever in Munich. But Harold was determined that Foster should hold onto the positive promise he had shown. In 2023, Sir Brendan remembered one gesture very clearly, even though we were speaking more than fifty years after the event. He explained:

*I liked Harold Abrahams and I still remember how kind he was to me. He gave me a photo to mark what I'd done at the Munich Olympics. It was a photo of the stadium scoreboard, with my name up there in lights in fifth place, and Harold wrote "British record-holder" on the photo.*

It was a lovely memento that helped boost Foster's confidence – and recognised that he was going places. Foster soon became the British athlete most capable of going in search of a medal at the next Olympics. In the meantime, Harold Abrahams showed further generosity with a medal of his own; a genuine original and not a reproduction.

He went to see Christina, his former fiancée. Later her daughter, Sue Smithson recalled the happy reunion. 'Harold came to my parents' house and my son Robert would have been about ten. He was running around the garden and Harold was there with his stopwatch, timing him. He gave Robert a medal. He said he would rather give them to someone than to have them stolen.'

Inscribed on the front, alongside the American and British flags and a runner, were the following words: 'OXFORD-CAMBRIDGE-PRINCETON-CORNELL'. On the back was written: 'TRACK AND FIELD MEET JULY 28, 1921 – TRAVERS ISLAND, USA'. And then there was the following inscription: 'Run Broad Jump Winner H.M. Abrahams CAMBRIDGE 21ft 8in'.

Was it just a coincidence that Harold selected a medal which he won at the very height of his romance with Robert's grandmother Christina, when they were engaged to be married? Whatever the truth, it was a poignant moment.

Seb Coe received his own memento from Harold Abrahams as an up-and-coming middle-distance runner. Lord Coe recalled, 'I did receive an award from him at one of the junior races at Crystal Palace. There was no mistaking you were in the presence of a very serious player in the sport. We knew and he knew who was in charge. I can remember that people were familiar with his story, were aware of being in the presence of someone quite extraordinary in the sport.'

That kind of respect and recognition wasn't always afforded

Abrahams, sadly. When living legends were invited to give away medals to the winning athletes at Crystal Palace on a summer's day in 1976, Abrahams was hurt by his treatment. He received no proper introduction to the crowd, and the organisers saw fit to have him present the medals for hammer-throwing, instead of the 100 metres which had preceded it.

Harold was understandably grumpy when he recorded a message for Rosemary, who had joined the army and was often away. 'To be asked to give away the "Hammer", when before that was the 100 metres! I would have liked the crowd to know – ninety per cent of them had never heard of me – that this bald old bugger had won a gold medal fifty-two years ago.'

Harold had earned the right to recognition – perhaps more than any administrator before or since. And ironically, if Abrahams were still alive to present medals at the Paris Olympics in 2024, he would be guaranteed a standing ovation. He was immortalised in *Chariots of Fire* barely five years after he complained that no one knew him.

Back in 1976 he consoled himself with his genuine delight in the progress of others. What other joy was there? Politics were taking over the Olympics – and that was tiresome to him. What was the point in banning a country from the Olympics when the whole idea was to bring countries together? Before the Montreal Olympics, at the 1976 IAAF Congress, Harold was the only delegate to speak in support of continued South African membership.

'If you want to change the laws of South Africa, certainly you will not do it if you isolate South Africa,' he claimed.

Time would prove him wrong on that one. However, anyone who tried to accuse Abrahams of being a racist supporter of apartheid would be laughed out of the room. His friendship with Jesse Owens was well documented. So was his respect for untapped Caribbean talent, an area in which he was way ahead of his time. Abrahams had known discrimination himself. But the Olympics were becoming a political football, a punchbag, a monstrosity of ulterior motives.

Abrahams reflected later:

*I have often wondered whether Baron Coubertin would ever have started the modern Olympics, if he would have seen just exactly how they would develop. In the past fifty-six years I have been to twelve Olympics and I have watched with increasing sadness and concern the effect of nationalism, professionalism, political interference and commercialism.*

Who would bring the Olympics back to basics and remind us of the sheer joy of running? Who would win GB's next track and field Olympic medal? One man answered that call, and it was Harold's bag-carrier. Abrahams had praised and celebrated Brendan Foster at the previous Olympics, when few others did. By the time Foster neared the finish of the 10,000 metres final in Montreal, he was out of the running for gold and silver. But the bronze medal he earned with his passion and sheer hard work stood alone. Incredibly, it was the only medal GB won in all Montreal's track and field competition. Brendan didn't lament his failure to win gold. He would go on to win so many of those in other major championships. In Montreal, he had done his best – and that was all that mattered.

'That's what *Chariots of Fire* is all about,' Sir Brendan said in 2023. 'It's being the best you can be – and that's what life is all about too.'

For all his faults, Harold Abrahams knew that as well. Whether you were Roger Bannister missing out on glory at Helsinki 52, or Brendan Foster missing out at Munich 72, he stuck with young athletes until they had their reward. That's why few could argue with the late Prince Philip's verdict on Abrahams. The Duke of Edinburgh put it like this in 2011:

*His dedication to the efficient administration of British athletics and his commitment to the welfare and development of individual athletes was complete.*

CHAPTER TEN:

# Puttnam Prepares to Take the Baton

In November 1976, Harold Abrahams was made only the sixth President of the Amateur Athletics Association since it began in 1880. After a lifetime's service to the sport, Harold followed in the footsteps of the Earl of Jersey, Viscount Alverstone, Sir Montague Shearman, Lord Desborough and his friend the Marquess of Exeter [formerly Lord Burghley – or "Lindsay" in *Chariots of Fire*], whose presidency had lasted some forty years. He couldn't have been more delighted.

'This is certainly one of the proudest moments of my life,' he said. 'To have been elected President of one of the oldest athletic associations in the world is a great honour – thank you very much.'

How he would have loved to share that sense of satisfaction with Sybil. And although she had been dead for fourteen years, Harold continued to visit her final resting place to mark each anniversary of her death. He recorded a message that summer to Rosemary, describing his feelings about these journeys back to Great Amwell:

*I went in the afternoon to visit Sybil's grave. It's funny because in a sense one doesn't know why one does it, because it isn't the only day of the year one thinks about Sybil. I think one rather has the feeling that she may know one's doing it, although that doesn't at all agree with my feeling that when one's dead, one's dead. It's a weird thing, you can't really contemplate extinction, and in a way nothing in this world can be destroyed, it merely changes its form. But I like to go out there in some ways; and I took some flowers from the garden and I like to think that perhaps she knows one's doing it, but of course it isn't the only time of the year I think about her.*

In his last public appearance, at Crystal Palace on July 22, 1977, it was Harold's duty and pleasure as President of the Amateur Athletic Association to read out the following royal message: 'I have been asked to convey to all the athletes and officials of the A.A.A. the warm thanks of the Queen for their kind and loyal message of Silver Jubilee greetings, which Her Majesty much appreciates. As patron of the Association, the Queen sends her best wishes for the success of the Nationwide Building Society Silver Jubilee A.A.A. Championships to all those taking part in them.'

Although the commercial element to that message may have stuck in his throat somewhat, this was still a grand way to leave the public arena, sixty-seven summers after his first appearance on another of the great old stages of London athletics, Stamford Bridge. Harold Abrahams had achieved so much between those appearances. Lord Coe, Chairman of the London 2012 Organising Committee, summed up his admiration for Abrahams and all he gave athletics with the following memorable line:

*Respect is not a strong enough word, actually.*

Behind the scenes, Harold wasn't finished just yet. He was ready to fight to the death, because he had recently been made aware of 'all these payments in athletics that are pretty extensive. I'm determined to do something to curtail them if I can, because it really is getting...'

Harold couldn't seem to find the right word, because his feelings were running so high in this latest recorded message to Rosemary. But he vowed, 'I'm going to have a crack at it, dear, because I think it is the only way in which we shall save athletics from being a very unpleasant thing.'

Harold's worst fears regarding the abuse of the amateur rules had been confirmed when he travelled to Turin for an athletics international between Italy, England and the USA. His Italian friend, the statistician Roberto Quercetani, met him there and recalled, 'The match was degraded by the absence of many leading athletes, attracted elsewhere by more fruitful commitments. Referring to promoters who would leave nothing untried to secure the best "stuff" available for their invitational meets, Harold jokingly asked: "Do you think they would pay $15 for an Abrahams vintage '24?"'

How times had changed. No wonder he still had affection for a bygone era. And soon everyone would, because an unlikely chain of events – leading all the way to *Chariots of Fire* – were set in motion by a housebound Englishman's boredom in LA.

David Puttnam explained, 'I was looking for a theme about someone doing something which was extraordinary.' As it turned out, Puttnam stumbled across exactly what he was looking for by chance. Here's the way he remembered it:

> It was rather embarrassing, I had rented a house in Pacific Palisades on the coast outside LA, from a guy who was a fanatical yachtsman. I was ill and I couldn't leave the house, so I was suddenly thrown back on what he had in his library.
>
> Every book seemed to be on sailing and navigation and I found the one book that wasn't – by Bill Henry. It was "An Approved History of the Olympic Games." So I started reading it and I got to page 116 about 1924. And I just found this extraordinary paragraph, not about Harold but about Eric Liddell refusing to run.
>
> And that's the bell that rung and I thought, 'Could you get the audience to accept the fact that someone couldn't run in the Olympics?' And that's where it started. But I also saw Harold Abrahams in the story and Douglas Lowe. And it was about this group of men, it was always intended to be about a group of men. From Day One I knew that Eric's story wouldn't hold a movie on its own. It's too thin. It's a one-line plot. So it was always going to be about relationships. And the film would have been a thin brew without Harold Abrahams.

Puttnam invited a writer to his home. His name was Colin Welland, a playwright with attitude. David gave him a newspaper cutting and a simple summary of the plot. What could Welland do with the story?

'I'd like to thank David Puttnam for having the wisdom to employ me,' said Colin so memorably on a Los Angeles stage about four years later.

Welland began to do some research. Puttnam remembered, 'Colin definitely did have a conversation with Harold. It must have been in the autumn of 1977.'

From left to right: Mrs Jenny Somerville (Liddell's sister),
Arthur Green (Vice President, Old Elthamians), Colin Welland,
Mrs Porteous, Headmaster Christopher Porteous and David
Puttnam visit Eric Liddell's old school, Eltham College.

It appears that Harold and Colin connected – and Abrahams was
enthusiastic about the idea of being immortalised on the silver screen.
To borrow some of Harold's previous words, suddenly everyone was
going 'to know that this bald old bugger had won a gold medal' more
than half a century earlier. As Puttnam wryly observed, 'there was never
for one moment any concern that Harold was not going to be happy
about the project at all.'

The reason Welland identified with Abrahams was that Colin – as
a northerner – also felt he had been the victim of prejudice. And as he
listened to the older man, he would have drawn parallels in their respective stories. That's one of the reasons why Lord Puttnam still felt lucky
decades later that he commissioned Welland.

He explained, 'In a way Colin was a masterstroke. It allowed him
to say things about being a northerner in the south; things that I think
he felt deeply about. Where I "lucked in" was that the Jewish outsider,
Harold, became the northern outsider, Colin, in the sense that in the
film Harold said what Colin felt.'

Rosemary Warne recalled, 'Harold told me that he'd got some interesting news to tell me in 1977 for Christmas – and then he didn't tell me anything. I found myself thinking, "Come on, what is this interesting news?" and he said, "No dear, I'm not telling you." I think he was probably going to tell me about it before the news came out. I think it was the film. He was very chuffed and bubbling because something was happening.'

And a few weeks before Harold Abrahams died, he wrote to Brian Marchant, Mussabini's grandson. Early research on the movie project by Colin Welland may have been the catalyst for contact between Abrahams and Marchant.

Harold wrote on November 23, 1977 – and expressed his gratitude towards old Sam Mussabini one last time. He gave Marchant a copy of that scarcely legible Mussabini note, sent from one Parisian hotel to another before the Olympic action began in that unforgettable summer of 1924. As considerate as ever, Harold added a "translation" in block capitals of what Mussabini had scrawled. That way Old Sam's grandson would not mistake a single word. Abrahams, of course, knew the contents off by heart.

Harold's accompanying note represented the last words he ever wrote on Mussabini and the most momentous time of his life.

*I can assure you that even after 53 years, I still have appreciation for all his help.*

There was something beautifully simple about that line.

Similarly, Mussabini's original note was so full of controlled passion that Welland used it for his screenplay. Sam's words are worth recalling one last time, and feature again on the next page.

Harold's correspondence proves that he kept Mussabini's little letter for more than half a century. And when Lord Puttnam saw Old Sam's handwritten message for the first time in 2010, he became quite animated and declared, 'It is exactly as we had it in the film! Word for word! Colin must have got this from Harold. It must have come from

Harold, because we didn't have any dealings with the Mussabini family, I'm ninety-nine per cent certain.'

```
                              ▉OTEL  FRANKLIN
                          RUE BOUFFAULT
                              PARIS
        JULY  7th.  1924

        DEAR MR. ABRAHAMS,
                  YOU MUST PLEASE PARDON MY NOT COMING TO SEE YOU, MUCH
        AS I WOULD LIKE TO DO SO.
                  HOWEVER - I BELIEVE AND HOPE YOU WILL WIN THE 100 METRES.
                  GO OUT DETERMINED TO DO YOUR BEST AND DON'T FORGET TO
        GO DOWN AT THE FIRST STRIDE.
                  A SPONGE AND SOME COLD OR PREFERABLY ICED WATER USED
        AROUND THE NAPE OF THE NECK, ▉▉▉  UNDER THE EARS AND AT THE WRISTS AND
        ELBOWS WILL BRACE YOU UP.
                     GET NICELY WARMED UP AND THEN RE-ACT TO THE GUN.
          I SHOULD USE THE SPRINGY OLD 6-SPIKED SHOES.

                       ALL THE BEST OF LUCK FROM
                            YOURS TRULY
                               S.A.MUSSABINI
        P.S.
            PLEASE WISH FRED GABY GOOD LUCK FROM ME.
```

Harold deciphers the scrawl for Sam Mussabini's relative.

They had some promising initial source material. But what should Puttnam and Welland call their film? They came up with one word that said everything,

"Runners."

That was the working title. And they felt excited about the creative challenges ahead. As it turned out, getting *Runners* made would take a minor miracle.

CHAPTER ELEVEN:

# Chariot For Mr Athletics

Time was short. Harold Abrahams had one Christmas left – and he spent it with Rosemary Warne in Bielefeld, Germany, where she was stationed.

'He seemed in very good form,' she recalled.

On his return to Winchmore Hill, where he was living with Alan and his wife Phyllis, Harold went back into battle one last time for the future of athletics. He seemed in good enough shape for the fight.

'He had just turned seventy-eight but he was still fit and would go on mile-long walks,' Alan explained. 'Right until the end, he kept working. Always busy, always with something to do. That's the way he liked it.'

On January 4, the last night of his conscious life, Harold called Robert Stinson, Honorary Secretary of the British Amateur Athletic Board. Stinson was a much younger man, and Abrahams had overseen his rise through the administrative ranks of athletics.

On December 30, Stinson had written to Harold. 'I would be grateful if you would find time to call me at home with regard to the Barry Williams problem,' he said.

The British hammer thrower was in hot water. Two articles in *The People* newspaper in 1976 had given the impression that Williams had taken anabolic steroids. As a result, he had lost his international eligibility. In a damage limitation exercise, Williams and the BAAB were in the process of retracting his previous remarks.

The Williams case had done nothing to dispel Harold's fears that the march towards professionalism was already turning athletics rotten; that drug use was bound to be the consequence of appearance money. How wrong he had been to dismiss doping as irrelevant back at the Amsterdam Olympics. But then again, in those days there was less incentive to take drugs. Now it was different. People were going to cheat if they thought they could get rich by cheating.

All Harold and Stinson could do, once the Williams case had been addressed, was try to prevent the floodgates from bursting open. If they crumbled, professionalism threatened to swamp the sport completely. By relaxing amateur rules where they could, so that athletes at least had money to train and travel, they might keep more competitors on their side. Maybe the pressure on those floodgates could be eased slightly, if they picked a way through the crisis carefully and set the right tone.

Harold had already ensured that athletes the world over could tap into trust funds – he called them "subventions" – set up by their national governing bodies. Stinson wondered whether there was anything else that could be done to make British athletes feel more valued, without giving way to full-blown professionalism.

The athletics writer Mel Watman pointed out, 'Probably more than most people, Robert Stinson was responsible for the liberalising of the amateur rules. And Harold was still forward-looking, even though he was tied to the amateur ethos of the day.'

As they talked that night, Abrahams and Stinson knew they were fighting a desperate rearguard action. Those floodgates still looked set to burst – and soon they would. Then the defences Harold had built to protect the purity of his sport might be swept away by the materialism of modern-day athletics.

'I think we should endeavour to retain the spirit of the old, while abandoning habits of thought and actions derived from a society that no longer exists,' Harold always said quite reasonably. You could almost hear him still trying to save the soul of the Olympic movement that night.

Retain the spirit of the old. That's what *Chariots of Fire* is all about. It would make Harold Abrahams a hero forever. But in his final days, he must have felt more like King Cnut, stubbornly defiant as the tide of change crashed in around his legs. The thought of track and field athletes poisoning his innocent world – and themselves – with drugs, in the shameless pursuit of appearance money was too much for Harold to bear.

Sue Stinson recalled, 'Robert suggested that Harold should go to bed because of the tiredness he could hear in his voice.'

The evergreen voice of athletics was finally weakening. The voice of the past; and the voice that had also pointed to an Olympic future way beyond Paris 2024. Robert Stinson said, 'Harold was the living embodiment of long-term progressive thought on athletics. I count myself fortunate that I was talking to him only thirty minutes before he suffered the stroke which proved fatal.'

His son Alan remembered that dreadful moment. 'We had finished dinner and he had gone upstairs to his office. We heard a crash. It was similar to my mother, the way he suddenly collapsed. He'd had a stroke.'

Harold was taken to Chase Farm Hospital in Enfield. Rosemary was informed, and Alan hoped she might hold the key to his recovery. Rosemary explained, 'Alan rang me, maybe on the fourth of January, told me the sad news and asked if it would be possible for me to come over, because they thought that familiar voices might assist in bringing him to. I managed to get compassionate leave and came over on a boat. When I reached the hospital, I talked to him about everything and played music. It is funny because you have a body lying there and you are not sure what they know, what they can hear and what they can't hear.'

Sue Pottle recalled, 'Many of us visited my father at his bedside, we sang him Gilbert and Sullivan and chatted about this and that – but no reaction.'

Rosemary remembered the underlying despair:

*It was very hard for me and the family. It was hard for all of us. I shaved him, because one of the things he was always so meticulous about was that he was always clean-shaven whenever one met him. He was meticulous about how he looked, personal hygiene and so on. And when I arrived, he hadn't been shaved for two or three days and he had got this awful stubble around him. And I thought maybe if I did that it would help because it was really quite soporific sitting around there. I think he had an electric shaver and I tried, I was probably pretty awful at it, but I thought he looked a little better and I thought maybe that would make him feel a little better. If it got through. One didn't know. That was it, really. There wasn't a lot else one could really do. He got pneumonia, I think I'm right in saying. He was certainly very chesty. He didn't come to.*

By now Alan had given up hope. 'After the first forty-eight hours, my view – and that of my wife – was that we kind of hoped he didn't wake up again. If you can get the patient back to consciousness within forty-eight hours there is a good chance of success. After that it is less likely.'

There was to be no awakening for Harold, and Alan pointed out, 'He was dead before he hit the ground in all but name. In practical terms he was dead. He had made it clear he didn't want to be a vegetable and wanted to go quickly. He didn't want to hang around. That was one thing he was scared of.'

Alan's sister Sue explained, 'I don't believe he would have wanted to wake in a paralysed state, because his brother Adolphe had been like that for about six months at the end of his life, and it had been very difficult.'

Harold Maurice Abrahams had come into the world early. It might be said that, following his collapse, he left just a little late – even for his own liking. He died on January 14, 1978 – almost thirty-three years after Eric Liddell.

Poor Rosemary Warne, whose army commitments had forced her back to Germany, scraped together enough money to head back to England again, following her heart. 'I remember going with the family from 42 Orpington Road. They very kindly let me ride in the car or one of the cars. We went to Enfield Crematorium. I don't really remember very much after that, I felt a bit miserable.'

Norman Cuddeford, the BBC commentator remembered the scene. 'It didn't seem to be a Jewish funeral. Nobody was wearing Jewish garb, it was a Christian funeral.'

Sue Pottle explained, 'The funeral was private – almost just family and Ken Gardner, who my parents had fostered during the war. Tony was there too and a few others.'

Harold would have been tickled that one of his former work colleagues captured the essence of his spirit as his once-athletic body finally returned to the elements. Cuddeford explained, 'Geoff Dobson, Harold's BBC radio athletics producer, was there. As the service came to an end, the coffin began its journey through the curtains. When it had disappeared, Geoff Dobson showed me his stopwatch. "That was 47.3 seconds. I think Harold would have been pleased with that."

Robert Stinson, who had heard Harold's last impassioned words on this earth, reflected sadly, 'Perhaps because he had been regarded as immortal, I fear too many of us had taken for granted the thoughtful influence that he exercised in the sport behind the scenes over the years.'

At least Harold never lived to see America's boycott of the 1980 Olympics. He had so hated those mass boycotts of 1976. And although he would have loved every second of Allan Wells' 100 metres gold medal run in Moscow, he might have had mixed feelings about the post-race interview. Scotsman Wells had become the first British man to win the Olympic 100 metres since the day Harold Abrahams had shocked the Americans in Paris way back in 1924. The 56-year wait wasn't lost on the journalist who reached Wells first after his historic achievement. Did Allan want to dedicate his win to Abrahams?

'No disrespect to anyone else, but I would prefer to dedicate this to Eric Liddell,' said Wells. 'This one's for Liddell.'

How would Harold have reacted to that, had he still been alive? He might have bristled a little, but understood that Wells, as a proud Scotsman, had grown up respecting his own national hero. Then a comforting thought might have drifted into Harold's mind.

'Ah yes, Mr Wells, but you didn't have to face and defeat the Americans for your 100 metres gold, did you?'

'And you didn't have to face and defeat Eric Liddell for your 100 metres gold, did you sir?' Wells could justifiably have replied.

Harold didn't live to enjoy that kind of banter with his champion-successor. But we will surely feel the presence of Abrahams at

Paris 2024 every bit as much as Liddell. It isn't a competition between these two. It hasn't been for a hundred years. They both took Paris by storm – and used victory wisely.

CHAPTER TWELVE:

## The Perfect Handover

In 1978, the very year that Harold died, someone else took the baton to keep alive the true spirit of the Olympic movement. David Puttnam had the vision. A shining film, full of purity and passion, bottling all that was best about the Games. And who would one of its main heroes be? None other than Harold Abrahams. The timing was exquisite. Even Harold, with his stop-watch precision, would have admired it.

If the handover happened anywhere, it was at Harold's Memorial Service, which took place at St Bride's – the "journalists' church" – just off Fleet Street on February 20, 1978. Colin Welland, chosen writer for the embryonic movie project, was there among the throng. And Harold's old BBC colleague Norman Cuddeford recalled a scene that would have been worthy of the film itself:

*I was an usher at the Memorial Service and it was packed. The music was beginning to fade away and the service was about to start when there was a kerfuffle outside and an old boy on sticks, who was also deaf, came in. I could see there was a small gap up in the choir stalls by Harold Evans of The Times, so I directed him there. As we made our way, he said loudly, 'Can I tell you a story about Harold?' I told him that he could tell me if he could be a little quieter, but he was deaf, as I say, so he still spoke loudly as he began, 'We always used to meet once a year for lunch. I was at Oxford, Harold was at Cambridge and we used to race. "Harold," I'd tell him, "I knew your backside better than your front side because I could never keep up with you."* A lot of people in the church heard him and they all laughed.

It summed up Harold's excellence on the cinders rather nicely. Cuddeford added, 'Looking back, it was the fact that the church was packed out which said more about Harold than any religion. The Marquess of Exeter represented the Duke of Edinburgh; Sir Roger Bannister was there, and Harold's fellow-medallist from 1924, Lord Porritt, read the lesson.'

But there were so many others who wanted to pay tribute to "Mr Athletics." Norris McWhirter delivered the eulogy and began like this: 'To deliver a remotely adequate address on the life and achievement of Harold would require an inordinate amount of time. In his life Harold timed everything and everybody. He quite unfortunately specialised on sermons and on addresses at memorial services . . .'

McWhirter later talked of the 'profound sense of loss' felt by 'all those whose lives were sometimes touched, sometimes transformed by the many kindnesses and the warmth of his feeling, particularly to those who, through youth or inexperience, or straitened circumstances lacked the wisdom or the substance of which he could and did so generously give.' Then he reminded everyone of Harold's 'immense achievement' in ensuring 'that track and field athletics today has the status of a national sport...Harold's memorials range from the permanence of his place in Olympic history to the near permanence of the IAAF rulebook, which he virtually wrote ...

'In giving thanks for his life and achievement of the incomparable Harold at the last we may all say as surely Harold can say, "I have fought the good fight, I have finished my course, I have kept the faith."'

Harold's life was over. Yet the telling of his story and that of Eric Liddell had only just begun. Colin Welland was sure by now the memorial service itself would be a good starting point for the movie. They had an idea for a final scene too – with Aubrey and Lindsay leaving the service and stopping outside the TV rental shop. The screens in the window showing a modern Olympics would be enough to attract their attention; though not enough to command it for long. And soon the elderly teammates from 1924 would shuffle off with a slight shake of their heads, reflecting on how times had changed. Was that ending too anticlimactic? They could work it out later. All storyline ideas were in their infancy at best.

Colin Welland had the bare bones of a story – and little more. Beneath their chosen title, *Runners*, Welland scribbled: "Three young runners, gentlemen in a gentlemen's world. But each with his own peculiar driving force, his own battle he has to win…and each with the one common aim…AN OLYMPIC GOLD!"

Charming enough; but would that sell the project to a bunch of hard-nosed movie people? David's trusted friend, the director Alan Parker, who had worked with him on the hit movie *Midnight Express*, was not enthusiastic.

'What? A bunch of toffs go to the Olympic Games? I'd move on from that idea,' he told Puttnam affectionately.

Even Eric Liddell's sister Jenny Somerville was not initially thrilled. 'It's so old,' she said. 'It all happened such a long time ago.'

But that was the beauty and innocence of it. And the producer was reluctant to move on from his idea, whatever anyone said. Instead, he asked to see Jenny's old collection of newspaper clippings about her brother. They just added fire to Puttnam's passion for the story.

'This is an expedient world,' Puttnam insisted. 'For people to behave in an unexpedient manner is extraordinary.'

He was determined to turn his gut feeling into a movie. But he knew he was fighting against huge odds. The story didn't easily capture people's imagination. Those who initially liked the sound of the film were few and far between. There didn't seem to be much to go on.

In the months after being commissioned, Welland had realized he needed more material, and put advertisements in London newspapers, asking for survivors from the era or their offspring to put flesh on the story. He struck gold when Evelyn Montague's son supplied him with the letters his father had sent home from the 1924 Olympics. They captured the collective innocence of the GB team.

'I was absolutely amazed by the naiveté of them,' Welland admitted, without meaning to be unkind. 'A 21-year-old man, writing in terms that in today's world would be naïve to the point of being ridiculous. It was rather like a 14 year-old writing.'

That "14-year-old" would go on to become one of the finest war correspondents of his generation, so those letters really did belong to a specific time of innocent hope and joy.

The backdrop and general mood for the movie were taking shape in Colin's head. That was all very encouraging, but David Puttnam needed something more specific to sell his vision to the right backers. A cleaner, clearer storyline would help.

Welland obliged to an extent, but he was not a man to let the creative juices flow too freely before the fruit was ripe. He explained where he was with the process in a handwritten note:

*I can't write a storyline as such...for this is primarily a film of three stories to be told both in parallel and interwoven – becoming progressively more interwoven as we move towards the climax in Paris. To work out the exact mechanics at this stage isn't the way I work. I prefer to set the script in motion then let the shifts in direction, pace and emphasis – even which events in the lives of our three to repeat or use – come instinctively. If everything is thoroughly researched and available – which it is, in the forms of letters, photographs, recordings and from cuttings, etc – imagination can take over and my script can evolve naturally, rather than be restricted slavishly to an artificially predestined course of events.*

*So what I have done is outline what I suspect will be the courses the three stories will take – outline them separately leaving the exact nature of their interaction until the moment of writing. There are of course other influences, other textures active in the movie – the British Ruling class in the person of Lord Birkenhead and his fellow Olympic Committee men – the United States athletic machine with its 'nice guys come last' motto, arriving in a specially chartered trans-Atlantic liner – and the women of the stories – mothers, sisters, girlfriends who wielded quiet but not great influence, being women of their time.*

*There is also the runners' world of the twenties – Varsity meets... considered comments...insights into the impressions the three giants are making on those about them.*

It was a little vague for a hard sell. And was there now enough to make an audience want to immerse itself in such an innocent and noble pursuit of sporting glory? What was the incentive? Doubts lingered.

The signs weren't good when one of the proposed movie's three main protagonists – and the last still alive by February 1978 – declined the offer to be portrayed in the film. Douglas Lowe, the 1924 800m gold medalist, was supposed to "star" alongside Liddell and Abrahams. But three runners became two when Lowe felt he wasn't offered enough money – and didn't particularly warm to the project anyway.

In 2023, Lord Puttnam remembered that rejection well.

*He was obviously a very gifted athlete, as he won the gold medal again in 1928. But my response from him was very grumpy and he rejected the £500 we offered him as being hopelessly inadequate.*

Was this the final straw? Two of the three leading characters had died, one just before writer Welland could fully bond with him. The last man alive had told Puttnam to get lost. It would have been enough to persuade most people to give up on the project.

Fortunately, David Puttnam had faith in his own creative judgement. He had trusted his instincts since the mid-1960s, when he had worked at an advertising agency called Collett, Dickenson, Pearce and Partners. Nearly sixty years later, he could still remember the first exciting realisation that he had genuine talent. But when did that come?

'Probably at around 23, when I was working at the ad agency as we started winning awards for work I was primarily responsible for – although it was mostly print at that time.'

Print turned to film. And Puttnam had been in the movie industry ever since a man called Sandy Lieberson had spotted his creativity and invited him to become a partner at a new production company – Goodtimes Enterprises – in 1970.

You didn't survive in that world if you didn't know what you were doing. David was still standing. *Midnight Express* had been magnificent. And he wasn't giving up on *Runners*.

CHAPTER THIRTEEN:

# The Hand of Liddell

David Puttnam met his writer again to see what they could salvage after Douglas Lowe's outright rejection of their movie.

Welland felt he could still work his magic with just the two main characters. And he was wondering whether one of the hymns sung at Harold Abrahams' memorial service might contain an alternative title. That hymn was *Jerusalem* – fitting given Harold's roots and his life as a true Englishman. One phrase stood out:

"Bring me my chariots of fire..."

Didn't that also perfectly encapsulate the passion of athletics?

Very well, they decided.

"Chariots of Fire" would make for a more distinctive title.

While many had turned their back on the project, one man was positive. As is often the case in the professional world, friendship did no harm. Sandy Lieberson, Puttnam's former production partner back in his first days in the business, had become Vice-President of European Production at Twentieth Century Fox. And unlike most, Lieberson quite liked the idea of this guy Eric Liddell taking a moral stand – and his rival Harold Abrahams sticking it to the bigots. But Sandy couldn't get the project over the line with his superiors.

Then, as if by a miracle, Lieberson suddenly didn't have any superiors. He was made President of Worldwide Productions for 20th

Century Fox. Now he could use his new position to do a provisional deal, so that *Chariots of Fire* at least had a chance of being made.

Puttnam looked back on the way things unfolded and declared, 'The film had no right ever to have been made. And in a well-run industry, it never would have got through. It's one of the aberrations of the industry that *Chariots* gets made.'

They weren't over the line just yet. There still wasn't enough money in the kitty. That Fox deal had been struck for $3 million; but even back in 1980, that wasn't enough money to make a really decent movie. Ideally, Puttnam needed another backer to match that $3 million. And the big players seemed to smell a "turkey" in the pipeline. Even Colin Welland, with all his love for the story, could understand it.

'Can you imagine going into a Hollywood mogul and saying, "I have this idea about two Olympic athletes from 1924…"?'

Most of the wisest men within the industry still didn't want to know. After four months of rejections, however, a company called United Star Shipping – run by a certain Mohamed Al-Fayed – came in with the cash. They had recently formed the Allied Stars production company – and identified with some of the *Chariots* themes as outsiders with attitude. Puttnam had exhausted all his options with more established backers by then.

He observed wryly, 'Believe me, you've been fairly well around the track before you get to Egyptian shipping lines.'

The investment came with baggage. Al-Fayed's son Dodi had a drug habit. Later, he allegedly brought cocaine onto the *Chariots* set and tried to share it with the cast, prompting his swift removal.

'He was a rather tragic figure,' Puttnam reflected in 2023.

Dodi's death in a Paris tunnel with Diana, Princess of Wales was the final act in a troubled story. And by Paris 2024, his father had also passed away. But the family share of *Chariots* profits was still paid out, dwarfing early estimates of a $6 million windfall for the Al-Fayed estate.

'His profit share is still being paid to the same company each year and is cumulatively way in excess of $6 million,' Puttnam said in 2023.

There was no promise of profit in the early eighties. Yet the Al-Fayeds were prepared to gamble; and that gamble allowed magic to be made. David Puttnam never forgot what they did, for all their imperfections. At the Oscars in 1982, he expressed his gratitude.

'Thank you, Mohamed and Dodi Al Fayed for putting your money where my mouth was,' David said memorably.

With the funding in place by the end of the 1970s. Inspired casting would be the next important element. David Puttnam had his eye on a couple of relatively unknown actors for the lead roles, because he felt a degree of anonymity would help the audience to accept the film's journey back in time.

Ian Charleson was an actor with pedigree. He worked with the Royal Shakespeare Company – but wasn't known to the average man in the street. He had a gentle charm that Puttnam thought might evoke the shy but stubborn essence of Liddell.

An actor called Ben Cross also had a classical background; but he was edgier; and Puttnam had a feeling he could bring that renowned chip on the Abrahams shoulder to life.

Both thespians might have thought twice about coming to the auditions if they had known the brutal training regime that awaited them.

Tom McNab, a former athlete and Olympic coach, was recruited as "Athletics Consultant." He gathered thirty-two actors to a cinder track in Putney in the middle of winter. Some hoped to be extras and others aimed to make the start line as supporting cast. At first, McNab wasn't told who the front-runners for the key roles were. The actors chosen by McNab had to look like athletes – and show enough ability to be trained as such.

'His judgement was crucial,' Lord Puttnam emphasised.

No one was fit enough to meet the athletic consultant's initial demands; and many were sick in the warm-up. But some actors showed more potential than others. McNab picked out Charleson and Cross as men who could cope with the rigours of a leading role. Puttnam breathed a huge sigh of relief. This was going to work. The ability of *Chariots* to convey sporting passion to millions of people around the world was thanks in no small measure to the wonderfully physical performances of Ben and Ian.

Tom particularly enjoyed knocking Cross into shape before filming, to ensure the actor really looked the part. McNab had coached genuine British athletes at a time when he felt the Harold Abrahams administration had blocked all progress. Poor Ben took the brunt of McNab's bitterness during this pre-shoot training.

'I used to make him do extra press-ups,' admitted the coach years later. 'Ben asked me why he had to do more than anyone else. I just looked at him and said, "I hated you, Harold Abrahams."'

As *Chariots of Fire* became a reality, David Puttnam began to count his blessings. The chance discovery of the story just because he was ill. The unlikely financing of the movie, thanks to the unexpected promotion of Lieberson to a lofty studio position. Additional funding from a surprising source. A screenplay writer from the north, with a chip on his shoulder as big as Harold's. Just the right actors coming through extreme athletic "auditions." It all seemed too good to be true. And maybe that's why David told a *New York Times* reporter what he thought was behind his extraordinary run of luck in getting *Chariots of Fire* off the ground. Maybe it wasn't luck at all.

'Eric,' Puttnam said.

Hugh Hudson, the film's director, heard this answer and raised an eyebrow at the thought that Liddell could have been watching over them. Puttnam stuck to his guns, though.

'He's kept his eye on the film from the first day,' David said. 'Someone has. Why not Eric?'

When reminded of this exchange in 2023, Lord Puttnam's opinion hadn't changed. It's quite a claim; but Puttnam had hinted at this strange phenomenon elsewhere. When he gave a talk at Edinburgh University in 2012, for example, he looked back on the making of *Chariots* and put it like this:

*At every turn, what I can only describe as a kind of hidden hand helped to provide the best possible solution to each seemingly impossible hurdle. Many, many times the film survived various crises – in terms of being financed, produced and distributed. It insisted on being made.*

He also marvelled at how a key member of the IOC broke ranks to give the movie the green light, even when her bosses were opposed to giving the project official Olympic blessing. Puttnam remembered this development with glee.

*There was the time when the IOC was trying to ban all reference to the Olympic Games in the film. But then Monique Berlioux, [Director of the IOC], stuck her neck out for us. She had been a member of the French Resistance, who took messages from one side of the Seine to the other by swimming across the river with a sealed container around her neck. Later she had represented France as a swimmer in the Olympic Games. She said we should press ahead with Chariots of Fire. If the film wasn't successful, the IOC would hardly know or care. If it was successful, they would bask in the limelight. Sure enough, later the IOC asked if they could please have a copy for their archives.*

And what were the chances of spotting a key movie location accidentally from the air, on the way back from scouting what had turned out to be an unsuitable one? Puttnam went on:

*When we wanted to use the track at Murrayfield for filming, the Scottish RFU that year were not the easiest people I'd ever dealt with in my life. So I took a little private plane with Hugh Hudson to look at a stadium on the Isle of Man, but it wasn't suitable. We were flying back to Liverpool when I spotted something below and said: "What's that?" It looked like a little stadium in the middle of nowhere. The pilot said it was somewhere on the Wirrall. We took bearings and went to find it after we landed. It was Bebington – and that became the location for the filming of the Stade Colombes scenes.*

Time and again, victory was plucked from the jaws of defeat in the strangest ways. Technical setbacks became triumphs. Puttnam recalled the famous title sequence at the start of the film, when his actors are running along the West Sands in St Andrews.

*We were filming the opening scenes of the GB team training on the beach and it was a beautiful sunny day. We got it all in the can. Then when we took a proper look, we found that sand had got into the works and scratched the negatives. That meant we had to do it all again the next day. It was blustery and windy and there were white horses on the waves. It was so much more atmospheric – another example of little miracles at work.*

And that was before Vangelis came crashing in at the last moment with the perfect music for that opening title sequence! They soon decided to use his iconic theme for the end credits too. It was inspirational; and it meant that the anticlimactic final scene outside a TV rental shop – the one they had shot while still unsure of the final message – had very wisely been discarded.

Everything seemed to fall into place – almost of its own accord – whenever the creative process was threatened. A positive force that refused to be beaten had driven everything.

'Eric Liddell's benign and supportive presence keeping an eye on us,' Puttnam repeated happily in 2023.

CHAPTER FOURTEEN:

# The Critics

In some ways the death of Harold Abrahams made life easier for David Puttnam.

Rosemary Warne explained, 'He would have hated the fact that Sybil was portrayed as being involved with him at university, because it wasn't true.'

Christina McLeod Innes was the real love interest – but she was left out. An intense intellectual student of Russian was less attractive to the film-makers than a glamorous stage performer

Puttnam was understandably unrepentant. 'We had to play a lot of games with time. We did know that Harold had a girlfriend during his running days. I never knew her name and I didn't know they had been engaged; I just knew there had been someone and he had been involved with her at the time. But the attraction of Sybil for us was this Mikado thing, and the notion of this exotic woman. Irresistible, frankly.'

Meanwhile the film showed Harold sprinting round Trinity Great Court in Cambridge, beating the chimes to great adulation. Abrahams never achieved this feat or even tried, though one of his best friends succeeded – Lord Burghley. Had he been alive, Rosemary felt that Harold would have refused to take the credit for something a good friend did. 'I think if Harold had seen the film, he would have been very upset about being given the credit for David Exeter's run. They were great friends.'

The movie portrayed Harold's Cambridge University elders as anti-semites, rushing to condemn Harold's use of a professional coach, Sam Mussabini. In fact, Harold wasn't trained by Mussabini while he was at university. That happened before – when he was just fourteen – and shortly after his Cambridge days, when he was twenty-three. Rosemary claimed, 'I think they overdid the antisemitism. I didn't feel – certainly not in his later years – that he was at all fussed about it.' This view that *Chariots* exaggerated the antisemitism was commonly held among friends and family. Yet Harold said in numerous interviews that anti-semitism had indeed motivated him. And Lord Puttnam insisted, 'The antisemitism is not exaggerated in the film. I am not suggesting he was repeatedly victimised, but it did exist; and it was a factor.'

The movie makers could have stuck rigidly to the truth in all areas of the story. But the Oscar-winning screenplay writer, Colin Welland, was a master dramatist. By not sticking strictly to the truth he created something truly beautiful. Some of the reasons behind the film's power and resonance lie in the subtle changes he made to what had been the real story.

As Welland himself said in a letter to Gladys Mussabini, the daughter of Harold's coach, Sam: 'Inaccuracies you refer to I freely admit but they were in most cases deliberate as sometimes events and details have to be reorganised in order to capsulate a range of happenings within the period of two hours.'

There's still so much about *Chariots of Fire* to celebrate and value. A few years before Sir Roger Bannister died, he said, 'It was one of the greatest films about sport. It took America by storm. It is a film portrayal and you would expect the producer to make some changes. I think Harold Abrahams would have enjoyed it and been interested in it.'

Harold would certainly have enjoyed what happened at a private viewing of the movie. Eric Liddell's widow Florence was there with members of her family. David Puttnam witnessed their emotional reaction, and watched as Florence spotted Ben Cross, who had come in late.

'Ah, Mr Abrahams, my husband spoke a lot about you,' she said.

It was her way of conveying to the actor – and anyone else who cared to listen – that Eric Liddell's respect for Harold Abrahams had lasted a lifetime. Liddell had even been heard praising Harold during his talks about the 1924 Olympics while interned in China. And over in England, Abrahams had often written glowing tributes to Liddell. They hadn't liked each other's running styles; but boy did they admire the fighting spirit.

Their mutual regard clearly endured. Florence wanted "Harold Abrahams" to know that – even though the real Harold had passed away two or three years earlier. And Flo also wanted the world to know that *Chariots of Fire* had successfully captured her husband's spirit on the big screen. She did add that Ian Charleson's Eric Liddell was a little 'solemn and preachy' compared to the real Eric. Perhaps she saw his playful side more than most. Opinions can be subjective; and different aspects of a personality emerge in different situations. All in all, there was widespread approval of the movie, even from Eric's sister Jenny, who never really opposed his running at all.

Sadly we would never hear the reactions of Eric Liddell and Harold Abrahams to this glorious film. But the man whose approval was most important to David Puttnam was still alive for the premiere and wider cinema release. That man was his father, Leonard, who had arranged his ticket for the London Olympics of 1948 – and thus sparked Puttnam's love for the Games.

David remembered, 'My father and mother were at the premiere and the celebratory dinner afterwards at the Savoy, as the film had been selected as the "Royal Film" for 1981, and the Queen Mum attended.'

The Royal Film Performance 1981
In the gracious presence of
Her Majesty Queen Elizabeth The Queen Mother.
To aid the Cinema and Television Benevolent Fund

CHARIOTS OF FIRE

Twentieth Century-Fox and Allied Stars Present An Enigma Production.
"CHARIOTS OF FIRE"
Starring: Ben Cross · Ian Charleson · Nigel Havers · Cheryl Campbell · Alice Krige
Guest Stars (in alphabetical order):
Lindsay Anderson · Dennis Christopher · Nigel Davenport · Brad Davis
Peter Egan · John Gielgud · Ian Holm · Patrick Magee
Screenplay by Colin Welland · Music By Vangelis · Executive Producer Dodi Fayed
Produced by David Puttnam · Directed by Hugh Hudson

CIRCLE   Odeon Leicester Square, on Monday 30th March 1981

*Chariots of Fire* Royal Premiere Invite.

Acclaim for the film was instant – and Leonard was able to savour the growing fuss with paternal pride. Then tragedy struck. Puttnam explained, 'My father lived to see *Chariots of Fire* become a commercial success in the UK and the USA – but died very suddenly of a heart attack on New Year's Eve of that year. He was 74.'

Christina McLeod Innes was from Leonard's generation – and went to see the film like any other cinema customer. Christina happily kept a low profile. Her daughter reflected, 'My mother must have been relatively newly widowed when *Chariots of Fire* came out. But she was absolutely determined to go and see the film. She would have been about eighty and we went up to London by train and by bus to the cinema. My mother and I went to see *Chariots of Fire* in a cinema in Regent Street.'

You had to wonder how Christina felt, watching Harold's story unfold in that West End cinema. Many a woman in her shoes would have been jealous at the way Sybil's character had usurped her place in history. This was fast becoming a nationally celebrated story, after all. Christina reacted quite differently. As she gazed at the screen, she became defensive of the real Sybil, whom she had known.

Sue Smithson remembered, 'My mother found it interesting, even though she said she didn't find it entirely true to what had happened. I remember my mother saying, "Ah, but that actress is nothing like Sybil was!" She certainly didn't like the actress who had been chosen to play the part of Sybil. She thought that was just crazy.'

It almost sounded as though she was trying to speak for Harold; imagining perhaps what his own reaction would have been, had he been sitting right there beside her. The real Sybil's sweet and supportive nature wasn't given the platform to shine in *Chariots* – but then again that wasn't the point of the film.

Sue Pottle said, 'The lady playing my mother was in all aspects totally unlike her and she played her more as a harpy or perhaps even a femme fatale – neither of which she was. The real Sybil was given to a gentle flirtation. I thought the film was a romanticised version of events, but a great film that we enjoyed.'

Christina did acknowledge that the Harold she saw up on the silver screen was essentially recognisable as the man she had once loved. Sue Smithson explained, 'I don't think she had any objections or criticisms about the portrayal of Harold's character. I think the antisemitism was probably exaggerated.'

But then Harold had exaggerated the antisemitism in his own mind at the time, as he later admitted. And although certain aspects of *Chariots of Fire* would have irritated him, the common consensus is that Abrahams would have enjoyed many of the film's more accurate elements. Above all, he would have loved the sheer passion for athletics that *Chariots* captured and generated. No doubt Christina loved that passion too, knowing what it meant to Harold, and having been his unofficial athletics photographer for a year or two at Cambridge. Christina, the remarkable survivor from the *Chariots of Fire* era, finally passed away on February 28, 2003. She was almost 101.

By then the movie had become an all-time classic. It won four Oscars, including Best Film. 'It is hard to imagine that Harold would not have enjoyed the chance to bask once more in the glory of his achievements,' admitted his daughter, Sue Pottle.

Lord Puttnam put it like this: 'My guess is that Harold would have done what Jenny Liddell did. He would have gone along with the film, but retained the right to criticise after it came out. I think he would have been pretty thrilled with the Oscar, though. He liked prizes.'

Both Liddell and Abrahams saw beyond prizes, one much sooner than the other. Yet they would surely have been gratified to learn that their story was gripping enough to win all those Oscars – even though Liddell never was much moved by a "corruptible crown."

For the record, *Chariots of Fire* began its honours parade at the BAFTA Awards, where it won Best Film for David Puttnam and Best Costume Design for Milena Canonero.

At the Oscars, David Puttnam also won Best Picture, and Canonero triumphed again for those fabulous costumes. Vangelis won an Oscar for Best Music, Original Score. Would he have picked up that gong had he not hunted down Puttnam and his wife Patsy at that Chinese restaurant a couple of years earlier? We shall never know. But the Oscar-winning screenplay writer, Colin Welland stole the show in Hollywood on that glorious night by warning the Academy: 'You may have started something. The Brits are coming!'

Puttnam wouldn't have minded being upstaged, for his joy was tinged with sadness that his father wasn't there to enjoy those big Oscar moments with him. In his moving acceptance speech for a lifetime BAFTA award many years later, Puttnam explained:

*The most admirable human being I ever met was my dad. My dad was extraordinary and like a lot of kids born during the war, I didn't meet him until I was five, so he was that much more extraordinary to me. And the only sadness I ever suffered…was that just a couple of weeks after I won the BAFTA award for Chariots, and then went on and won it in Los Angeles, the Oscar, my dad died. And so, this charismatic, this extraordinary man and I never had the opportunity to exchange that glance or hug each other. And that left a hole…*

There were some uplifting moments for David Puttnam and everyone else associated with the movie, though; for example when a world leader used the film to illustrate a new initiative for world peace. That's precisely what US President and former film star Ronald Reagan did on June 3, 1988.

Making a speech to highlight how Mikhail Gorbachev, then President of the Soviet Union, was seeking 'serious reform' in Moscow, Reagan captured the mood of optimism like this:

*And here is a story, one last story that can remind us of what we are about. It is a story that a few years ago came in the guise of that art form for which I have an understandable affection – the cinema. In one unforgettable scene, Eric Liddell reads the words of Isaiah. 'He giveth the power to the faint, and to them that have no might, he increaseth their strength . . . but they that wait upon the Lord shall renew their strength; they shall mount up with wings as eagles. They shall run and not be weary.' Here is our formula for completing our crusade for freedom. Here is the strength of our civilisation and our belief in the rights of humanity. Our faith is in a higher law . . . 'Come, my friends,' as it was said of old by Tennyson, 'it is not too late to seek a newer world.'*

As the countdown to Paris 2024 began, *Chariots of Fire* had lost none of its power to inspire. It has stood the test of time and served the Olympic movement with great distinction

EPILOGUE:

# The Olympic Survival Relay

'Never in my wildest dreams did I ever imagine the film would become so big,' Lord Puttnam admitted modestly in 2023.

*Chariots of Fire* was huge on both sides of the Atlantic and around the wider world. It transcended the Olympic Games; and yet it was quintessentially Olympian in spirit. And that's why the amiable producer deserves a place in our thoughts alongside Liddell and Abrahams in this Paris Centenary Year.

If anything, David always saw himself as a vehicle for the good sporting vibes that seem to surround his movie. He never tried to project himself as some kind of Olympic hero.

'I was terrible at running – especially hating cross country!' he pointed out amusingly, possibly unaware that Lord Sebastian Coe was trying to engineer an Olympic comeback for the cross country, for the first time since those Chariots of Fire Games in 1924. But you could understand his point. He didn't feel he could be placed on a podium with Liddell and Abrahams.

Was he right, though?

Being hopeless at running didn't erase the part he had played in saving the soul of the Games. With Liddell and Abrahams, Puttnam contributed most vividly to the positive energy it took to carry the Olympic movement through from 1924 to 2024. Every time an Olympic Games comes around, *Chariots of Fire* takes us somewhere beautiful, beyond the doping, commercialism, boycotts and bans. *Chariots* can't stop those things from happening. But it does to help us stay in love with the Olympics.

And Games organisers seem to know it.

In 2008, the host nation China naturally embraced Eric Liddell as one of their own. They also circulated a story claiming he had stayed in that Japanese-run internment camp when he could have left, his potential release personally negotiated by Sir Winston Churchill. The Chinese said Liddell had sacrificed himself so that a pregnant woman could go free instead. Although doubts were later cast on the veracity of this story, it was precisely the sort of thing Liddell would have done, even in his own hour of need. Words can scarcely convey the saintly quality of the man.

London 2012 continued the *Chariots* love affair. The film's influence could be seen even before the Olympics started. When the torch relay came to Britain, they didn't run along the beach at Broadstairs, where GB's 1924 Olympic team really trained. The location chosen was West Sands, St Andrews, where Puttnam had filmed his memorable opening scene.

*Chariots* featured in the 2012 opening ceremony, where its theme tune and title scenes were hilariously undermined by Rowan Atkinson's Mr Bean. We heard the *Chariots* music at medal ceremonies all through the Games. And when those Olympics touched the soul of the host nation and the world beyond, we had David Puttnam's glorious movie to thank as much as any other factor.

In the year of the Paris Centenary, *Chariots of Fire* would never be more important. As Lord Puttnam once said:

*We're in a bad place. We're dealing with corporatism, consumerism, celebritism. We have to navigate ourselves back to a place that isn't rotten. We need foundations to find the best of ourselves. Eric Liddell's values and beliefs provide about as good a foundation as you're likely to find.*

*Chariots of Fire* remains a refuge for anyone who cares about the soul of sport and doesn't want darker forces to take over. Maybe that's why everyone still loves the film so much.

When Seb Coe watched the movie with his children in the early 2020s, he was relieved to sense they loved it almost as much as he did. And that only served to confirm what he already suspected:

*The values are timeless and not past their sell-by date. I don't know whether David Puttnam saved the soul of the Games; but the film brings to life a huge part of the Olympic treasury. It very much represents who we were, where we were heading and what we left behind.*

It's a good description. But like Harold Abrahams and Eric Liddell, many people wanted to hold onto the best of what was being left behind. How far would the Paris 2024 Games organisers embrace *Chariots of Fire*? Only time would tell us to what extent the French would be prepared to celebrate a British movie. The signs were looking good in the build-up to the Games – and rightly so. The events depicted in the film took place on Parisian soil, after all.

Whatever was destined to unfold in the French capital, the movie's re-release in cinemas in the UK and Ireland was anticipated, pencilled in to coincide with the Olympics. In anticipation of a fresh audience, the film had been further enhanced by 21st-century technology.

Sadly, hardly anyone from the original *Chariots* family had survived to look forward to the festivities.

'I'm the only one left, along with Nigel Havers,' reflected Puttnam in late 2023.

And yet the show must go on.

The Olympic Survival Relay started with the selfless spirit of Eric Liddell – and continued with the protective instincts of Harold Abrahams. Puttnam took up the fight through his marvellous movie, maintaining momentum all the way to Paris 2024.

This trio have preserved the true spirit of the Olympic Games for a hundred years between them.

But it normally takes four people to run a relay.

Who will take the baton from David Puttnam as we race into the future?

*Fin*

# Index